United States taxes and tax policy

United States Taxes and Tax Policy supplements and complements the theoretical material on taxes found in public finance texts using a combination of institutional, factual, theoretical, and empirical information. By adding flesh to theoretical bones, this textbook provides insight into the behavior of individuals in both the private and public sectors.

Specifically, the economic effects of taxes and tax policy are stressed and, as a result, students will gain an appreciation and understanding of how tax policy actually affects the economy. For example, where many texts typically stop with a rather pristine treatment of the income and substitution effects of a tax, *United States Taxes and Tax Policy* goes further by examining econometric studies of the supply of labor, and the relationship of this work to taxes, the Laffer Curve, and the role and magnitude of the underground economy. Using this approach, Professor Davies brings life to what can be a dull subject.

Using language that is straightforward and nontechnical, *United States Taxes and Tax Policy* is a textbook designed for students and intelligent laymen. It is pitched at a level for junior-senior introductory courses in public finance or taxation, but can be used as well for courses of public policy, education finance, law, and political science.

The author is professor of economics at Duke University. He has written over 60 articles for such journals as *The Journal of Political Economy, The American Journal of Economics and Sociology,* and *The American Economic Review,* and has served as an economic consultant to a variety of organizations including the United States Agency for International Development and the United States Treasury.

United States taxes and tax policy

DAVID G. DAVIES

Duke University

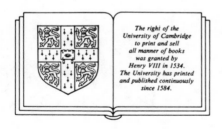

The right of the
University of Cambridge
to print and sell
all manner of books
was granted by
Henry VIII in 1534.
The University has printed
and published continuously
since 1584.

CAMBRIDGE UNIVERSITY PRESS

CAMBRIDGE

LONDON   NEW YORK   NEW ROCHELE

MELBOURNE   SYDNEY

Published by the Press Syndicate of the University of Cambridge
The Pitt Building, Trumpington Street, Cambridge CB2 1RP
32 East 57th Street, New York, NY 10022, USA
10 Stamford Road, Oakleigh, Melbourne 3166, Australia

First published 1986

Printed in the United States of America

Library of Congress Cataloging-in-Publication Data

Davies, David G.
    United States taxes and tax policy.
    Bibliography: p.
    Includes index.
    1. Taxation – United States.   I. Title.
HJ2381.D38   1986   336.2′00973   85-31414

British Library Cataloguing in Publication Data

Davies, David G.
    United States taxes and tax policy.
    1. Taxation – United States.
    I. Title
    336.2′00973   HJ2381

ISBN 0 521 30169 6   hard covers
ISBN 0 521 31769 X   paperback

To Carol, Richard, and Lynn,
with they know what
and they know why.

Contents

Preface

The main purpose of this book is to outline recent developments and ideas about taxes, tax policy, and theory in the United States. To begin to understand the crosscurrents of thinking about these issues, it is helpful to know something of the economic background and problems besetting the American economy.

Since the early 1970s, the large industrial sectors have suffered a long and debilitating recession. Traditional large-scale industries, such as mining and steel, are all but dying out and being replaced by more efficient foreign competitors. Moreover, rapidly growing industries, such as communications and computers, do not require vast amounts of the output of traditional sectors.

Large-scale shifts in the configuration of modern products and services have been taking place for some time. Nevertheless, it is now more than a decade since the American economy turned sour, and the growth in real per capita income has continued to sputter along with general economic conditions. Recoveries are relatively short-lived, and economic indicators are often lower than during the preceding upturn in activity. The economy appears to be in a long period of decline, relieved by periodic but anemic recoveries. Some of the ground lost during recession is regained, but advances are neither robust nor lasting. No single factor is responsible for this poor economic performance. Worldwide shocks to the system, such as the Viet Nam War, the movement to a generalized, floating foreign exchange, and the oil embargoes, have had notable effects.

Additional important factors responsible for the lackluster economic performance are our own government's policies in relation to inflation, saving and investment, productivity, and the regulation of economic activity. We examine the overall tax aspect of these issues in Chapter 1; the remainder of the book examines how particular taxes relate to these important policies.

United States Taxes and Tax Policy introduces the student and intelligent layman to an analysis and description of this subject. It is both a supplement and complement to the traditional theoretical material on taxes found in public finance texts. It offers a combination of historical, institutional, factual, theoretical, and empirical information.

This mixture of elements is important because it helps individuals better understand the subject of public finance and bridges the gap between the real world and the theory found in texts. By adding flesh to theoretical bones, this book provides insight into the behavior of individuals in both the private and public sectors, including households, businesses, government agencies, and legislatures. Information in this book will also prepare individuals to make more informed and intelligent decisions. Although I am continually impressed by the native intelligence and goodwill of my students, I am equally impressed, and sometimes appalled, by their ignorance of the world in which we live. For example, they initially reject the fact that the upper 50 percent of all income earners pay about 93 percent of all federal individual income taxes. By giving students factual information of this type, *United States Taxes and Tax Policy* supplements much of what traditional texts offer.

At the same time, this book stresses the economic effects of taxes and tax policy. Evidence and the testing of hypotheses are emphasized, and it is in this exciting area that younger economists are making giant strides toward understanding individual taxes and their effects. They are beginning to quantify and systematically relate relevant variables. For example, we now have estimates on how inflation has affected capital assets, the change in nominal value of these assets, and their taxation. Researchers are beginning to clarify the thorny econometric issues surrounding the effect of income taxes on consumption, saving, work, and leisure.

This provocative work is being carried on in universities and research centers throughout North America, the United Kingdom, and Australia. The intellectual leader in these efforts has been Harvard's Professor Martin Feldstein, former chairman of the Council of Economic Advisers to the President and longtime president of the National Bureau of Economic Research. Much innovative work has also been done at Stanford University, The Brookings Institution, Harvard, Princeton, Duke, the University of Western Ontario, the American Enterprise Institute, and private consulting firms.

Much of the thinking and many of the results of this quantitative research are reported in this book. Consequently, readers will gain appreciation and understanding of how tax policy actually affects the economy. For example, texts usually stop with a rather pristine treatment of the income and substitution effects of a tax; *United States Taxes and Tax Policy* goes further by examining econometric studies of the supply of labor and leisure, the relationship of work to taxes, the Laffer Curve, and the effect of taxes and inflation on corporate income, capital gains, and investment. Many individuals find that this approach enlivens what can be a dull subject.

This book is designed for the interested layman and students; it is not intended to impress colleagues with a virtuoso display of technical analysis. Some professors and noneconomists will, however, be very interested in the many modern research studies I have culled, reported, and discussed.

United States Taxes and Tax Policy is aimed at the level of junior–senior introductory courses in public finance or taxation, but it could also be used for pertinent courses in public policy, business administration, education finance, law, law and economics, political science, and public administration – anywhere that the subject of taxation is examined. The language is generally straightforward and nontechnical, and interested lay readers can gain much from this book.

A Preface is the traditional place to express an author's appreciation to the many individuals who helped in some direct way to complete the work. I follow this custom and thank first Professor Russell Mathews, director of the Centre for the Study of Federal Financial Relations at the Australian National University, who suggested the need for a monograph to inform Australians of the intricacies of United States taxes and tax policy. The writing of the monograph gradually changed over time, and the result is this larger, more comprehensive work. Without the encouragement of Professor Mathews, the project would neither have been started nor completed.

I owe a debt to my professional colleagues, especially Charles Clotfelter of Duke University and Lloyd Valentine of the University of Cincinnati, who read and criticized parts of the manuscript. I almost always took their advice. Thanks also to George Whitehouse, my reliable, conscientious, and ever-helpful tax expert and friend on the 1983–84 Jamaican Tax Mission. The thirty-four years spent with the IRS made him a veritable encyclopedia on tax matters. I always took his advice about the technical aspects of United States taxes. I also wish to express my appreciation to my many interesting and intellectually curious students at Duke University, with whom it has always been a pleasure to work. I especially want to thank my research assistants for efforts above and beyond the call of duty: Ritson Ferguson, my coauthor on expenditure taxation; Richard Winter and Jesus Lopez-Herrida for their excellent research on sales and value added taxation; Julie Puffer for her work on the property tax; and, finally, Jim Jackson, Michael Womack, and Kent Wicker for reliable, outstanding, and timely general research assistance. They were always there when I needed them. I, however, bear full responsibility for the contents of this book.

I must not forget those magicians of the word processor: Wanda Jedierowski, Pat Johnson, Forrest Smith, and, especially, Gwendolyn Gore and Judith Dixon of Duke University and Maxine Langott of Kingston, Jamaica. Their good humor was exceeded only by their efficiency, and neither ever waned.

I would also like to record my appreciation to Roy Weintraub for his kind help and support. Lastly, I must not forget my understanding editor, James Mason, and, especially, my editorial director, Dr. Colin Day. Their patience, availability, and knowledge made working with Cambridge University Press a genuine pleasure.

David G. Davies

Cutlass Bay
Ocho Rios
Jamaica, W.I.

CHAPTER 1

Economic foundations of U.S. tax policy

From the late 1930s until sometime in the 1970s, the exact date is too nebulous to pin down, the major influence on U.S. stabilization and tax policy was Keynesian aggregate theory. As we shall see in the forthcoming sections, Keynesian macrothought and policy has since been challenged by the monetarists, the rational expectationists, and the supply-siders.

Monetarists believe that appropriate control of the money supply will help foster the conditions necessary for the growth of a healthy economy. In the short run, changes in the stock of money are crucially important in determining fluctuations in real output and employment. In the long run, however, the quantity of money can only influence nominal gross national product (GNP). Real income is affected by many of the same elements that supply-side, neoclassical economists emphasize. These micro-economic factors include such real variables as the suppliers of labor, raw materials, and capital, the state of technology, the amount and quantity of human capital, the health and resourcefulness of individuals, a sound legal framework, and a stable and constructive public policy that contains the incentives necessary to put productive resources to efficient use (Meiselman 1982:9).

Monetary macromodels have not been especially successful in predicting the path and turning points of such important economic variables as consumption, investment, saving, and GNP. Moreover, the Federal Reserve has not followed the macrorecommendations of monetarists because it has been unwilling or unable to follow a consistent policy of steady growth in the stock of money. For the purpose at hand, monetarism per se has little to say about tax policy, although it is certainly true that counterproductive fiscal policy can make the monetary authorities' job much more difficult.

The rational expectationists, led by Robert Lucas, Neil Wallace, and Thomas Sargent, believe that short-run stabilization policies are generally doomed to failure. They will have no impact on economic activity or real GNP if the policies are applied when the public expects them.

The rational expectationists argue that people learn from experience and then act intelligently in their own interests; they consider all available information bearing on the future, including knowledge of the predictable response and action of policy makers to a recession, for example, and then adjust their behavior accordingly. When people do this, they are likely to nullify policy actions. For example, if unions expect that the government's stimulative policies to fight the recession will increase inflation, this expectation will be worked into their contracts.

Businesses may find that the government's stimulus increases the money demand for products, but if wages and other costs increase in anticipation of the policy of expansion, businesses may not perceive any greater opportunities for profit. Consequently, there is no incentive to increase production. Moreover, higher money wages are not likely to induce more time and effort from workers who expect inflation and increased taxes to vitiate the monetary gains.

The rational expectationists conclude that employment and output will remain virtually unchanged if individuals correctly predict government actions. In fact, government policies designed to expand real output may lead only to accelerated inflation. There is evidence to support the views of the rational expectationists, but many of the implications for tax policy have not been developed.

The decline of Keynesian economics

The negligible real rate of growth of the U.S. economy over the past two decades has led to growing disenchantment with the long-reigning Keynesian economic policies associated with liberal orthodoxy. Many analysts trace the roots of current economic problems to these policies that were adopted by government. An increasing number of academics, congressmen, leading businessmen, and independent researchers question the wisdom of government tax and expenditure programs that call for massive recurring deficits despite the existence of record levels of employment and near-capacity use of plants and equipment.

According to Keynesian doctrine, employment and gross national product are determined by aggregate demand. Low rates of economic growth and unemployment are caused by insufficient spending.

Conventional Keynesian economics requires policymakers to manage aggregate demand by using fiscal and monetary policy to influence the spending of consumers, businesses, and governments. If the problem is unemployment, the normal remedy requires the central government to stimulate demand by increasing its spending, reducing taxes, and incurring a budgetary deficit. Keynesians believe that the gross national product will rise by some multiple of the increase in public sector expenditure. If the economy is overheated, policy dictates that taxes be increased so the budget will manifest surpluses. In most cases, it is assumed that aggregate supply will somehow automatically and passively accommodate changes in demand.

This orthodox liberal view of how the economy operates has been embedded in the influential macroeconometric models that the U.S. Congress and Executive Branch have used to formulate and implement policy. The models, however, have not been very successful in forecasting economic variables over the past several years. They have been unable to come to grips with declining productivity, capital stock, and purchasing power. They cannot explain the economic stagflation of the past decade that continues to plague the U.S. economy in the 1980s.

Failure of the Keynesian models

The failure of these models has led to the conversion of an increasing number of economists to modern neoclassical or supply-side economics (Day 1980:11). The spirit and thinking of these converts is perhaps best represented by Michael Evans, who was one of the most noted Keynesian econometric model builders in the United States. He formulated and estimated the original equations for both the highly influential Wharton and Chase Econometrics models. Evans (1980:14–18) now freely admits that he used outmoded Keynesian theory to make predictions about the economy.

He notes that the Keynesian preoccupation with demand virtually blinded model builders to the need for analyzing the effect of changing tax rates on productivity, investment, and incentives to work. Moreover, saving was a negative factor in the Keynesian model, leading to a diminution in output. Keynesian econometricians either did not recognize the central role saving plays in allowing real capital to grow or they could not incorporate this behavior into their equations. Keynesian policy led us to the somewhat absurd conclusion, at least for the long run, that government spending does more for the economy than a cut in taxes because the government has a marginal propensity to spend, which is at least unity, whereas the private sector cuts down on aggregate investment, productivity, and income through its habit of saving. Thus, even though saving is a necessary act to create either human or physical capital, Keynesian policy makers believed that it inhibited full employment and the attainment of a healthy economy. Evans (1980:15–16) emphasizes and analyzes in some detail the crucial importance of saving to increased productivity and long-term economic growth. He notes that in existing Keynesian-type models, the rate of taxation has no independent effect on saving other than its usual direct impact on disposable income; but recent more sophisticated research confirms that the saving rate is influenced by the net rate of return to savings, a position that neoclassicists have held for years. Contemporary researchers have also discovered that an increase in savings unequivocally depresses interest rates, which, in turn, causes investment to rise; but these complex relationships are not included in current macroeconometric models (Evans 1980:15).

Roberts's critique

Paul Craig Roberts (1978:21–22), another strong critic of Keynesian models, shows that the large-scale econometric programs used by government neglect the impact of tax rates on an individual's choice between work and leisure. He argues persuasively that high marginal tax rates alter the relative price between labor and leisure. An increase in taxes increases the cost of working and simultaneously reduces the cost of leisure. At the same time, the cost of current consumption relative to saving falls because the future income from current saving bears higher future taxes. Because it is a well-accepted theorem in economics that when the price of something rises a smaller amount will be taken, Roberts believes higher taxes cause work effort, savings, and investment to decline. The result of the tax disincentive is declining production and income, an alien conclusion in macroeconometric models, but one that recognizes the simple, real-world fact that fiscal policy influences supply as well as demand.

These theoretical relationships between tax rates and work effort are supported by recent empirical studies. In modern economies not only are independent professionals (e.g., doctors, lawyers, dentists, accountants, and consultants) able to vary hours worked, but other individuals also do much the same thing by taking more vacation and sick time, increasing their rate of absenteeism, altering time spent at moonlighting, working at jobs with a shorter week, or simply dropping out of the work force. Households vary hours worked when different members enter and withdraw from the labor force in response to changing incentives. Evans (1980:15) reports that a survey of government income maintenance programs revealed that for every 10 percent increase in tax rates, there was a 1 percent drop in the amount of labor offered in the market.

Inflation and macromodels

Evans (1980:18) argues that even if tax rates do not increase, inflation pushes workers into higher and higher progressive income tax brackets so that individuals not only tend to work less but also bargain for higher nominal wages to try and preserve real incomes in spite of the upward drift in taxes. Although these forces exacerbate inflation, they have only recently been accounted for in current macromodels (Vanderford 1980:29).

Inflation along with a tax policy that requires depreciation allowances to be based on historical rather than replacement costs has a depressing effect on investment. Inflation causes nominal profits to rise. The phantom profits are subject to increased taxation. Real after-tax profits fall as larger and larger amounts of company income must be set aside to help replace the capital that the small, outdated, historical cost allowances will not cover. Because of tax rules and tax rates set by federal, state, and local governments, profits must rise about twice as fast as inflation so that firms can provide enough funds to replace capital. If profits do not increase fast enough, firms raise the required rate of return for many specific investment projects, and this increase causes a decline in capital spending (Evans 1980:18).

Neo-Keynesian econometric models, on the other hand, generally forecast declines in investment and gross national product as a result of a tax cut that increases the profitability of investment. This strange result occurs because investment is postulated to be very sensitive to changes in interest rates and relatively insensitive to after-tax profits. The models are also static so that a cut in tax rates always leads to a decline in government revenue, which, in turn, causes budgetary deficits, Treasury borrowing, and upward pressure on interest rates (Roberts 1978:27–8), the latter causing investment to fall.

Stagflation and the long run

Keynesian models have not explained and cannot explain stagflation because they do not incorporate the pertinent supply-side relationships. They do not have, for example, any relative price effects of changes in effective tax rates (Keleher 1979:2). Increasing aggregate demand in the short run may increase output and employment, but increasing demand in the long run, without accounting for the proper incentives to increase supply, leads to inflation and slow economic growth in output and employment.

Paul Roberts (1978:29) underscores the crucial difference between Keynesian macromodels and the emerging supply-side theories, noting that the long run consists of a series of short runs. Policies that are beneficial in the short run but that have deleterious long-run effects sooner or later will provoke a crisis. Many critics now believe this process accurately depicts the history of the United States economy during the past twenty years.

The modern neoclassical view of tax policy

Two analytical approaches are associated with the neoclassical view of the economy. I identify the group led by Paul Craig Roberts, Robert Mundell, Norman Ture, Arthur Laffer, Jack Kemp, George Guilder, and Jude Wanniski as supply-side economists. The loosely knit group led by Martin Feldstein, Michael Boskin, Charles McLure, and Michael Evans I call modern neoclassicists. Both groups could be labeled incentive economists because of their heavy emphasis on the effect of incentives on individual economic behavior. The principal difference between the two schools is that modern neoclassicists recognize the importance of aggregate demand in the short run, while emphasizing long-run policies to encourage growth. They do not believe that tax reductions will increase productivity and production sufficiently in the short run to curb inflation. They see the necessity of relying on monetary and fiscal policy to foster stability in income. The supply-siders risk committing the Keynesian error of largely ignoring one of the two fundamental determinants of income, but in their case aggregate demand is pushed into the background.

There is fair agreement between the groups on advocating specific types of tax reductions to encourage work, saving, and investment. However, modern neoclassicists see the effects of these actions happening over a longer time span. Although exceptions are associated with particular taxes, modern neo-classicists do not generally believe, on the basis of current evidence, in the Laffer effect (a reduction in tax rates will actually increase revenues). They embrace neoclassical economics, as do the supply-siders, but they have a greater appreciation for the remnants of modern macroeconomics.

Current tax policy

Current tax policy appears to rest more on neoclassical ideas than on any other body of thought. Consequently, the balance of this chapter examines the principal ideas of this somewhat diverse movement.

As the failures of orthodox policy became more obvious, interested parties repeatedly called for deep, searching, and pervasive examination of the tax structure and its impact on the economy. Fortunately, there has been an ongoing research effort into the relationship between taxes and the economy's performance since the mid-1970s. This work has been led by brilliant younger economists who understand that the current techniques of managing the economy, which were developed during the Great Depression, are no longer suited to the problems of the 1980s. Although most of these modern neoclassicists and supply-side economists understand Keynesian analysis, the theory of rational expectations, and monetarist theories, they emphasize none of them. Because they are interested in the problems that currently challenge us, they consider a longer time span than neo-Keynesian economists and politicians.

These incentive economists concentrate their investigations on economic efficiency and growth. They view positive incentives to production as the driving force in a robust, healthy, and growing economy. Their analysis is concerned with evaluating incentives and their impact on human behavior and the resulting supply of goods and services. In order to achieve the goals of efficiency and growth, most of the supply-side economists concentrate their recommendations for government policy and action on tax matters.

The most serious threats to incentives to produce are government policies with respect to inflation, government benefits, and taxation. Modern neoclassical and supply-side economists reason that the impact of inflation with its concurrent enormous distortions, due in part to historical cost-accounting procedures, inhibits saving and investment. Their empirical studies show that in some cases effective rates of taxation on capital gains and profits can and do exceed 100 percent, and this implies diminution of capital. Inflation also causes an upward drift in personal income tax brackets so that individuals must, without statutory changes in tax rates, pay over to governments higher and higher proportions of their real wages and salaries.

Importance of high marginal tax rates

As previously noted, aggregate demand is the driving force in neo-Keynesian analysis, and those variables that impinge on demand are considered the keys to successful management of the economy. Until capacity is reached, supply is a passive force that responds mechanically to the stimulus of demand.

Incentive economists take a different position. They reason that to obtain an increase in real income, production must rise. Consequently, they argue for a reduction in taxes not because aggregate demand is enhanced, but because productive activity is encouraged. A cut in the rate of taxation permits individuals to retain a larger share of their earnings. This, in turn, alters the tradeoffs or relative change in price between and among work and leisure, saving and investment, and, consequently, the level of production.

High marginal taxes encourage individuals to decrease their productive efforts in favor of leisure. It is estimated that the marginal tax rate on an average American worker exceeds 45 percent (Browning and Johnson 1979:69). Under these conditions, opportunities for overtime or moonlighting are foregone, retirement may come at an earlier age, more sick leave and absenteeism occur, vacation and time between jobs become longer, and risky investment projects are avoided when the personal return is significantly reduced (Gwartney and Stroup 1980:276).

High marginal taxes cause distortions in the market because they inhibit or eliminate both specialization and exchange, two powerful forces that lead to efficiency and notable increases in output. An experienced automobile salesman facing a 40 percent marginal tax rate, for example, would probably hire a professional to paint his house if the going rate for painters were no more than $60 a day. For every additional $100 the salesman earns before tax, he is allowed to keep $60. If his marginal rate is boosted to 45 percent, his after-tax earnings are only $55 and he saves $5 by painting his own house while refraining from selling cars. Moreover, the tax base shrinks by $160 because the salesman foregoes $100 in earnings and the painter who is not hired loses $60 in wages (Roberts 1978:13).

High marginal taxes affect the volume and quality of tax-deductible and nondeductible goods as well as the quantity of saving and investment. In addition to taxes on corporate earnings, owners are subject to personal income taxation on the dividends paid out of after-tax company earnings. Assuming that the marginal tax on dividend income is 45 percent (Browning and Johnson 1979:69), the combined corporate and individual marginal rate on income generated by a corporation would exceed 70 percent.

The high tax rate on corporate earnings creates a strong incentive for owner-managers and managers to spend company funds for tax deductible, business-related goods and services that also yield personal satisfaction to individuals. It should not be surprising to observe corporate jets, helicopters, gymnasiums, tennis courts, swimming pools, golf courses, chauffeured limousines, country club memberships, three-martini lunches, and business-related meetings (vacations) in exotic locations. The aggregate personal cost of every $100 spent is only about $30, and the cost to any one owner is in proportion to the normally very small percentage of total shares the individual owns.

Modern neoclassical and supply-side economists believe that the two uses of income, consumption and savings/investment, are altered by taxes. The price on consuming income in the present is a diminution in the amount of future income. It follows that the higher the taxes, the less after-tax future income will be sacrificed and the lower the price of present consumption. Under these conditions, current consumption will increase at the cost of less investment.

Paul Craig Roberts (1978:24) uses this type of analysis to explain some observed behavior in England. An individual Englishman may face the choice of saving $50,000 and receiving an estimated 17 percent return. His gross income would be $8,500 on his investment. But with a 98 percent marginal tax, the after-tax income is only about $170 per annum. The opportunity cost of spending $50,000 is only $170 per year, and this fact explains to Roberts's satisfaction why there are so many Rolls Royces and other examples of conspicuous consumption in England today.

Another rather obvious effect of high marginal tax rates has been the rapid growth of the tax shelter industry. The current tax structure along with inflation has caused even moderate income families to seek legal ways of shielding income from current taxation. Valuable resources with alternative economic uses are increasingly being used to seek loopholes in the law and to lobby for schemes that will blunt the effect of high taxes (Noble 1984:25–6). The tax shelter industry, which exists because of high marginal rates, is one in which there is a preponderence of human capital. It employs many of the economy's brightest and most highly trained lawyers and accountants, who could work more profitably and productively in other, more beneficial activities if tax rates were lower (Gwartney and Stroup 1980:227:8).

Importance of government benefits

As the result of empirical studies, incentive analysts believe that such government benefits as unemployment and welfare payments have become very important factors impinging on the incentive to work and to produce. The gaps between after-tax wages and these benefits have become so small that leisure rather than work is encouraged. Marginal rates of effective taxation on prospective lower-income earners who could enter the labor force often exceed 70 percent when free benefits, foregone because of reemployment, are added to the tax liability that could be incurred by finding and working at a job. If a prospective worker's expenditure for clothing, transportation, time, and other costs associated with holding a job are also considered, the effective marginal rate of taxation of returning to work can easily exceed 100 percent.

Importance of saving and capital formation

The modern neoclassical and supply-side economists emphasize the importance of increasing the share of resources devoted to investment to foster economic growth, but not solely or even chiefly by increasing aggregate demand with policies that encourage consumption. Increased saving plays a crucial role in their prescriptions for economic growth with price stability. Additional saving permits faster growth and a permanently higher standard of living because saving allows scarce resources to be devoted to more and better buildings, equipment, education, research, and technology. Empirical studies support the idea that as relatively larger amounts of investment increase the capital-to-labor ratio, a nation's real national product and per capita income grow.

Martin Feldstein (1979a:15), Professor of Economics at Harvard University, President of the National Bureau of Economic Research, and one of the leaders of the new school of incentive economists, has emphasized the point that the United States saves too little for future investment and spends too much on current private and government consumption. Since 1960, Americans have saved 8 percent of their income, about half the rate of saving in the twenty-three other industrially advanced countries that are members of the Organization for Economic Cooperation and Development. In 1978, the saving rate dropped to less than 6 percent ("The U.S. Bias . . ." 1978:90–6); the ratio of savings to disposable income fell to 3.3 percent in the last quarter of 1979, almost half the fourth-quarter rate that existed in the 1950s, 1960s, and most of the 1970s (Day 1980:11).

Feldstein (1979a:15) states that one of the major bars to increased savings is the social security system. Due to increasing intergenerational transfers of income, the social security tax rate has had to be increased by more than 600 percent, and current statutory provisions will cause the rate to rise to more than 20 percent of income in order for benefits to keep pace with the rising proportion of retirees in the population. Feldstein's research indicates that high benefits and tax rates have caused a notable decrease in private saving. The incentive to save is blunted by the fact that, on average, social security pays on retirement 80 percent of a worker's maximum after-tax income to a married couple. He notes that social security tax payments were greater than $100 billion in 1978, an amount that exceeded all corporate saving and pension contributions as well as all saving by individuals (Feldstein 1979a:15).

Social security and saving

The social security system not only depresses private saving, but unlike private pension plans it also provides no saving for capital formation. Social security is financed on a pay-as-you-go basis so that taxes collected from workers are immediately disbursed to the retired beneficiaries, who maintain high rates of consumption. The system could be reformed by giving employees the opportunity to join private retirement schemes, which can provide equal benefits at lower cost, and by retarding the constantly escalating level of benefits that will apply to individuals who retire in the future. Each of these changes would allow the nation to increase its savings and investment and provide high incomes in the future.

Taxes and saving

Another factor inhibiting capital formation that the incentive economists stress is the structure of American tax laws and rules that penalize saving and reward spending. This philosophy, which is embedded in the fabric of government economic policy, stems from economic thinking emphasizing that short-run demand should be constantly pumped up to avoid recessions and loss of votes to the ruling party. Its effect has been to encourage American consumers to borrow to a degree unequalled anywhere else in the world or anytime in their history. Consumers today almost entirely substitute borrowing for savings as the way to maintain living standards and gain control over such assets as housing, consumer durables, and even soft goods. The United States consumer, for the first time in any business cycle, has chosen the course of increasing spending while decreasing saving during a period of rising prices (Day 1980:11).

This uncharacteristic behavior is encouraged by the perverse incentives that exist. An individual who saves and purchases a $10,000 certificate of deposit at 8 percent, for example, will receive a pre-tax income of $800; but with a marginal federal, state, and local tax of 45 percent, the after-tax income is only $440, or 4.4 percent. This rate of return is not very attractive, especially when it is less than the rate of inflation. On the other hand, if an individual borrows and spends $10,000, the interest paid to the lender is deductible from income and reduces the income tax liability of the borrower.

The effect of the tax laws and rules is to increase the cost of saving and decrease the cost of borrowing. It is not surprising that saving and investment rates are declining whereas borrowing and spending are rising.

The plight of the saver is even more daunting. Government policies that have led to startling and sustained increases in the price level have forced savers to subsidize borrowers. After permitting a borrower to use one's money for a year, the lender's $10,000 certificate of deposit is worth something less than $9,000 due to inflation. After two years, the real value of the certificate is less than $8,000. These kinds of capital losses are, of course, stunningly unfair and help explain the falling rate of saving in America.

The low and negative returns on saving also inhibit individuals from risking their funds in corporate shares. A study by the National Bureau of Economic Research indicates that inflation has substantially reduced the after-tax return on investment. In 1977 alone, inflation was responsible for a real tax increase of $32 billion. This large sum represented an increase in the effective tax rate on corporate investment of approximately 50 percent, an increase due solely to inflation as the U.S. Congress passed no such tax law. Taxes paid by shareholders and the creditors of corporations now take fully two-thirds of real corporate income. Incentive economists argue that this state of affairs does not provide the necessary incentives for individuals to save and invest (Feldstein 1979a:15).

Reducing taxes on savings and the income from capital would increase the quantity and quality of capital, making workers more productive, real wages higher, and the country richer. Some modern neoclassical economists estimate, for example, that eliminating taxes on savings accounts would increase the rate of return to the average saver by 40 percent, which would produce between $30 and $40 billion more in personal savings each year. Increased savings would put downward pressure on interest rates, making investment and capital formation more attractive (Boskin 1978a:43–6).

Budget deficits and saving

The new school of incentive economists points to the increasingly important factor of government budgetary deficits as another reason for the diminution in private saving and investment. The politically attractive option of spending more money than there is income available for spending means, of course, that the government must run deficits. During the past five years, the federal government alone, despite record levels of tax receipts, has had to borrow more than $675 billion, and the projected deficits for the years 1985–89 total

$1067 trillion ("Administration . . ." 1984:3). In order to finance these unprecedented deficits, government normally borrows funds from private capital formation. These huge deficits have been extremely detrimental to the long-run health and growth of the U.S. economy by diverting funds away from productive investment and into current consumption.

In addition, unlike private individuals who spend more than they can afford, the state can finance increased expenditures by printing more money. This creation of money helps to cause inflation because disbursing these funds increases the stock of money and nominal incomes, but not goods and services on which the money is spent. Inflated incomes subject taxpayers to higher and higher marginal rates of taxation even though their real incomes may be steady or even falling. These increased tax revenues are then available for more political spending, and no senator or representative has had to vote for an increase in taxes to obtain these funds, which can be and are spent to benefit special interest groups that support the incumbent politician.

Modern neoclassical models

Incentive economists hypothesize a strong direct connection between effective tax rates and the aggregate supply of an economy. The general relationship is based on the assumption that some very basic public goods and services are necessary for an economy to produce marketable output. When tax rates are zero and there is no revenue or government output, the economy lacks such traditional public services as defense, internal law and order, and a legal system, which are complimentary to the private sector.

As public spending and taxes increase, the disincentives and inefficiencies associated with a larger government become more important. The degree to which public and private output complement each other declines as government provides fewer essential goods and services; at some point, government may reach diminishing total returns, and expenditures may actually diminish productive activity in the private sector. Transfer payments that permit workers to withdraw from the labor market at little or no cost, for example, are incompatible with economic growth.

At the same time, higher taxes levied to finance higher expenditures reduce the net after-tax rewards from saving, investing, and working for taxable income. These changes in relative prices alter the incentive structure so that individuals will save less and consume more; develop, seek, and invest in tax shelters (Noble 1984:25–6); invest less; choose more leisure; and/or work more in such nontaxable activities as charities and nonprofit organizations. People will also evade taxes by engaging in the illegal subterranean economy. All of these activities tend at some point to cause output to decline. As effective tax rates approach 100 percent, aggregate supply approaches zero.

The specific relationship between output and the tax rates that provide the funds for government spending depends on the supply of the various factors of production. The sensitivity or elasticity of these factor supplies depends on such things as the work and savings habits of the society, the time period under consideration, the importance of international trade, and the particular functions government finances with the tax revenues. As usual, anything that expands the number, importance, and intensity of alternatives for the owners of productive factors increases their elasticity of supply and sensitivity to changes in tax rates.

The wedge model

Incentive economists have developed a *wedge* model to help explain the behavior of production factors. They start with the assertion that the supply of a factor is determined in part by the owner's predicted after-tax earnings. The supply curve of labor, for example, is positively sloped in the normal Marshallian fashion. The choice between working and taking leisure is governed largely by the relative price of these two activities. Since the price of leisure is the income given up by not working, it follows that an increase in taxes on labor income leaves less net income to the worker and lowers the price of leisure. Conversely, a tax cut increases the amount of after-tax income from working, increases the price of leisure, induces individuals to substitute work for leisure, and increases the supply of labor and real output.

Supply-side economists believe that the substitution effect generally dominates the income effect. Some scholars, however, argue conversely that when taxes increase and the price of leisure falls, workers will choose more work and take less leisure. The proponents of this position assert that individuals have a target income and will labor longer to maintain their level of money income if income taxes are raised; they will work less and consume more leisure if taxes are cut, and their nominal income rises. This latter point may, of course, be possible for an individual with a backward bending supply curve, but it is illogical to argue that aggregate income can increase if all individuals reduce their amount of work.

Jude Wanniski (1979:84), a leading proponent of supply-side economics, disagrees with the target income theory and states the modern neoclassical position quite clearly. "People work when work is more attractive than non-work. The more a worker is rewarded for non-work and penalized for work, the less he will work." If increased income is a goal, government policy can help society achieve this end "by lessening the burdens of regulation, taxation, or tariffs. It can make non-work less attractive, first by reducing non-work subsidies" and by increasing penalties on those individuals who evade taxes, engage in illegal bartering, and maneuver in the underground economy.

Like Keynesian economists, modern neoclassicists believe that government policy also affects the demand for factors of production, but they do not confine their thinking to an analysis of the impact of shifts in aggregate demand and disposable income. Changes in relative prices are important to those firms demanding labor because the price of labor is a cost to them. Moreover, the law of demand, which states that the quantity desired varies inversely with price or cost, holds for labor markets. It follows that increases in taxes and government-mandated and other imposed costs increase the cost of employment labor. The results are that firms will demand fewer workers and output will tend to fall.

The labor wedge model

The wedge model was developed to analyze, illustrate, and compare pre-tax and post-tax situations. Before the time taxes are imposed, the wage workers receive equals what companies pay for labor. After taxes are imposed, however, the amount firms pay exceeds the amount laborers actually receive. This difference between what the buyer pays and what the seller of labor receives is called the wedge.

The wedge causes firms to demand less labor; at the same time, because rewards are less, suppliers of labor use several means to decrease the quantity of labor supplied to the market. Workers may labor less intensely, take more leisure, or engage partly or wholly in the less efficient but higher paying illegal subterranean economy where they pay no taxes.

Figure 1.1 contains the essential elements of the wedge analysis. The pre-tax situation is illustrated by an equilibrium in which the real wage is RW_0 and the quantity of labor demanded is Q_0. On the imposition of a tax, firms, at least initially, must pay a higher wage RW_1, but labor receives only RW_2, and workers offer only Q_1 of work. The wedge at the new equilibrium in the labor market is equal to $RW_1 - RW_2$, or the difference between demand and supply curves at Q_1, and represents the governmentally imposed cost (tax).

The lined area forming a triangle in Figure 1.1 has been described variously as deadweight loss, welfare loss, excess burden, distortion, an unneutrality, and a tax-induced inefficiency. This area can and has been measured in dollar terms for various taxes in the United States. Estimates are reported in Chapters 3, 4, and 6.

It is important to realize that virtually all taxes are responsible for a certain amount of inefficiency. The challenges are to choose taxes and arrange the tax structure to minimize deadweight losses and distortions that affect the choices of individual decision makers.

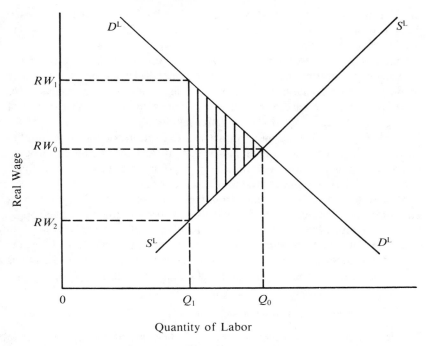

Figure 1.1. Labor wedge model

The capital market wedge model

Modern neoclassical economists use essentially the same thinking in their analysis of capital markets as they do for labor markets. Instead of work – leisure choices, decisions about the supply of capital revolve around the use of funds for consumption or for savings and investment (future income). The price or cost to an individual of increasing current consumption is a diminution of current savings and, therefore, a larger amount of foregone future income. There is a negative correlation between consumption and the net real rate of return on savings and investment. Current consumption falls and savings and investment actively increase when the rate of return rises. When the rate of return falls, the price of consumption decreases; and, as with other economic goods, the quantity of goods and services currently consumed rises, and long-term growth is inhibited.

The net rate of return on savings – investment activity is also important in decisions regarding the use of funds in either market- or nonmarket-oriented investment. A reduction in the rate of return lowers the relative price of investing in domestic and international tax shelters. Conversely, an increase in the net market yield causes more funds to be allocated into productive market investments.

Changes in effective tax rates play a crucial role in altering relative prices between consumption and savings – investment and between investment in productive taxable enterprises and nontaxable tax shelters. Increasing taxes lowers the price of leisure and encourages consumption at the expense of savings and investment. Higher taxation also makes the use of funds for investment in tax shelters more attractive. Tax rate reduction, on the other hand, not only increases the supply of capital through a reduction in consumption and an increase in saving, but also produces a shift of capital funds out of tax shelters into more productive market-oriented investment.

Modern neoclassicists conclude from the wedge theory that tax rates affect both the supply and demand of productive factors and the aggregate supply of an economy. Fiscal policy changes that alter relative prices and have an impact on aggregate production are largely ignored in Keynesian income expenditure models. Incentive economists contend that policy prescriptions that do not consider these important fiscal effects are destined to fail.

Role of modern neoclassical models

The decline of Keynesian economics has left the study of macroeconomics in a state of chaos. As Robert Lucas (1982:5) has perceptively observed, "Everyone has their own theory now, and since orthodoxy has no way of discriminating, all get a fair hearing." With this prevailing state of affairs, it is not surprising that the familiar sounding neoclassical principles, dressed up to some extent in supply-side garb, should reemerge in the forefront of research and policy.

U.S. tax policy in the 1980s is based largely on the time-tested, neoclassic, microeconomic principles that encourage productive behavior by relying on enhancing incentives at the margin of economic activity where individuals make important decisions. Current policy focuses on the individual's costs and benefits associated with the taxation of an extra dollar of saving or investment or an additional amount of work (Krieger 1982:7–8). The desired goal of this microapproach is, of course, to produce salutary macroeffects on the economy.

Two principal dangers are associated with the current neoclassical supply-side position. One related problem is the fact that the position may be discredited if it fails to deliver on the excessive claims promised by some of its more extreme advocates (Krieger 1982:7–8). The second danger is endemic to any coherent policy subject to the pulls and tugs of special interest groups. It may be compromised to the point of ineffectiveness or even become counterproductive, as happened with some misapplied Keynesian prescriptions. It should also be stressed that an unceasing amount of high-level empirical work is required if modern neoclassical economics is to provide the profession and country with a continuing basis for an effective tax policy.

Principles of sound taxation

The original and still primary goal of taxation is to raise revenue. Taxes transfer resources from the private to the public sector to enable government to perform a variety of functions. In performing this transfer task, care must be taken so the economy is not unduly disrupted. Sound tax criteria are required to help accomplish this goal. Consequently, it is advisable to explore several generally accepted tax principles before investigating the various individual taxes.

Fortunately, Adam Smith (1937:777–8) and Break and Pechman (1975: 4–10) laid down several generally accepted principles of good taxation. These principles are equity, simplicity, fiscal economy, and certainty. To these four tenets economists have more recently added a fifth and most important canon, economic efficiency.

Economic efficiency

The traditional interpretation of economic efficiency implies that ideally a tax should be neutral with respect to its effect on economic behavior. For example, a newly introduced tax should not lead individuals to alter their choices, to save more or less, to work more hours or take increased leisure, or to change the pattern of their investment and consumption decisions.

In the real world, perfect economic efficiency is obviously impossible. But the goal of neutrality, of minimizing both the misallocation of resources and the altering of economic decisions, is a very important ingredient of sound tax policy.

Equity

Tax equity has to do with fairness, and it is a highly subjective concept. Nevertheless, there is general agreement that a tax structure ought to treat similarly those individuals who are in approximately the same economic situation and, at the same time, account for differences among people who are in dissimilar circumstances. The first idea is referred to as horizontal equity, the latter as vertical equity.

It is easier to fulfill the goal of horizontal equity; but neither ideal is simple to apply, especially with more than a hundred million taxpayers in the world's largest and most complex economy. It should be noted that the goal of vertical equity, which implies the desirability of progressive tax structures, has in practice made more difficult achieving other tax objectives, such as, economic efficiency, simplicity, certainty, fiscal efficiency, and perhaps equity itself.

Until recently, much of the discussion about U.S. taxes and tax policy centered on the question of equity. Because of the slow growth of the economy coupled with rather dim prospects for the future, scholars, politicians, and others are now researching and concentrating more attention on the principle of economic efficiency.

Simplicity

"Every tax ought to be levied at the time, or in the manner, in which it is most likely to be convenient for the contributor to pay it" (Smith 1937:778). This principle of taxation implies that tax laws and regulations should be simple and easily understood. Average taxpayers should be able to prepare their own tax returns without the need for costly professional advice and assistance. Similarly, business firms should easily be able to provide accounting and other necessary records required for the proper assessment of taxes. Moreover, Break and Pechman (1975:9) point out that simplicity has an added virtue because it enhances equity by enabling individuals with limited educational backgrounds to compute their tax liabilities as correctly as persons with more knowledge and expertise.

Fiscal economy

"Every tax ought to be so contrived as both to take out and keep out of the pockets of the people as little as possible, over and above what it brings into the public treasury" (Smith 1937:778). This means that not only the government's cost of the administration should be considered in evaluating the fiscal efficiency of a tax, but also the time and expense of the taxpayers should be included. Moreover, present-day economists would argue that these costs should not necessarily be minimal but actually optimal. The preferred policy would reveal that the marginal social costs of administration are just equal to the marginal benefits derived from proper assessment, compliance, and tax collection activities.

Certainty

Adam Smith (1937:778) noted that the time of the tax payment, the manner of payment, and the quantity to be paid should be certain, clear, and plain to the contributor and every other person. Moreover, the auditing of taxpayers' returns, as well as other administrative procedures requiring the time and expense of the taxpayer, should be conducted in the most professional and expeditious manner possible. Legal redress through the judicial system should be made as certain as possible for the taxpayer.

Avoidance, evasion, and tax effectiveness

Tax evasion can be defined as fraudulent underpayment of taxes. Tax avoidance is the attempt to decrease tax liabilities within the law. Recently, Russell Mathews (1982:1–26) analyzed several factors contributing to economic inefficiency and inequity in tax structures when tax avoidance and evasion can no longer be considered minor aberrations from normal taxpayer compliance.

This analysis led Mathews to contribute a set of specific recommendations that, if adopted, would greatly enhance both the efficiency and equity of tax systems. His tax rules provide us with a valuable additional set of detailed, operational tax principles to help evaluate present-day tax structures. They are derived (holding other factors constant) for various types and forms of taxation where opportunities for avoidance and evasions are considered together.

Tax effectiveness criteria

Mathews (1982:9) notes the following:

Irrespective of the form of activity on which a tax is imposed – production, income, sales, expenditure, consumption, wealth, transfers – a broad-based tax imposed at a low rate is likely to achieve a higher score on an index of tax effectiveness than a selective tax imposed at a higher rate. A tax imposed at a uniform rate will be more effective than a tax with a progressive rate structure. A tax collected at the source of transactions by a party other than the ultimate taxpayer will rank higher on the index of tax effectiveness than a tax which depends on a declaration of liability by the taxpayer himself.

Taxes levied on the benefit principle or earmarked for particular expenditure programs, such as local government property taxes, education levies and motor taxes, will be subject to fewer leakages than taxes credited to general revenue. Taxes with exemption provisions or which permit deductions from the gross revenue base will be less effective than taxes imposed unambiguously on strictly defined bases. Taxes which are obtained from a few collection points, such as customs duties on exports and imports, excise duties and tolls, will be more effective than taxes which have to be collected from widely diffused sources; for the same reason, taxes imposed on manufacturers or wholesale distributors may be expected to rank higher on the effectiveness index than retail sales taxes. Cascaded turnover taxes will be less effective than single-stage or value-added taxes and income taxes based on a separation of company and personal incomes will be less effective than those which successfully integrate the two sources.

The formidable conceptual and administrative difficulties of measuring income, especially under conditions of changing prices, mean that income taxes will be less effective than either taxes on wealth or taxes on transactions such as cash flows or expenditures. Measurement problems, especially in relation to unrealized capital gains, will make capital gains taxes less effective than annual wealth taxes; while measurement and assessment problems together will tend to place annual wealth taxes in a lower position on the index of tax effectiveness than death duties.

CHAPTER 2

The individual income tax

Historical background

The fascinating early history of the U.S. income tax centered on three main factors:

1. budgetary deficits and surpluses;
2. the redistribution of income;
3. the question of direct versus indirect taxation.

Each of these issues proved to be important forces in the final and permanent adoption of the individual income tax.

Budgetary deficits and surpluses

In many instances throughout history, war proved to be an important factor in revolutionizing the fiscal system of a country. The Civil War was no exception. Tariffs, which had been the principal form of federal taxation until 1861, proved to be an inadequate revenue source for a government struggling with seceding southern states (Paul 1954:7).

A rather vague revenue law passed by Congress in 1861 committed the North to the use of an income tax. It was strengthened in 1862 when the levy was made mildly progressive, and provisions for withholding taxes at the source, including interest and dividends, were instituted (Paul 1954:7; Groves 1964:162–4).

After the usual administrative difficulties associated with introducing a new levy, the income tax proved to be a substantial source of revenue. Because funds were needed to prosecute the war, rates were increased and made more progressive in 1864. During the postwar period, Congress increased the personal exemption, made the tax proportional, and twice reduced rates. Nevertheless, large budgetary surpluses emerged, exercising a strong fiscal drag on economic activity (Olson 1973:8; Paul 1954:12–13).

Redistribution of income

Individuals and groups who favored redistributing income from higher to lower income classes strongly supported retaining the income tax. Opponents cited its detrimental effect on saving, capital formation, risk taking, and economic growth, as well as the depressing economic impact of continuing, large, and increasing budgetary surpluses that were responsible for withdrawing funds from the private sector (Paul 1954:22–9). In light of the budgetary deficit problems of the 1970s and 1980s, it is interesting to note that starting in 1866, the federal government realized an unbroken string of annual surpluses until 1894, the year following the Depression that began in 1893 (Studenski and Krooss 1952:171).

Opponents of the income tax finally won the debate, at least temporarily, when Congress permitted the tax to expire in 1872 (Paul 1954:27). Advocates for the progressive individual income tax did not give up. Over the next twenty years, they introduced sixty-six separate bills in Congress to reestablish the levy. Finally, in 1895, the House and Senate passed an act that taxed all forms of individual and corporate income. The law also defined gifts and inheritances as income (Studenski and Krooss 1952:222).

Direct versus indirect taxation

The new legislation was immediately challenged in the courts on the grounds that an income tax is a direct tax (Paul 1954:59). The Constitution required that a federal direct tax be apportioned according to the population of the various states and not in relation to the income or wealth of a state.

This requirement meant, for example, that if the state of New York had 20 percent of U.S. income but only 10 parcent of the population, just 10 percent of the total revenue from a federal income tax could be taken from New York residents. Since the per capita income of New York was higher than that of Mississippi, for example, federal income tax rates would have had to be lower for New York than for Mississippi in order to satisfy the apportionment clause in the Constitution. But differential federal tax rates between and among states would have clearly violated other parts of the Constitution. In effect, the Constitution prohibited the use of federal direct taxes.

In a landmark case, the Supreme Court noted that the Revenue Act of 1895 involved a direct tax, and because it was not apportioned among the states in accordance to their respective populations, the Court ruled by a vote of five to four that the law was unconstitutional (Studenski and Krooss 1952:224). Redistributionists reacted by beginning a campaign that culminated in 1909 with congressional approval of the Sixteenth Amendment to the Constitution. In 1913, the amendment became part of the Constitution when, as required by law, a minimum of three-fourths of the states ratified it (Olson 1973:8).

Congress wasted little time in passing a mildly progressive income tax law that same year. Provision was made for collecting taxes at the source on wages, salaries, rent, and interest, but this part of the new law was repealed

Table 2.1. *Income tax rates and revenue, 1914*

Normal tax:	$12.7 (millions)
Surtax:	
$ 20,000–$ 50,000 at 1 percent	$ 2.9 (millions)
50,000– 75,000 at 2 percent	1.6
75,000– 100,000 at 3 percent	1.3
100,000– 250,000 at 4 percent	3.8
250,000– 500,000 at 5 percent	2.3
Over 500,000 at 6 percent	3.4
	$28.3 (millions)

Source: Paul Studenski and Herman E. Krooss, *Financial History of the United States,* McGraw-Hill, New York, 1952, p. 274.

in 1916 (Paul 1954:104). The 1913 Revenue Act imposed a 1 percent rate on corporate income and on all personal income in excess of $3,000, and surtaxes ranging from 1 percent on incomes of $20,000 to 6 percent on those over $500,000. Table 2.1 shows the rates, incomes, and revenues for 1914 (Studenski and Krooss 1952:273–4).

When the country entered World War I in 1917, surtax rates were increased to a minimum of 40 percent, and the initial base against which these rates applied was decreased drastically from $20,000 to $3,000. Receipts from the income and profits tax increased from $28 million in 1914 to $2,850 million in 1918 (Studenski and Krooss 1952:274, 295).

Tax cuts in the 1920s

Federal expenditures declined after the end of World War I, but receipts continued to rise. In fact, revenues climbed to a record high of $6.7 billion in 1920, $2 billion more than 1919 and more than $2.5 billion more than the last year of the war. Federal revenue would not reach this unprecedented level again until the first year of World War II (Studenski and Krooss 1952:308, 450).

There was a great deal of debate over the disposition of these surpluses. Positions ranged from increasing expenditures to retiring the debt to reducing taxes. The controversy about which policy to adopt was settled soon after Andrew Mellon was appointed Secretary of Treasury in 1921. He recommended that Congress repeal the excess profits tax, cut the corporate income tax to 2.5 percent, and reduce the maximum surtax rate on personal income from 65 to 32 percent (Studenski and Krooss 1952:310).

Secretary Mellon continued to use neoclassical reasoning and recommended tax cuts in 1924, 1926, and 1928 that he believed would encourage

Table 2.2. *Share of income tax paid by income groups*

Income group	1920	1925	1929
Under $ 5,000	15.4%	1.9%	0.4%
$ 5,000– 10,000	9.1	2.6	1.0
10,000– 25,000	16.0	10.1	6.0
25,000– 100,000	29.6	36.6	27.4
Over– 100,000	29.9	48.8	65.2

Source: Paul Studenski and Herman E. Krooss, *Financial History of the United States,* McGraw-Hill, New York, 1952, p. 314.

saving, investment, and economic growth. Compromise again ruled the day in 1924, but Congress finally enacted most of his suggestions in the tax reduction acts of 1926 and 1928 (Studenski and Krooss 1952:312).

Despite the four tax reduction laws Congress passed in the decade of the twenties, the inexorable move toward increased reliance on federal direct taxes that had begun with the sixteenth Amendment continued unabated. Personal and corporate income taxes produced a significantly higher share of total revenue than they did before World War I and nearly as much as at the peak of the war. Moreover, as indicated in Table 2.2, the proportion of the income tax paid by the relatively high income recipients increased dramatically during the 1920s (Studenski and Krooss 1952:314).

The depression years

Although there was some support for the idea of running budgetary deficits in the face of a notable deflation of the currency and falling aggregate demand and employment, both the Democratic Congress and Republican administration favored reducing government spending and raising taxes in 1932. In fact, the Revenue Act that emerged from Congress that year represented the largest peacetime increase of taxes up to that time.

The newly elected Roosevelt administration lost little time in raising taxes. The Revenue Act of 1934 increased corporate and personal income taxes, making the latter more progressive. When these measures failed to balance the budget, the President recommended to Congress a general reform of the tax structure. The 1935 law narrowed the tax base and increased further the rates on middle and especially higher incomes. The following year, Congress, at the urging of the administration, passed the undistributed profits tax, and the President lost much of the remaining confidence and support that he had from the American business community. Moreover, in 1936 and 1937, taxes to support the newly created social programs for unemployment insurance, social security, and railroad retirement took effect (Studenski and Krooss 1952:420–2).

Taxpayers reacted to the series of New Deal tax acts with an enormous increase in tax avoidance. Randolph Paul, special tax consultant to the President and Treasury at the time, gives a particularly graphic account of the extent, variety, and ingenuity associated with the development of tax shelters in 1936 and 1937, including the establishment of "companies" in the Bahama Islands (Paul 1954:199–208), a ploy also used today. Congress acted swiftly and enacted a statute that closed many, though not all, the loopholes and inequities.

The war years

The revenue acts passed to finance World War II imposed an excess profits tax, increased the normal corporation income levy, and increased rates on personal incomes. They also broadened the tax base tremendously by lowering exemptions. After extended and acrimonious debate throughout the winter and spring of 1943, Congress also enacted the Current Tax Payment Act, which reinstated and broadened the Civil War and World War I policies of withholding taxes at the source and time of income (Paul 1954:326–49). This pay-as-you-earn method continues to this day.

Postwar federal spending did not decline to prewar levels and neither did taxes. In fact, nonmilitary expenditures began to rise before the war with Japan was concluded. Much the same general fiscal pattern characterized the movement in spending and taxation during America's military involvement in Korea and Viet Nam and afterward.

The postwar peacetime years

The Eisenhower and Kennedy–Johnson administrations recommended and obtained from Congress notable reductions in the marginal rates of taxation on personal incomes. There were no significant cuts in these marginal rates for the vast majority of taxpayers between 1965 and 1981. The top rate on income was 70 percent in both years, though the highest marginal rate on so-called earned income, which does not include interest and dividends, was reduced to 50 percent in 1971 (under the provisions of the Tax Reform Act of 1969).

Congress did reduce taxes several times between 1965 and 1979, but the main device to accomplish this goal was an increase in personal deductions and tax credits. This strategy offered a slight temporary reduction in current tax liabilities; but because marginal rates remained virtually unchanged, inflation boosted taxpayers into higher and higher tax brackets. The result more than offset the effect of increased deductions.

The combination of inflation and the progressive income tax structure rapidly increased government revenues in the sixties and seventies, but reduced the real income of millions of taxpayers. This phenomenon of inflation-induced but unlegislated tax increases together with Congressional insensitivity to the problem were important causes for the fiscal unrest in the decade of the seventies and at the beginning of the 1980s.

Anatomy of the income tax

When viewing income taxation from a historical perspective, it is difficult to describe *the* income tax. It has changed so radically during the seventy-odd years it has been in use in the United States that the original proponents would hardly recognize it.

"The belief that the individual income tax is the fairest of all taxes" (Goode 1964:11) no longer holds in the United States, if indeed it ever did prevail. The annual polls of the Advisory Commission on Intergovernmental Relations reveal that Americans believe the federal income levy is the least fair and the worst of all taxes. Perhaps of greater significance, it is progressively losing the support of the lower middle-income class and blue-collar workers (Advisory Commission on Intergovernmental Relations 1980:1–2). Changes in tax statutes and the economic environment help to explain the disenchantment with the contemporary levy.

Growth, pervasiveness, and disenchantment

The original law taxed only a very small minority of individuals who had relatively high incomes. It was easy for the majority of voters to support an arrangement whereby relatively few persons paid for a substantial part of federal expenditures.

Today, the picture is vastly different. Most voters must pay, and some with taxable incomes in excess of only $1,700 pay a marginal rate of 12 percent. In addition, forty-four states use the individual income tax. The tax rates are substantial, and most of them are progressive. In California, for example, incomes above $26,000 bear a tax rate of 11 percent; the marginal rate in Delaware reaches 19.8 percent. Moreover, more than 4,000 local governments also levy income taxes, many of them progressive. Rates in the District of Columbia range from 2 to 11 percent. New York City rates rise to 4.3 percent, which is in addition to the maximum state rate of 14 percent. These state and local levies are in addition to the federal income tax.

The persistent rise in the price level of the past fifteen years is another factor that has led to the electorate's disenchantment with income taxation. Inflation has exacerbated the pervasiveness, progressivity, and burden on the tax. Individuals and families with modest incomes have been automatically forced up into relatively high marginal tax brackets, even though their inflation-adjusted incomes have remained constant or actually fallen. The United States individual income tax was neither intended nor structured to cope with marked increases in inflated wages, salaries, interest, and rent.

Capriciousness of the income tax

Another factor that has caused the average income earner to express disappointment in the levy is its capriciousness. Individuals in similar circumstances pay vastly different amounts, and some people are able to escape paying quite large sums. For them, the income tax has become largely a voluntary tax. Moreover, since the tax is to a certain extent self-assessed, publicity concerning its capriciousness has led to increased dissatisfaction, avoidance, and outright evasion.

R. L. Mathews's (1980:28) research on this topic is instructive. He notes that the personal income tax has become largely a levy against wage and salary earners. The ''upper and lower ends of the income scale have been able to take steps to avoid or evade tax.''

Mathews (1980:30) supports his claims with an analysis of Australia's personal income and tax liabilities over a recent fourteen-year period for which data were available. He found that in fiscal 1965–66, wage and salary earners, who have their taxes withheld at the source, earned 65.7 percent of total personal income and paid 67 percent of total individual income taxes. By 1978–79, wage and salary earners' share of personal income had fallen slightly to 63.3 percent, but their tax liabilities as a share of total individual income taxes had increased sharply to 81.2 percent.

These figures indicate that nonwage and nonsalary individuals increased slightly their share of total personal income over the years; at the same time, they substantially reduced their taxes from 33 percent to only 18.8 percent of total individual income taxes paid. If the 1965–66 tax share of each income class had remained constant, wage and salary earners would have paid some $1.8 billion less to the government, but the tax liability of nonwage and nonsalary earners, who do not have their taxes withheld, would have been more than 75 percent higher than they actually were in 1978–79 (Mathews 1980:3). These and other data in Table 2.3 make it clear that there is massive avoidance and evasion of the individual income tax.

Similar calculations for the United States are unfortunately unavailable because the Treasury does not report taxes paid by wage and salary earners.

Table 2.3. *Income tax paid by wage and salary earners and other individuals*

Fiscal year	Individual income tax				Personal income			
	Tax on wage and salary earners (1) $m	Tax on others (2) $m	Total tax (3) $m	(1)/(3) (4) %	Wage and salary earned (5) $m	Other personal income (6) $m	Total personal income (7) $m	(5)/(7) (8) %
1965–66	1,160	571	1,731	67.0	10,674	5,583	16,257	65.7
1966–67	1,323	599	1,922	68.8	11,640	6,289	17,929	64.9
1967–68	1,508	670	2,178	69.2	12,650	6,177	18,827	67.2
1968–69	1,727	652	2,379	72.6	13,982	7,189	21,171	66.0
1969–70	2,084	774	2,858	72.9	15,671	7,649	23,320	67.2
1970–71	2,432	746	3,178	76.5	17,946	8,212	26,158	68.6
1971–72	2,889	880	3,769	76.7	20,067	9,474	29,541	67.9
1972–73	3,161	929	4,089	77.3	22,375	11,433	33,808	66.2
1973–74	4,238	1,252	5,490	77.2	27,596	14,294	41,890	65.9
1974–75	6,071	1,643	7,714	78.7	35,409	16,442	51,851	68.3
1975–76	7,020	2,200	9,219	76.1	41,445	19,925	61,370	67.5
1976–77	8,529	2,525	11,054	77.2	46,880	23,526	70,406	66.6
1977–78	9,639	2,490	12,129	79.5	51,548	26,420	77,968	66.1
1978–79	10,398	2,406	12,804	81.2	55,879	32,022	87,901	63.6

Source: Russell Mathews, "The Structure of Taxation," Centre for Research on Federal Financial Relations, The Australian National University, Canberra, Reprint Series, 34, p. 29. Reprinted from the Proceedings of the Australian Institute of Political Science Summer School on *The Politics of Taxation*, Canberra, 26–28 January 1980.

The tax base

It is apparent that many exemptions, deductions, exceptions, and loopholes are associated with the individual income tax. To understand better how the levy works in practice, it is instructive to explore the basis of the tax.

In his excellent treatise on the individual income tax, Richard Goode (1964:14) points out that legislators have not tried to present a general definition of income. Unlike economists, who do begin with a very definite overall notion of income (Haig 1959:59; Simons 1938:50), lawyers have been content to enumerate what specific items are to be included or excluded for purposes of taxation. Many decisions concerning what is and is not subject to the tax are made by bureaucrats, judges, and juries. Unhappily for taxpayers, a decision regarding taxable income by a court in one jurisdiction is not necessarily binding in another area.

The two principal kinds of income with which taxpayers grope are adjusted gross income (AGI) and taxable income. Incomes from a variety of specific sources comprise AGI. Some of the sources are wages, salaries, tips or gratuities, interest, dividends, rent, royalties, alimony, business income, a portion of capital gains, certain prizes, awards, gambling winnings, court-awarded punitive damages and compensation for lost profits, damages received for patent or copyright infringement, sale of such personal items as cars, refrigerators, furniture, hi-fis, jewelry, or silverware on which there is a gain (losses are not deductible), illegal drugs, and so on (U.S. Department of Treasury 1980:52–60).

Cash income that is not considered part of AGI and, therefore, not taxed includes interest on tax-exempt securities, most social security payments, railroad retirement, federal employee retirement, certain prizes, workmen's compensation, cash rental allowances for members of the clergy, unemployment compensation (partially), payments to reduce the cost of winter energy consumption, black lung benefits, mortgage assistance payments, public welfare benefits, and so on. Income set aside for payments into individual retirement and Keogh retirement accounts is not taxed until withdrawn. Noncash income that escapes taxation includes unrealized capital gains, Medicaid, imputed rent on owner-occupied housing, in-kind rental assistance, imputed rental allowance for the clergy, food stamps, and so on (U.S. Department of Treasury 1980:52–60).

After taxpayers discover the size of their AGI, they are permitted to make various deductions. These may be itemized if it benefits the taxpayer. Some people choose the much simpler zero bracket amount that used to be called the standard deduction. Some expenses incurred in earning income are deductible from AGI whereas others are not. Deductions include such items as contributions to churches, universities, and charities, certain taxes paid on outstanding loans, and major medical expenses that exceed 5 percent of AGI.

A deduction of a different sort may be subtracted from AGI to derive taxable income, or TI. The personal exemption allows deduction of $2,000 if married, $1,000 for a single person, and $1,000 for each dependent. A multitude of rules and conditions that determine whether an individual is a dependent under tax law and regulations. Certain classifications, such as the blind and individuals sixty-five old and older, receive double personal exemptions (U.S. Department of Treasury 1980:17–22).

After adding the various items that qualify as income and then subtracting the appropriate deductions, taxpayers can find their tax liability by consulting the pertinent tax tables supplied by the Internal Revenue Service. Three such tax rate schedules for federal income tax rates in 1984 are shown in Table 2.4. The Revenue Act of 1981 changed the higher marginal rates on interest and dividend income by cutting the maximum to 50 percent. In addition, the law reduced the entire rate schedule at every income level by about 23 percent in three separate steps over the thirty-three-month period that started in October 1981. Beginning in 1985, the individual income tax was indexed to neutralize the effect of inflation. The reader should consult the section entitled Indexing in Chapter 3 for insight into this concept.

Revenue productivity of the income tax

Table 2.5 shows that income tax collections have increased dramatically over the years. Part of the reason for the revenue growth was the increase in real incomes over time. The major reason for the sharp rise in collections was inflation. Nominal incomes have increased rapidly, and even without the progressive feature of the U.S. income tax, total revenue would have risen along with inflation. The progressivity of the tax, however, tended to exacerbate the rise since nominal incomes were pushed up into higher and higher income tax brackets where, until recently, the marginal rate of taxation reached as high as 70 percent.

Distributional effects of deductions, exemptions, and tax credits

The 1970s witnessed a particularly strong and increasing dispersion in the federal tax burden among households. This change in the distribution of taxes and income was due primarily to inflation and congressional action.

Tax deductions

The standard deduction, which Congress first introduced in 1944 to simplify the calculation of tax liabilities for lower income recipients, is subtracted from income earned when deriving taxable income. In 1970, the minimum standard deduction was increased to between $200 and $1,100, depending on the tax-

Table 2.4. *Federal income tax rate schedules*

Married taxpayers filing together

Over	Not over	Pay +		of the amount over
$ 0–	$ 3,400	$ 0 +	0%	$ 0
3,400–	5,500	0 +	11%	3,400
5,500–	7,600	231 +	12%	5,500
7,600–	11,900	483 +	14%	7,600
11,900–	16,000	1,085 +	16%	11,900
16,000–	20,200	1,741 +	18%	16,000
20,200–	24,600	2,497 +	22%	20,200
24,600–	29,900	3,465 +	25%	24,600
29,900–	35,200	4,790 +	28%	29,900
35,200–	45,800	6,274 +	33%	35,200
45,800–	60,000	9,772 +	38%	45,800
60,000–	85,600	15,168 +	42%	60,000
85,600–	109,400	25,920 +	45%	85,600
109,400–	162,400	36,630 +	49%	109,400
162,400 and over		62,600 +	50%	162,400

Married taxpayers filing separately

Over	Not over	Pay +		of the amount over
$ 0–	$ 1,700	$ 0 +	0%	$ 0
1,700–	2,750	0 +	11%	1,700
2,750–	3,800	115.50 +	12%	2,750
3,800–	5,950	241.50 +	14%	3,800
5,950–	8,000	542.50 +	16%	5,950
8,000–	10,100	870.50 +	18%	8,000
10,100–	12,300	1,248.50 +	22%	10,100
12,300–	14,950	1,732.50 +	25%	12,300
14,950–	17,600	2,395.00 +	28%	14,950
17,600–	22,900	3,137.00 +	33%	17,600
22,900–	30,000	4,886.00 +	38%	22,900
30,000–	42,800	7,584.00 +	42%	30,000
42,800–	54,700	12,960.00 +	45%	42,800
54,700–	81,200	18,315.00 +	49%	54,700
81,200 and over		31,300.00 +	50%	81,200

Single taxpayers

Over	Not over	Pay +		of the amount over
$ 0–	$ 2,300	$ 0 +	0%	$ 0
2,300–	3,400	0 +	11%	2,300
3,400–	4,400	121 +	12%	3,400
4,400–	6,500	241 +	14%	4,400
6,500–	8,500	535 +	15%	6,500
8,500–	10,800	835 +	16%	8,500
10,800–	12,900	1,203 +	18%	10,800
12,900–	15,000	1,581 +	20%	12,900
15,000–	18,200	2,001 +	23%	15,000
18,200–	23,500	2,737 +	26%	18,200
23,500–	28,800	4,115 +	30%	23,500
28,800–	34,100	5,705 +	34%	28,800
34,100–	41,500	7,507 +	38%	34,100
41,500–	55,300	10,319 +	42%	41,500
55,300–	81,800	16,115 +	48%	55,300
81,900 and over		28,835 +	50%	81,800

Source: 1984 Federal Income Tax Form 1040, Department of Treasury, Washington, 1984.

Table 2.5. *Federal and state local individual income tax receipts*

Year	Federal tax	State-local tax	Total tax receipts
1960	$ 41.8B	$ 2.5B	$ 44.3B
1961	42.7	2.8	45.5
1962	46.5	3.2	49.7
1963	49.2	3.4	52.6
1964	46.0	4.0	50.0
1965	51.1	4.4	55.5
1966	58.6	5.4	64.0
1967	64.4	6.3	70.6
1968	76.5	8.1	84.6
1969	91.5	10.1	101.5
1970	88.8	11.1	100.0
1971	85.7	12.7	98.3
1972	102.7	17.5	120.2
1973	109.5	19.1	128.6
1974	126.4	20.6	147.0
1975	120.8	22.8	143.6
1976	141.5	26.8	168.3
1977	162.7	30.9	193.6
1978	189.4	35.5	224.9
1979	225.7	33.8	259.5
1980	251.0	44.9	295.9
1981	289.0	51.9	340.9
1982	310.4	50.8	361.2
1983	295.3		
1984[a]	302.1		
1985[a]	340.8		

[a] preliminary estimates
Source: Survey of Current Business, U.S. Commerce Department, Washington, various issues, and *Economic Report of the President,* Washington, 1984, pp. 309, 311.

payer's income and number of dependents. By 1979, it had been increased seven times and stood at $3,400 for married persons. As a result of these increases, more people took the standard deduction than previously. In 1970, for example, about 52 percent of the individuals submitting tax returns used the standard deduction; by 1978, more than 73 percent took advantage of this provision in the tax code. Moreover, since upper income classes are more likely to itemize deductions, higher standard deductions have not benefited them, and the large tax savings from congressional manipulations of the standard deduction have accrued to individuals in the lower and lower middle-income classes (Palash 1980:17–18).

Table 2.6. *Deductions and exemptions as a proportion of income*

Year	Deductions (1)	Exemptions (2)	(1) + (2) (3)
1965	11.9%	17.3%	29.2%
1966	11.8	16.7	28.5
1967	11.9	15.5	27.8
1968	12.2	15.0	27.2
1969	12.8	14.5	27.3
1970	13.4	13.9	27.3
1971	14.9	14.1	29.0
1972	15.7	14.1	29.8
1973	15.5	13.1	28.6
1974	15.8	12.6	28.4
1975	16.0	10.7	26.7
1976	16.2	10.0	26.2
1977	17.1	8.8	25.9
1978	18.7	8.2	29.9

Source: Carl J. Palash, "Recent Trends in the Federal Taxation of Individual Income," *Quarterly Review,* Federal Reserve Bank of New York, Autumn 1980, pp. 15–20.

Personal exemptions

The shift in the tax bite to middle and upper middle-income groups was enhanced and exacerbated by the decline in the value of personal exemptions. Since they are fixed dollar amounts, inflation erodes their real worth over time, and Congress has not increased them fast enough to vitiate the effect of rising prices. The value of exemptions as a percentage of income has fallen drastically over time. In 1965, they represented slightly more than 17 percent of income; but despite several legislative increases, exemptions were only 8 percent of income in 1978 (Palash 1980:18–20).

The effect of the declining value of personal exemptions relative to income has had a greater impact on middle and upper income groups because, on average, they have more exemptions than lower income recipients. The main reason for this circumstance is that there are many more single taxpayers in the lower income groups.

Table 2.6 records the relative value of exemptions over time. It also shows deductions and the combination of deductions and exemptions as a percentage of income.

Tax credits and rates

Income taxes due the government are computed by applying the appropriate tax rate to taxable income and then subtracting any eligible tax credits. As with changes in the standard deduction and personal exemption, tax credits have also played an important role in changing the distribution of the tax burden.

Tax credits for individuals became important in the mid-1970s, when Congress introduced the per capita credit and the earned income credit. The per capita credit was replaced by an increase in the personal exemption in 1978. The earned income credit was designed to reduce the impact of rising social security taxes as well as alleviate tax-induced work disincentives on the lower income groups. Other tax credits exist for child care, retirement income, energy efficient expenditures, and work incentives.

The combination of inflation and statutory changes in the 1970s altered the distribution of the tax burden in a way that increased the progressivity of the individual income tax. By 1978, the lowest 20 percent of the taxpayers paid only 0.5 percent of their incomes in income taxes. In 1969, this figure stood at 2.9 percent. The top quintile of taxpayers was the only income group to pay relatively more income taxes in 1978 than in 1969.

If the effect of increases in social security rates and tax base are included in calculations, only the top 40 percent of taxpayers incurred relatively greater tax liabilities in 1978 than in 1969. The largest increase in the amount of income and social security taxes paid was sustained by the highest 20 percent of the taxpayers.

Perhaps of greatest fiscal importance from the supply-side perspective was the general rise in the marginal rates of income taxation between 1965 and 1978. Although the lowest quintile of taxpayers actually faced lower rates at the end of this period, the top 20 percent experienced an increase in the marginal rate of taxation of more than 40 percent. All of these trends were modified slightly by legislation in 1978 and significantly by the Economic Recovery Act of 1981.

Additional problems of the income tax

Several problems have plagued income tax authorities during its history in the United States. Among them are the marriage tax problem, the averaging of irregular incomes, so-called automatic stabilization, and society's cost of administering the levy.

The marriage tax problem

The history of the tax treatment of married couples typifies the zigzag pattern of shifts in federal income tax policy and illustrates well the complexities, discrepancies, inconsistencies, and capriciousness (Brazer 1980:224, 231) that characterize the individual income tax. This section briefly traces the history of the United States marriage tax (Munnell 1980:247–78) and investigates economic and other effects of the tax on married and single individuals.

Early history: All taxpayers were treated as individuals in the statute passed by Congress in 1913; due to progressive rates, however, a single worker paid a higher tax than a married couple, both of whom worked and together earned the same income as the unmarried individual. Because the law stipulated that the individual was the basic unit subject to taxation, the progressive income tax was capricious. The system ignored the aggregation of income by the married couple.

This fundamental problem was exacerbated over time as more states passed community property laws. The courts ruled that married couples in such states could divide their income for tax purposes, even if only one partner earned all of it. In effect, the tax law was not only unneutral between single and married persons, but also between married couples with identical incomes.

Congress belatedly recognized the problem in 1948 and moved to eradicate the so-called geographical inequity that was due to community property laws. It passed a law that permitted all families, both single- and double-earner households, to split income for tax purposes. Income splitting also ensured that two-worker married couples paid the same amount of taxes as two single individuals earning the identical income. Because the resulting progressive tax appeared to be neutral regarding two-earner married couples or two unmarried persons, there appeared to be no marriage penalty.

Taxpayers soon discovered, however, that there was now a tax on remaining single. An unmarried taxpayer earning the same income as one who was married, but whose spouse remained at home, paid a higher tax because, unlike the income-splitting married couple, the single person could not split income to take advantage of lower marginal rates (Merry 1981c:28).

Recent history: The changing mores of the 1960s, along with an increasing general awareness of the unfair ''single tax,'' contributed to growing pressure on Congress to rectify once again the inequities built into the individual income tax. The fate of unmarried workers was ameliorated in 1969 by creating separate tax rate schedules for single and married person.

Unfortunately, this change in the revenue law created what is now widely known as the marriage penalty. Actually, whether marriage, divorce, legal separation, or remaining single causes taxpayers' liabilities to rise or fall depends on a host of complex factors. For example, Harvey Brazer's research (1980:223–24) shows that aggregate income, its distribution between husband and wife, whether deductions are itemized, how medical expenses and capital losses are actually distributed between marriage partners, and eligibility for tax credits (e.g., those for child care and earned income) are among those variables that determine whether getting married will increase or decrease a couple's combined tax liability.

There is no doubt that the legislative efforts of 1969 resulted in the capricious treatment of individuals whose only difference was marital status. Congress needs to realize that no law can achieve mutually exclusive goals. As Brazer succinctly puts it, "it is possible to tax equally a two-earner married couple and two cohabiting single persons when each pair has the same aggregate income." On the other hand, "it is also possible to tax equally one- and two-earner married couples having the same income. But it is not possible to do both (Brazer 1980:224)" and also maintain a progressive tax structure.

Economic effects: Fairness aside, there are other very undesirable economic characteristics of the marriage tax. One exceptionally objectionable feature requires the second partner in the marriage, very often the wife, to pay tax on her first dollar earned at the husband's relatively high marginal rate. Labor econometricians have generally established that the supply elasticity or responsiveness to changes in net wages of female second earners is relatively large. That, together with the marriage tax, is doubtless responsible for holding down the production of goods and services in the marketplace.

The marriage tax causes a distortion in the pattern of output and the distribution of income by encouraging the overproduction of services performed in the home. Moreover, when individuals choose alternatives that offer after-tax rewards in place of those with higher pre-tax compensation, welfare losses are created (Brazer 1980:227). Boskin and Sheshinski (1979) examined a model of indentical families that included primary and secondary workers. Their goal was to derive a tax treatment that would minimize tax-induced inefficiencies between market and nonmarket activities. They demonstrate that the theory of optimal taxation shows that the workers with the greater supply elasticity should bear lower taxes in order to mitigate distortion in the individual's choice of type of work. Their sensitivity analysis indicates that primary workers, customarily husbands whose labor supply elasticity is very low, could bear twice the taxes of secondary workers in order to minimize the inefficient use of labor.

Brazer (1980:230, 236, 245–6) has worked out several tax illustrations that incorporate the many and varied circumstances in which married couples find themselves. No matter what the situation, the progressive personal income tax generally penalizes marriage. Table 2.7, which reflects the general pattern of the tax, compares married couples and pairs of single persons when each set of individuals has two dependents. The excess tax or marriage penalty of the married persons rises from $200 at an income of $5,000 to $920 at $8,000, and on up to nearly $7,000 extra tax at an income of $100,000.

Congress has appeared to be generally unaware of the intricate relationship

Table 2.7. *Illustrative tax liabilities of married couples and pairs of single persons, two dependents, selected levels of income, 1978[a] Dollars*

Aggregate adjusted gross income	Tax liability		Difference in tax liability[c] (3)	Present value of difference, life expectancy of 30 years[d] (4)
	Married couple, joint return, two dependents (1)	Two single heads of house-holds, one dependent each[b] (2)		
5,000[e]	−300	−500	200	3,920
8,000[e]	120	−800	920	18,032
12,000[e]	822	168	654	12,819
20,000[f]	2,330	1,960	370	7,252
30,000[f]	4,520	3,770	750	14,700
40,000[f]	7,310	5,880	1,430	28,029
60,000[f]	14,380	11,000	3,380	66,249
100,000[f]	31,420	24,426	6,994	137,085

[a] The two dependents are children under fifteen years of age for whom there is no child care; no medical expenses are included in itemized deductions.
[b] Each single person receives half the pair's aggregate income.
[c] Column 1 minus column 2.
[d] Computed using an interest rate of 3 percent a year.
[e] Personal deductions not itemized.
[f] Itemized deductions equal to 20 percent of adjusted gross income. At $20,000 married couples itemize, single people do not.
Source: The Economics of Taxation, Henry J. Aaron and Michael J. Boskin, Editors. Copyright © 1980 by The Brookings Institution, Washington, D.C. Table A-2.

between the income tax and the fundamental social and economic changes that have been occurring over the past several decades. The nature and composition of the family have undergone dramatic change. The traditionally married, one-earner family represents a declining portion of the population. Between 1940 and 1978, the female labor force participation rate doubled in the United States, and the rate for married women tripled. Between 1966 and 1978, the divorce rate doubled (Munnell 1980:253) and individuals were postponing marriage and childbearing. In the last three decades, the percentage of families with a female head increased by more than 60 percent (Boskin 1979:5).

Tax policy is only one factor affecting the marriage decision, but it is noteworthy that the number of unmarried cohabiting couples under the age of forty-five increased by almost 700 percent in the 1970s (Munnell 1980:253). Couples can, of course, escape the tax penalties induced by income tax rate schedules, deductions, and various tax credits by divorcing or refraining from marriage. In any case, the policy of maintaining the family rather than the individual as the unit subject to taxation has become increasingly difficult to defend because it leads to gross inequities and inefficiencies.

Reform once again: Among industrially advanced countries, the trend is definitely toward the individual as the unit for taxation. Alicia Munnell and Harvey Brazer have made eloquent arguments for individual taxation, but Joseph Pechman (1977:94–7) has made an equally effective case for choosing the family as the basis for personal taxation. Michael Boskin and Eytan Sheshinski (1979) have demonstrated that large economic costs are associated with the present system. Most economists are in favor of some type of reform.

Researchers are discovering, however, that reform of the marriage tax is a very complicated problem. In a National Bureau of Economic Research Paper, David Feenberg and Harvey Rosen (1980:1–58) simulated the effect of the following four alternative tax policies:

1. An exemption from taxation of 25 percent of the first $10,000 of secondary workers' earnings.
2. A tax credit of 10 percent on the first $10,000 of secondary workers' earnings.
3. Taxation of the husband and wife as single individuals with the tax base of each being half of total family income ("income splitting").
4. A choice between taxation of the husband and wife as single individuals, with the tax base of each spouse being his or her own earnings plus one-half of family unearned income.

The first two schemes generally follow the traditional approach of maintaining the family as the unit of taxation. The objective of these two alternatives is to mitigate the effects of high marginal rates on married second earners. Policies (c) and (d) move toward making the individual the unit of taxation.

Feenberg and Rosen find that the modest tinkering manifested in alternatives (a) and (d) does not stimulate much extra work and there is no Laffer effect, whereby revenues would actually increase with a decline in the rate of taxation. One very important finding is that labor supplies for different income groups will not change in the same direction with a given tax change. In general, secondary workers in upper income groups tend to substitute work for leisure whereas income effects dominate the behavior of lower income class secondary workers, who reduce their hours of work when taxes are reduced (Feenberg 1981:1–2). It seems clear from their research that a complicated model incorporating many subtle tax intricacies is necessary in order to analyze the empirical effects of personal tax changes.

Marriage tax provisions in the 1981 Revenue Act: As part of the new tax code in 1981, Congress passed a provision designed to mitigate the effect of the income tax marriage penalty for some 17 million, married working couples who paid more taxes than if they had been single ("Reagan Signs Tax Bill" 1981:2A). Under the new law, two-income couples received a tax deduction in 1982 of 5 percent from the salary of the lower-paid partner, up to a maximum of $1,500. The phasing in of the offset to the marriage penalty was completed in 1983, when the figures rose to 10 percent and $3,000 (Klott 1984:50; "Making the Most" 1981:127).

It was estimated that this new provision would reduce Treasury revenue by about $7 billion in fiscal 1983 (Merry 1981b:3). The bulk of the benefits go to two-worker families with joint incomes between $20,000 and $50,000 (Anderson et al. 1981:29). Another effect is that a one-earner family would pay higher taxes than a two-earner family with equal size and income. The incentive for a second-earner adult to remain at home is reduced. Knowledge of the net effect on the supply of labor to the market place must await econometric testing.

The irregular income and averaging problem

A progressive income tax structure causes individuals with a fluctuating income to pay more taxes over a period of years than a person with an equal but steady income over the same time span. For example, a single individual with a taxable income of $25,000 in each of two successive years incurs an annual tax liability of $5,952, or a total of $11,904 for the two years. Another individual who is subject to an irregular income and earns $50,000 in one year but nothing in the next one pays a tax of $18,067.

This inequitable consequence highlights one weakness in using annual income as a measure of ability to pay (Davies 1980:204–7) and quite obviously violates the principles of horizontal equity. Moreover, because the tax increases the cost of engaging in economic activities that generate irregular income, fewer of those creative activities will be performed. As a result, the progressive tax becomes repressive and produces an economic inefficiency.

In a dynamic economy, a wide variety of tasks and individuals fall into the category of fluctuating income. A few examples are authors, lawyers, professional sports figures, musical performers, composers, entrepreneurs, inventors, actors, consultants, professional risk underwriters, and venture capitalists. Several of these activities are very important in developing the conditions, techniques, and products necessary for robust growth and economic progress.

Researchers have formulated various averaging techniques to try to mitigate some of the inequities and repressive economic effects of the progressive income tax. Early averaging devices were far from perfect. The state of Wisconsin, a pioneer in the use of the income tax, instituted a system of averaging in 1927 but abandoned it in 1934 because of its inherent defects and the vicissitudes of the economic depression (Groves 1946:226).

Henry Simons (1938), Harold Groves (1946), and William Vickery (1947), all eminent fiscal economists, have been strong proponents of income averaging schemes. The current Treasury method of averaging fluctuating incomes is a variation of Simons's (1938) proposal. The basic technique was adopted by the federal government in 1964 (Goode 1964:237) and revised in 1969.

The general idea behind averaging incomes is to permit taxpayers to add their actual tax liabilities over a period of time, calculate what their taxes would have been if their incomes had been evenly distributed over that period, subtract the calculated taxes from the liabilities, and receive a refund for the difference. The actual process of calculation is complicated by a number of administrative definitions and provisions, some of which are designed to prevent taxpayers from averaging incomes when the income variation over time is relatively small.

The government's method of averaging has had its critics. A research group led by Martin David (1970:275–95) concludes that administrative rules promulgated to prevent averaging when there are relatively minor variations in income discriminates against low income recipients. They also note that the law is "unnecessarily complex" and "excessively restrictive." In a more recent article, Steuerle, McHugh, and Sunley (1978) find the benefits of income averaging do not accrue to the individuals the law intended to help. Moreover, the most recent statute introduced new inequities into the system. There is, however, little sentiment for altering the present system.

The problem with automatic stabilization

Until recently, analysts generally believed that the progressive feature of the income tax, which allows individual personal tax payments to increase or decrease more rapidly than the changes in individual incomes, encouraged consumer demand in recessions and dampened purchases during periods of excessive demand. Therefore, they thought that the tax system automatically promoted stability in the movements of GNP, and that the untimely, discretionary decision making of policy makers, which so often led to cocyclical rather than anticyclical economic behavior, could largely be avoided.

However, several serious problems are associated with the idea of automatic stabilization or built-in flexibility. The first problem centers on the persistent existence of long-term rising prices over the past fifteen years. The self-fulfilling prophecy of inflationary expectations that drives people to buy now before prices rise, and thereby helps cause prices to increase, has tended to overpower the demand-dampening effect of relatively rapid rising taxes.

As a result, taxpayers earning constant real gross incomes have been pushed into higher marginal tax brackets; expenditures on consumption have risen and savings have fallen to extremely low historical levels. These results have procyclical effects on GNP.

A second, more serious criticism of built-in flexibility involves the downward rigidities in American wages and salaries. As a recession ensues and GNP falls, inflexible individual wages and salaries no longer tend to decrease as they formerly did. Therefore, the progressive tax continues to take relatively large amounts in taxes from households at precisely the time aggregate demand is declining. The decrease in GNP is reflected in the laying off and furloughing of workers who then have no earned income to be taxed. As a result of this contemporary tendency of some workers to maintain their income while others have none, the automatic stabilizing feature of the progressive income tax is largely inoperative.

A third and critical problem with automatic stabilization centers on the role of the progressive income tax as the economy emerges from the bottom of a recession. As soon as incomes begin to rise, tax liabilities begin to rise more rapidly than incomes. This more than proportionate increase in taxes acts to depress individual and aggregate demand through its dampening effect on consumption, saving, and investment. The progressive income tax chokes off economic recovery at the most critical stage of the business cycle, long before high employment levels can be attained and unemployment reduced to acceptable levels. In fact, unemployment at the beginning and during the early stages of economic recovery following each economic recession since the mid-1960s has been higher than in the preceding one, a condition exacerbated by the so-called automatic stabilizing and anticyclical properties of the progressive income tax.

The cost of administration

One of Adam Smith's (1937:778) famous canons of taxation states that "every tax ought to be so contrived as both to take out and keep out of the pockets of the people as little as possible, over and above what it brings into the public treasury." Proponents of the income tax intimate that it fulfills Smith's tenet, pointing out that the cost of administering it is exceptionally low. These primary costs associated with the efficient operation of the Internal Revenue Service, however, are a small fraction of the total costs of extracting revenue from taxpayers.

Secondary costs: The secondary costs incurred directly by the public are enormous. These costs include those associated with acquiring information, filling out various tax forms, and taking legal steps to minimize tax liability. Secondary costs are so high because of two fundamental reasons. The first reason is the incredible complexity of the tax laws and amendments and their accompanying rules and regulations. The second factor is the strong incentive that encourages and rewards bureaucrats for the growth in federal bureaus.

The complex legal underpinning of the federal income tax has fostered a growing tax-avoidance industry inhabited by some of the country's sharpest, most imaginative, and talented legal and accounting minds. High marginal statutory rates of taxation have been tempered by special provisions or loopholes, which Congress has passed into law to shield certain categories of income from those very same rates. Clever tax experts then discover ways to avoid or minimize tax liability on other forms and kinds of income. Over time, the consequence of this repeated process is a code and set of tax provisions that is so incredibly complex and unwieldly that no individual or group of individuals anywhere completely understands it. Individuals with identical incomes can and do pay vastly different amounts of taxes.

An important way to decrease taxes owed is to convert ordinary income into capital gains that carry significantly reduced tax rates. Perhaps a more wasteful method of avoiding taxes is the investment in tax shelters, the most rapidly developing sector of the tax-avoidance industry (Noble 1984:25–6).

Tax shelters normally involve investing funds in activities in which the before-tax return is below other alternatives but the after-tax yield is higher. Imaginative vehicles that lawyers and other private tax experts have devised to minimize taxes include investments in certain types of oil, real estate, printing, research and development, low-income housing, coal, commodity, cattle feeding, and groves, orchards, and vineyard shelters ("Tax Briefs" 1982:61). It should be noted that there are also alterations in employment choices due to the differences in the amount of income that can be sheltered in various occupations and firms (Goode 1964:71).

Costs and changes in tax laws: The costs of administering, complying, and avoiding taxes always jump dramatically when tax forms, law, or regulations change. Such changes have noticeable effects on the tax advising and preparation industry as well as on individual and business taxpayers.

The original 1913 income tax law required 26 printed pages. Due to changes, hundreds and hundreds of pages in the Internal Revenue code are now devoted to income taxes. Tax experts pay millions of dollars for tax publication services to try to keep abreast of the latest developments. One such service used 400 pages to explain the original law in 1913; sixty years later, it took more than 30,000 pages to do the job (Olson 1973:8).

The Tax Reform Act of 1969, a law ostensibly designed to close those ubiquitous but elusive loopholes, changed the tax law, forms, and regulations. It was so complex and difficult to understand that it became facetiously known as the Accountants' and Lawyers' Relief Act. The average taxpayer was thoroughly confused by the new tax forms and proliferation of schedules as well as the myriad instructions written in typical bureaucratese. As a result, the tax preparation industry greatly benefited. The 4,400 tax offices of H & R Block, Inc., for example, just about doubled their revenues from 1968. Thousands of other tax experts and tax preparation firms similarly benefited by assisting individuals and businesses through the labyrinth of federal tax forms. In explaining the growth and good fortune of the tax compliance industry, the head of one accounting firm notes, "every time the government makes a change to simplify things, it's good for business." He estimates that the average return now requires about double the work of a few years ago (Morganthaler 1982:33).

The 1913 Form 1040, the basic format for describing an individual's income and tax situation, consisted of one page. Today the booklet of forms and instructions the taxpayer receives contains 48 pages, and the IRS suggests that one consult the very helpful 192-page publication entitled, *Your Income Tax*. Less than half a million individuals, or about one person in 270, were required to fill out Form 1040 during the first year of the individual levy against income (Olson 1973:8). Currently, there are approximately 100 million individual returns ("Help the IRS Reform Tax Code" 1985:128), about 2 of every 5 Americans. This vast number of taxpayers, coupled with the many changes in the code and regulations over the years, has dramatically increased the cost of compliance.

Bureaucratic incentives and costs: The second major factor responsible for the high secondary costs associated with the administration of the income tax is suggested by James Bennett and Manuel Johnson (1979:27–43). Implicit in their discussion is the well-supported idea that most individuals are interested in their own welfare and will take steps to enhance their position. Government workers are no exception, and because their rewards of more pay, prestige, and authority largely depend on the number of fellow workers and size of their budget, there are strong incentives to enlarge the agency.

Growth can be achieved by initiating "needed" programs to solve social and economic problems. However, because a government agency normally does not produce an easily measured service, bureaucrats provide paperwork as tangible evidence that the organization is successfully and conscientiously performing its tasks. Paperwork becomes the more easily monitored criterion of production and the basis for an increase in next year's appropriations.

But whatever the rate of agency growth, budgets are limited. Consequently, to preserve as many bureau funds as possible to spend on purposes that will directly and indirectly enhance the personal satisfaction of bureaucrats, agency heads divert much of the paperwork cost to the private sector.

Moreover, because a bureau does not compensate individuals and businesses for the time and effort expended on completing government forms, the cost to decision makers in the agency for demanding more and more information is zero. It follows from the second law of economics that a bureau will demand paperwork up to the point at which the marginal value to the bureau of the last forms approaches zero. The incentives embedded in this kind of institutional setting clearly foster an increasing volume of paperwork and privately borne costs.

Officials at the U.S. Treasury are much like the rest of us and not exempt from pursuing courses of action that will enhance their lives. In a report now ten years old, testimony before a congressional committee revealed that the individual income tax form accounted for more than 73 million returns a year, and Form 1099, the information form for dividends and interest that businesses must submit, accounted for more than 100 million additional responses. These figures, however, were only a fraction of the various other forms companies must complete. The cost to small businesses dealing with Form 941 alone exceeded $235 million (Bennett and Johnson 1979:39–40); it is estimated to exceed a half billion dollars today.

Further evidence: Perhaps because the subject is mundane, surprisingly little research has been done on the costs of administration of and compliance with federal taxes. The bits of information that do exist, however, indicate that costs are quite large. The total administrative expenses of the Internal Revenue Service average around 0.5 percent of total tax collections (*Monthly Tax Features* 1979:3). Richard Goode points out that allocation of expenses for the various tasks is not available, but it is very likely that the IRS expense of administering the income tax is as high as 1 percent of income tax revenue (Goode 1964:33). The actual IRS budget in 1985 was about $3.5 billion, and the work force totaled 87,743 ("Taxman" 1985:9B).

These primary costs are much less than the secondary costs that are borne directly by individual taxpayers and businesses. The Tax Foundation estimates that business firms collect 87 percent of all federal tax revenues (*Monthly Tax Features* 1979:3). The following anecdotal information gives a different perspective on the magnitude of secondary costs. After passage of the Economic Recovery Tax Act in 1981, H & R Block, Inc., arranged to run new, eight-hour tax seminars to acquaint each of its 40,000 tax-preparing employees with the implications of the new law. Other tax firms such as Seidman and Seidman prepared and sent a series of letters and bulletins to their clients. Peat, Marwick, Mitchell and Company, the giant accounting firm, prepared several alternative tax pamphlets, one for each of the several versions of the tax bill that was making its way through Congress so that the firm was able to produce 120,000 copies the day after the final bill was passed ("Tax Briefs" 1982:61).

Further evidence reveals that companies typically pay $25,000 for a "tax physical." Price Waterhouse & Company predicted that its revenues would, as a result of the new tax law, increase by 33 percent in 1982. Moreover, individuals pay approximately $3,000 each for a tax checkup, and because major firms service thousands of individual taxpayers, millions of dollars of additional revenue will accrue to each firm ("Tax Briefs" 1982:61). The annual revenues of H & R Block, Inc., were running at the rate of $365 million in 1985. (Wilke and Harris 1985:109). These kinds of revenues and costs do not include the receipts of the highly lucrative tax-avoidance industry, which is dominated by expensive lawyers, accountants, and entrepreneurs who use their skills to find imaginative ways of escaping tax liabilities.

A more comprehensive view of compliance costs can be gained by examining the number of hours the private sector uses to complete tax forms. Bennett and Johnson cite a 1978 government report indicating that according to the IRS "its reporting and recording requirements result in about 613 million hours of burden annually on business and individuals" (Bennett and Johnson 1978:39).

Assuming that the opportunity cost or foregone best alternative use of that time is equal to the average American wage for nonsupervisory workers, recording and reporting taxes amounted to approximately $3.5 billion. This estimate undoubtedly is low because the assumed wage is not high enough to represent the pay of tax preparers and taxpayers, especially those with high incomes and more complicated returns. Moreover, the IRS estimate of hours is probably too low. A more recent study by the Government Accounting Office estimated that individuals and businesses spend 975 million hours annually working on tax forms ("Tax Forms Billion-Hour . . ." 1982:10A). This figure is about 60 percent greater that the one for 1978 and represents real costs to society of at least $7 billion. Converting this time into work years yields another perspective on costs. A total of 975 million work hours is equivalent to 485,000 individuals working 40 hours a week for 50 weeks a year.

No one knows the cost to the private sector of keeping records, processing information, completing tax forms and schedules, and filing returns. It seems clear, however, that very crude estimates, which would include the costs associated with the tax avoidance industry, set the lower limit somewhere between $7 and $10 billion. Perhaps more important are the additional costs incurred by the actual employment and investment changes individuals make to avoid paying income taxes.

There is little doubt that high, progressive marginal rates, numerous exclusions, various deductions, and other special provisions in the law are largely responsible for the high cost of administering and complying with the current income tax law. Prospects for reform are dim. In addition to the numerous special interests that have succeeded in securing special tax legislation from Congress, the tax preparation and avoidance industries themselves are now very strong lobbies. They would lose much if a genuinely simplified tax code were ever adopted.

CHAPTER 3

Economic effects of individual income taxes and inflation

The economic history of the world's nations reveals short-run fluctuations in the purchasing power of money with a persistent long-run upward trend of inflation. Governments from ancient China, Egypt, Greece, and Rome to those that exist today simply cannot resist paying their bills by debasing their currency through inflationary policies. The United States is no exception, and these policies have had a profound effect on our income tax.

Bracket creep

For purposes of calculating income tax liabilities, Congress has constructed numerous tax brackets, each normally including small ranges of income and an associated amount of tax on a given income that is due the government. Because the federal income tax is progressive, that is, the higher the level of income the greater the average rate of taxation, higher incomes that are in higher brackets are subject to higher rates of taxation.

Congress has defined these income tax brackets in current or nominal dollars. They are unadjusted for inflation. This means that as wages and prices increase, taxpayers are automatically boosted into higher tax rate brackets, even though their real incomes may remain constant or even decline. This phenomenon, in which individuals' taxes increase more rapidly than their current income, is known as bracket creep. An important consequence of bracket creep is that taxpayers find themselves paying larger and larger shares of their earned income over to the federal government.

The arithmetic of bracket creep

The following examples illustrate the mechanics and effects of bracket creep. Even before the strong inflation of the late 1970s, the problem existed, as shown by the following figures. A family of four with an income of $15,000 in 1955 would have had to increase earnings by 120 percent, or $32,900 in 1976, just to stay even with inflation. Taxes on this family, however, would have increased from $1,540 to $6,600, or by 330 percent. The family was pushed from a bracket in which the marginal rate of taxation was 22 percent into one in which it was 36 percent, *even though there was no increase in*

Table 3.1. *The inflated 1980 salary required to equate 1972 income*[a]

1972 income	1980 income	Percent change
$10,000	$19,860	+98.6%
20,000	39,720	+98.6
30,000	59,580	+98.6
40,000	79,440	+98.6

[a] Actual 9 percent inflation rate for 1972–1980.
Source: "Mr. Congressman," *The Wall Street Journal* July 14, 1981, p. 9. Reprinted by permission of *The Wall Street Journal,* © Dow Jones & Company, Inc. 1981. All Rights Reserved.

Table 3.2. *Bracket creep with higher money but constant real pre-tax income*

1972 income	1980 income[a]	Average rate of taxes		Percent change in rate due
		1972	1980	Bracket creep
$10,000	$19,860	7.5%	10.0%	+33.3%
20,000	39,720	11.8	15.7	+33.1
30,000	59,580	14.7	21.0	+42.9
40,000	79,440	17.6	25.0	+42.6

[a] Inflated 1980 salary required to equate 1972 income.
Source: "Mr. Congressman," *The Wall Street Journal* July 14, 1981, p. 9. Reprinted by permission of *The Wall Street Journal,* © Dow Jones & Company, Inc. 1981. All Rights Reserved.

real purchasing power. In fact, the combination of inflation together with the progressive feature of the federal income tax decreased the family's real after-tax income by 11 percent (Citibank 1977:12–14).

A more recent study illustrates more specifically the interrelationships among inflation, bracket creep, and real income. Table 3.1 shows the percentage increase in money income required to keep pace with the actual rate of inflation between 1972 and 1980.

Table 3.2 shows clearly how the progressivity of the income tax combined with inflation automatically boosts all taxpayers into higher brackets. Bracket creep subjects individuals to high marginal rates of taxation, as shown in the right hand column of Table 3.2.

Table 3.3 illustrates why taxpayers were worse off in 1980 than in 1972, even if they received salary increases equal to the rate of inflation. The culprit is bracket creep, which reduces the after-tax purchasing power of the 1980 income below that of 1972 for all income groups.

Table 3.3. *Bracket creep and declining real income, 1972–1980*

1972 pre-tax income	1980 pre-tax income	After-tax purchasing power		Percent change in purchasing power
		1972	1980	
$10,000	$19,860	$ 9,247	$ 8,998	−2.7%
20,000	39,720	17,640	16,862	−4.4
30,000	59,580	25,588	23,708	−7.4
40,000	79,440	32,972	29,948	−9.2

Source: "Mr. Congressman," *The Wall Street Journal* July 14, 1981, p. 9. Reprinted by permission of *The Wall Street Journal,* © Dow Jones & Company, Inc. 1981. All Rights Reserved.

Table 3.4. *Inflation, progressive taxes, and bracket creep[a]*

Present taxable income from all sources	Increased income needed to keep up with 10% inflation	Rate of tax on increased income	Total increased income needed to offset inflation and taxes
$15,000	$1,500	19.13%	$1,855
20,000	2,000	23.95	2,630
25,000	2,500	28.00	3,472
30,000	3,000	32.00	4,412
35,000	3,500	37.00	5,556
50,000	5,000	49.00	9,804

[a] It is assumed that spendable income is equal to federal taxable income, and that the family breadwinner has a spouse, and both are under 65, with two dependent children who live at home.
Source: "The 'Infla-tax' Treadmill," *Letter from the Lion,* The Dreyfus Corporation, Winter 1981, p. 2.

The Research Department of the Dreyfus Corporation has released figures that examine the problem of bracket creep, which they call the "infla-tax" treadmill, from a slightly different perspective. They analyze different income levels and the tax status of various married couples with two dependents in an economy with a 10 percent annual rate of inflation (Dreyfus Corp. 1981:2).

Table 3.4 illustrates the dramatic impact of inflation coupled with the progressive feature of the income tax and how these two elements automatically boost average and marginal tax rates without any legislative consideration or vote.

Table 3.5. *The effects of inflation on the tax liability of persons in different economic circumstances, 1980*

Adjusted gross income	Current tax (1)	Effective tax rate (2)	Tax after 13.3% inflation[b] (3)	Effective tax rate after inflation (4)	Amount of tax increase (5)	Increase as a percent of original tax liability (6)
		Single person without dependents				
$ 5,000	$ 250	.05	$ 362	.07	$ 112	44.8%
10,000	1,177	.11	1,392	.14	215	18.3
15,000	2,047	.14	2,445	.16	398	19.4
25,000	4,364	.17	5,234	.21	870	19.9
50,000	12,559	.25	15,273	.30	2,714	21.6
100,000	31,424	.31	36,442	.36	5,018	16.0
		Joint return without dependents				
$ 5,000	$ 0	—	$ 37	.01	$ 37	—
10,000	702	.07	941	.09	239	34.0%
15,000	1,624	.11	1,947	.13	323	19.9
25,000	3,399	.14	4,116	.16	717	21.1
50,000	10,183	.20	12,385	.25	2,202	21.6
100,000	28,694	.29	33,712	.34	5,018	17.5
		Joint return with two dependents				
$ 5,000[a]	$ -500	-.10	$ -500	-.10	$ 0	0.0%
10,000	374	.04	587	.06	213	57.0
15,000	1,233	.08	1,527	.10	294	23.8
25,000	2,901	.12	3,556	.14	655	22.6
50,000	9,323	.19	11,525	.23	2,202	23.6
100,000	27,714	.28	32,732	.33	5,018	18.1

[a] Qualifies for the maximum amount of the earned income credit.
[b] Assumes incomes increase as much as the rate of inflation.
Source: Congressional Budget Office, *Indexing the Individual Income Tax for Inflation*, Washington, D.C., September 1980, p. 6.

The Congressional Budget Office has constructed a table that illustrates how inflation together with the tax system increases the share of a taxpayer's income that must be paid to the federal government. Perusal of Table 3.5 shows that single taxpayers earning $15,000, for example, would pay $398 more in taxes if their incomes increased by a 13.3 percent rate of inflation. The rise in taxes, which is due entirely to inflation and the progressive rate structure of the income tax, represents a 19 percent increase. A comparison of columns (2) and (4), the before- and after-inflation effective tax rates, confirms the fact that taxpayers are paying an increasing share of their income in taxes. Column (3) shows the absolute amount of the increase.

Effects of bracket creep

The two principal initial effects of bracket creep are:

1. a general increase in the marginal tax rates for taxpayers; and
2. a more rapid rise in government revenues than in the rate of inflation.

Edgar Browning and William Johnson (1979:70) have calculated marginal rates for each of ten income deciles in the United States. Their figures are actually effective marginal rates because they include in their analysis government transfer programs that directly effect the marginal rate of taxation. These are the appropriate rates to examine when the analyst is interested in production incentives.

Browning and Johnson (1979:70, 11) find that the two lowest income deciles are confronted with the highest effective marginal rate of 63 percent. The next two lowest deciles have the next highest rates. The tenth or highest income decile has the fifth highest effective marginal rate of taxation. The lowest 40 percent and highest 10 percent of the income earners face rates close to or exceeding 50 percent. The overall average marginal rate is approximately 45 percent.

The Browning and Johnson study is based on 1976 data. Inflation and large increases in the social security program since that time have no doubt caused marginal rates to rise.

A study by the First Chicago Bank (1980:2) shows what has happened to the economically important marginal rate of taxation over time. In 1965, about 81 percent of the federal taxpayers faced a marginal rate of less than 20 percent, and 19 percent had marginal rates in excess of 20 percent. By 1976, 58 percent of the taxpayers were confronted with rates more than 20 percent.

By 1980, the fastest growing item in the family budget was personal income taxes (Flanagan 1980:28). The big gainer when government debases the currency, inflates prices, and exacerbates bracket creep is the government. Bracket creep, automatic increases in social security, and inflation-induced business taxes caused the tax burden to increase by $200 billion during President Carter's administration. This enormous amount represented an increase of about 50 percent in the federal tax burden, significantly higher than the rate of inflation ("Review and Outlook" 1981:28).

The Congressional Budget Office estimated that bracket creep alone would generate an additional $115 billion between 1979 and 1985, and this increase would not require legislative consideration (Runyon 1982:1). Moreover, the Tax Foundation (1982a:1–2) notes that the price index increased from 115.7 (1967 = 100) in 1970 to 247.4 by the fourth quarter of 1981, while real GNP rose from 107.3 to 149.5 and federal taxes from 127.5 to 424.4. Statistical estimates of the elasticity of federal taxes with respect to income cluster around a figure of 1.6 (Greytak and McHugh 1978:168–80; Von Furstenburg 1975:117–25). A 10 percent inflation means that federal government revenues will increase by 16 percent. The nature of this kind of tax system presents a strong incentive to members of Congress and other governmental officials to continue to pursue their inflationary policies.

Changes in the distribution of the tax burden

Mathews (1975:20–76) found that the average rate of taxation rises for all levels of income during an inflationary period, but because of the particular provisions in the tax code, the rate of increase in tax rates varies among different taxpayers. Consequently, the distribution of the tax burden among individuals changes with inflation.

The mechanism through which redistribution occurs rests partly on the nature of deductions and exemptions from gross income that are allowed by the law. The most important of these are the personal exemption for taxpayers and their dependents and the standard deduction, or what has recently become known as the zero bracket amount. Interest payments on mortgages and consumer loans, state and local government taxes, charitable contributions, and medical expenses are principal deductions for taxpayers who itemize deductions in lieu of the zero bracket amount.

Because all deductions and exemptions are specified fixed amounts of current dollars, inflation automatically decreases their real value. Consequently, taxpayers entitled to deductions for dependents find their taxable income increasing more rapidly than their net income. Even though real income may remain unchanged, a larger portion of net income is subject to higher progressive rates.

The more dependents in a family, the greater the relative increase in taxes. Moreover, given the number of dependents, the lower the income of the family, the larger the proportionate increase in taxable income during inflation.

The figures in column 6 in Table 3.5 show clearly the differential effects of inflation and taxes on individuals with and without dependents. The joint return with two dependents shows that the increase in postinflation taxes as a percentage of the original preinflation tax liability is higher for all income classes except the very lowest, which qualifies for the maximum amount of the earned income credit. The differentials are greatest for the lower income groupings.

A reduction in the purchasing power of the dollar erodes the real value of the zero bracket amount so that the lower the income of the family, the greater

Table 3.6. *Growth in federal spending, 1950–1980*

	Annual rate of growth			
	1950–59	1960–69	1970–79	1980
National defense	19.8%	6.3%	4.1%	15.4%
Nondefense	6.2	8.6	13.7	18.0
Total	9.8	7.3	10.4	17.4
	Share of GNP			
	1950–59	1960–69	1970–79	1980
National defense	10.0%	8.6%	6.0%	5.3%
Nondefense	8.2	10.8	14.9	17.3
Total	18.2	19.4	20.9	22.6

Source: "Growth in Federal Spending," *Economic Review,* Federal Reserve Bank of Atlanta, October 1981, p. 22.

the proportionate increase in taxable income. For any specified proportionate increase in income, large, low income families suffer the greatest commensurate rise in taxable income. At the same time, proportionately larger amounts of cost-of-living adjustments will normally be taxed away from middle and higher income individuals than from others (Congressional Budget Office 1980:5).

Effects of inflation and income taxation on resource allocation

The preceding sections indicate how inflation has been an important factor in the swift rise in federal tax collections. Rapidly rising revenues have, in turn, facilitated brisk growth rates in government expenditures. As a result of this activity, the size of the public sector has increased compared to the private economy.

The annual rate of growth of resources under the direct and indirect control of the federal government has grown from 9.8 percent for the decade of the 1950s to 17.4 percent in 1980. Federal government expenditures as a proportion of GNP have increased from approximately 18 percent for the 1950s to almost 23 percent in 1980. This pattern means, of course, that government spending has been growing more rapidly than private spending.

Table 3.6 shows the annual rate of growth for both defense and nondefense purposes over a thirty-year period. It also includes the total share of GNP devoted to the federal government, as well as the breakdown between defense and nondefense functions. All of the data confirm the substantial relative growth in the federal government.

Inflation and macroeconomic stability

Most of the many macroeconomic effects of inflation are not yet well understood. Part of the reason for this state of affairs is that macroeconomic theory is in a state of flux; many analytical issues still need to be worked out before economists can grapple more successfully with some of the aggregative effects of inflation. Consequently, only a few conjectures will be made here.

At this time, no strong evidence exists to indicate that there are short-run significant differences between changes in real and nominal income on the magnitude of changes in tax revenues. As indicated earlier, estimates of the GNP elasticity of federal income tax revenue center around the value of 1.6. This relationship means that taxes will increase by 16 percent for every 10 percent increase in income.

An implication of this elasticity coefficient is that in the long run government expenditures will grow more rapidly than private sector spending. This process per se may foster inflation because the marginal propensity of the government to consume is at least equal to unity whereas that of taxpayers is less than one.

Perhaps more important for long-run aggregate growth is that the federal government is more service oriented than the private economy. The creation of services implies labor intensive modes of production and lower increases in productivity. These results means a lower rate of growth in GNP and, with a given monetary policy, a higher price level.

It is fair to say that contemporary evidence appears to support the notion that inflation exacerbates the drawbacks of automatic stabilization mentioned earlier in this chapter. Moreover, recent experience demonstrates that the federal government will not necessarily withdraw additional tax revenues from the income stream during inflation. Neither will increased person tax rates necessarily have a restraining influence on all disposable incomes. Labor unions and other well-organized groups have been able to vitiate to a large extent the effects of increased tax rates by aggressively pursuing wages and imaginative fringe benefits.

There has been a strong tendency during the past twenty years for central governments not only to spend all of their tax revenues but also to have to borrow money to meet their rapidly growing expenditures. The United States government is no exception. In most cases, macropolicy appears to have been unrelated to the goal of stabilizing the national income. Furthermore, gathering evidence indicates that government policies have contributed to inflation and lagging production.

Indexing

The United States tax system was not designed for inflationary periods. Consequently, many serious problems have emerged during the past fifteen years of rapidly rising prices. Charles Clotfelter (1982a:4) has substantiated that one of the most important effects of inflation and bracket creep is to make the structure of marginal tax rates more progressive. Furthermore, this change in the structure of rates is permitted to happen without explicit congressional action. The result is that the government takes an increasing share of personal income over time.

Another effect of inflation already noted is that it changes the distribution of the federal tax burden among taxpayers in a rather capricious way. A final major problem centers on the relationship among inflation, taxes, and expenditures that has allowed the federal government to grow more rapidly than the private sector.

Advocates of indexing the tax system believe that appropriate allowances for inflation would go a long way toward mitigating these serious problems. Opponents argue that indexing the tax system would impair the flexibility of Congress to resolve and determine the many issues encompassed in the federal budget. Moreover, they claim that indexing would weaken the stabilizing properties of the income tax by reducing its effect during inflationary times. It is also alleged that indexing would inhibit and limit the possibilities of reviewing and altering the tax code (Congressional Budget Office (1980:17–18). Although there are elements of truth in these objections, the benefits of indexing probably exceed the costs. Some fifteen countries have adopted some form of indexation for their tax systems in recent years.

The elements of indexation

There is fairly general agreement that the goal of indexation is to vitiate the impact of inflation on the real income of individuals (Mathews 1975:20–76; Fellner, Clarkson, and Moore 1975; Aaron 1976; Fuerbringer 1984:37). Consequently, some measure of the changes in prices or in the cost of living would be most effective in adjusting the tax system for the effects of inflation. Most countries use some version of a consumer price index to adjust for increasing prices. It has the twin virtues of being known to consumers and available from the appropriate government bureau.

Full indexing requires that all references to fixed dollar amounts in the tax laws be adjusted for inflation. There are at least eighty-two such provisions in the Internal Revenue Code, but, as Pechman points out, indexing personal exemptions, the standard deduction, the per capita credit, the earned-income credit, the low-income allowance, and the rate brackets would mitigate sig-

Table 3.7. *Selected tax brackets and taxes for family of four, 1984*

Taxable income brackets	Amount tax is	Plus	Rate on excess[a]
$11,900–$16,000	$1,085	+	16% excess of $11,090
16,000– 20,200	1,741	+	18 excess of 16,000
20,200– 24,600	2,497	+	22 excess of 20,200
24,600– 29,900	3,465	+	25 excess of 24,600

[a]Excess is the amount that the taxpayer's income exceeds the lower number in the bracket (e.g., $11,900). For example, if taxable income is $12,600, the tax owed is $1085 plus 16 percent of ($12,600 − $11,900), or $1,085 + $112 = $1,197.
Source: Based on 1981 tax law.

Table 3.8. *Selected indexed tax brackets and taxes for 10 percent inflation and family of four, 1984–85*

Original taxable income brackets	Same brackets but indexed	Indexed amount of tax is	Plus	Rate on excess[a]
$11,900–$16,000	$13,090–$17,600	$1,193	+	16% excess of $13,090
16,000– 20,200	17,600– 22,220	1,915	+	18 excess of 17,600
20,200– 24,600	22,220– 27,060	2,747	+	22 excess of 22,220
24,600– 29,900	27,060– 32,890	3,811	+	25 excess of 27,060

[a]Excess is the amount that the taxpayer's income exceeds the lower indexed number in the indexed bracket (e.g., $13,090). For example, if post-inflation taxable income is $13,860, the tax owed is $1,193 plus 16 percent of ($13,860 − $13,090), or $1,193 + $123 = $1,316.
Source: Based on 1981 tax law.

nificantly the distortions caused by the fixed-dollar designations in the laws. For purposes of illustration, only the exemptions, standard deduction, and brackets are included in the following discussion.

Table 3.7 displays several selected tax brackets, taxes, and how tax liabilities were calculated for joint returns scheduled to be in force in 1984. It forms the basis for further calculations and comparisons in Tables 3.8 and 3.9.

Table 3.8 shows the same tax brackets adjusted for an assumed 10 percent inflation between 1984 and 1985. The amounts of taxes have also been modified to account for inflation. The marginal rates of taxation do not change when brackets and amounts of taxes are indexed.

Table 3.9 illustrates the effect of indexing the income of a four-member family for a general 10-percent rise in prices. Gross income in the base year of 1984 is $20,000. The taxable income of $12,600 is found by subtracting the standard deduction of $3,400 and four exemptions at $1,000 each. The

Table 3.9. *Effect of indexation on family of four with a gross income of $20,000 and 10 percent inflation, 1984–85*

| Item | 1984 level | 1985 level equals 1984 level plus 10 percent inflation | |
		Unindexed for inflation	Indexed results
Gross income	$20,000	$22,000	$22,000
Minus standard deduction	3,400	3,400	3,740
Minus personal exemptions	4,000	4,000	4,400
Taxable income	12,600	14,600	13,860
Amount tax[a]	1,197[a]	1,517[a]	1,316[b]
Effective rate[c]	5.98%	6.90%	5.98%

[a] Based on Table 3.7.
[b] Based on Table 3.8.
[c] Tax owed divided by gross income.
Source: Based on 1981 tax law.

tax liability of $1,197 is derived from Table 3.7, as described in note (a) of that Table. The effective tax rate is 5.98 percent.

After one year and a 10-percent inflation, the family's nominal income rises to $22,000. If the standard deduction and exemptions are not indexed, taxable income rises to $14,600 and the $1,517 that would be owed to the government is calculated from Table 3.7 as follows: $1,085 plus 16 percent of ($14,600 − $11,900), or $1,085 plus $432 equals $1,517. Even though the family's real income remained constant, its tax rate increased 6.90 percent.

Indexation appreciably alters these figures. When the standard deduction and exemptions are adjusted to account for the general rise in wages and prices, taxable income is only $13,860. Moreover, because the tax bracket is indexed by 10 percent, the tax liability is calculated as follows: $1,085 (from Table 3.6) plus 10 percent of $1,085 for a total of $1,193. To this amount, indexing requires that we add 16 percent of the difference between $13,860 and the new, lower indexed bracket of $13,090 (from Table 3.8), or 16 percent of $770, which equals $123. The sum of $1,193 plus $123 equals $1,316, which is the tax liability of the family of four after indexing for 10-percent inflation. The effective tax rate is 5.98 percent, which is equal to that of 1984 when the real income of the family was identical to its 1985 real income.

These examples illustrate that indexing can virtually eliminate most distortion in the individual income tax code that are caused by inflation. Bracket creep is eliminated, real tax burdens do not increase, there is no capricious redistribution of the tax load among taxpayers, and the share of personal income claimed by the government remains relatively constant.

Table 3.10. *Rate of saving in leading industrial countries*

Country	1967	1977
Japan	18.5%	21.5%
France	15.9	16.1
West Germany	11.3	14.0
Great Britain	8.5	13.9
Canada	6.2	9.8
United States	7.5	5.1

Source: Alfred Malabre, Jr., "Americans Save Far Less of Their Earnings Than Citizens Elsewhere and the Gap Grows," *The Wall Street Journal.* Reprinted by permission of *The Wall Street Journal,* © Dow Jones & Company, Inc. All Rights Reserved.

Tax cuts and tax effects

As discussed in Chapter 1, modern neoclassical economists believe that tax rates are an important key to controlling the economy. Tax rates affect the amount of labor, saving and investment, and the resulting productivity, production, and GNP.

The pressure for tax cuts

Chapter 1 noted several negative features concerning the lack of economic progress in the United States during the past fifteen to twenty years. Real incomes rose modestly over the period and hardly at all during the 1970s. Productivity was actually negative during part of that decade. Inflation, bracket creep, and increases in social security, state and local income, sales, fuel, and property taxes had definite deleterious effects on the private sector. Income and social security taxes as a percentage of personal income increased from 13.2 in 1965 to nearly 20 in 1981 and has been projected to 23 percent by 1985.

By the latter part of the 1970s, the United States had by far the lowest official saving rate in the industrialized world. Japan's rate of about 21.5 percent led France, West Germany, Great Britain, and Canada, the last maintaining a saving rate out of disposable income of 9.8 percent. The figure for the United States was 5.1 percent, and nearly half of that was for residential housing. These figures dispel any mystery surrounding our long-term, low rate of investment in human and physical capital. Table 3.10 compares rates of saving among countries between 1967 and 1977.

It should be noted that despite the many new changes the Reagan administration introduced to encourage saving, the decade of the eighties shows no

Table 3.11. *Marginal tax wedge in New York, 1978*

Taxable income	Social security	Federal	New York	Total
$ 1,000	12.1%	16%	2%	30.1%
2,000	12.1	19	3	34.1
3,000	12.1	19	4	35.1
4,000	12.1	21	4	37.1
5,000	12.1	21	5	38.1
6,000	12.1	24	5	41.1
7,000	12.1	24	6	42.1
8,000	12.1	25	6	43.1
9,000	12.1	25	7	44.1
10,000	12.1	27	7	46.1
11,000	12.1	27	8	47.1
12,000	12.1	29	8	49.1
13,000	12.1	29	9	50.1
14,000	12.1	31	9	52.1
15,000	12.1	31	10	53.1
16,000	12.1	34	10	56.1
17,000	12.1	34	11	57.1
18,000	12.1	36	11	59.1
19,000		36	12	48.0
20,000		38	12	50.0
21,000		38	13	51.0
22,000		40	13	53.0
23,000		40	14	54.0
24,000		40	14	54.0
25,000		40	15	55.0
26,000		45	15	60.0
32,000		50	15	65.0
38,000		55	15	70.0
44,000		60	15	75.0
50,000		62	15	77.0

Source: Congressional Record, Vol. 124, No. 6, January 26, 1978.

signs of a revival in the rate of saving. The United States personal savings rate averaged less than 4.5 percent for the first eight months in 1985. In August the rate dropped to 2.8 percent. This figure represents the lowest rate ever recorded in the United States (Economic Diary 1985:24).

Kemp–Roth I

Americans began to express discontent as they saw a rapidly increasing share of their nearly constant real incomes taken by government. Table 3.11 illustrates the marginal tax wedge faced by New York residents in 1978. Moreover, projections based on laws then in force revealed that taxpayers earning $8,000 in 1978 would find themselves in the 50-percent marginal tax bracket by 1982 (Congressional Record 1978: No. 6).

Representative Jack Kemp from New York and Senator William Roth of Delaware responded to voters' appeals by introducing the first Kemp–Roth Bill in 1977. It provided an across-the-board reduction in tax rates. By eschewing tinkering with exemptions, deductions, and various credits to achieve tax relief, Kemp–Roth I altered the structure of tax rates. Marginal rates, so crucial for economic decisions, were reduced. Lowering marginal tax rates will unambiguously lead to a more efficient use of resources. This strategy is consistent with the neoclassical supply-side approach, which emphasizes increasing the incentives to work, save, and invest.

Specifically, Kemp–Roth I provided for a 10-percent reduction in individual income tax rates in each of the three years following passage of the bill into law. It also decreased the corporate tax rate on the highest income bracket from 58 to 45 percent and raised the surtax exemption for small businesses from $50,000 to $100,000. The highest individual tax rate would be cut from 70 to 50 percent, the lowest from 14 to 8 percent, and all other rates by a comparable amount (Congressional Record 1977: No. 119).

Despite 151 cosponsors in the House of Representatives, Kemp–Roth I did not pass the Congress in 1977; it was reintroduced in 1978 and 1979 as Kemp–Roth II. Although similar in nature, the latter bill included a provision that would limit federal spending to a declining share of the GNP in 1980, 20 percent in 1981, 19 percent in 1982, and 18 percent in 1983.

Kemp–Roth II also provided for indexation of the tax code. Tax brackets would be adjusted by the consumer price index so that taxes of individuals would not increase in real terms unless income increased. Table 3.12 shows the effect of the Kemp–Roth II tax reduction bill over the years in comparison with tax increases caused by inflation and scheduled increases in the social security system.

Despite 194 votes cast for Kemp–Roth II, it met strong resistance in the House of Representatives and the Senate. Democrats feared that tax reduction would slow the rate of increase in government spending. Republicans were concerned that the budget deficit would be increased, further augmenting the national debt.

It became clear to the Kemp strategists that something more than the appeal of enhancing incentives and, therefore, production and employment would be required if Kemp–Roth II were to become law. Arthur Laffer, a controversial supply-side advocate who strongly believed in the tradition of Adam Smith and John Baptiste Say that government regulations and high taxes drastically decrease work effort and reward, supplied this additional rationale for the Kemp–Roth tax cuts.

Table 3.12. *Tax increases vs. Kemp–Roth II*

Budget year	$ billions				
	1981	1982	1983	1984	1985
Tax increases:					
income tax	$14.6	$37.4	$62.7	$ 91.6	$125.0
social security	9.8	17.5	20.5	23.4	36.4
Total tax increases	$24.4	$54.9	$83.2	$115.0	$161.4
Kemp–Roth[a] tax cut	$19.8	$52.4	$95.4	$136.0	$174.6

[a] Assumes no increase in work and investment and thus no feedback of additional taxes.
Sources: "Kemp–Roth II, The Tax Rate Reduction and Spending Limitation Acts," mimeo from office of Representative Kemp, 1979, and on the work of Joint Committee on Taxation, U.S. Congress.

The Laffer Curve

Supply-side wedge theory recognizes that changes in tax rates affect the use of factors of production. The inputs largely determine the magnitude of aggregate supply that forms the basis for taxation. An important relationship therefore exists between tax rates and the tax base, which together determine the amount of tax revenues.

The most publicized version of this relationship has been called the Laffer Curve. The idea behind the curve goes back at least to the fourteenth century (Laffer and Seymore 1979:5). Its general form is illustrated in Figure 3.1.

The Laffer Curve, *ABC*, shows that at point *A*, where tax rates are zero, tax revenue will also be zero. As governments begin to tax at low rates, public revenues begin to rise. Additional taxes levied at higher rates cause government receipts to increase even more, but at a decreasing rate as the curve begins to level off in approaching point *B*. Increases in rates beyond point *B* carry such strong disincentive effects that the tax base and the revenues it produces actually decline. Laffer calls this area, *BCF*, the prohibitive range.

Tax receipts will decline due to an increase in leisure as its price falls and because saving and investment will fall as the net rate of return is reduced. Taxes will also decrease because of an increase in tax evasion and the development of a robust illegal cash or underground economy. At point *C*, tax rates are 100 percent, production in legal markets ceases, and exchange reverts to bartering because government would take all the earnings of the factors of production.

Several implications can be drawn from the Laffer Curve. First, there is a set of taxes that will, for a given economy, maximize government revenues.

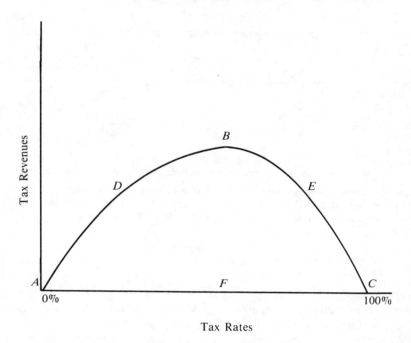

Figure 3.1. The Laffer Curve

This point is located at *B* in Figure 3.1. Secondly, except for point *B*, two rates, one relatively high (point *E* for example) and one relatively low (point *D*), will produce the same amount of tax revenue. Finally, if an economy is located any place between points *B* and *C*, the government can increase its revenue by actually reducing tax rates; between *A* and *B*, tax rates and revenues are positively correlated.

A growing number of economists have come to appreciate the necessity of incorporating the theory and measurement of supply-side effects into the body of macroeconomic theory, but there is considerable disagreement about some aspects of the Laffer Curve. Differences are not so much directed at the issue of incentives and their relationship to production, the tax base, and government revenues, but to the location of point B and the magnitude of supply-side effects.

Empirical evidence

Systematic empirical evidence on these points is relatively scarce. This is due partly to the economics profession's long and almost exclusive preoccupation with macroeconomic expenditure models. Supply-side hypotheses are also very difficult to test, but the evidence is beginning to grow. Evans Econometrics and Data Resources, two prominent research firms, are developing and testing supply-side models. Higher quality statistics and new econometric techniques promise to improve the estimation of various relationships and magnitudes.

Anecdotal evidence on the Laffer Curve

Led by Jude Wanniski's research, several supply-side analysts have compiled a history of cases that purport to support the idea behind the Laffer Curve. The two most prominently mentioned accounts center on the series of tax cuts made in the 1920s, on the advice of Secretary of Treasury Andrew Mellon, and the 1964–65 Kennedy tax cuts.

Tax reduction in the 1920s: As noted earlier in Chapter 2, Congress passed four separate tax reduction laws in the 1920s. Normal and surtax rates were cut from a postwar high of 67 percent to 25 percent during the decade, with most of the reduction occurring between 1921 and 1926. The 1920s were indeed prosperous years, and pure supply-side analysts attribute much of the growth in national income to tax policy. It is interesting to note that the share of income taxes paid by persons with incomes in excess of $100,000 increased steadily from 29.9 percent in 1920 to 65.2 percent in 1929, despite drastic cuts in the maximum rate of taxation. Those individuals with incomes of $300,000 or more paid $77 million in taxes in 1922, but $230 million in 1927 (Evans 1978:10).

At the same time, the proportion of the total income tax paid by the lower income groups diminished dramatically. Between 1921 and 1925, the amount of tax paid by those in the $0–$5,000 group decreased by 85 percent; by 72 percent in the $5,000–$10,000 group; 57 percent in the $10,000–$15,000 group; and 39 percent in the $15,000–$20,000 group. Revenues collected from taxpayers in the $20,000–$50,000 group remained about the same, but the proportion increased for all those about $50,000. The increase in personal exemptions in 1925 alone decreased the number of taxpayers by 44 percent. The changes in the tax laws during the decade of the 1920s produced a revolution in the distribution of the tax burden (Mueller 1981:24).

The Kennedy tax cut: In 1963, the highest marginal tax rate was 91 percent and the lowest stood at 20 percent. President Kennedy proposed that they be lowered to 70 and 14 percent, respectively. He also recommended that the top corporate tax rate on income be decreased from 52 to 48 percent. Congress followed these recommendations by reducing rates to 77 percent in 1964 and 70 percent for 1965 and the year following.

Personal income tax revenues declined from $51.5 billion in 1963 to $48.6 billion the following year. Tax collections began to rise thereafter, resulting in a $3 billion surplus by the middle of 1965. The cause of any increase after 1965, however, is somewhat clouded by the escalation of the conflict in Viet Nam.

In assessing the effects of the Kennedy tax cut, Michael Evans (1978:10) makes the point that the impact of the reduction on incentives should manifest itself most clearly in the upper income groups, where taxes and tax rates are highest. The evidence he gathers on this hypothesis is impressive. Evans discovered that there was virtually no growth in taxes paid by individuals with incomes in excess of $100,000 for the three years before the lowering of taxes. Although the rate reductions did not take effect until March 1964, tax collections for the years 1964–1966 increased by an average of 49 percent over three pre-tax years for these upper income classes. Taxes paid by individuals earning more than $1 million annually nearly doubled during the two years rates were being reduced. These changes probably reflect the fact that upper income persons have much more flexibility in manuevering their assets among tax-free and tax-sheltered opportunities (Roberts 1981:26). Further details on the upper income groups are presented in Table 3.13.

It is instructive to examine the impact of the tax cut on important macrovariables. Counter to Keynesian thinking and predictions, real consumer spending fell as a proportion of income, but saving and investment increased rapidly. The rise in real personal saving equaled about 75 percent of the reduction in taxes in each of the three years following the tax cut. The marked turnaround in the saving rate occurred almost simultaneously with the lowering of taxes and preceded the effects of the military build-up in Viet Nam (Roberts 1981:26).

These changes in consumption, saving, and investment increased the capacity of the economy to grow and produce. Economic growth was most pronounced in the corporate sector, but the rate of change in production was most notable in the noncorporate, small business sector. Their spending on real investment increased from less than 1 to 11 percent a year.

The kinds of changes in tax burdens that took place among income groups in the years 1964–66 happened again in the early 1980s. The portion of federal income taxes paid by Americans with incomes less than $19,000 dropped from 17 percent in 1980 to 12 percent in 1983, a decline of 28 percent. These taxpayers filed 66 percent of the returns in 1980, but slightly less than 60 percent three years later. The taxes actually paid by this group fell by 22 percent during this period.

In contrast to these figures, individuals and couples with incomes higher than $75,000 paid a little more than 20 percent of federal income taxes in 1980, but nearly 26 percent for 1983, an increase of more than 25 percent.

Table 3.13. *Effect of Kennedy tax cut on upper income groups*

Year	Maximum tax rate	Taxes paid by $1,000,000 class	Taxes paid by $500,000–1,000,000 class	Taxes paid by $100,000–500,000 class	Total by upper groups
1961	91%	$342	$297	$1970	$2609
1962	91	311	243	1740	2294
1963	91	326	243	1890	2459
1964	77	427	306	2220	2953
1965	70	603	406	2752	3763
1966	70	590	457	3176	4223

Source: Michael K. Evans, "Taxes, Inflation, and the Rich," *The Wall Street Journal*, August 7, 1978, p. 10. Reprinted by permission of *The Wall Street Journal,* © Dow Jones & Company, Inc. 1978. All Rights Reserved.

These changes occurred following the Reagan administration's tax program enacted in 1981, which included a 23-percent reduction in tax rates for most Americans. Moreover, it also contained an extra tax cut for upper income taxpayers since the maximum rate on investment income was reduced from 70 to 50 percent ("Higher-Bracket . . ." 1985:10A).

Vedder and Gallaway (1985:30) found changes in taxes paid by income groups as a result of the Reagan tax-rate cuts in 1981 similar to those discovered by Evans. All income classes below the $50,000 level experienced reductions in the amount of taxes paid as well as their share of total income taxes collected from all individuals. The upper income groups paid higher amounts after the cut in tax rates. Between 1981 and 1983, the $50,000–$100,000 and the $100,000 income classes increased their share of total income taxes collected from 17.9 to 19.4 percent and from 15 to 19.6 percent, respectively. Taxpayers earning over $1 million saw their taxes more than double from $4.9 billion to over $10.2 billion.

Additional anecdotal evidence: Supply-side advocates cite a long list of other cases that they believe support the Laffer hypothesis. Representative Kemp notes the sixty-year period of robust economic growth in Great Britain following Parliament's abolition of the income tax in 1815 (Congressional Record 1978: No. 6). Bruce Bartlett relates the account in which tobacco tax revenues "shot up" in 1827 following Parliament's reduction of the tax by one-fourth (Bartlett 1978:1334).

At about the same time, Britain began reducing tariffs on imported products. Elimination of the tariff on silk, which had been the most protected of all domestic industries, caused the output of manufacturers employing silk to nearly double within a decade. Silk exports tripled, and employment and wages in the industry increased steadily. Under Gladstone's leadership, tariffs were decreased on a wide range of products in the 1840s, and, as in the case with silk, production grew rapidly and government revenue increased. Later, Gladstone lowered the rate of taxation on income and once again production and government revenues grew (Rabushka 1978:6).

Supply-siders cite many more cases of the Laffer Curve besides those in nineteenth-century Britain. According to Representative Kemp (Congressional Record 1978:No. 6), post–World War I events in France and Italy paralleled the U.S. experience of the 1920s. He also cites the economic miracles of both West Germany and Japan following World War II.

Jude Wanniski (1979:248, 256), in an extensive investigation of third world countries, finds not only that the poorest of them have steeply progressive individual income levies, but also that the threshold or income points at which the rates reach very high levels are quite low. The marginal rates in Pakistan, for example, range from 10 percent on $200 of income, to 50 percent on $3,500, and up to 70 percent on $10,000. India's marginal rate is already 80 percent at $12,500, and the top marginal rate in Tanzania is 95 percent on an income of $2,386.

Wanniski's (1979:251–6) most interesting account cites Robert Prinsky's comparison of Ghana and the Ivory Coast, neighboring countries that have much the same physical characteristics and broadly comparable populations. The tax structures are drastically different. Ghana's is much more progressive and has notably lower threshold incomes that are subject to its relative high rates. Although each country reported about equal per capita incomes in 1965, Ivory Coast's record shows that its per capita GNP was more than three times that of Ghana's by 1975. The explanation by Wanniski for the remarkable economic change lies, of course, in the Laffer Curve.

Perhaps the most compelling anecdotal case of the effect of tax reduction on economic growth in the third world involves Puerto Rico (Wanniski 1978: Ch. 12). In 1977, the government eliminated the notorious "la vampirita" 5-percent surtax, which was adopted in 1974 on the recommendation of Yale economist James Tobin (Simon 1980). Arthur Laffer observes that after this across-the-board reduction in income taxes, the Puerto Rican deficit vanished and was replaced by a slight surplus (Laffer n.d.: 7–8). The cut in tax rates was associated with increased revenues of $15 million in fiscal 1978, a decrease in inflation, an increase in business activity, and a decline in the unemployment rate (Carnes 1978:9C).

Further reductions in rates occurred in 1978 and 1979, and income tax collections were more than 13 percent higher in fiscal 1980 than in 1979. Buoyed by these experiences in tax reduction, the government approved a tax decrease of 15 percent to be enacted in three equal increments over the years

1980–2. There has been a concurrent increase in economic growth along with these tax cuts. Moreover, in fiscal 1980, the Treasury Secretary reported that 100,000 more taxpayers were on the rolls than in the previous year (Simon 1980).

Evaluation of anecdotal evidence: In attempting to draw conclusions and generalizations from historical examples, situations, and cases, the analyst always risks committing the error of *post hoc ergo propter hoc*. It is deceptively easy to mistakenly attribute cause to a factor that may only be associated with the phenomenon that requires explanation. The difficult problem of sorting out explanatory variables exists for all sciences with empirical content; economics is no exception.

Anecdotal evidence on the Laffer Curve is somewhat disquieting because tax rates are emphasized whereas the effects of other possible explanatory variables are largely ignored. Nagging doubts about the Laffer explanation would be diminished if, for example, the pertinent Kennedy–Johnson years could be modeled in a sophisticated way; then analysts could account for changes in important variables that have not been controlled for in the anecdotal evidence.

Laffer (1981:18–20) himself cites with approval the time-series work of Canto, Joines, and Webb (1979) who, after extensive statistical analysis, concluded that the change in tax collections occasioned by the Kennedy–Johnson tax cuts were statistically insignificant. In other words, the cumulative effect of the tax cuts through 1966 caused no decline in the revenue government collected.

Canto, Joines, and Webb (1979) used a one-variable Box–Jenkins, time-series model to produce their estimates. It has been shown that a univariate model can be used successfully to map a time series when only the history of that one variable is known. A study by Charles Nelson (1973 and 1972:902–17) indicates that, in general, this one-variable technique will produce predictions as accurate as forecasts obtained from complicated econometric models.

Nevertheless, testimony by economists on the Laffer-inspired, Kemp–Roth tax reduction bill revealed a wide diversity of opinion on the expected results. Few analysts, however, shared the optimistic prediction of the bill's sponsors that the tax cut would pay for itself in the short run. Several researchers took issue with the supply-siders' evidence drawn from such anecdotal illustrations as the Mellon and Kennedy cases (Committee on Ways and Means 1978:17–104). On the other hand, economist and psychologist George Katona of the University of Michigan Survey Research Center concluded that the 1964–5 tax cut did indeed pay for itself. From data and surveys conducted by Katona and his collegues during the Kennedy–Johnson era, the Michigan group concluded that the sequence of developments in that period makes it probable that the decrease in tax rates led to greater public confidence, which, in turn, fostered improved business conditions and higher incomes (Koretz 1981b:16).

What is to be concluded from this discussion on anecdotal evidence? Unfortunately, economics is generally unlike sciences in which experiments can be controlled and replicated. Consequently, economists are limited by history's single run of data. Therefore, when cases are repeated within the same country over time or among several different countries, with allowances made for institutional and other important differences, the investigator should take notice. In this context, the great number and variety of anecdotal situations that supply-siders cite are suggestive.

Also, remember that the validity of the Laffer Curve is not so much at issue as is the location of the region on the curve where tax rates can be lowered and tax collections increased. Indeed, one contribution derived from Laffer's ideas is that static models, such as those the Treasury has used, yield seriously flawed predictions about expected revenues. It is now more widely recognized and accepted that decreasing tax rates will alter incentives and encourage economic activity, and increased production will lead to higher tax collections than predicted by static models. As a result, models builders have removed unrealistic and unhelpful assumptions that do not permit feedback into the system from changing variables. Tax policy can now be based on firmer estimates of the amount of expected tax revenues.

Some further economic effects

The following sections focus on some additional economic effects of the income tax. To a limited extent, they help further assess the ideas of supply-side analysts regarding the efficacy of tax rate reductions.

The personal income tax has two profound effects on the incentives of individuals. It reduces the financial rewards for saving and risk taking and distorts the choice between present and future consumptions. The tax also reduces the compensation for work and distorts an individual's choice between labor and leisure. An analysis of the effect of the tax on saving and consumption is discussed more appropriately in the following chapters on expenditure, capital gains, and corporation taxation. Its influence on work, leisure, and tax revenues is discussed here.

Income tax and work – leisure incentives

The income tax reduces the price or opportunity cost of leisure because it lowers the marginal reward for working. Economic theory indicates that an individual will tend to substitute lower cost leisure for relatively higher cost, less remunerative labor. Leisure simply becomes more attractive because at the margin workers now sacrifice less net income when they take more leisure. This substitution effect occasioned by the tax causes the output of legally produced goods and services in the market to fall.

At the same time, the income tax produces an income effect that tends to counteract the results of substitution. Because of reduced net incomes, taxpayers will decrease all normal items of consumption. However, the preferences of taxpayers may be such that they will respond to the tax and lower net income by working more in order to maintain their previous higher standard of living. These individuals are sometimes referred to as target income earners.

The net effect of an income tax on the labor–leisure choice, in the short run, depends on the magnitude of the two competing forces impinging on the taxpayer. If the substitution effect outweighs the income effect, workers will tend to work less and consume more leisure. If the income effect dominates, taxpayers will work more at the expense of leisure time.

Economic theory per se cannot tell us whether the substitution or income effect is the stronger force. To find the answer, researchers must rely on empirical investigations.

Empirical evidence about the income tax and labor supply

There are two main approaches to the empirical study of the effect of the individual income tax on the labor supply. The interview method uses a battery of questions put to taxpayers concerning the effect of the tax on their economic behavior. Certain procedures and checks on answers are followed in an attempt to produce a valid study. An alternative approach, typical of applied research in economics, ignores what individuals say about their behavior and tries to examine directly what people actually do.

Interview studies: Brown and Jackson (1979:271) have cataloged a number of interview studies associated with taxpayers in both low and high income groups. Unfortunately, not a great deal can be learned from these investigations. Different studies used different techniques, and there were no consistent results concerning the magnitude or importance of either the substitution or income effect. About the best that can be said of these inquiries is that they consistently reveal that the effect of taxes differs for different individuals. Because of the disadvantages and lack of consistent results associated with interview studies, recent research has used econometric techniques to try to sort out the net effects of income taxation on the supply of labor.

Earlier econometric studies: Cain and Watts (1973:332–5) report results from many early econometric studies on the income and substitution effects in the labor market. A remarkable variation is found in the coefficients scholars obtained. Some of the early problems that produce the notable differences in estimates centered on the interdependent labor supply decisions among members of the same household and the impact of nonemployment income. Moreover, the average rather than the proper marginal wage rate was used as the basis of estimation. Earlier researchers were no doubt constrained by the availability of desired data.

Subsequent research began to grapple with some of these problems, but as Brown and Jackson (1979:279) note, correctly specifying and estimating labor supply econometric models still involves formidable problems. Moreover, these problems are apt to increase as work progresses on multiworker households, women, the elderly, and high income groups.

Ongoing econometric research: Two recent studies, one by an English economist and one by an American, integrated labor supply data with tax information and derived several implications on the performance of the economy.

Michael Beenstock (1979:9) reports on the differences in English worker behavior between upper and lower income groups. His somewhat tentative conclusion suggests that the income effect dominates the behavior of lower income workers whereas the substitution effect holds for higher income workers.

Beenstock (1979:10–12) goes on to estimate a Laffer Curve over the period 1946–77 for the United Kingdom. His data and regression equation reveal that the apex of the Laffer Curve is reached when the aggregate tax rate is 60 percent, although the curve begins to flatten out as the tax rate approaches 45 percent. He concludes that in terms of maximizing revenue, the British tax system is very close to its limit. In addition, Beenstock interprets his estimated curve as reflecting the disincentive effects of taxation, and, although the British economy is presently on the normal range of the curve, it is near the point at which disincentives begin to manifest themselves.

In a subsequent article, Atkinson and Stern (1980:43–51) criticize Beenstock's work on a number of technical points. They point out, inter alia, the formidable difficulties involved in aggregating diverse taxes in order to estimate a Laffer Curve.

Don Fullerton (1980), formerly of Princeton University and the National Bureau of Economic Research, has investigated the relationship between tax rates and government revenues in the United States. He reports that most empirical work on labor supply indicates that there is a difference in the response of prime-age males and secondary workers to changes in after-tax income. Secondary workers, most of whom are still females and teenagers, have elasticity of supply of about 0.9. This means that for every 1 percent drop in after-tax income, these workers reduce their hours of work by about 0.9 percent. According to econometric studies, primary workers are quite insensitive to changes in their after-tax incomes. The elasticity of workers in general has been estimated at only 0.15 (Koertz 1981a:12).

Using a general equilibrium model, Fullerton (1980) constructed a Laffer Curve for several alternative elasticity values. He finds that the United States could possibly be operating in the prohibitive range of the Laffer Curve, but it is far more likely that the marginal tax rates and/or labor supply elasticities would have to be considerably higher than most present research suggests.

Charles Stuart (1981:1020–38), in a careful and suggestive study of Sweden, notes that the average effective marginal tax rates on labor income there increased from 50 to 80 percent between 1959 and the present. With the help of his model, which allocates labor to taxed market uses or to untaxed (largely household) activities, he estimates that the long-run effect of the increase in rates explains up to 75 percent of the relatively recent decline in GNP.

Stuart (1981:1020, 1031–2) also derives the point of total maximum tax revenue or the peak of the Laffer Curve. It stands at about 70 percent, or about 10 percentage points higher than the peak for the United Kingdom. Perhaps more disquieting is the fact that the actual rate in present-day Sweden is 80 percent, indicating that the marginal social costs of additional revenues have become enormous.

Stuart's (1981:1032–8) model predicts values for various variables that are quite accurate. Between the early 1960s and late 1970s, when marginal tax rates increased by an average of 1.5 percent per year, moving from about 55 to nearly 80 percent, annual growth rates dropped from 4.4 percent to 1.4 percent. Employment in the market also declined during this period, and the model accurately predicts the declines in output and hours worked.

Stuart makes no attempt to gauge the inhibiting impact of such social institutions as the forty-hour week on the process of adjusting to higher and higher marginal rates of taxation. The presumption is that less legal and market production would take place in Sweden. There are a number of indications, however, of pressure for changes in the older institutions. Maternity leaves have been increased, the annual vacation now allows five rather than four weeks, the demand for part-time jobs is increasing, and a commission is considering the possibility of instituting a thirty-hour work week. It appears that Swedish workers are on average substituting nonmarket activity for taxed market activity as marginal tax rates now leave the "representative" Swedish workers only twenty cents out of the last dollar earned (Stuart 1981:1034).

The work of Jerry Hausman (1981:61) is perhaps the most original and ingenious study of labor supply and the tax system. Although not primarily interested in the revenue effects of taxes, his estimates show that the federal tax system has a notably depressing effect on the number of hours workers desire to labor. Using data from the mid–1970s, Hausman discovered that the tax structure annually reduced the number of hours worked by almost 9 percent of total desired hours. One significant consequence is that the average expected welfare or deadweight loss is 28.7 percent of tax collections and 4.3 percent of after-tax income.

The distribution of the deadweight loss among different wage level groups is marked. It rises very sharply from $78 a year in the lowest group, with wages ranging from $2.25–$4.23 per hour, to more than $1,000 for workers whose wage rate exceeds $7.57. Hausman (1981:62) concludes that one cannot say how rapidly the tax-induced loss should rise in a system with progressive taxes, but the startling increase supports the notion that the tax system has a pronounced negative effect on economic behavior and may serve as a rationale for tax reform.

Evaluation of labor supply and tax research

Research on the supply of labor has made considerable progress during the past decade (Rosen 1980:171–6). Early research concentrated on regressing hours of work on wage rates, income, and control variables to derive estimates of wage and income elasticities.

Most economists presently working in the area of labor supply appear to agree that econometric analysis has produced two notable stylized conclusions: (1) the substitution effect of changes in after-tax income for prime-age males is relatively small, but (2) married women are very responsive to changes in net wages. There is a recognition, however, that more careful investigation of the alternative ways laborers can vary their work should be on the research agenda. They can respond to an increase in taxes, for example, by working slower or less intensively, by working few hours per week or moonlighting, by exchanging a full time for a part-time job, increasing their absenteeism, taking more sick leave, bargaining for more vacation time, starting work later in life, or retiring earlier. Also, a spouse or some other member of the household may withdraw from the labor force.

Recently, analysts have been integrating the behavior of working and nonworking spouses, the effects of social security and aid programs, and the impact of progressive income taxes into their models; but much work needs to be done. The interaction of husband and wife on labor supply decisions also requires consideration. Moreover, important factors influencing long-run policy regarding taxes and economic growth need to be addressed.

Rosen (1980:172) notes that the emphasis in the labor supply literature on hours of work is understandable because it is an important variable. It also appears to be a relatively easy one to measure. The introduction of long-run considerations, however, illustrates that the idea of labor supply is much broader than just number of hours worked per week per year. Workers can vary not only their hours, but also their career choices and the amount of education and training they undergo.

Human capital and labor supply: Investment in human capital immediately moves the issue into a longer time horizon than one year. T. W. Schultz has argued forcefully that our tax laws discriminate against the formation of human capital (Rosen 1982:6). Boskin (1975b:5) has challenged this view, but Rosen (1982:6) shows in a more sophisticated model, which includes the ideas of uncertainty and the use rate of capital, that one cannot know a priori whether a proportional tax on wages is neutral with respect to human capital. The related question of on-the-job training decisions raises somewhat similar problems, but Rosen (1982:6–7) has found that the income tax actually tends to increase the probability that a worker will use on-the-job training.

Tax avoidance and labor supply: Another problem that labor econometricians must soon address is the avoidance and evasion of taxes and the impact of this kind of behavior on the total legal and illegal supply of labor. Tax avoidance occurs when individuals shift their activities from higher to lower or untaxed endeavors. Avoidance is not illegal. A familiar example concerns substituting home production or other nonmarket work, such as the case described in Chapter 1, in which the automobile salesman chose to refrain from selling cars in order to paint his house because of high marginal tax rates.

We have observed that in the short run lowering the after-tax rate may either increase or decrease work in the legal market. Introducing into the analysis the realistic possibility of nonmarket work, such as doing one's own painting, repairing, gardening, or volunteer work, adds a further dimension to the substitution income choice facing workers that reduces the incentive to undertake work in the market. When income taxes are increased, the net wage for paid work in the new equilibrium will be below the marginal product of home or volunteer work. This result causes the decision maker to increase nonmarket labor and reduce market production until the marginal product of nonmarket work falls to that of the market sector.

The increase in income taxes leads to a welfare loss. The reason for this loss is that individuals undertake activities at home in which their marginal product is below what it would be in the market. The tax, however, drives a wedge between what workers are worth in the market (their gross wage) and what they actually receive (their net after-tax wage) (Brown and Jackson 1979:279–81).

Using the Harberger general equilibrium model, Michael Boskin (1975a:11) estimated U.S. welfare losses due to the differential tax treatment of market and nonmarket activity. The estimates ranged from $22 to about $45 billion for the year 1972; they are probably more than double those figures today. Moreover, the welfare loss due to the income tax should include figures for the vast undergound economy, but there are no estimates for these losses.

Taxes are also avoided when labor is completely withheld from the market because of increased leisure. The result, of course, is a reduction in the output of goods and services. To counteract diminished production, supply-side economists recommend that marginal income tax rates be reduced. As an alternative, Nobel laureate James Tobin (1980:42) has asked ". . . what about taxing commodities complementary to leisure – hammocks, coffee, boats, skis?" It is interesting to note that the Swedish government made a similar proposal to tax hobbies and leisure activities in an attempt to counter high marginal rates (Guilder 1979:22) but later withdrew it.

Tax evasion and labor supply: High marginal tax rates create incentives to evade taxes even though criminal penalties include stiff fines and prison sentences. Based on careful research, Charles Clotfelter (1982b:1–22) has demonstrated that the level of marginal tax rates have a significant impact on the amount of tax evasion. His simulations, however, suggest that the revenue effects of reductions in the marginal tax rate are likely to be relatively small.

Evasion of taxes is illegal and represents money due but not paid to government. Evasion may be less of a problem for the growth of the economy than avoidance because both legal and illegal market production of goods and services continues even though income taxes are not being paid by the producers. At the same time, productivity is apt to be lower than if marginal rates were lower. Evasion of taxes, whether on legal or illegal activities, entails a less efficient use of resources because covert activities are costly. Moreover, optimal specialization and market exchange activities will be blunted in the case of illegal underground production (Moszer 1981:23–44). What needs to be recognized is that both the avoidance and evasion of taxes has a large impact on the legal supply of labor.

Conclusion on labor supply and taxes: Despite the rather general acceptance by labor economists of the two stylized "facts" that primary-age males have a low sensitivity to changes in net wages and females are quite sensitive to tax-lowered incomes, caution must be used in formulating tax policy toward labor income. The elasticity coefficients derived from the array of regressions labor and other econometricians have produced are short-run estimates concentrated almost exclusively on the number of hours worked per week. The quality and intensity of work and long-run considerations associated with investment in human capital, including on-the-job training, require new, imaginative research and consistent estimates of their impact on lifetime supply. In addition, an enormous amount of fundamental work on labor supply, taxes, and the underground economy awaits exploration. Until we learn more than we now know, policy makers and legislators should proceed cautiously when formulating major changes in the income tax structure.

Conclusion

The vast majority of Americans supported the progressive income tax for many years. They felt it was an equitable tax. Moreover, it proved to be a prodigious provider of revenue for government. Now however, a large and continually growing body of evidence suggests that people no longer respect the revenue laws as they once did. The reasons for this state of affairs are not difficult to find.

The progressive income tax was not designed to work in an inflationary environment, so it should be no surprise that it is operating poorly. Bracket creep has pushed relatively modest real incomes into unprecedentedly high marginal rates of taxation, causing resentment on the part of many taxpayers.

The income levy has become a capricious and unfair tax, shot full of loopholes, special exemptions, deductions, and credits attained and protected by powerful special interest groups in all income classes. Individual Retirement Accounts (IRAs) and Keogh Plans, which are schemes designed by Congress to increase savings, are cases in point. How they work and affect individuals and families are fairly well known (Nash 1984:19), but researchers do not yet know whether these plans have been responsible for a significant increase in the aggregate supply of savings. It is known that many taxpayers have switched funds from other taxed assets into these two tax shelters, and others have borrowed significant amounts to fund their IRAs or Keoghs (Hamilton 1984:18). Each of these strategies vitiates the intent of Congress and adds nothing to the nation's pool of savings.

The progressive income tax penalizes marriages in which both members of the family work. Its progressivity along with inadequate provisions for handling losses and for averaging income over time helps reinforce feelings of unfairness about the tax. Taxpayers with the same income pay vastly different rates and amounts. Many higher income recipients who can afford high-priced lawyers and accountants are able to avoid paying large tax bills, whereas lower income groups who must legally have their taxes withheld at their place of work have less opportunity to take advantage of certain provisions in the law and minimize their tax liability.

Administration and collection of the tax have imposed enormous costs on society (Hall and Rabushka 1983:5–7). These costs promise to grow as Congress has required more and more paperwork of private individuals and companies, and more and more IRS inspectors, auditors, and accountants are hired to halt the widescale cheating caused largely by high marginal rates of taxation.

As noted in this text, the progressive income tax creates many excess burdens on individuals and society. As a result, there are large welfare losses, and the free choices of people are distorted by the tax.

The tax no longer works well as an automatic stabilizer, if it ever did. As presently constituted, the tax code favors consumption over saving. Its capricious ad hoc provisions with respect to capital and income from capital do not encourage investment and economic growth. They also have a depressing effect on the capital-to-labor ratio and, therefore, on real wages.

Without doubt, cheating is widespread on income taxes. Investigations by private researchers and information from official government reports confirm a vast and growing dishonesty among legally employed Americans regarding their taxes. The Internal Revenue Service claims that the average American cheats the government out of nine dollars in income taxes for every one dollar that criminals fail to pay on their illicit activities. Estimates of the amount of income produced that illegally escapes income taxation range from 10 to 27 percent of GNP, or between about $300 billion and $1 trillion annually.

American behavior in the underground economy is strong evidence of the disenchantment, disrespect, and disdain taxpayers hold for the progressive hybrid income tax as it now exists. This failure is especially critical because, to a large extent, the American income tax is a self-assessment levy that requires a high degree of good will and honesty on the part of taxpayers. The progressive income tax of the 1980s no longer enjoys the confidence of a broad cross section of Americans.

CHAPTER 4

Expenditure versus income taxation

Expenditure taxation has a long and noble lineage. Thomas Hobbes is generally credited with fathering the modern view of the levy on expenditures. His idea was honed and developed further by several of the most notable economists in the history of the profession.

John Stuart Mill, Alfred Marshall, A. C. Pigou, Irving Fisher, Luigi Einaudi, Nicholas Kaldor, J. E. Meade (Davies 1961:584), John Maynard Keynes (Kaldor 1955:12), and Martin Feldstein "Why Washington Likes . . ." 1983:80–2), all of whom bring impeccable credentials to the discussion, are proponents of the expenditure tax. The main reason for their advocacy is the strong technical appeal of the tax. An appropriately designed expenditure levy is superior to an income tax on both efficiency and equity grounds. This notion will be developed further in this chapter.

Issues in income and expenditure taxation

Cursory examination of the arguments for and against an expenditure tax indicates that it, more than an income tax, could approximate the ideals of efficiency and equity. There is even general evidence that a cash-flow tax would be easier to administer than a comprehensive income tax, although account must be taken of the potential transition and international problems arising from a switch in the tax base.

Equity issues

The equity issue suggests that the burden of the tax should be distributed across the whole population in such a way as to cause the least hardship. The view that the aim of a revenue-raising tax is the curtailment of private expenditure in favor of public expenditure indicates that the most equitable tax should consider the individual tax unit's expenditure pattern.

Proponents of the income tax, however, believe that the accretion of economic power during a tax-accounting period, regardless of whether it is allocated to either consumption or saving, represents a better measure of one's ability to pay than does consumption. The latter is merely a component of total accretion, although, at times, due to net dissaving, this component may

77

be larger than the whole (Davies 1959:72–8; 1960a:229–95; 1960b:987–95).

A personal consumption tax, also called an expenditure tax or cash-flow tax, differs from an income tax because it exempts net saving and investment from the tax base and taxes individuals only on what they spend ("Britain . . ." 1983:22). Although the details of the design of consumption tax are discussed later, the tax base of an expenditure levy is roughly determined by adding up gross receipts, which include wages, tips, salaries, dividends, interests, and other sources of income, and then subtracting the money that went into stocks, bonds, savings accounts, and the repayment of loans and mortgages (Lee 1983:34). The cash-flow levy would be a tax on an individual's standard of living. A credit or exemption for some level of consumption similar to the present income tax standard deduction could easily be incorporated into the law (U.S. Department of Treasury 1977:139).

A reform that bases tax liability on personal expenditures largely avoids the intractable problem of trying to measure income. Under a cash-flow, personal consumption levy there is no rational basis for special rates of taxation on capital gains, for the exemption of interest earned on municipal bonds, or for any of the other almost endless provisions in the present law that currently favor high-income taxpayers (Feldstein 1976a:15).

The Hobbesian view of taxation holds that it is more equitable to tax an individual on what one withdraws from the economic pool in the form of consumption rather than on income, a measure of what one contributes to the economic pool in productive performance (Bradford 1980a:102). A consumption tax would exempt those who contribute to the productive potential of the economy by saving. An expenditure tax could also eliminate the intertemporal bias of an income tax and eliminate much of the discrimination between different types of assets, including human capital, that exists under the current tax structure.

The life-cycle view

Expenditure tax proponents view the lifetime of the tax unit as the only relevant period for assessing ability to pay. Events over a short time period are not an adequate basis for determining the relative ability of two persons to pay (Bradford 1980a:107). Similarly, tax payments over a short time period do not constitute an adequate basis of comparison for the burdens borne by people (Davies 1980:204–7). Advocates of an expenditure tax propose a life-cycle model of savings and consumption. To understand this life-cycle model, assume individuals enter the labor force with a given set of skills and ability, earn a constant wage throughout their lives, and invest and/or borrow at a constant rate of interest. This approach is similar to assuming perfect certainty and perfect capital markets over the life of the taxpayer. Under this set of circumstances, a person's endowment or basic wealth can be defined as the discounted stream or present value of future wage payments (Mieszkowski 1978:30).

If the model is further restricted to exclude the possibility of gifts or bequests to the person or by the person, then the endowment is equivalent to the present value of a person's consumption. Though the issue of bequests and gifts is a complex matter, gifts may be included in the life-cycle model without compromising its conclusions by considering bequests as consumption of the donors and income of the recipients. This procedure maintains the fundamental notion that lifetime income equals lifetime consumption.

Taxing consumption rather than income is more equitable from a life-cycle perspective. If income were taxed, persons with the same endowments but different time preferences would be taxed differently. Persons with high rates of time preference who save little will pay little, if any, tax on interest income because their savings will be small. On the other hand, individuals who save by deferring present consumption for larger amounts of future consumption will bear a greater tax burden due to their tax liability on interest income (Mieszkowski 1978:30). The greater tax burden incurred is not due necessarily to any increase in the second individual's present value of consumption, which may, in fact, equal that of the first individual. In contrast to an income tax, a consumption-based system is neutral with respect to the taxpayers time preference for consumption (Mieszkowski 1978:34). That is to say, the price of future consumption is not altered by an expenditure tax.

A related shortcoming of an accretion-type income tax is that it discriminates between two people with different earning patterns. An individual who earns income sporadically with intermittent periods of very high and very low income may actually pay more tax than a second individual who has a steady income level, even though their overall income levels and consumption patterns are identical.

Many types of income, including royalties and capital gains, are sporadic and uncertain and may be real or nominal depending on inflation. According to the Kaldorian argument, "income measured as a flow is a highly imperfect measure of a person's permanent spending power or ability to pay taxes" (Mieszkowski 1978:28–9). The argument that favors a consumption base on equity grounds reflects the idea that an individual's consumption is much more stable than his income over the period of a lifetime (Mieszkowski 1980:181).

The case for a life-cycle model approach to taxation and for an expenditure tax is strongest in a world of perfect certainty. Indeed, although perfect certainty is unrealistic, there have been a number of recent trends that favor a life-cycle approach. For instance, medical advances have increased average life expectancy and made life more predictable. As a result, planned retirement is now much more widespread, with significant growth of private and public retirement pensions. Moreover, with general increases in real income levels, a growing fraction of the population can acquire significant savings. However, even if we allow for uncertainty in the life-cycle model, the equity arguments for an expenditure tax are not changed in any essential way (Mieszkowski 1980:180, 182).

Critics of the life-cycle model question its validity and applicability on the grounds that people are irrational and capital markets are inefficient. They maintain that people do not plan their consumption patterns over a lifetime in a fully rational manner (Mieszkowski 1980:182). The rise in popularity of private pension funds and the availability of public pension funds such as social security tend to negate this criticism.

Musgrave and Musgrave (1980:246) assert that lower income consumers have less access to loanable funds or have to pay higher interest rates and are disadvantaged under a consumption tax, especially in periods when high outlays are needed. However, this alleged bias in the important cases of borrowing to increase human capital as well as obtain home ownership has been largely vitiated by an array of government-guaranteed loan programs. Moreover, under a consumption tax, characteristics of the capital markets need not be any more burdensome to the poor than under an income tax, given certain averaging options of an expenditure.

Further equity advantages and objections to expenditure taxation

Another equity advantage of the expenditure tax, unrelated to the life-cycle model, is the relative neutrality it has for different types of investment. For instance, under an income tax, the deferral of the tax on capital gains until the asset is sold substantially raises the net rate of return that holders of these types of assets can earn, relative to those who invest in such fixed-income assets as saving accounts and pay tax annually on income from interest. The preferential treatment of capital gains is the most important way in which current tax law reduces the obligation of the wealthy (Feldstein 1976a:14–15).

The expenditure tax would also eliminate the bias that exists under an accretion-type income tax against risky investment (Kaldor 1955:118). An investor could realize substantial gains on a risky asset and incur no tax liability under a cash-flow tax, provided all proceeds were reinvested. Only those proceeds used to finance current consumption would be subject to tax, whereas an income tax is levied on all of the return regardless of whether it is reinvested. Under the present progressive tax structure, the larger the yield realized, the larger would be the percentage taken out by taxes and hence the disincentive to take risks. Klein (1977:461–81) notes that the income tax also biases capital accumulation toward investment in human capital, for example, a college education, and away from physical investment because most human capital is financed out of tax-free foregone earnings. The expenditure tax, however, taxes returns on this type of investment when realized as higher wages spent on consumption; there is none of the bias that is built into the income tax.

A traditional objection to an expenditure tax on grounds of equity is that it would permit the accumulation of vast wealth, which would provide the owners not only potential future consumption capability but also "power over the economic and political life of the nation" (Pechman 1977:67). As Andrews (1974:1170) points out, although an accretion-type tax may somehow get at disparities in wealth better than a consumption tax, the most adequate way to tax wealth is not with an income tax but with a separate wealth tax "with its own set of exemptions and rate structure to reflect attitudes about the distribution of wealth."

Much of the literature in favor of an expenditure tax also recognizes a need for a supplemental tax on wealth. Mathews (1975:37–42) is quite specific about this point in his recommendation of a broad-based, consumption-type tax. Another suggestion is to retain and revise current estate and gift taxes that would bear directly on intergenerational transfers of wealth (U.S. Department of Treasury 1977:139). Kaldor even argues that an expenditure tax in and of itself would be an implicit tax on current wealth (Feldstein 1976a:16). Taxing consumption would curb extravagant expenditure by the rich who receive favorable tax treatment currently by living on inherited wealth, capital gains on accumulated wealth, investments in tax-exempt municipal and state bonds, borrowing against their wealth and using the interest liability that results to offset and reduce tax liabilities on earnings from investments, and other wealth investments yielding tax-sheltered income.

One criticism of a cash-flow levy is that it would place a heavier burden on the young and old as compared with the middle aged (Goode 1980:54). Although it is true that retired persons living off savings would pay higher taxes than under the current system, this would be offset by the lower taxes paid during their working lives when the savings or pension benefits were accumulated. As for the young who characteristically borrow for consumption and purchase a disproportionate share of consumer durables, the liability under a consumption tax could be mitigated through simple averaging.

Another common criticism of the expenditure tax is that it would be regressive. Based on the notion that the saving rate tends to increase with the level of income, it is charged that the burden of an expenditure tax would fall heaviest on those with lower income levels and lower rates of saving (DeFina 1980:24). Some economists, most notably Milton Friedman, argue that the assumption that the saving rate varies with the level of income is erroneous as it is based only on single-year survey data. If taken as a proportion of permanent income, these theorists believe that saving would prove to be a nondeclining function of income. However, Friedman's theory has been subject to much debate and inconclusive testing.

But even if saving is an increasing proportion of income as the level of income rises, the expenditure tax need not be regressive. As Seidman (1981:6–7) noted, the tax rate structure could be progressive. To approximate the same proportions of tax return drawn from different income classes, it would be necessary to adopt a steeper rate schedule. To insure that the same amount of tax revenue was attained, it would be necessary to adopt generally high tax rates for each income level to compensate for the loss of saving from the tax base. Laborers would stand to gain in the long run from a higher expenditure tax that allows for forgiveness of taxes on saving and the positive implications thereof for the growth in investment and the real wage rate. The long-run transfer of income from capital to labor must be considered against the short-run gain to capital from the interest income exemption.

As expenditure tax might at first glance impose a greater burden on larger families with higher household consumption ratios than smaller families, but this could be overcome easily, as under the income tax, with an exemption for each family member or dependent. In general, the cash-flow tax would not be more of a burden for the poor relative to a comprehensive income tax, although it would favor those individuals at each income level who choose to postpone consumption. This redistribution horizontally (within income classes) from nonsavers to savers and the potential it could provide for economic growth and real returns to labor led Lawrence Seidman (1980:15) to characterize a move to a progressive consumption tax as "an anti-poverty policy."

Efficiency, savings, and economic growth

The adoption of an expenditure tax would eliminate the bias toward current consumption that exists under an income tax and would redistribute disposable income from low to high savers within each income class. It is generally accepted that this redistribution would bring about a change in the capital – labor ratio and a greater share of real income for labor.

Income taxes and incentives

Proponents of the expenditure tax believe that the income tax adversely effects the incentive to save and invest ("Why Washington Likes . . ." 1983:80; "Better Taxes" 1983:17, 22), and that only by removing this disincentive can private saving be increased and, in turn, the level of output and income stimulated. In what Seidman (1980:14) calls the "growth path of the real wage of labor," a higher saving or investment rate implies a higher growth path for the capital – labor ratio. Empirical analysis of a cross-section of countries in any given year, or a time series for a single country, reveals a strong positive correlation between the capital – labor ratio and the real wage of labor. In the standard neoclassical model, a higher capital – labor ratio implies a higher marginal product of labor and, therefore, a higher real wage.

An income tax negatively affects the growth of saving and the capital – labor ratio in two ways. By taking the return on capital, the income tax not only reduces the rate of return but also makes the before-tax and after-tax rate of return unequal. In addition, since the marginal propensity to invest out of government revenue is less than that in the private sector, transferring resources from the private to public sector reduces and further affects the national saving rate (Boskin 1978b:S5). The extent of this distortion and the loss of economic efficiency is determined by the extent to which private saving depends on the real or after-tax rate of return, the interest elasticity or sensitivity of savings to changes in interest rates, and the difference between the public and private propensities to save.

Measures taken to correct these distortions would be superior to plans to redistribute income through taxes and transfers (Seidman 1980:16). First, taxes and transfers represent artificial economic behavior and only serve to bring about greater distortions. Second, from a psychological standpoint, an increase in wage earnings brought about by greater economic efficiency would be more satisfying than a gift or transfer of equal magnitude. Finally, the extent of such redistribution is constrained by the attitude of the taxpayers.

Taxes and saving

All important taxes violate the basic economic principle of efficiency by distorting economic choices. The marginal evaluation consumers place on a commodity are no longer equal to the marginal cost of producing that commodity once a tax is imposed. The income tax, unlike the expenditure tax, specifically distorts the choice between intertemporal consumption patterns due to a distortion of the return of saving. Although the degree of distortion is greater for larger values of the interest elasticity of saving, some economists feel that even should this elasticity be zero, substituting consumption for income taxes could bring about positive economic growth.

Another way substituting expenditure for income taxes can raise aggregate saving, even without a significant interest elasticity of saving, is the "horizontal redistribution effect" (Seidman 1980:12–13). By redistributing income within each income class, from low savers to high savers, and assuming that the income tax is replaced by a consumption tax of equal progressivity, aggregate saving will generally increase.

According to a study for the Board of Governors of the Federal Reserve System, there is substantial variation in the annual average propensity to save of households within an income class (Seidman 1980:13). Calculations based on these findings suggest that the increase in saving resulting from a redistribution of tax burdens would range from 60 to 10 percent of the total tax yield involved in the switch (Break 1974:119–237).

Total saving can be expected to increase in the event of a tax substitution for two reasons:

1. An increase in the after-tax rate of return to saving, assuming a positive and significant interest elasticity of saving.
2. Redistribution of disposable income from spenders to savers within each income bracket.

Although tax proponents do not question that the rate of return on saving would be higher under a consumption tax, they do question the validity of the assertion that a higher rate of return will generate increases in aggregate saving, and they oppose granting saving and investment preferential treatment. Before turning to the larger and more important matter of the interest elasticity of saving, let us examine this latter point.

The ideas of the income tax theorist concerning saving are embodied in these words of Richard Goode (1980:56): "I would stress that both consumption and wealth accumulation [saving] are exercises of economic power; . . . private investment, no less than consumption is a withdrawal from the pool, a form of utilization of production . . . motivated not by benevolence, but by the self-regard that Adam Smith relied on to induce the butcher, the brewer, and the baker to supply him his dinner." Though Goode and others like him are no doubt correct in stressing that both saving and consumption are motivated by self-interest, it does not follow that the consequences are irrelevant to equity and efficiency and that only motivation should matter (Kaldor 1955:53).

Most economists would now agree that the once popular argument that saving is doubly taxed under an income tax is sterile, and that only new income generated for investment is taxed. However, it can be argued on equity grounds that there should be a lower tax on high savers because their contribution to social welfare is greater than the low savers or high consumers (Seidman 1980:15). The implication of this argument, according to Kaldor (1955:53), is that when considering what constitutes the fairest tax system, "one cannot stop short of reflection on the social consequences of individual behavior, and the effects of the tax itself".

Interest elasticity of savings

Empirical studies that analyze the impact of changes in the interest rate on aggregate savings fail to provide a consensus. A large body of economists have long believed that the interest elasticity of saving is zero and, despite changes in the rate of interest, aggregate saving will remain fairly constant. A cursory look at the figures over the period 1929–69 for gross private saving (GPS) and gross national product (GNP) tends to support this belief. There is general agreement that except for the deep depression years, this ratio has remained fairly steady. However, the more meaningful ratio of GPS and disposable income as a measure of the saving preference of the individual consumer shows that for the same time period this ratio has risen steadily (Boskin 1978b:S9). Boskin (1979b), Wright (1967:854), Boskin and Lau (1978:3–15), and Summers (1978) have questioned the validity of the traditional assumption that the interest elasticity of saving is zero. Their empirical results suggest that it is not a useful assumption, and that the interest elasticity of saving is positive and significant.

Wright (1967:854) has estimated the value of the interest elasticity of saving as somewhere between .19 and .24. To explain the relative constancy of the saving–income ratio over time, he suggests that the income and substitution effects were offsetting, but that a substantial substitution effect did exist.

Intuitively, it is easy to grasp the concept of the substitution effect of saving as interest rates rise. As the rate of return rises, savers get more for their money relative to present consumption than before the rise in interest rates, and the inclination is to trade off current consumption for saving. The income effect of a higher interest rate is less clear. Andrews (1974:1173) suggests, "for one who is saving to meet some particular objectives, a rise in the interest rate would make it easier to obtain that objective and would therefore operate to allow the individual to spend a higher portion of his current income."

Boskin (1978b:S3–S27) criticizes Wright's figures as not being fully compensated to eliminate the income effect and to obtain a pure estimate of the substitution effect or interest elasticity of saving. Wright (1967:854) admits this may be a legitimate shortcoming of his results despite efforts to overcome it and obtain a fully compensated elasticity estimate. The implication of this fault, as Boskin bears out in his comprehensive treatment of the topic, is that the interest elasticity of saving is actually greater than .25. In a variety of different regression analyses using alternative sample periods, various consumption functions, and instrument variables derived from the Hickman–Coen macroeconomic model, Boskin (1978b:S16) concludes that the interest elasticity is important and his preferable estimate on statistical grounds is .40.

Furthermore, production function analysis suggests that policies that increase capital accumulation and growth of the capital–labor ratio will increase labor's gross share of national income.

The current tax treatment of income from capital decreases the net rate of return to capital accumulation. Boskin's estimate of the elasticity of saving and the elasticity of capital substitution has been used to derive an elasticity of the net rate of return with respect to capital income tax rates. This result implies a substantial tax-included decrease in the rate of saving and the capital intensity of production, a reallocation of consumption from the future to the present, and a lower capital-to-labor ratio resulting in a substantial transfer of gross income from labor to capital (Feldstein 1978a:S29–S51). Based on his estimates of the rate of return on capital (.40) and the interest elasticity of saving (.40), Boskin (1978b:S19) estimates the annual welfare loss due to the distortion of the income tax on the rate of return of savings at $60 billion.

The present value of these costs for the future is a large multiple of this annual cost figure. There is some cause to temper Boskin's estimate of $60 billion annually because it includes the distortions of the corporate income tax.

Howery and Hymans (1980:1–31) have investigated the sensitivity of saving to changes in the rate of return, but they eschew examining the traditional measures of saving in favor of their own concept, which they call personal cash saving. They note that if their view is correct, empirical evidence of studies such as Boskin's are not relevant to the issue of the elasticity of saving with respect to rates of interest. Boskin's (1980a:34–41) extensive reply indicates a variety of reasons that the Howery–Hymans estimates miss the mark.

Excess burden of income and expenditure taxes: Robert Hall (1969:124–45) has also investigated the excess burden of income and expenditure taxes. Using Tobin's (1967:237) generalized version of the Ando–Modigliani (1963:55–84; 1964: 111–13) life-cycle model, Hall (1969:139) concludes that his general equilibrium analysis supports the partial equilibrium claims of the proponents of the consumption tax. At the same time, he suggests that the magnitude of the deadweight loss associated with an income tax is "hardly large enough to cause serious concern." Mieszkowski (1980:188) points out, however, that Hall's own figures imply that the excess burden of the income tax is about 10 percent of the revenues, a figure compatible with Boskin's estimate. If the correct figure were even half of Boskin's and Hall's implied estimates, the excess burden would appear to be highly significant.

In other work on excess burden, Lawrence H. Summers (1978) uses a multiperiod life-cycle model to make comparisons among taxes and finds consumption taxes superior to those on wages. Building on Boskin's work, Fullerton, Shoven, and Whalley (Boskin and Shoven 1980:169) also discovered that adoption of the expenditure tax would improve economic efficiency. Interestingly, their research indicates no increase in efficiency as a result of current policy that permits some saving to be sheltered from current taxation. Of equal interest is Gordon and Malkiel's (1981:3–15) discovery that if an expenditure tax were adopted without eliminating the levy on corporate income, tax-induced distortion would actually increase. As a result, they suggest that proposals for an expenditure levy be accompanied by the elimination of the corporate tax, or at least a reduction in the bias favoring debt financing.

Summary of research on consumption taxes and efficiency: Capital market imperfections cast doubt on the size of the net gain in economic efficiency attained by a move to the expenditure tax, but they do not compromise the argument that the expenditure tax is more efficient than the income tax. If there is a need to increase saving as an impetus to long-run economic growth, as declining productivity figures would suggest, then the adoption of an expenditure tax that would encourage individuals with the resources and incentive to increase saving seems preferable to the erosion of the income base by exemption saving under the current tax system. The latter action would create unwarranted distortions in favor of certain investment assets (Thuronyi:1980:276).

The efficiency arguments in favor of the expenditure tax are compelling. Recent findings of significant positive estimates of the interest elasticity of saving suggest that the move to a cash-flow tax and the subsequent higher, real after-tax return on saving would eliminate substantial welfare losses under the current tax system. As Boskin and Lau (1978:3–15) contend, even a modest elasticity of saving with respect to interest has drastic implications for the comparison of income and expenditure taxes.

Implementation of the tax

Critics of a consumption-type personal tax charge that it would involve all the practical difficulties of the existing personal income tax in addition to new problems involved in getting from an income base to an expenditure base. However, the Meade Committee Report, the Mathews Study, and the work by William Andrews (1974:1149) and Hall and Rabushka (1983:32–52, 68–77) show that the administration of an expenditure tax may be superior to that of an income-based tax.

Administrative mechanics

An expenditure tax base would be calculated by adding up all income receipts for the year, including wages, dividends, business profits, sales proceeds, and borrowing, and then subtracting amounts saved, paid to acquire assets, and repaid on loans. All these calculations would be based on money transactions for the current year; they would be much simpler than either making adjustments to include imputed appreciation under a comprehensive income tax or living with the complexity and distortion that result from the existing hybrid treatment of accumulation (Andrews 1974:1149). By including all monetary receipts for a year in the tax base, including gifts received, and allowing for the deduction of saving and assets purchased, the annual consumption of the tax unit could be computed without directly monitoring the purchase of all goods and services.

There is no reason to anticipate major changes in the definition of the taxable unit or personal deductions. Although it would be more efficient to tax individuals, administrative ease dictates that the family unit remain the taxable unit. Considerations for different rate structures for married persons filing jointly (to try to create a marriage-neutral tax), single persons, and single persons as heads of households would be as admissible and workable under an expenditure tax as under an income tax.

Deductions for each dependent family member would likely be continued to account for the effect of family size on the ability to pay. Personal exemptions, a standard deduction, and ordinary personal deductions for alimony payments, medical expenses, and charitable contributions would have the same justifications and problems as under the existing tax scheme (Andrews 1974:1151). Deductions for business expenses, including travel, meals, lodging, and entertainment, would pose a traditional problem in calculating tax liabilities and should be more limited as part of any tax reform. Source withholding would be a bit more difficult under the expenditure tax, but it could be continued and even extended to include some minimum amount of dividend and interest payments on a presumed income–consumption relationship.

It would be necessary to have a complete recording of cash balances at the outset of the new tax administration to ensure the tax liability for future consumption financed with these balances (Musgrave and Musgrave 1980:457). Under the expenditure tax system, the taxpayer would have to report the acquisition of all assets during the taxable period that constitute savings, all lending and borrowing activity, the value of all gifts made that might be deductible, cash on hand, and bank balances at year's end (Kelley 1970:241).

All this information, with the exception of cash and bank balances, is necessary to some degree under the present income tax. Interest paid on loans, for example, is deductible, and interest earned on loaned funds is taxable as income. Moreover, reporting the sale of assets would be no more burdensome than the compliance for capital gains income reporting under the present system. Various reporting devices of channeling information from third parties into the tax administration could aid in uncovering unreported consumption financed from unreported cash balances or receipts, but the administrative cost and complications involved might outweigh the benefits realized. These additional reporting agencies would not be essential to the effective implementation of the expenditure tax.

The elimination of corporate income taxes: The expenditure tax would improve on the present income tax base in two important respects. It would eliminate the corporate income tax and the need to value assets through time. Dividends paid by corporations from profits would be reported as individual receipts, and unrealized capital gains, obtained through retention of profits or otherwise, would be considered as reinvestment and exempted from any tax liability (Musgrave and Musgrave 1980:457). In effect, the corporate income tax is merged with the personal income tax, providing a gain in efficiency and equity as well as simplicity over the present system.

There would be no need for the periodic revaluation of assets, as with a comprehensive income tax, because only the purchase outlays would be taxed by a cash-flow system. A taxpayer might be required to submit a yearly statement of assets and liabilities, a personal balance sheet, to enable verification by the authorities that all transactions have been reported (Kelley 1970:242). Such a statement would show only the valuation of assets at the time of purchase because all changes in their value before disposition would be irrelevant in calculating the expenditure of the tax unit.

Summary

A cash-flow expenditure tax has administrative advantages over an income tax. By exempting all forms of saving from the tax base, it would render some of the most difficult problems of income measurement irrelevant. Depreciation schemes, inflation adjustments, allocation of undistributed corporate income, and evaluation of capital gains would have no place in an expenditure tax system as accruing wealth is wholly irrelevant. Undistributed corporate income would no longer be taxed because the adoption of a cash-flow levy implicitly assumes the elimination of both personal and corporate income taxes. Only the cash-flow spent for consumption would be taxed.

Despite the relative simplicity of the personal consumption tax, there would be many technical questions and details to be resolved if the levy were to be successfully adopted and administered. Fortunately, Mathews (1975), Meade (1978), and the authors of *Blueprints for Basic Tax Reform* (U.S. Department of the Treasury 1977) address many of these issues and offer sound practical suggestions on how they can be handled. Others have also contributed solutions to the problems of adopting and implementing a personal consumption tax (Bradford 1980a:75–110; Graetz 1980:161–276; Kelley 1970:241; Miesz-kowski 1980: 179–201, 1978:30–41; Peacock 1978:31–5).

The evidence would appear to favor the personal consumption tax on the grounds of both equity and efficiency. Moreover, relative to the current, extremely complicated income tax law, the administrative simplicity of a cash-flow tax as proposed by the Mathews Committee (in *Blueprints for Basic Tax Reform*) and the Meade Committee seems superior. The present hybrid income tax no longer merits nor has the solid support of the tax-paying public. The welfare loss to society of this tax appears abnormally high.

CHAPTER 5

The taxation of capital gains

Nature of capital gains

According to United States tax law, capital is defined as any property except that held for sale in the ordinary course of business. Inventories, depreciable business property, real property used in a trade or business, and debt obligations sold or exchanged by financial institutions are not normally subject to the capital gains tax, but they may be subject to income and property taxes.

Capital gains taxation is concerned mainly with individuals but also with certain types of businesses that own property. When the nominal value of property rises above the price paid its owner, there is a capital gain; the increase in value of the asset is subject to capital gains taxation when the asset is sold. For example, the owner of a house purchased in 1975 for $50,000 and sold in 1986 for $115,000 realized a $65,000 capital gain, which in most cases is subject to taxation.

A more precise determination of a capital gain (or loss) involves the difference between the amount realized, which is the gross amount received for the sale of property less commissions and other selling expenses, and what the Treasury calls the adjusted basis. The latter normally includes the original cost of property augmented by improvements but adjusted downward for depreciation.

Reasons for capital gains

Capital gains are generated in several ways. Assets can fluctuate in value if there are changes in the traditional factors that determine the level of demand. Changes in income, population, the prices of related products and services, the distribution of income, and tastes or preferences of individuals can affect the future earnings of an asset and thus its present value.

Factors that influence supply can also cause the value of capital assets to rise and fall. Changes in technology, the quantity and quality of the labor force, and the discovery of natural resources can generate capital gains that are subject to taxation.

A third factor causing changes in the value of assets is the movement of interest rates. A $1,000 bond at an interest of 10 percent per annum produces a gross income of $100 per year. If interest rates decline to 8 percent, for example, prospective buyers will have to pay $1,250 for a bond that will yield $100 per year. Current owners of bonds will have realized a capital gain of $250, which is subject to taxation if the owner sells the security.

A final cause of capital gains is the increase in the general level of prices. Indeed, during the decade of the 1970s and into the 1980s, inflation has been the most important source of increases in the price of assets. Although these changes are phantom and not gains in the real value of assets, the government taxes these inflated increases in the value of property. As discussed later in this chapter, the practice of applying a capital gains levy to nominal gains causes serious violations not only of the principles of horizontal and vertical equity but also of economic efficiency.

Brief history

The United States Congress, following the passage of the Sixteenth Amendment to the Constitution in 1913, passed an income tax law that took effect the following year. The original statute taxed ordinary income on wages, salaries, dividends, and interest and capital gains at the same very low rates. Since then, the taxation of capital gains has been a continuously controversial subject.

The strong inflation of World War I produced pressure not only to reduce tax rates but also to tax capital gains at preferentially lower rates than those on ordinary income. Both of these goals were accomplished in the early 1920s. The levy on capital gains was changed several times in the 1920s and 1930s (Seltzer 1951:20–4); from the late 1940s until 1969, rates remained virtually unchanged (David 1968: Minarik 1981:241–77).

Throughout most of the history of capital gains taxation, statutory rates have been lower than those on ordinary income. A change in the fundamental relationship between these two types of taxes began in the 1960s with an increase in egalitarian pressures on Congress. Between then and 1978, there was a continuing and substantial drive to reduce the differential between the two sets of tax rates by increasing those on capital gains.

Recent rate structure

The Tax Reform Act of 1969 increased the marginal rate of taxation on large long-term gains, which were those in excess of $50,000 and held more than one year. The rate structure was increased again by the Tax Reform Act of 1976. Marginal rates gradually increased from 25 to 49.1 percent by 1978.

Before 1978, capital gains tax liability was calculated by reducing any long-term gain by 50 percent and paying a tax on the remaining 50 percent at a rate

Table 5.1. *Tax treatment of capital gains in selected advanced industrial countries*

Country	Highest rate on long term gains	Holding period[a]
Australia	exempt	one year
Belgium	exempt	none
Canada	22 percent[b]	none
Germany	exempt	six months
Italy	exempt	none
Japan	exempt	none
Netherlands	exempt	none
Sweden	23 percent[b]	two years
United Kingdom	30 percent	none
United States	20 percent[b]	six months[c]

[a] The minimum period an asset must be held in order for it to qualify as a capital gain rather than ordinary income.
[b] Excluding provincial, state, and local tax.
[c] For assets acquired after June 22, 1984, and before January 1, 1988.
Source: "Footnote to the Above", *The Wall Street Journal*, May 8, 1978, p. 20, and United States Tax Code. Reprinted by permission of *The Wall Street Journal*, © Dow Jones & Company, Inc. 1978. All Rights Reserved.

governed by the taxpayer's marginal rate of taxation on ordinary income. Under certain circumstances, the law also provided for a minimum tax of 15 percent on the excluded portion of capital gains.

President Carter's tax program for 1978 contained, among other things, strong recommendations to increase the rates on capital gains that had already been increased in 1969 and 1976. A contrary view, based on recent economic research at the National Bureau of Economic Research and political pressures from the tax and spending revolts in the various states, prevailed in Congress. The result was a sharp rebuff to the President and Treasury because both the Senate and House of Representatives agreed to reduce the levy on capital gains. Various provisions liberalized the law so that tax liabilities decreased for all owners of taxable property. The top rate was reduced from approximately 49 to about 28 percent.

Status of capital gains taxation in other industrial countries: The information in Table 5.1 shows the maximum rate levied by central governments on long-term capital gains for several leading, economically advanced countries. It also reveals the minimum holding period required before an asset can be considered a long-term investment. It is suggestive and interesting to note that all countries that tax capital gains have experienced very little change in their growth rates during the past several years, whereas, with the exception of Australia and the Netherlands, all the countries that exempt capital gains from taxation have had notable increases in their gross domestic product. Note that although Australia does not have a capital gains tax, an individual may not buy and sell more than a very few financial instruments in a given year without being declared a trader. The tax authorities are not exactly clear on how many transactions can be made, but if one is declared a trader by the tax administrators, gains on any transactions are treated as income for taxation purposes.

Table 5.1 makes it clear that investors can realize large tax savings if they pay careful attention to the timing of their purchases and sales. Such various arcane techniques as selling "calls," delay delivery and payment of shares (up to sixty days), use of put options, plus other esoteric alternatives can turn short-term gains, which are taxed at higher rates, into long-term gains (Blumstein 1984:22).

Problems of capital gains taxation

Several serious problems are associated with the taxation of capital gains. These include:

1. the bunching of capital gains in one particular year;
2. the existence and impact of inflation;
3. the estimation of revenue; and
4. the effects on economic efficiency and growth.

Bunching

Most tax experts agree that the appreciation of capital, if it is to be taxed, should ideally be taxed, like other income, as the value of an asset accrues. This approach implies that assets should be revalued constantly, otherwise unrealized gains could accrue over a number of years. The objection to this procedure is that, in the absence of exchange in the market, the cost of determining value is prohibitive. As a result, evaluation of the magnitude of capital gains occurs in practice only when an asset is sold.

The problem associated with bunching arises because of progression in the tax rate structure that applies to ordinary income. It is this rate that governs in determining the tax liability on capital gains. Calculating and paying taxes at the time of sale can easily result in a larger tax bill than in a hypothetical case in which gains would have been taxed as they accrued. An individual who acquired an asset in 1975, for example, could be subject to a low tax because of relatively low income. However, as years pass and the person's income increases, the taxpayer is subject to higher and higher rates of taxation, and this rate may be at its highest when the asset is liquidated and taxes are due on the gains. On the other hand, investors in effect receive interest-free loans from the Treasury as the assets they hold appreciate in value (Wetzler 1977:115–53).

The problem of bunching could be largely alleviated by an appropriate income-averaging scheme. The use of proportional tax on income would eliminate the problem of bunching.

The existence and impact of inflation

The structure of taxation in the United States was not designed for an inflationary economy. When inflation rates averaged less than 2 percent per annum, as they did between 1952 and 1969, taxing capital gains was not a major issue, even though there has always been wide agreement that inflation-created increases in the value of capital assets should not be taxed (Eckstein 1979:87). Inflationary gains in those years were somewhat offset by the fact that half of any long-term gain was excluded from the tax base.

The rapid inflation of the past decade drastically altered the situation as the consumer price index (CPI) increased by about 100 percent between 1970 and 1980. This means, of course, that an asset that cost $100,000 ten years ago now must be worth about $200,000 in order simply to maintain its consumer purchasing power. It also means that without any form of legislative action, effective tax rates on the illusory and inflated capital gains (and other forms of income too) were constantly and dramatically increased by this unprecedented peacetime rise in the general level of prices.

Low de jure rates of taxation on capital gains turn out to be quite high de facto rates. In some cases, the actual effective rates of taxation exceed 100 percent, and owners consequently suffer real losses as the amount of their capital is not even maintained. This confiscatory effect occurs because government has not permitted adjustment of money or nominal values to allow for the rate of inflation. This whole problem was doubly compounded by the increases in statutory tax rates in 1969 and 1976 and the rising rates of inflation, exacerbated by the government's simultaneous war on poverty and involvement in Viet Nam.

Taxing gains in asset values, which reflect only a general increase in prices when there are robust inflationary pressures, has deleterious effects on the economy as well as on individual owners. Indeed, altering tax and accounting rules to account for inflation represents the most fundamental tax problem affecting capital formation today (Feldstein 1979b:55).

National Bureau of Economic Research study

The first comprehensive, rigorous, and systematic empirical research relating inflation and the capital gains tax was conducted at the National Bureau of Economic Research by Martin Feldstein and Joel Slemrod (1978a:107–10). Their imaginative work has given us much insight into and understanding of the fundamental relationships among inflation, capital gains taxation, the distribution of the tax burden, the price of shares, and several important aggregate economic effects.

The empirical basis of their studies was a special Treasury sample of 30,000 individual tax returns for 1973. These taxpayers had engaged in some 230,000 stock sales. By applying the consumer price index for the pertinent years of the stock purchases by the various individuals in the sample, Feldstein and Slemrod (1978a:107–10) calculated the real capital gains in 1973 dollars, as well as the actual taxes paid on the nominal gains. They also figured the taxes that would have been paid had individuals been taxed on real rather than inflationary gains.

The results of this NBER study are most revealing. The researchers found that individual investors paid capital gains taxes on $4.6 billion of nominal gains. However, when the cost of all these shares were adjusted for inflation, there were no real gains; instead, investors lost nearly $1 billion of their assets.

The illusory gain of $4.6 billion due to inflation provided $1.1 billion in taxes to Treasury. Some taxpayers did, of course, have real capital gains. The researchers were able to calculate these gains, and the taxes due on these real or price-adjusted gains would have been only $661 million. They concluded that inflation raised tax liabilities by approximately $439 million.

Further research indicated that although adjusting for inflation decreased the nominal gain in value of assets for every level of income analyzed, the effect of the adjustment resulted in a distorted pattern of taxes on the various income classes. The impact of the false measurement of gains was most severe for individuals in the lower income classes and easiest on persons with incomes in excess of $500,000.

Table 5.2 shows the NBER comparisons between nominal and real capital gains and the corresponding tax liabilities for various income classes. The figures reveal that taxpayers with adjusted gross incomes (AGIs) below $100,000 have negative real capital gains after allowing for inflation. Although the nominal figures appearing on Treasury tax forms exhibit about $1.3 billion in aggregate gains for all income classes up to $100,000, after adjustment for inflation, these taxpayers suffered capital losses in the amount of $4.3 billion. The corresponding figures for individuals with incomes above $100,000, on the other hand, show money gains of about $3.4 billion and positive real gains of $2.4 billion.

Table 5.2. *Capital gains and associated tax liabilities by income class – Adjusted Gross Income Class*

	Less than zero	Zero to $10,000	$10,000 to $20,000	$20,000 to $50,000	$50,000 to $100,000	$100,000 to $200,000	$200,000 to $500,000	More than $500,000	All
					Millions of Dollars				
1. Nominal capital gains	86	77	21	369	719	942	1,135	1,280	4,629
2. Real capital gains	−15	−726	−895	−1,420	−255	437	839	1,125	−910
3. Tax on nominal capital gains	1	−5	23	80	159	215	291	374	1,138
4. Tax on real capital gains	0	−25	−34	−52	58	141	235	337	661

Source: Martin Feldstein and Joel Slemrod, "Inflation and the Excess Taxation of Capital Gains on Corporate Stock," *National Tax Journal*, Vol. 31, no. 2, June 1978, p. 109.

The more wealthy were somehow not only able to protect capital, but they also actually managed some growth in their real assets. In general, the higher the income class, the smaller the difference between nominal and real capital gains. Individuals with incomes below $100,000 suffered real capital losses, but Treasury nevertheless levied taxes against their money gains. At the same time, there was virtually no difference between nominal and real gains in the highest, $500,000 income class.

The difference between rows 3 and 4, tax on nominal gains and what the tax on real capital gains would be, indicates the amount of excess tax liabilities borne by individuals. The NBER study shows that the extent of the excess tax decreases absolutely and relatively as income increases. For example, the $50,000–$100,000 class paid $159 million, but only $58 million would be paid on real capital gains. Therefore, they paid 159/58 or about three times the appropriate tax. The highest class paid $374 million instead of $337 million. Thus, they paid only 11 percent more than the tax on real gains. This effect of government policy on different income groups violates any generally accepted notion of vertical equity.

In addition to unsatisfactory relationships between income classes, tax laws in combination with inflation are also responsible for introducing arbitrary and capricious effects within income groups. Feldstein and Slemrod (1978a:107–18) report that taxpayers who are subject to the same statutory rates of taxation pay widely differing effective rates because of differences in the time capital assets held. For example, they found that about 45 percent of the total taxes paid by the $20,000–$50,000 income class were incurred by persons whose liability on real gains would have been between 80 and 100 percent of the actual tax on nominal gains.

On the other hand, about 55 percent of the taxes paid by this income group were paid by individuals whose liabilities on real gains would have been less than 80 percent of what they actually paid. As a result, their effective rates on real gains were considerably higher than those of their fellow taxpayers, and adjustment for inflation would have been highly beneficial in reducing these higher effective rates.

An even wider variation exists among individuals in the rates of tax liability on nominal gains within the $10,000–$20,000 income class. It is clear that taxing inflationary rather than real gains is of small consequence to some taxpayers but of immense importance to others. These distortions within income classes violate the generally accepted idea of horizontal equity, that is, individuals in similar circumstances should be treated equally.

Some conclusions of the NBER study

Feldstein and Slemrod (1978a:107–13) point out that according to the Standard and Poor's Index the price of a diversified portfolio of shares increased by about 100 percent between 1957 and 1977. At the same time, the Consumer Price Index also doubled, so there was no increase in the real value of the portfolio during the two decades. As a result of this relationship, any tax on the nominal gain represents a real loss to the investor. An effective levy of 20 percent, for example, means an erosion of approximately 10 percent in capital. The problem of capital erosion was much worse in the decade of the 1970s because stock prices increased much less than in the period 1957–77, but the CPI doubled during the decade.

On the basis of extensive evidence, the National Bureau of Economic Research Study shows that the tax on capital gains is grossly distorted because tax rules, which have not been formulated to permit adjustments due to inflation, cause a significant mismeasurement of gains. The resulting excess taxation is not associated with any particular era but is embedded in the existing tax structure.

Feldstein and Slemrod (1978b:21–22) calculate that the real value of share prices should increase at an average rate of approximately 2 percent per annum because of the positive effect of retained earnings. If, after one year, an effective levy of 20 percent is applied to a $100 original investment, the net after-tax gain is ($100 × .02) − ($2 × .20) = $1.60, or 1.6 percent per year. If, however, inflation is running at the rate of 6 percent, then share prices would rise by 8 percent. Therefore, 2 percent in real terms in addition to the 6 percent tax on the 8 percent return leaves a residual of ($100 × .08) − ($8 × .20) = $6.40, or 6.4 percent in nominal terms, but only $2.00 − $1.60 = $.40, or .4 percent net after-tax gain. Expressing the tax of $1.60 as a percentage of the real gain of $2.00 leaves an effective tax rate on real gains of 80 percent.

If the CPI is 8 percent, share prices should increase by 10 percent; and with a 20 percent statutory tax rate, the after-tax nominal gain is ($100 × .10) − ($10 × .20) = $8, or 8 percent per annum. This return only equals the rate of inflation. The effective tax rate on real gains is $2 in taxes due the Treasure divided by $2 in real gains – or 100 percent. Rates of inflation greater than 8 percent per annum would bring effective rates of taxation in real capital gains in excess of 100 percent. Table 5.3 presents the details of these calculations. The reader is invited to make additional comparisons.

Indexation of capital gains

The distorting effect of inflation combined with tax laws could be rectified by permitting the investor to increase the original cost of an asset in accordance with the rate of inflation at the time of transfer of ownership. This procedure would not only protect real rates of gain but also permit more active trading of shares as individuals' incomes and preferences for risk change. Moreover,

Table 5.3. *The effect of taxation of inflated capital gains*

Alternative possibilities		A		B		C		D	
Row	Item	$	%	$	%	$	%	$	%
1.	Original investment	100		100		100		100	
2.	Real annual rate of gain		2		2		2		2
3.	Real capital gain	2		2		2		2	
4.	Rate of inflation		0		6		8		10
5.	Inflated capital gain	0		6		8		10	
6.	Real + inflated rate of gain[a]		2		8		10		12
7.	Total capital gain[b]	2		8		10		12	
8.	Statutory tax rate		20		20		20		20
9.	Amount of tax[c]	.40		1.60		2.00		2.40	
10.	Real + inflated after-tax gain[d]	1.60		6.40		8.00		9.60	
11.	Real + inflated rate of after-tax gain[e]		1.6		6.4		8		9.6
12.	Effective tax rate[f]		20		80		100		120
13.	Real after-tax gain[g]	1.60		.40		0		(−.40)	
14.	Real rate of after-tax gain[h]		1.6		.4		0		(−.4)

[a] Rows 2 + 4
[b] Rows 3 + 5
[c] Row 7 × row 8
[d] Row 7 − row 9
[e] Row 10/row 1
[f] Row 9/row 3
[g] Row 3/row 9
[h] Row 13/row 1

Source: M. Feldstein and J. Slemrod, "How Inflation Distorts the Taxation of Capital Gains," *Harvard Business Review*, September–October, 1978, pp. 21–22.

according to the NBER study cited previously, the poor suffer relatively greater capital losses due to inflation than do the wealthy; indexation would largely correct this inequity.

Unaccountably, there has been little support for the indexation of any United States taxes until relatively recently. The Treasury in the past has consistently and strongly lobbied against the slightest hint of any adjustments for inflation in tax liabilities. In 1978, however, Congressman Archer, a conservative member of the House of Representatives Committee on Ways and Means, the organization that introduces all federal tax legislation, formulated a proposal to adjust capital gains for the impact of inflation before calculating tax liabilities on gains. His measure was to be part of a bill that reduced capital gains tax rates, a bill that ran counter to the position of President Carter and Treasury. In a very strange roll call of votes, liberals and certain other members of the Committee voted in favor of the Archer amendment, whereas most

Republicans opposed the proposal. The liberals apparently hoped that the Archer measure, along with the proposed reduction in rates, would make the bill too attractive for investors and that Congress would reject the Committee's recommendation and vote against the entire bill. Much to everyone's surprise, the legislation not only passed through committee, but the House also overwhelmingly supported the bill. The entire idea of indexation was dropped, however, when the House and Senate bills reached conference.

Problems with the estimation of revenue

Having examined the problems of bunching and inflation, it is appropriate to consider some other effects associated with capital gains taxation. The first of these effects is the question of revenue.

Important legislation on the taxation of gains due to changes in the value of assets was passed by the U.S. Congress in the autumn of 1978. Before November 1, 1978, a taxpayer calculated tax liability by decreasing the long-term gain by 50 percent and paying a tax on the other 50 percent. On sales of taxable assets after October 31, 1978, the long-term gain was reduced by 60 percent, and tax paid on the remaining 40 percent. If, for example, the marginal rate of taxation on the individual's wage or salary was 40 or 50 percent, then the calculated, nominal effective tax rate on long-term gains turned out to be 16 or 20 percent, respectively (40 percent $\times$ 40 percent marginal rate $= 16$ percent; 40 percent $\times$ 50 percent marginal rate $= 20$ percent).

Although the effective tax base was only 50 percent of a long-term gain before November 1, 1978, a taxpayer could be liable for taxes for as much as 50 percent of the full capital gain. This could result due to a special minimum tax of 15 percent and a marginal rate as high as 70 percent, as well as other esoteric provisions in the former law.

Provisions in the 1978 Act limited the top rates of tax on long-term gains. Even if the marginal rate on an individual's so-called earned income exceeded 50 percent, the statutory income tax rate to be applied to capital gains could not exceed 50 percent. The idea of a minimum tax was retained so that the highest rates on long-term gains were limited to 50 percent of the gain in addition to a minimum tax on the 60 percent "untaxed" part of the gain. Together, these levies resulted in a top marginal rate of approximately 28 percent on the total market long-term gain. As explained in the previous section, however, inflation can and does cause effective real rates to exceed 100 percent in some circumstances.

The 1978 scenario: President Carter, his close advisers, and the Secretary of Treasury and his staff proposed an increase in the taxation of capital gains in

1978. They were opposed to proposals circulating in Congress that recommended cuts in the rates. They believed that Treasury would lose large amounts of revenue, and that the rich would be favored. In April 1978, the Treasury Department stated that capital gains tax relief would "cost" $2.2 billion in lost revenue and that "over four-fifths of the benefits would go to persons with incomes near $100,000" (Pollock 1980:2).

Treasury's estimate of $2.2 billion proved wildly off the mark. Michael Boskin (1978a:237–8) points out that the Treasury model on which revenue estimates were based is merely a cross-tabulation of tax returns by various types of characteristics, such as level of income. Until recently, no behavioral relationships have been included in Treasury's model. It is assumed that every firm and every household will continue behaving in the same way after the imposition of a change in taxes as they did before the tax alteration. This means that if a tax is doubled, or even increased to 100 percent, individuals will not alter their behavior in response to such changes. Boskin notes that under Treasury assumptions, government revenue experts would figure the impact on tax receipts of a proposed doubling of the capital gains tax base, for example, by simply adding to the tax base extra gains that are now excluded from the base, after which they would calculate the tax. Martin Feldstein (1979b:56) also points out that Treasury ignored important behavioral responses when it tried to analyze the impact of the proposed tax cuts on capital gains in 1978.

The position of private research organizations, such as the National Bureau of Economic Research, Data Resources, Inc., and Chase Econometric Associates, was contrary to that of the government. They all believed that revenue would decrease very little if any rates were reduced. Oscar Pollock, of the firm Ingalls and Snyder, conducted a study of the effect of the increase in capital gains taxes in 1969, which took effect in 1970. He concluded that the record suggested that returning to the old pre-1970 tax law would more likely increase rather than reduce government receipts ("Footnotes to the Above" 1978:20).

Treasury officials attacked analysts who reasoned that reducing the maximum rate on capital gains would unlock unrealized gains that had been building since the rate increase in 1969. The notion of private analysts was that tax reduction would encourage realizations while simultaneously permitting investors to realign their portfolios in accordance with their preferences for risk and wealth. This sort of activity would act as a counterbalance to the revenue "lost" due to lower rates. But the Treasury's position was that "this theory did not match the facts" (Pollock 1980:2).

Later in 1978, when consideration of tax reduction moved from the House Ways and Means Committee to the Senate Finance Committee, Treasury officially conceded (after Senator Long insisted that feedback effects of changes in the law would be significant) that effective tax rate reduction could possibly bring added realization, which could conceivably offset part of the revenue loss resulting from lower rates. Indeed, Treasury experts then calculated that the net loss in revenue would be $1.7 billion, not the $2.2 billion they had estimated less than three months earlier (Pollock 1980:2–3, 6–7).

In response to the sharp questioning of Congressman James R. Jones of the House Budget Committee, Assistant Secretary of Treasury Donald C. Lubick wrote to the Congressman on February 13, 1980, stating that the projected realizations due to the 1978 tax cut would increase by $8 billion in both 1979 and 1980. These figures led Treasury officials to revise upward the increases in expected revenue from their former estimates of $573 million for 1979 and $535 million for 1980 to $900 million for each of these years. These newer numbers represented increases of 57 and 68 percent, respectively, over their previous predictions made a few months earlier (Pollock 1980:2–3, 6–7).

But even these figures were seriously flawed. Revenue estimators in Treasury's Office of Tax Analysis suddenly assumed, for purposes of analyzing the tax cut, an effective tax rate for 1979 and 1980 that was far below the historical trend. Table 5.4 highlights the dramatic change between 1978 and 1979. Moreover, as Oscar Pollock has demonstrated in one of his careful pieces of research, Treasury analysts exacerbated the errors in their projections by grossly underestimating the realizations that would take place by individuals with relatively high incomes (Pollock 1980:7–9).

More recent statistics from Treasury and analysis by Pollock show that Treasury officials in the Carter administration made egregious estimating errors (Pollock 1980, 1981a, 1981b). Far from a reduction in revenue resulting from the 1978 tax cut, revenues paid by individuals actually increased by about $1.6 billion, or 19 percent, the largest absolute gain in the history of the capital gains tax. Tax receipts were $3.5 billion, 56 percent higher than Treasury analysts predicted.

In 1979, taxpayers with adjusted gross incomes exceeding $100,000 doubled their 1978 realizations. Lower income groups only moderately increased realizations. The notable rise in realizations by the high income group, which was subject to appreciably higher average and marginal tax rates, tended to vitiate the reduction in the overall effective tax rate, even though statutory rates declined (Pollock, 1980, 1981a, 1981b).

It should be remembered that these results were an admixture of short- and long-run effects, and there is insufficient evidence at this time to support or negate the Laffer hypothesis that when tax rates are relatively high, reduction in rates will actually increase revenues. Some of the increase in realizations in late 1978 and all of 1979 were due to the unlocking of ownership in shares as individuals found it less costly to rearrange their portfolios in order to be

Table 5.4. *Total capital gains and the effective tax
rate on capital gains for returns with net capital gains
only (individual only) (1955–1980)*

Year	Total[a] gains	Taxes paid on capital gain income	Effective tax rate
1955	$ 9.9	$1.2	12.0%
1956	9.7	1.1	11.8
1957	8.1	0.9	11.1
1958	9.4	1.1	11.1
1959	13.1	1.6	11.8
1960	11.7	1.4	11.6
1961	16.3	2.0	12.4
1962	13.5	1.6	11.8
1963	14.6	1.7	11.9
1964	17.4	2.2	12.7
1965	21.5	2.8	13.1
1966	21.3	2.7	12.8
1967	27.5	3.9	14.0
1968	35.6	5.2	14.5
1969	31.4	4.4	14.1
1970	20.8	3.0	14.6
1971	28.3	4.3	15.2
1972	35.9	5.6	15.7
1973	35.8	5.3	14.9
1974	30.2	4.3	14.3
1975	30.9	4.5	14.4
1976	39.0	6.2	15.9
1977[b]	45.9	7.3	15.8
1978[b]	48.0	7.4	15.4
1979[b]	59.3	6.4	10.8
1980[b]	63.9	7.0	11.0

[a] Net long-term gain in excess of short-term loss plus short-term capital gain.
[b] Estimates.
Source: Office of Tax analysis, U.S. Department of Treasury, February 13, 1980.

more compatible with their preferred wealth and risk positions in the post-tax situation. Table 5.5 illustrates many of these points.

Effects on economic efficiency and growth

The conclusions of most modern economic research on the taxation of capital gains indicate the existence of a *lock-in* effect (Seltzer 1951:167–72, Holt and

Table 5.5. *Revenue effect of 1978 capital gains tax cut for individuals*[a] *(billions of dollars)*

Year	Actual gains	Treasury's prediction in 1980	Percent error	Taxes paid	Treasury's predictions in 1980	Percent error
1976	$39.0			$6.2		
1977	45.9			7.3		
1978	51.5	$48.0[b]	−7.4%	8.3	$7.4[b]	−12.2%
1979	70.5[c]	59.3[b]	−18.8%	9.9[d]	6.4[b]	−54.7%
1980	64.4[e]	63.9	−0.8%	9.0[d]	7.0	−28.6%

[a] The maximum rate on capital gains was reduced from approximately 50 to 28 percent on November 1, 1978.
[b] Treasury estimates made in February 1980.
[c] Final return by Office of Tax Analysis, U.S. Department of Treasury, April 22, 1982.
[d] Author's estimate.
[e] Preliminary return, Office of Tax Analysis, U.S. Department of Treasury, April 22, 1982.
Sources: Oscar S. Pollock, "The 1978 Capital Gains Tax Reduction: An Emerging Breakthrough in U.S. Tax Policy," June 11, 1980, "Revenue Effects of the 1978 Capital Gains Tax Reduction: New and Important Data," February 12, 1981, and "The 1978 Capital Gains Tax Reduction: A Breakthrough in U.S. Tax Policy," April 9, 1981, Ingalls and Snyder, New York; and Office of Tax Analysis, "Capital Gains and Realizations," U.S. Department of Treasury, April 29, 1982.

Shelton 1962:337–52, Fredland, Gray, and Sunley 1968:467–78). This term describes an investor whose assets have increased in value, but who, because of taxes, has little incentive to sell them and actually realize the gains. The lock-in effect is exacerbated by inflation, which can cause effective rates of taxation to exceed 100 percent.

The lock-in occurs because capital gains are taxed only when property is actually sold and the gain realized. Holding or not selling assets means that increases in value are untaxed, and these increases are in a sense reinvested free of taxes. Because of this tax deferral, there is a tax-free compounding of capital.

An important macroeconomic result of the lock-in effect is the prevention of the development of socially and otherwise economically desirable projects because of the inability of entrepreneurs to raise the required capital. The lock-in effect also creates inefficiency for individual investors because it inhibits making changes in one's portfolio, and this constraint causes a misallocation of risk.

Lower tax rates on capital gains encourage a more flexible attitude toward the choice of portfolio investments and, consequently, more sales of assets (Green 1978:79). By painstakingly processing, adjusting, and analyzing thousands of bits of data, Feldstein (1978b:507–8) and his coworkers discovered that individual investors were sensitive to tax rates on capital gains. Their analysis revealed a high degree of sensitivity to capital gains realizations with respect to the marginal rate of taxation on gains. Therefore, they concluded a reduction in rates would actually stimulate realization to the extent that Treasury would ultimately gain revenue.

Readers interested in exploring further implications of econometric research on the lock-in effect are urged to examine Appendix A. It includes additional findings of work done at the National Bureau of Economic Research and Data Resources, Inc., as well as critiques of this research by such scholars as Pechman (Zucker 1978:24), Yinger (1978:428), Auten and Clotfelter (1982:613–32), Minarik (1981:241–77), and Wetzler (1981:280–1).

Other economic effects of capital gains taxation

Several other economic effects flow from the taxation of capital gains. One of the most important is the impact on the market for shares of company stock.

Importance of the share market: Economic research undertaken during the past two decades strongly confirms the idea that the share market can have important effects on the overall economy. Current thinking identifies three principal channels by which the share market influences the economy. Otto Eckstein (1979:87) identifies them as follows:

1. It is an important factor influencing the cost of capital that enters into decisions regarding the amount and type of business fixed investment;
2. Since ownership of stock comprises a relatively large and volatile component of household financial assets, change in values notably affects consumer spending; and
3. Its behavior has a direct impact on portfolio decisions between stocks and bonds.

The share market affects important sectors of the economy in several other ways, but as Eckstein (1979:88) points out, they have to this point been difficult to model. Nevertheless, there is fair agreement that a broad share market enhances the position of smaller companies that require capital formation. These smaller enterprises are often innovative firms that use the venture capital the share market provides in ways that often importantly affect the rate of technological progress. Behavior in the stock market may also determine the degree of attractiveness to foreign investors of investment in the United States economy. Moreover, evidence suggests that a strong share market strengthens the dollar and reduces inflation.

Effects of the capital gains tax on the share market: Prices of assets are, of course, intimately related to the subject of capital gains taxation; it is price fluctuations that give rise to gains and losses in the value of assets. There is general agreement among economists that a reduction in the capital gains tax will increase the price of shares. Brinner and Brooks (1981:218–9) note that the price of stocks will increase because the after-tax rate of return will rise following a cut in the levy on gains. Lower taxes will also encourage increased selling of stocks because the reduced tax cost on realized gains in the value of assets will make the share market more attractive to investors, and the more buoyant environment may cause the price of shares to rise.

In 1978, Otto Eckstein estimated a range of values for the increase in prices. For example, he predicted the stock market would rise by 4 percent with a tax reduction of 25 percent. Using an alternative model with different assumptions, Chase Econometrics Associates, Inc., estimated the rise in share prices could be as high as 40 percent by 1982, a figure that was exceeded in October 1980. Martin Feldstein, who agreed that the stock market would rise, did not give a firm quantitative estimate (Brinner and Brooks 1981:218–19).

Higher share prices mean that the market values the assets of companies at a higher level. Some analysts believe that this gives firms a greater incentive to invest in new plants and equipment. According to this line of reasoning, the capital investment boon of the 1960s was enhanced because the share market valued company assets 40 percent above the cost of replacing them. In 1978, on the other hand, the market valued each dollar of corporate assets at only eighty-five cents, which created the incentive to buy existing companies rather than expand by building new plants and purchasing equipment (Brinner and Brooks 1981:218–19).

In more recent work, Joel Slemrod (1982:3–16) attempted to analyze the effect of the 1978 cut in capital gains taxation on the volume of stock transactions. As shown in Table 5.6, the absolute numbers indicate that transactions were significantly higher on both the New York and American Stock Exchanges as well as for over-the-counter operations after passage of the Revenue Act of 1978. Slemrod notes that the data include figures on the sales and purchases by institutions for which marginal rates of taxation were unaltered. Therefore, much of the volume change between years is probably due more to a shift in behavior by individuals rather than by institutions.

In order to control for other economic factors that might distinguish the pre- and post-tax periods, Slemrod (1982:8–13) introduces several explanatory variables into his analysis, including the change in share prices. He finds that a substantial increase in the amount of stock transactions can be associated with the tax cut per se. Volume for the period 1979–81 was 119 percent higher on the American Stock Exchange than it would otherwise have been, if there had been no tax cut; and 91 and 50 percent higher, respectively, for

Table 5.6. *Share transactions*

| Year | Millions of shares traded[a] | | |
	New York Stock Exchange	American Stock Exchange	Over the Counter
1972–77	17.9	2.8	6.6
1978	28.5	3.9	10.9
1979	31.9	4.3	14.4
1980	45.0	6.6	26.7
1981[b]	48.1	6.1	32.3

[a] Daily average.
[b] Through May.
Source: Joel Slemrod, "Capital Gains Tax Reduction," *Public Finance Quarterly,* (January 1982); p. 5. Copyright © 1982 by Sage Publications, Inc.
Reprinted by permission of Sage Publications, Inc.

over-the-counter trades and the New York Stock Exchange. Consequently, the revenue cost of the tax rate reduction is diminished by the increased activity of individual traders. Currently available evidence did not permit Slemrod to test the Laffer hypothesis that the revenue cost would actually be negative.

The issue of equity versus capital formation

Otto Eckstein (1979:19) argues that two basic issues are embedded in the question of capital gains taxation. One is taxpayer equity, and the other is the most appropriate strategy on savings and capital investment that the United States economy could best follow.

Congress increased the statutory rates of taxation and generally tightened various provisions with respect to capital gains in 1969 and then again in 1976. President Carter and Treasury demanded further increases in 1978, but because of the foundering economy and substantial popular opposition, Congress did not support the administration's proposals. Instead, the Investment Incentive Act of 1978, commonly called the Steiger–Hansen bill, was introduced in an effort to alter the incentives of savers and investors. Supporters of this legislation believed that returning to the pre-1969 rate structure, which, in comparison with the 1977–8 position favored the higher income groups, would help shield the return to individuals from inflation and encourage investors to put their funds to the most efficient use in various areas requiring new capital.

Eckstein's assessment is clearly correct. The issues surrounding the proposals for the tax legislation of 1978 centered directly on the question of equity versus capital formation and economic growth. Yet, if the conclusions of current research completed by several independent organizations are accepted, this is a tragically false choice when the long-run is considered. Recall that, according to the NBER studies, inflation together with the higher tax rates legislated in 1969 and 1976 caused both large vertical and horizontal inequities. A policy that would introduce indexation and an appropriate reduction in tax rates would resolve both the issues of equity and capital formation. Moreover, capital gains realizations are sensitive to increases in tax rates, and a reduction in these rates may actually generate larger receipts for Treasury in the long run. The relationship among capital gains taxation, saving, investment, and economic growth is analyzed in later sections of this chapter.

Capital gains taxation and the distribution of share ownership: There is no doubt that the rapidly rising levels of taxation on capital gains between 1969 and 1978 altered appreciably the distribution of share ownership. The proportion of stocks owned by nontaxable institutions, such as pension funds and nonprofit organizations, increased sharply. At the same time, some 6 million small investors dropped out of the capital markets as the taxes on capital gains doubled between 1969 and 1978 ("What President Carter Can Learn . . ." 1978:5).

Yet, although share ownership is highly concentrated, it has been estimated that approximately 40 percent of all stock held by individuals is owned by families with adjusted gross incomes of less than $25,000 (Blume, Crockett, and Friend 1974:16–40). It was shown previously that inflation in capital gains hits these middle and lower income classes the hardest, with effective tax rates on real gains often exceeding 100 percent. This situation provides a strong incentive for these income groups to withdraw their capital from the share market.

Capital gains, saving, and capital formation

The government's treatment of capital gains can have a very direct and important impact on the rate and amount of saving and capital formation. A discussion of the relationship between capital gains and personal saving as well as the link between gains and company saving and investment follows.

Effects of capital gains taxation on personal saving: The structure and pattern of capital gains taxation can affect personal saving in at least three ways. First, many economists believe that a close, positive functional relationship exists between income and saving such that a decline in income brings a corresponding reduction in saving. An increase in capital gains taxation reduces net income and therefore saving.

Income can be divided into transitory and permanent components. It has been argued that individuals behave differently regarding changes in transitory income than they do with similar changes in permanent income. The marginal propensity to consume out of transitory income is thought to be relatively low and its complement, the marginal propensity to save, to be high. If, as economists believe, capital gains probably contain a larger component of transitory than permanent income, then an increase in capital gains taxation will reduce saving. Note, however, that empirical studies estimating the magnitude of the marginal propensity to save out of capital gains have not been conclusive (Wetzler 1977:141; Bhatia 1972:866–79).

A second way that a capital gains tax can affect personal saving is through wealth effects. Increasing taxes on assets with anticipated gains will normally cause a decline in the price of the asset. This reduction in price will reduce the wealth of these investors but will normally be partially offset by the increase in demand for other assets. The net reduction in private wealth may cause householders to increase saving until the pre-tax wealth position is reached (Friend and Lieberman 1975:624–33). Inflation, however, can cloud these economic decisions; consequently, a household's nominal saving may increase but its real saving decline. Evidence of the effect on saving of changes in wealth is not conclusive.

Finally, an increase in capital gains tax directly effects saving because it decreases the rate of return to savers. Until recently, many economists thought that saving was insensitive to changes in the rate of return and interest earned on assets. Recent empirical research by Michael Boskin (1978b:S3–S27), however, indicates there may be substantial sensitivity to these important variables. According to his estimates, increases in taxes on capital income significantly decrease saving.

Boskin's (1978c:45; 1978b:S3–S27) interest elasticities imply that a 10-percent increase in the after-tax rate of return would increase private saving by about 4 percent. He estimates that the heavy taxation of capital relative to labor has inhibited its accumulation, with the result that the capital/labor ratio has been reduced by 30 to 40 percent. He concludes that the distortion in choice between consumption and saving caused by taxes on capital has led to a dead weight loss of the enormously large sum of between $50 and $60 billion annually. There is some uncertainty concerning Boskin's estimates, but even if they are twice the true figures, the losses are still dauntingly large.

Capital gains taxation and corporate saving: Since dividends paid by a company become ordinary income to individuals and customarily bear higher tax rates than capital gains, there is, in the absence of inflation, an incentive for corporations to save by retaining earnings rather than to pay out income in the form of dividends. Increased taxation of capital gains would shift incentives and encourage companies to declare larger dividends. There would be a consequent diminution in aggregate saving because of the marginal propensity to consume out of dividends received by individuals, and a lesser amount of a given corporate dollar of income earned would be saved (Feldstein 1973:170).

A policy recommendation

Available evidence on the effects of an increase in the taxation of capital gains indicates that both private and company saving would be reduced. At a time when there is widespread concern about the lack of saving, investment, capital formation, and consequent increases in productivity, increasing capital gains taxes is a counterproductive policy. Increased equity for middle and lower income groups, who are suffering real losses because of the combination of capital gains taxation and inflation, could be achieved by not only lowering rates for the higher income groups (who bore the brunt of the tax rate increases in 1969 and 1976), but also legislating reductions for all income classes. More fundamentally, equity and long-term economic growth could best be enhanced by effectively indexing capital gains for purposes of taxation.

Investment in new firms

The development and survival of new businesses is crucial for a dynamic economy in which economic growth is an important goal. Successful small firms in the United States have been responsible for the development of recent technological breakthroughs in minicomputers, plain-paper copiers, and instant photography. As one astute observer of the business scene noted, "The life-blood of this economy has been in backing new ideas, and a lot of the best have come from individuals who couldn't sell them within their own organizations" (Bulkeley and Richert 1979:42).

Unfortunately, most young firms do not have the capital to develop new ideas and concepts. The pay-off to investors often takes five to ten years. It is in this crucial area that venture capital and the firms that specialize in raising such funds from individuals play such an important role in the implementation of ideas, the success or failure of which can provide notable benefits to society.

Successful investments in new business lead not only to beneficial changes in technology, increases in production, new and improved products and services, and the growth in GNP, but also to large capital gains for individual investors. Note, however, that losses on new ventures occur much more often than gains.

A direct connection exists between the net rate of return and the supply of venture capital. Because of the possibility of investment losses, there is risk associated with supplying assets to entrepreneurs. Capital gains taxation decreases risk taking by investors for two reasons (Green 1978:87). First, as noted, a tax increase on assets that gain in value causes a shift in investment away from risky new ventures to older enterprises that pay a larger share of earnings in the form of dividends. New firms are usually small companies that pay no dividends in their early development.

A second factor that inhibits risk taking is the loss-offset provisions in the tax law. They are favorable to Treasury but disadvantageous to the investor. Current legislation allows long-term capital losses to be offset by long-term capital gains, but only one-half of net long-term capital losses can be written off against ordinary income, and then only up to a maximum of $3,000. This "heads I win, tails you lose" attitude increases Treasury revenue in the short run in comparison with a situation in which gains and losses are treated equally. As a result, private saving and investment are developments that, because they are new, carry an exceptionally high degree of risk for venture capitalists. The asymmetrical treatment of losses by government makes the odds on risky ventures longer and less attractive. As a result of these factors, which favor the government's rather than the investor's side of the balance sheet, new issues of shares by small companies came to a virtual standstill for most of the 1970s.

Note that capital gains are not levied against the estate of the deceased owner; but property acquired from a decedent, when sold, can be taxed on any gain in value while it was held by the decedent's recipient. This factor probably inhibits sales and enhances the lock-in effect during the lifetime of asset holders. In general, the basis of the value of the property for calculating gains is the fair market value at the date of the decedent's death, but there are esoteric exceptions to this rule. In any case, full loss offsets would be more acceptable to the Treasury if capital gains were properly accounted for and taxed at death.

Empirical relationship between capital gains taxation and venture capital

There have been no systematic studies of the relationship between changes in the laws on capital gains taxation and changes in the supply of venture capital. This is due partly to the extreme difficulty in accounting for the many other economic, legal, and psychological variables that have an impact on the market for risky capital. Nevertheless, sketchy bits of data as well as anecdotal information indicate a definite relationship between taxes on capital gains and the supply of capital for new and risky developments.

Theodore Levitt has noted the negative effects of the tax laws of 1968 and 1976 that drastically reduced the returns from capital gains by increasing the maximum rate by 100 percent while decreasing the amount of losses that could be offset against income. He found that in 1968, more than 300 high technology companies, firms that are generally quite risky, were founded in the United States; but in 1976, not one such firm was established ("Footnotes to the Above" 1978:20).

Other evidence comes from a study by the American Electronics Association on small but growing electronics firms. The chairman of the task force that undertook the research testified before the House Ways and Means Committee that data from their survey showed that a notable decrease in capital gains taxation could actually cause federal tax revenues to increase. It was claimed that this Laffer effect would result from the unique ability of these types of firms to generate production and employment, which would give the Treasury a proportionately higher tax base.

Evidence in mid-1979 indicated that the venture capital market was suddenly booming again. Mr. Reid Dennis, chairman of the National Venture Capital Association, reported that the industry was more active than at any time since 1969 (Bulkeley and Richert 1979:42). By the end of 1979, investment in venture capital had increased to $1 billion from the $300 million average for the years 1974 through 1977 ("The 40% Solution" 1980:34). Among the reasons for this prosperity were increasing corporate acquisitions of small new firms, the spectacular success by some new companies financed by venture capital, and the growing importance of firms that specialized in supplying venture capital in exchange for equity in fledgling companies.

The emergence of these specialized companies that fund prospective businesses has helped encourage new investment by reducing the cost of monitoring risky ventures. Individual investors in venture capital firms rely on them to monitor the new operating enterprises. Venture capital firms also spread the risk by relying on many individual investors for funds.

Although these factors are important in helping to explain the resurgence of venture capital, it is no coincidence that the market was more buoyant in 1979 than at any time since 1969. Capital gains taxation was increased in 1969, effective in 1970, and again in 1976. However, the 1978 legislation reduced the tax on any gains in the value of assets. According to many of the firms that specialize in venture capital, the most important factor in the recovery of this important investment was the reduction in the maximum tax on capital gains on investments held over a year, which Congress passed in the autumn of 1978 (Bulkeley and Richert 1979:42).

Additional empirical evidence on the efficacy of tax reduction

Edward O'Brien (1979:24) has presented the most thorough survey of evidence on the effect of the 1978 cut in capital gains taxation. Remember that the period he examines, November 1978 to September 1979, was marked by increased interest rates, accelerating inflation, and impending recession.

O'Brien examines three principal indicators in evaluating the effects of the

Revenue Act of 1978 on investment. They are: substantial increases in share prices for small businesses, a rise in the new offerings of stock by small enterprises, and the sharp increases in investment just discussed.

Differential increases in share prices: Share markets offer a full portfolio of investments that range from those with low risk and return to those that are riskier and carry a higher rate of return. The larger, safer corporations are predominant in the Dow Jones Average and also in Standard and Poor's 500; the lower-capitalized, riskier firms are more heavily represented in the American Stock Exchange and NASDAQ indices.

The portfolios of institutional investors, many of whom are exempt from federal taxation of income and capital, are dominated by the higher-capitalized issues, whereas individuals tend to invest in relatively lower-capitalized businesses. O'Brien hypothesizes that any reduction in the tax on gains in the value of assets, which affects mainly individuals, should produce a differential impact on the two different types of issues.

The evidence strongly supports his thesis. Between November 1, 1978, when the Revenue Act of 1978 took effect, and September 30, 1979, the American Stock Exchange Index rose by 57 percent. The NASDAQ increased by about 31 percent. The record of the Dow Jones Average and Standard and Poor's during the same time period reveals increases of only 6.1 percent and 12.9 percent, respectively. Slemrod's (1982:3–16) more recent study on the effect of the 1978 capital gains tax reduction on the volume of stock transactions indicates a similar performance for the longer period 1979–81. The value of the American Stock Exchange Composite Index in May of 1981 was 150 percent higher than at the end of 1978; the indices of NASDAQ and Standard and Poor's were 98 and 38 percent higher.

Table 5.7 shows the sensitivity of both the number of new issues of stock and their magnitude to the sharp reduction in the maximum rate of taxation on capital gains in the autumn of 1978. As previously mentioned, the Ways and Means Committee and the entire House of Representatives approved reductions in taxation in the summer of 1978. There was, consequently, widespread anticipation by investors that tax rates would be decreased. The result was a marked increase in the issue of new shares. Approximately 75 percent of the value of these new public offerings in 1978 were issued in the last half of the year. The number of these issues doubled and their value trebled in comparison to the first six months of the year. The value of new initial issues of shares for 1979 increased at a rate approximately 600 percent that of the five years following the 1973–4 recession, and the increase for the first nine months of 1980 was about 700 percent greater.

The preceding material on venture capital, behavior of share prices, and new issues of shares provides us with a variety of evidence. All the available

Table 5.7. *Initial offerings of shares*

Year	Share value ($m)	Number of issues
Jan.–Dec. 1974	$117	55
Jan.–Dec. 1975	236	25
Jan.–Dec. 1976	271	45
Jan.–Dec. 1977	276	49
Jan.–June 1978	54	18
July–Dec. 1978	160	40
Jan.–June 1979	256	59
July–Dec. 1979	336	85
Jan.–Sept. 1980	800	182

Source: Edward I. O'Brien, "Reduction of Tax on Capital Gains Spurs Invest-ment," *The Wall Street Journal,* October 31, 1979, p. 24; and Tim Metz, "New Issues Become the Rage Again, Riding on Stock Market's Strength," *The Wall Street Journal,* November 17, 1980. p. 31. Reprinted by permission of *The Wall Street Journal,* © Dow Jones & Company, Inc. 1979, 1980. All Rights Reserved.

figures indicate a case for the success of the policy of reducing taxes on capital gains. Despite many negative factors in the economy, the 1978 legislation achieved the goal of increasing investment, especially in the smaller and more dynamic companies.

Capital gains taxation and inequities and inefficiencies in housing

Capital gains taxation as traditionally applied to residential housing exempli-fies many of the deficiencies in this type of levy. It is responsible for inequi-ties, lock-in effects, and inefficiency in the distribution of space among fam-ilies and individuals. The tax on nominal gains in the value of homes has caused overconsumption of housing by older individuals and underconsump-tion by many younger, larger families.

Inflation and, to a much smaller extent, increases in population have caused home owners to accumulate large nominal profits. As with other assets, the law requires that these nominal gains in value be subject to taxation. The tax can often deplete what would have been a substantial portion of a family's retirement funds (Cook 1978:12A).

Just as young couples find it very difficult to purchase their first house, older people find it economically punishing to sell their next-to-last or last one. As Kenneth J. Thygerson, an economist with the U.S. League of Sav-ings Association, reports, "Housing is the only asset most people have that has risen faster than inflation'' (Cook 1978:12A). If a house were bought five years ago for $25,000 and sold $50,000 today for the nominal profit would be $25,000; yet the seller probably would have to use that profit, along with the original $25,000 and possibly more, to replace the house.

The government, however, exacerbates the problem confronting the home seller by levying a capital gains tax against the phantom profit of $25,000. Therefore, replacing the house, even with a smaller structure, could involve substantial losses to the family. The law does permit postponement of the tax if a replacement house of equal value, $50,000 in the example, or higher, is purchased or built within twenty-four months of the original sale. This provision in the old tax code was of little help to an older couple, whose children had grown and left home, and who desired a smaller living space. They were inhibited by the prospect of substantial economic loss in their choice of whether to move to an apartment, buy into a retirement complex, or simply purchase a small house. This situation was a classic case of the lock-in effect caused by capital gains taxation.

The problem of efficiency in the housing market has been exacerbated by inflation. Middle income families have discovered that housing and land are about the only assets within their power and economic capacity that afford them a hedge against inflation. This investment possibility has spurred sharp increases in the demand for residential structures, pushing the price of housing even higher.

There is no place in America where inflation and increasing population have had more impact on the rapidly rising prices of housing than in California. These factors, combined with the capital gains tax, were underlying causes of the tax revolt of 1978. In some cases, older home owners saw the value of their homes double in as short a period of time as four years. A well-meaning but ill-advised state law required reassessment of residential housing at full market value for purposes of levying and collecting property taxes. The result was that many home owners, especially those retired and living on relatively fixed incomes, simply could not pay the rates unless they sold their homes. At the same time, the capital gains tax exerted enormous pressure inhibiting the sale of housing through the lock-in effect. The net receipts from sale after capital gains taxation, not to mention real estate brokers' and legal fees, stamp taxes, moving expenses, and so forth could leave prospective sellers in a devastating economic position.

The result of this dilemma is history. Despite vigorous opposition by the governor and most other politicians, the bureaucracies in many different governments, the business community, and the special interest, minority, and ethnic groups, as well as dire warnings of governmental collapse, Proposition 13, which placed a limit on rates, passed with an unprecedented majority of two to one.

California residents passed Proposition 13 in June 1978. United States congressmen and senators, who quickly understood its political overtones, reacted with unusual speed. The Federal Tax Revenue Act of 1978, passed in October of that year, included some relief from the taxation of capital gains on housing. A home owner fifty-five years or older, who meets certain residence requirements, can now exempt the first $125,000 in gains on the sale of that home. This exemption is permitted once in a lifetime.

In time, inflation will erode and neutralize this exemption. But for now, this exemption removes the lock-in effect for most homeowners. It permits a more efficient distribution of housing space among younger and older families and individuals and reinstitutes a degree of equity that inflation had eradicated under the old law.

Capital gains and numismatic, philatelic, and other collections
as investments

A rapidly increasing problem associated with inflation and capital gains taxation is the relatively recent predilection of individuals to invest funds in such nonfinancial and largely nonproductive assets as rare stamps, coins, paintings, tapestries, china ware, and antique furniture. An entirely new industry of privately owned mints and studios has been spawned to produce and distribute limited editions of expensive glassware, plates, porcelain, sculpture, and commemorative medals and coins (Harris 1980:64–7; "Boom in Coin . . ." 1980:17; "When to Put . . ." 1981:158–61).

These items are particularly attractive to investors and prospective taxpayers because they appreciate in value as the currency is debased, and the exchange of these wares is difficult for governments to trace. Avoidance, and more particularly evasion, of taxation on any nominal or real gains in the value of these assets is relatively safe and easy to accomplish. As a consequence, economic inefficiencies abound because large and increasing amounts of otherwise valuable and productive time are spent in nonproductive and clandestine activity. Undoubtedly, some individuals derived genuine consumer satisfaction from these items, but in addition to time, there is a waste of other resources.

Conclusion and summary

The taxation of capital gains has waxed and waned throughout its more than seventy-year history in the United States. Until recently, there had been no systematic empirical information on the impact of the nature and changes in the levy on behavior of individual investors. Instead, decisions about policy and legislation rested largely on unscientific value judgements. Arguments regarding the levy were put forward by proponents concerned mainly with the equity of the levy as well as opponents who believed that investment in new productive capacity should be encouraged and not inhibited by disincentive taxation.

At the same time, Treasury has alertly guarded against diminution of tax receipts by lobbying against proposals to liberalize the rate structure and other legal provisions that determine the tax liability of savers and investors. Recent research indicates that the trade-off between equity and investment, and also between more and less revenue to Treasury, may be more of a short-run problem and not as serious as most interested observers have believed. Several econometric studies indicate sufficient sensitivity of investors to lower rates to permit a substantial growth in investment, employment, and the capital/labor ratio. Consequently, the real wage rate is such that tax revenues to Treasury may rise. If such results should transpire, the debate on the issue of equity would tend to become moot. However, researchers need to undertake additional, careful theoretical and empirical work on this issue because no general agreement now exists as to whether the elasticity of realizations with respect to the tax rate per se exceeds or falls short of unity.

The overriding current problem with capital gains taxation centers on the existence of inflation. The tax structure of the United States was not designed for an economy with a substantial rate of inflation. Research confirms that taxes on capital gains, which sometimes accrue over a decade or more, along with inflation can and do cause effective rates of taxation to exceed 100 percent. This situation not only manifests strong inequities but also has a deleterious effect on capital formation, productivity, and economic growth. Some form of indexation of capital gains must be adopted on a permanent basis.

CHAPTER 6

The corporation income tax

The United States corporate income tax was passed into law in 1909, predating the individual income tax by more than four years. This tax has been an integral part of the federal revenue system for almost fifty years but has been declining as an important source of revenue since the Korean War. In 1950, it accounted for 28 percent of total federal receipts; in 1960, 23 percent; and in 1970, 17 percent (U.S. Bureau of Census 1974:222). By 1982, the figure had dropped to 12 percent (U.S. Bureau of Census 1983:4). The estimated figure for 1985 was also 12 percent (Council of Economic Advisers 1984:220, 304–5).

Introduction

Currently, the corporate tax is the center of much attention because many analysts believe it to be both inequitable and inefficient. They argue that it has inhibited economic growth by stifling capital formation, and that the net real rates of return provided by investment are not sufficiently high to attract the funds of investors. Moreover, the enormous and continuing federal budgetary deficits have created extremely large demands in the money and credit markets, driving up interest rates, attracting the relatively small amount of savings now available, and generally exacerbating the problem of capital formation. The issue of economic growth has caused analysts, investors, and politicians to focus attention on the nature and structure of the corporate income tax.

Four fundamental problems are associated with the corporation income tax. They are shifting and incidence, double taxation, investment incentives, and the impact of inflation. These major issues are discussed following a review of the nature, structure, and revenue productivity of the tax.

Reasons for the corporation income tax

One reason given for the corporation income tax centers on the perception of the corporation as a legal entity with an existence of its own. Proponents of the tax argue that the corporation is an important economic and social force, managed by professionals who are subject to little stockholder control. They

119

also argue that the corporation is much more than a conduit for personal income that is distributed through dividends and capital gains. Advocates of the tax conclude that the incorporated business has a separate taxable capacity all its own, which should be subject to a tax over and above that paid on dividends and capital appreciation by individual owners. It is important to note that this separate entity view assumes that the corporate tax falls on shareholders and is not shifted forward to consumers or backward to the owners of factors of production (Musgrave and Musgrave 1980:400–1).

Another rationalization for the tax rests on the benefit principle. State and federal governments provide a wide array of services that assist business. These range from police and fire protection, street and road facilities, and statistical services to legal, marketing, and financial matters. All of these services tend to reduce costs, but they are not confined to corporations as proprietorships and partnerships also share in the use of these governmentally provided services. A more appropriate base for benefit taxation might be a combination of property and value-added taxes (Musgrave and Musgrave 1980:401–2).

Brown and Jackson (1979:362) point out that a very cogent reason for the levy is simply that there is income that can be taxed. There is some truth to the saying that an old tax is a good tax because individuals and businesses have long since adjusted to major changes in this levy. An alternative tax to replace the revenue lost as a result of eliminating the corporation income tax would have associated with it the new and relatively high cost of change and adjustment.

A fourth factor that could be used to rationalize the corporation income tax is the issue of regulation. Government could use some form of the levy to control monopoly, restrict the absolute size of firms, and change incentives for saving, investment, and economic growth. Governments have, in fact, used the excess profits tax in time of war to control rates of return. Musgrave and Musgrave (1980:403) note, however, most regulatory objectives would be better served by tools or instruments other than a profit tax.

Most corporations do not pay out all their current net income in dividends to the owners. Dividends are, of course, taxed at personal individual income tax rates; but without a corporation tax or an effective capital gains tax, a substantial share of income would not be subject to taxation. Such a state of affairs would create a strong incentive for corporations to retain a higher proportion of their income than is presently the case. In addition to permitting shareholders to reap large returns through untaxed capital gains, companies would be even more protected from meeting the tests of money markets when new investment decisions arise. Consequently, firms might begin projects that promise less than the optimal rate of return on funds and scarce resources.

The structure of the corporation income tax

The structure of the corporation income tax is influenced by corporate tax rates, taxable income, the tax base, and the resultant revenue.

Tax rates: The corporate income tax is levied on incorporated private enterprises. In 1985, it was levied at five different rates, depending on the size of the entity's income:

first	$25,000	15 percent
second	$25,000	18 percent
third	$25,000	30 percent
fourth	$25,000	40 percent
more than	$100,000	46 percent

Taxable income: In principle, taxable income is calculated by deducting the costs incurred in producing goods and services from the gross income. In practice, determining taxable income can be very complex and difficult. Different firms and industries present unique problems so that uniform tax treatment of such diverse industries as aerospace and banking is virtually impossible (Musgrave and Musgrave 1980:397). Issues concerning exactly what items can and cannot be deducted from gross income as legitimate business expenses often form the basis for governmental administrative hearings and rulings and sometimes for cases in court.

The corporate income tax has often been accused of harboring a plethora of loopholes. Whatever the merits of that criticism, it is evident that "a fair corporation tax cannot be a simple tax" (Musgrave and Musgrave 1980:397). A number of exemptions, credits, and allowances have been introduced to the tax code in order to change corporate behavior. For example, accelerated depreciation or an investment tax credit can be used to stimulate investment by raising a company's after-tax return. These provisions have effect because the corporation is itself a taxable entity, and these tax preference items are enjoyed by corporations as well as other types of businesses.

The tax base: The number of corporate tax returns is much smaller than the number of individual taxpayer returns. The number of yearly returns reporting net income has averaged approximately 1,100,000 during the past decade.

The pattern of returns reveals that small firms compose the vast majority of the total number of corporations reporting net income. Conversely, a large proportion of the tax is paid by a very small number of businesses. Musgrave and Musgrave (1980:398) report recent data indicating that enterprises with assets in excess of $250 million comprise less than .01 percent of the tax returns, but they pay 65 percent of all corporate income taxes. Firms with assets of more than $25 million submit just a little more than .05 percent of the corporate returns, but their federal income tax liability composes 78 percent of the corporate tax. These figures indicate a concentration of wealth in a relatively few, very large enterprises, and for all practical purposes they comprise the corporate income tax base.

Corporate tax revenue: Revenue generated by the corporation income tax during the past decade is shown in Table 6.1. Taxes collected for the budget accounts of the U.S. government as well as corporate tax accruals are displayed. All figures are in nominal terms.

Generally, the raw data reveal a constant but irregular increase in the amount of tax collected until the end of the decade. From 1980 to 1983, both revenue concepts showed a decline. Corporate taxes as a proportion of budget receipts declined on average over the decade, falling to a low of 6.2 percent in 1983. A similar pattern with slightly higher percentages held for corporate tax accruals as a share of total tax accruals in the national income amounts. Corporate taxes in the budget and in the income accounts as a share of GNP held fairly steady until 1980, when the numbers began to decline. Estimates for 1985 revealed the possibility of a reversal in all of these declining figures (Council of Economic Advisers 1984:220, 304–5, 309).

The data in Table 6.2 permit a comparison over selected years of the relative importance of the corporate levy among the world's industrially advanced countries. In comparison with other countries, the United States levy ranks relatively high as an important part of the tax system. No clear overall trend emerges in the statistics, although evidence suggests a slight decline over time in the importance of the tax for the majority of countries. Note that the data in Tables 6.1 and 6.2 are not strictly comparable because U.S. and OECD (Organization for Economic Cooperation and Development) definitions differ.

Because corporate tax revenues are a function of corporate profits, another way to view the revenue potential of the levy is to examine the behavior of profits over time. The trend in corporate profits has been downward since the Korean War. In the 1950s, corporate profits before taxes were 11.5 percent of GNP, but the ratio declined to 9.8 percent in the following decade and to 8.6 percent in the 1970s. If before-tax profits are adjusted for rising prices in order to allow for nominal inventory profits and inadequate allowances for depreciation, the ratio of profits to GNP fell by 29 percent during the three decades, with almost all of the decline occurring in the 1970s (First Chicago Bank 1979:7).

Although the ratio of before-tax profits to GNP declined after 1950, after-

Table 6.1. *Federal corporate income tax revenue in the federal budget national income accounts, 1971–1985* [billions of dollars/fiscal years]

	Budget accounts				National income accounts				
	(1)	(2)	(3)	(4)	(5)	(6)	(7)	(8)	(9)
Year	Corp. tax	Budget receipts	Corp. tax ÷ receipts	Corp. tax ÷ Ind. tax[a]	Corp. tax ÷ GNP	Corp. tax[b]	Nat. income tax receipts	Corp. tax ÷ receipts	Corp. tax ÷ GNP
1971	$26.8	$188.4	14.2%	31.1%	2.5%	$31.9	$192.4	16.7%	3.0%
1972	32.2	208.6	15.4	34.0	2.7	34.2	213.4	16.0	2.9
1973	36.2	232.2	15.6	35.1	2.7	43.4	240.7	17.0	3.1
1974	38.6	264.9	14.6	32.4	2.7	43.4	271.6	16.0	3.0
1975	40.6	281.0	14.4	33.2	2.6	41.8	283.4	14.7	2.6
1976	41.4	300.0	13.8	31.4	2.4	52.5	314.9	16.7	3.0
1977	54.9	357.8	15.3	34.8	2.8	58.8	365.9	16.1	3.1
1978	60.0	402.0	14.9	33.1	2.8	67.2	414.2	16.2	3.1
1979	65.7	465.9	14.1	30.2	2.7	75.8	480.7	15.8	3.1
1980	64.6	520.0	12.4	26.5	2.4	70.6	527.3	13.4	2.7
1981	61.1	599.3	10.2	21.4	2.1	70.5	610.3	11.6	2.4
1982	49.2	617.8	8.0	16.5	1.6	51.3	627.8	8.2	1.7
1983	37.0	600.6	6.2	12.8	1.1	54.3	630.7	8.6	1.6
1984[c]	66.6	670.0	9.9	22.7	1.8	74.8	691.3	10.8	2.0
1985[c]	76.5	745.1	10.3	23.3	1.9	93.5	779.2	12.0	2.3

[a] Individual income tax payments [b] Corporate profits tax accruals [c] Estimated
Source: Council of Economic Advisers, *Economic Report of the President*, Washington, D.C., 1981, pp. 233, 314–15, and 319, and 1984, pp. 220, 304–05, and 309.

Table 6.2. Corporate income taxes as a percentage of total taxes

Country	1965	1970	1972	1974	1976	1978	1980	1982
	%	%	%	%	%	%	%	%
Australia	16.1	16.7	15.1	13.8	11.7	10.6	12.0	10.0
Austria	5.4	4.4	4.1	3.9	3.4	3.2	3.5	2.9
Belgium	6.2	6.8	7.2	7.8	6.8	6.0	5.7	6.0
Canada	15.1	11.3	11.1	12.9	11.6	11.4	11.6	8.0
Denmark	4.5	2.6	2.2	3.2	3.8	3.2	3.2	2.6
Finland	8.3	5.5	4.6	4.6	4.4	4.3	4.4	4.5
France	5.3	6.3	5.7	7.9	5.8	4.7	5.0	5.1
Germany	7.8	5.7	4.6	4.9	4.6	5.8	5.5	5.1
Greece	1.9	1.7	4.0	4.6	3.2	—	3.8	4.0
Ireland	9.1	8.8	5.6	6.9	4.4	5.0	4.5	4.7
Italy	6.9	6.6	7.4	5.4	6.1	8.8	8.1	8.0
Japan	17.8	20.1	17.5	22.1	15.7	18.4	21.8	19.7
Luxemburg	11.0	17.0	13.9	21.3	17.1	21.4	16.8	15.4
The Netherlands	8.0	7.7	6.7	6.7	7.0	6.3	6.6	6.8
New Zealand	20.9	18.4	14.6	15.0	12.7	8.0	7.8	7.9
Norway	3.8	3.2	2.5	3.3	4.0	4.6	3.3	6.5
Spain	10.2	8.7	8.1	8.5	7.3	5.4	5.1	4.7
Sweden	6.1	4.4	3.9	3.4	3.6	3.0	2.5	3.3
Switzerland	7.1	7.6	7.8	7.8	7.7	6.3	5.8	6.2
Turkey	4.1	5.7	4.3	4.8	4.0	4.4	4.7	12.7
United Kingdom	6.3	5.1	7.4	9.7	5.0	7.2	7.7	9.6
United States	15.8	12.7	11.2	11.0	10.3	11.4	10.2	7.0

Source: OECD, Revenue Statistics of OECD Member Countries, 1965–1979, Paris, 1980, p. 46, and 1984, pp. 36–45.

tax profits increased from 4.8 percent of GNP to 5.6 percent in the 1960s. The main reason for this shift was the liberalization of tax laws in 1962 and 1964. However, if inventory profits and depreciation allowances are adjusted for inflation, the ratio of after-tax profits to GNP declined by a dramatic 37 percent between the 1950s and the decade of the 1970s. The major factors responsible for this record drop were the increased tax liabilities resulting from inflated profits due to a rise in prices rather than an increase in real values (First Chicago Bank 1979:7).

Shifting and incidence

Changes in the allocation of resources as a result of adopting or changing the corporation tax depend in the first instance on how the owners of resources react. To determine what the economic effects will be, it is mandatory to know who actually bears the burden of the levy. However, a major problem with the tax on corporation income is its incidence. Crucial questions are: Is the tax shifted? If it is, by how much and to whom? The answers to these questions are perhaps the most diverse in the entire economics literature.

The short run

The classical short-run position on shifting and incidence of corporation taxes assumes full employment of the factors of production and that all firms, competitive and monopolistic, seek to maximize profits. Because under these conditions businesses will attempt to produce a rate of output at which marginal cost and marginal revenue are equal, levying a corporate tax gives managers and owners no incentive to change the rate of output. Post-tax profits, although lower because of the tax, will be maximized at the same output as pre-tax profits.

There is, as a result, no shifting of the tax forward to consumers through increased product prices; nor is there a shifting of the levy backward to labor and other owners of resources by decreasing the corporation's wage, rental, and other payments. Richard Goode (1951:71–2) best summarizes the conclusion of the classical position when he states, "The initial or short-run incidence of the corporate income tax seems to be largely on corporations and their stockholders."

The sales maximization model: William Baumol (1965:198–9) introduced the sales maximization model to the economic profession. Because of monitoring and policing costs, Baumol eschews the traditional profit maximization assumption and substitutes the sales of firms as their objective function. The pertinent constraint on a firm's sales is the minimum profit necessary to keep owners from withdrawing their capital and shifting their investment to other enterprises.

The firm reacts to an increase in the corporation tax by reducing sales, with the result that prices rise as output is reduced. The decrease in the quantity of goods and services produced and sold implies that suppliers of resources, including labor, will bear part of the burden of the tax through the receipt of reduced payments from the corporation. The higher prices imply that consumers will also bear part of the burden of the levy. Exactly how much of the tax will be borne by the various individuals will depend on the elasticity of the pertinent supply and demand curves.

The Baumol model allows the tax to be shifted backward and forward. His model and the classical case made it clear that the short-run impact of the levy on the allocation of resources and the distribution of individual income is a direct result of whether business enterprises attempt to maximize profits.

Econometric research: Pioneering econometric work on the short-run effect of the corporate levy revealed very surprising results. Krzyzaniak and Musgrave (1963:19) concluded on the basis of their model and statistical analysis that the tax was completely shifted. In some cases, more than 100 percent of the levy was shifted. This meant that owners of the enterprise succeeded in shifting the tax to consumers, labor, and owners of other resources, and the after-tax rate of return on capital did not decline.

Critics soon found many problems with the Krzyzaniak–Musgrave analysis. There were difficulties with both the model and the econometric work. Other empirical studies followed, but they added little knowledge to or help in understanding the shifting and incidence of the corporate income tax. However, the seminal research of Arnold Harberger (1962:215–40), and later of Charles McLure (1975:125–61), greatly advanced on the theoretical work on the incidence of the levy. Analysis is now on much firmer ground, but extremely difficult problems in satisfactorily combining theoretical and empirical research remain.

The Harberger long-run model: Serious general equilibrium analysis of corporate income tax incidence really began with the research of Harberger (1962:215–40). The long run in his model is defined as the allowance of sufficient time for capital to move in and out of firms, industries, and economic sectors. He assumes the following:

1. Corporations are entirely financed with equity funds;
2. perfect competition, and thus mobile factors of production;
3. certainty;

4. two goods being produced; and
5. all changes that occur are small in size.

When the tax is increased, the net rate of return to assets in the corporate sector decines in the short run. As time passes, capital moves out of the corporate sector, output declines, and prices rise. As investment funds and resources move into the untaxed, unincorporated sector, quantity there rises and prices fall. In the long run, the rate of return on equity funds for the entire economy declines, and the burden of the corporate tax falls on all owners of capital, incorporated and unincorporated.

Because the average price of capital declines, the income to those who own capital will fall relative to labor. If, as is often assumed, the marginal propensity to save out of capital income is higher than that for labor income, aggregate saving for the economy is likely to fall. According to the modern neoclassical model, the capital-to-labor ratio will then decline, labor will become less productive with less capital to assist in production, real wages will fall, and economic growth will be inhibited.

Another deduction that flows from Harberger's model involves a mixture of welfare gains and losses to consumers. Ceteris paribus, individuals and households that spend a relatively larger proportion of the budget on corporate goods will find their real incomes lower because there are now less of these items and they sell at higher prices. Conversely, individuals and households who purchase relatively more of their consumer goods from the unincorporated sector will realize gains because the influx of capital has caused output to increase and prices to decline.

An increase in the corporate tax rate has generated a new set of incentives, and investors have responded by transferring capital from higher productive uses to activities in which capital has a lower productivity. This specific effect can be theoretically measured and empirically estimated, and it constitutes a real loss in economic efficiency as a whole (Harberger 1964:58–76).

Criticism of the Harberger model: The strongest criticism of the Harberger model has come from J. E. Stiglitz (1973:1–34) and M. A. King (1977:246), each separately concerned essentially about the same sort of considerations. Stiglitz (1973:32) asserts in the concluding remarks of his stimulating paper that in analyzing the effects of the levy against corporate income, one must examine all pertinent provisions of both the personal and corporate tax code. M. A. King (1977:246) echoes this thought about the necessity of analyzing the detailed provisions of the tax system concerning depreciation and investment incentives, as well as alternative methods of financing and the institutional and legal constraints.

Stiglitz (1973:32) demonstrates the importance of the relationship between the relative tax saving on personal borrowing as compared to corporate borrowing. If the additional individual income tax rate is greater than that on corporate income, there is a strong incentive for the firm to use retained earnings to underwrite as much new capital as possible, and any additional investment should be financed by debt.

The fact that the law treats interest payments on borrowed money as an expense of doing business is important for Stiglitz (1973:31–32) because it permits the imposition or change of the corporation income tax without causing intersector inefficiency or misallocation between safe and risky industries. He believes that Harberger and other economists have confused the average with the marginal cost of capital.

In considering a new investment on the margin, for example, a firm, if it can attract debt finance, need only generate a return equal to the rate of interest that is deductible under current law. This rule of investing up to the point at which the marginal return on capital equals the rate of interest applies with equal force to the unincorporated sector of the economy.

The fundamental difference between the Harberger and Stiglitz–King position centers on their assumptions with regard to method of financing. In Harberger's model, corporations are financed 100 percent by equity funds, but any new investment by Stiglitz or King's firms is financed entirely by debt. This difference and the results obtained highlight the crucial importance of assumptions in corporate income tax analysis.

It should be pointed out that Harberger (1974:123) is, of course, well aware of the role of debt financing in the corporate sector. He states explicitly that by the very definition of the tax on corporate income, "all unincorporated activities are exempt; and even with the corporate sector of the economy, the tax falls more heavily on activities with low ratios of debt to equity (because interest on debt is a deductible expense)."

Further criticism of the Harberger general equilibrium model centers on the assumption of competition that, among other things, implies in the case at hand that there is intranational, intersectoral mobility of the factors of production (Brown and Jackson 1979:372–3). It is not clear, however, that results would change radically if the competitive assumption, which clearly violates conditions of the real world, were replaced by a given degree of monopoly.

Interestingly, M. A. King (1977:248–9) offers a related criticism. He states that in terms of his model, the corporate profits tax may have a direct effect on incentives by its effect on the cost of capital. There may also be an indirect effect due to the impact of the tax on either the marginal rate of return or the rate of interest. He notes that all general equilibrium models assume a closed economy, even though capital is the most internationally mobile of all the factors of production. If one key to the incidence issue is the effect of the tax on the interest rate, then omitting international capital movements could lead to misleading conclusions.

Despite these thoughful critiques, it is fair to say that Harberger has led the way with his seminal research on corporation income taxes. His model has subsequently become the foundation of all serious, modern analytical and empirical work on the shifting and incidence of the tax.

Long-run simulation results: John Shoven of Stanford University and John Whalley of the University of Western Ontario (1972:281-321) have constructed a medium-size econometric model that appreciably expands the scope of Harberger's work. They were able to incorporate several economic sectors, consider the distribution of income, account for individual and societal choice between work and leisure, and allow for the effects of several taxes simultaneously.

Shoven and Whalley (1972:281–321) derive results from their research similar to Harberger's position that owners of capital in general, both corporate and noncorporate, tend to bear the burden of the tax on corporations. In addition, although couched in a kind of sensitivity analysis framework, their estimates of the efficiency cost of the tax to the economy are similar to Harberger's numerical answers.

More recently, Don Fullerton joined Shoven and Whalley (1978:23–58) to construct a numerical equilibrium model of the entire U.S. economy and taxation system. Their scheme used many of Harberger's assumptions but extended many of the relationships among sectors and variables while providing extensive statistical content, using 1973 data to estimate parameters. They incorporated consumer and producer behaviors, savings and investment activities, foreign trade activities, and government policies regarding the purchase of goods and services.

The model was able to generate information on the extended and pervasive effects of such changes in government policy as a reduction in the tax rate on corporate income. Fullerton, Shoven, and Whalley (1978:23–58) provided numerical estimates of returns to capital and of taxes on corporate income as well as those on property, unincorporated income, and the corporate franchise.

This work represents a magnificent accomplishment. The structure of the model increases the richness of our understanding, surpassing previous work. At the same time, as the authors note, it should be regarded as a pilot model that provides a foundation for future developments.

Empirical estimates of the equity impact

Musgrave and Musgrave (1980:425) believe that the equity of the tax should be evaluated in terms of its impact on individuals and households and not on

Table 6.3. *Effective rates of the corporation income tax, by income class, 1970*

Income class[a]	If half the tax is borne by owners of capital and half is shifted forward to consumers	If the tax is borne by owners of capital in general	If the tax is borne by stockholders
0–3	4.6%	3.1%	0.8%
3–5	3.5	2.9	0.6
5–10	3.1	2.2	0.7
10–15	2.7	1.8	0.6
15–20	2.6	1.9	0.8
20–25	2.5	2.0	1.3
25–30	2.6	2.3	1.7
30–50	2.9	3.3	2.9
50–100	3.8	5.5	7.0
100–500	5.0	8.2	14.1
500–1,000	7.7	12.1	27.6
1,000 and over	8.6	13.4	32.0
All classes[bc]	3.0	2.8	2.4

[a] In thousands of dollars. Income is defined as money factor incomes plus transfer payments, accrued capital gains, and indirect business taxes.
[b] The average burden of the corporate income tax is different under the different assumptions because the portion of it borne by the tax-exempt sector (and therefore not included in the household sector) varies.
[c] Includes negative incomes.
Source: Federal Tax Policy, by Joseph A. Pechman. Copyright © 1977 by The Brookings Institution, Washington, D.C. Table 5-2.

business firms. However, because there is no generally, empirically supported and accepted theory of the incidence of the corporate levy, no definitive statements can be made concerning the burden of taxation borne by individuals.

Joseph Pechman and Benjamin Okner (1974:25–72) have attempted to handle this problem by preparing an array of assumptions and then calculating the effective rates of taxation by income class. When it is assumed that half the levy is borne by consumers through higher prices of corporate products (the Krzyzaniak–Musgrave effect) and half by the owners of capital in general (the Harberger effect), the tax is slightly regressive for individuals and families with incomes up through the $10,000–$15,000 income class. The most progressive structure is derived from the assumption that corporate taxes are borne by shareholders (the Goode effect). For a detailed analysis of income under three assumptions, see Table 6.3.

Concluding remarks

Debate over the shifting and incidence of the corporate income tax is not settled, although differences in conclusions stemming from alternative theories can, in some cases, be attributed to differences in initial assumptions. Despite theoretical and econometric problems, however, many economists are gravitating toward the position that forward or backward shifting of the tax in the short run is not likely. Charles McLure (1981c:3) believes that most public finance specialists would probably agree that there will be long-range shifting to owners of capital outside the corporate sector through the Harberger mechanism, with effects on both capital formation and wage rates.

Further economic effects of the tax

We have examined the current prevailing views of the impact of the corporation income tax on the allocation of resources between the corporate and noncorporate sectors. Further economic distortions exist between dividends and retained earnings, debt and equity financing, and present and future consumption and savings and investment. The levy also effects the distribution of incomes to individuals and households.

Present and future consumption and saving and investment

As observed in the preceding section on shifting and incidence, if it is concluded that the tax cannot be shifted directly forward or backward and that investment is financed by equity capital, one effect of the corporate levy is to decrease the net rate of return of capital in both the corporate and unincorporated, untaxed sectors. As a result, the net rate of return to savings will fall, increasing the cost of saving or future consumption. Present consumption becomes more attractive and individuals and households increase their rate of consumption while reducing their rate of saving.

Modern neoclassical economists believe that aggregate saving will then fall and that fewer resources will be for use in investment. The ratio of capital to labor will decline; and with less capital to assist workers in producing, the marginal product and real wages of labor will fall. This whole process will have deleterious effects on economic growth and per capita real income.

Dividends and retained earnings

Other things equal, the corporation income tax reduces the amount of equity capital available for business investment. However, as Pechman (1977:139) points out, other factors have not remained constant. Empirical research indicates that the high rates of taxation against individual income, combined with relatively lower rates on capital gains, have encouraged corporate managers to increase business rates of saving in the form of retained earnings, which are then used for investment. Morover, although the evidence is not clear on the issue, it is quite possible that some investment projects funded by retained earnings would not be profitable and undertaken if the firm were forced to seek funds from competitive capital markets.

Note that recent high rates of inflation have turned formerly favorable statutory rates on capital gains into relatively high de facto rates. Although marginal tax rates may fall below effective tax rates, some individuals have paid effective tax rates that exceed 100 percent. This fact could tend to diminish corporate rates of retained earnings.

Tax-induced nonneutrality between debt and equity financing

Two main sources of investment capital are available to corporations: equity funds supplied directly or indirectly (retained earnings) by stockholders and debt instruments that pay interest to investor-creditors. As noted, interest owed to creditors is treated as an expense and is deductible from corporate income before calculating the firm's tax liability. There is, as a result, an incentive for managers to increase the debt-to-equity ratio.

The process, however, has its limits. Brown and Jackson (1979:374) note that as the debt-to-equity ratio rises, individuals in the capital market see an increase in probability of bankruptcy because interest payments, unlike dividends, must be paid. This raises the cost of both debt and equity as prospective creditors and shareholders will demand larger returns to compensate for the greater risk.

Double taxation and corporate tax integration

As Michael Boskin and John Shoven (1980:168) point out, the U.S. tax system is extremely complex and does not even vaguely incorporate the Haig–Simmons notion of income. In particular, income from capital is taxed in a wide variety of ways with no obvious overall rationale guiding tax treatment. One of the most troublesome and capricious problems is the double taxation of corporate income. This section examines some difficulties and effects that result from the problem and some possible alternative solutions.

The mechanics of double taxation

The different treatment of income derived by labor and income derived by capital has long been criticized by academics. These differing treatments were caused by political influences on taxation policy rather than by the traditional policy concerns of equity and neutrality. An anomalous result of the system of taxing labor and capital income differently is the double taxation of corporate dividends.

Double taxation of corporate dividends occurs because dividends, in the form of corporate income, are initially subject to the corporate income tax. Once distributed, these dividends are taxable as ordinary income in the hands of the recipient shareholders. The total burden of taxation may be severe. Shareholders who are subject to the 20-percent marginal rate of the personal income tax, and who receive a dividend of $54.00, actually sustain a tax burden of $56.80. First, in order to grant a dividend of $54.00, the corporation had to pay corporate income tax of $46.00. Shareholders are not credited with any payment of this tax, despite the fact that it directly subtracts from the amount of dividend they receive. The $54.00 they receive make taxpayers liable for $10.80 in personal income tax. Thus, taxpayers are left with $43.20 in disposable income and a combined tax burden of $56.80, essentially taxing the dividend at a rate of 56.8 percent. Taxpayers in the 50-percent bracket keep only $27.00 out of what was originally $100.00 in corporate income.

Profits that are not distributed by a corporation to its shareholders are retained earnings. Retained earnings accrue to stockholders in the form of capital gains when they sell their stock. Sixty percent of long-term capital gains are exempted from personal income taxation; the remainder are taxed at the shareholder's marginal rate. This practice adds another dimension to the patchwork of taxes falling on corporate income. One dollar of personal income, for example, can be earned in several ways: by an unincorporated individual; by a corporation that retains its income; by a corporation that distributes its income; or by some combination of the latter two ways. Such income may be treated vastly differently by the tax code. Unincorporated individuals are taxed at their bracket rate, from zero to 50 percent. Retained earnings are initially taxed at 46 percent, and the addition of an individual's capital gain tax liability can drive the rate significantly higher. These widely varying possibilities substantially influence the way a taxpayer chooses to realize income. They also significantly influence the progressivity of the individual part of the federal income tax system (Christian 1977:7)

Considerable debate has ensued over how to eliminate these disparities in corporate and shareholder taxation. One method discussed is the integration of corporate and personal income.

Assumptions of integration

A major assumption of those favoring integration is that the incidence of the corporate income tax falls on the owners of the corporation. If the corporate tax is shifted to the consumer or to the wage earner or other suppliers, then the shareholder does not actually suffer double taxation. The corporate tax would be similar in nature to the sales tax, and its crediting to the dividend recipient would be inappropriate. Integration would therefore result in substantially lower taxes on profit income and could represent a windfall to the shareholder (Christian 1977:7).

Another major belief of integrationists is that corporations have no independent taxpaying ability and are merely conduits through which earnings pass to shareholders. The conduit theory is implicit in the calculations of taxation that appear in the introduction to this section of the chapter. In those calculations, the corporation's tax burden was attributed to the shareholders. Under this assumption, it is clear that the combination of corporate and personal income taxes yields tax rates that are inequitable and capricious when compared to the statutory personal rate structure.

McLure (1979:22) notes that if corporations are not conduits for earnings to pass to shareholders, then attributing the corporation income tax to shareholders is fallacious. Realistically viewed, the conduit theory is at least an oversimplification. Because of the separation of ownership and control, the interests of corporation managers may often be different from those of the shareholders. Conflicts can occur over dividend policy itself. This difference makes the existence, nature, and level of the corporate tax essentially irrelevant for appraising the personal income tax.

It is interesting that the West German government, which has totally eliminated the double taxation of dividends, rejects the conduit theory. It viewed the decision to maintain, reduce, or eliminate double taxation as one governed by expediency (McLure 1979:44). Integrationists in the United States would do better to support integration for its effect on allocation of resources and corporate financial structures rather than on the conduit theory.

Benefits of integration

Musgrave and Musgrave (1980:410) note that integration is meant to achieve basically three goals:

1. Restore horizontal equity by having capital income taxed no more heavily than labor income;
2. Remove distortion resulting from the singling out of capital income from the corporate sector; and
3. Increase overall level of investment.

Integration would improve capital market efficiency by eliminating the distortions resulting from singling out capital income from the corporate sector.

Double taxation distorts investment in favor of noncorporate activities. The cost of this misallocation has been estimated at .05 percent of the gross national product. The waste is equivalent to throwing away more than 10 percent of the revenue produced by the corporate tax. Feldstein and Frisch (1977:38–41) conclude that double taxation also causes distortions between dividends and retained earnings and between equity finance and debt finance. The effect of removing these distortions is difficult to quantify, but it is expected to be positive.

Integration advocates claim that because the corporate tax is a cost borne ultimately by capital, integration would result in an increase in overall investment. Feldstein and Frisch (1977:40–4) tested this hypothesis through an econometric simulation and found no way to predict the effect of integration on overall investment. They determined that the effect of an expected decrease in corporate savings would be to reduce savings, because one dollar of retained earnings adds approximately twenty-five cents more to private saving than one dollar of dividends. Additionally, net return on savings would increase, but the effect of this could vary. They found no clear evidence that integration would aid the overall level of investment.

Integration could be expected to increase the progressivity of the tax system. Feldstein and Frisch (1977:44–8) tested both partial and full integration. The partial integration method was to cut the corporate tax to 15 percent and to treat all of the remainder as personal income. Both types of integration increased progressivity by modestly helping bottom and middle bracket taxpayers and substantially increasing the burden on upper bracket taxpayers.

Methods of integration

Integration methods fall under the broad categories of full or partial integration. Full integration eliminates or substantially reduces the double taxation of dividends and retained earnings. Partial integration only eliminates or substantially reduces only the double taxation of dividends. Partial integration is often known as dividend relief.

One method of full integration is to treat shareholders as if they were partners in an unincorporated business. The corporate income tax would be abolished, and the total profits would be imputed to the shareholders. The profits, both distributed and retained, would be taxed as ordinary income in the hands of the shareholders. The use of the partnership method necessitates the periodic write-up of the basis of the stock to avoid double taxation. Double taxation would occur if retained earnings, which had already been taxed, were accrued by the shareholder as capital gains. Assessment of a capital gains tax would then result in double taxation. A slight variation of this method retains the corporation tax as a source-withholding tax. The corporation's payments would be in the account of the individual shareholder. Those shareholders in brackets below the 46-percent corporate rate would be entitled to refunds; those in brackets above 46 percent would be liable for the remainder of the tax (Musgrave and Musgrave 1976:408).

Another method of full integration is the capital gains method. This requires first the abolition of the corporate income tax. Dividends would be treated as ordinary income. Capital gains would be fully taxed, even if they are unrealized. In this manner, both dividends and retained earnings would be taxed. Retained earnings would be taxed according to the price appreciation of the stock (Musgrave and Musgrave 1976:409).

It is appropriate to note here that both integration methods abolish the corporate income tax. Without such a tax, it is impossible to grant exemptions, credits, or preferences to corporations; there is simply no corporate tax against which these items can operate. They might have to be replaced by granting similar concessions to shareholders or by giving a direct subsidy to the corporation.

Partial integration provides tax relief on dividends only. One method of partial integration is to exclude dividends from ordinary income taxation. All corporate income would be taxed by the corporate income tax regardless of whether it was distributed or retained. Because the total corporate tax would be the same whatever amount is distributed or retained, financial considerations rather than tax consequences would govern the distribution process (Christian 1977:18).

This scheme could be regressive. Certainly there are stockholders in brackets below the 46-percent corporate rate. A simple palliative would be to exclude only the first $500 or so of dividend income from ordinary income taxation, adjusted annually for inflation. This would, of course, leave a significant amount of dividends still subject to double taxation, albeit at a somewhat lower rate (Christian 1977:18).

Another method of partial integration is to allow corporations to deduct dividends from corporate income. This procedure would cause all dividends to be taxed at the shareholder's ordinary income rate. In this way, dividend taxation would be as progressive as the personal income tax. This method would not allow shareholders to benefit directly through dividend receipts from corporate tax credits because only undistributed earnings would benefit from these exemptions.

Feasibility of full integration

Full integration, under any system, would be an administrative challenge. It would have to accommodate two formerly distinct areas of taxation whose independence has led to the development of practices that would be difficult to reconcile within a single system.

One difficulty of imputing all of a corporation's earnings to its shareholders is that stock sales and transfers occur within the tax year. Within a given year, there may be several owners of a block of stock, all of whom cannot be imputed the corporation's income. The burden of estimating exactly how much income should be imputed to each would be heavy. For example, a shareholder may own stock for six months. During those two quarters, the corporation merely breaks even. In the next six months, someone else owns the stock and the company makes a profit. Do the owners split the imputed earnings, or is quarterly performance examined to impute all the income to the second shareholder? The first option is inequitable, the second difficult to achieve (McLure 1979:146–69).

Obtaining personal tax information from corporations in time to file a personal return would be difficult under full integration. Corporate and taxpayer fiscal years often do not coincide. Integration could then require some adjustment by corporations. Corporations are also shareholders, and the performance of their portfolios may greatly affect their year-end position. Therefore, shareholder corporations cannot report accurate earnings until they receive earnings estimations from such companies. But what if those companies are also shareholders who are waiting for this kind of information? Meanwhile, the individual shareholder is waiting at the end of this line, and millions of returns could be delayed.

The lack of finality of corporate returns could wreak havoc with the finances of individual investors. It is not uncommon for reported corporate income to be subject to audit adjustments. Additionally, amended returns sometimes create significant changes in reported corporate income. These adjustments can be made as much as five years after the first return. It is difficult to imagine that integration schemes would allow the shareholders to suffer such uncertainty as to their eventual tax burdens (McLure 1979:146–69).

Tax preferences also pose administrative problems. A tax preference is any provision that requires tax liability to be less than if the standard corporate tax rate were applied to economic income of the corporation. If there were no corporate tax, all tax preferences would vanish because there would be no liability against which to operate. They could only be replaced by preferences for shareholders or by direct subsidies to corporations.

If a corporate tax were retained for withholding purposes, the preferences would still operate. This would lead to a problem in identifying the tax paid on each dollar of distributed income. The question would be whether that dollar bore the tax or was immunized from the tax. Countries that have adopted dividend relief generally consider preference-shielded income to be "stacked" last in distributions. If preference income is distributed, a tax is imposed on it that "washes out" the preference. Thus, only the corporation can enjoy the preferences. This method is considered the likely treatment of preference if dividend relief were adopted in the United States. There is general agreement that any rule that involves stacking preferences first or prorating preferences is not administratively feasible (McLure 1979:146–69).

These problems are only a few of the many noted by economists contemplating integration. The feasibility of integration is so questionable that no country has adopted full integration. Integration advocate Charles McLure believes that the decision to have integration or dividend relief may hinge on the solution of these technical and administrative problems (McLure 1978b:331).

Conclusion

Integration is very attractive to most economists because it eliminates what they view as a clumsy, bifurcated system. Yet it seems clear that due to technical problems, the best that can be realistically expected to become law is partial or full dividend relief. If this is true, those reformers most concerned with equity and symmetry will have to settle for a system that preserves a significant amount of those inequities they attack.

Does evidence support the view that a half step toward integration is a step forward? Actually, the hard evidence says very little. Much is made of a previous argumentation in economic literature, but the little empirical research that has been done is conflicting. Feldstein and Frisch (1977:39–52), for example, discern no probable effect on the overall level of investment from integration. However, this major purported benefit of integration may or may not accrue.

Given that full integration appears unrealistic at this time, policymakers should wait until better information is available to turn to partial integration. One thing is certain – without any form of integration, it is still possible to ameliorate some disadvantages of the current system through preferences and shareholder credits.

The anatomy of investment incentives

There has been constant concern with negative incentive effects of the corporation income tax ever since it became law. More recently, the concern increased as lawmakers finally became more aware of the plight of U.S. business and the economy.

The most direct approach to the incentive problem would be simply to reduce the general rate of taxation on capital income. Significant reductions in this rate would most likely, at least in the short run, entail a sharp decrease in revenue. As a result, economists, accountants, and lawyers have continuously searched for selective ways to tax business income effectively and equitably without causing substantial losses to the Treasury. After a brief description of the process of depreciation, proposals concerning accelerated depreciation and investment tax credits will be discussed.

Depreciation

The amount of a corporation's income tax liability depends on its net pre-tax income, which is a function of its gross income and costs. The single most important problem in determining costs centers on the depreciation of business assets that have life in excess of one year.

If a new $1,000 machine has a life of ten years, in order to calculate net income properly, managers should subtract the cost of the machine from gross income sometime during the ten-year period. They would prefer to deduct the $1,000 sooner rather than later because such a strategy would increase current cash flow immediately. This preference arises because an extra dollar of cash flow earned in the present, due to the present depreciation allowance, is worth more than a dollar earned sometime in the future. As a result, the present value of the firm is higher when depreciation can be deducted sooner rather than later during the life of the machine.

The part of the tax law that deals with depreciation is concerned with the manner in which allowance is made for the wearing out of plant and equipment. The two major factors considered are the number of years allowed to business for the purpose of writing the expense of capital off the accounts and the pattern of year-to-year deductions that a business can use.

Until recently, good business practice required a firm to write off an asset over a period of time equal to the life of the asset. This job was not easy because it required estimates about obsolescence, current and future maintenance practices, and the quality of the new asset. Businesses have had little control over the number of years over which depreciation could be calculated, and this factor has been a continuing source of friction between private enterprises and the government. Until 1962, when the rules were liberalized slightly, the period allowed by the Treasury was based on the actual, past average life of the pertinent asset. Because of the constant clamor of the business community, Treasury issued a new set of rules in 1971 that permitted firms to reduce the tax life of equipment by 20 percent. Buildings and other assets did not qualify for this more liberal treatment (Brannon 1971:13). These rules, called Asset Depreciation Ranges, still governed depreciation practices as recently as the summer of 1981.

Until 1954, managers had no control over the time pattern for depreciating capital because it was governed solely by Congress and the Treasury (Brannon 1971:14). The law required that a constant amount of depreciation be deducted as a cost from gross income over the useful life of the investment. In the case of the aforementioned $1,000 asset, $100 depreciation would be deducted in each of its ten years of existence. This method of allowing for the wearing out of capital is called straight line depreciation.

In the major revision of the tax code in 1954, Congress introduced two additional formulas governing the time patterns of depreciation. Each of these methods, *sum or years digits* and *double declining balance*, permitted larger amounts to be depreciated in the early years of the asset's life and smaller amounts in the later years. This law introduced the idea of accelerated depreciation to the United States, and it is the precedent and basis for current efforts to liberalize further allowances for depreciation.

The investment tax credit

In 1962, at the urging of the Kennedy administration, Congress passed an investment tax credit act. It was replaced in 1969 but later restored. Unlike accelerated depreciation, the investment credit provides a direct and immediate tax reduction. Accelerated depreciation tends to favor long-term investment, such as that found in the oil, rail, mining, and steel industries, whereas the credit favors shorter-term capital expenditures, which are found in the electronics, aerospace, and computer industries. The shorter-lived asset can, of course, be replaced more often, and this alleged advantage permits businesses more frequent use of the tax credit.

Under the U.S. federal income tax law that was in force in 1981, however, the amount of the credit permitted to be taken against taxes owed depended on the useful life of the asset. No credit was allowed on investments with expected lives of fewer than three years; those with expected durability between three and five years qualified for a credit of 3.5 percent; those between five and seven years, 6.66 percent; and those with seven or more years, 10 percent. These tax credits were ignored, however, in deriving depreciation allowances.

David Bradford (1980b:282) points out that both tax credit and accelerated depreciation have an impact on the choice of an investor. The progressive rates of tax credit favor very durable assets compared with a flat rate credit; disallowing the incorporation of the credit in calculating depreciation tilts the scale on the side of capital with a relatively short useful life. Interestingly, Emil Sunley (1978:1–17) concludes from his analysis that neutrality requires a structure of tax rate credits similar to those in force in the 1970s. Bradford (1980b:282) gives a qualified confirmation to this view.

Economists R. E. Hall and D. W. Jorgenson (1967:391–414) were the pioneers in the study of the effects of investment tax credit on the purchases of new capital goods. They discovered in their experiment that after one year, a 7-percent tax credit was responsible for increases of more than 40 percent in equipment investment in the manufacturing sector and 48 percent in the total nonfarm sector.

Although the Hall-Jorgenson study has been criticized (Eisner and Nadiri 1968:369–82), subsequent research has supported its general conclusion that the investment tax credit can have a notable effect on the amount of spending for capital assets (Rossana 1981:16). Most recent studies indicate that the impact of the credit is smaller than the original Hall–Jorgenson figures indicate. Auerbach and Summers (1979:1–9) show, however that where decision makers perceive the change in the tax credit as permanent rather than transitory, the effect on asset purchase is even larger than the Hall–Jorgenson results.

Comparison of accelerated depreciation and investment tax credit

If the investment stimulus per dollar of revenue loss is the criterion for judging, both credit and depreciation are superior to tax rate reduction. The former can easily be limited to new investment, but a reduction in the rate would apply to income from all capital, new and old. Ceteris paribus, accelerated depreciation increases the rate of return on investment and tends to favor assets with a long life. The credit also enhances profitability but tends to discriminate in favor of short-lived capital.

Rate reduction does not violate the principle of neutrality, but both types of investment incentives probably do have distorting impacts. It is useful here to cite Bradford's (1980:282) conclusion that, in general, it is impossible to formulate a neutral rule for calculating the credit if the pertinent interest rate and detailed pattern of capital returns are unknown. Both Bradford (1980b:281–98) and Harberger (1980:299–313) have demonstrated, however, that it is possible to conceive of schemes under which neutrality could be achieved.

Proponents of the tax investment credit rightfully claim that it is a more flexible fiscal tool. Individuals who favor accelerated depreciation note that its stability and permanence provide a more conducive environment for business planning.

At this time it is virtually impossible to state with any precision what the equity effect is of investment incentives. Theoretical and statistical problems inhibit analysis. The Musgraves (1976:438) believe, however, that the effect favors individuals in high income brackets. If this is correct, then short-term distributional goals and economic growth may be in conflict.

Tax policy for research and development

Price-adjusted expenditures for research and development were fairly constant between the mid-1960s and mid-1970s. They reached their peak in 1964, when they amounted to almost 3 percent of GNP. They declined thereafter, but all of the reduction can be accounted for by the drop in federal spending for R and D in the defense and space industries.

Although only one of many factors helping to generate growth, R and D funding is a key ingredient. Several studies have shown that the funding reduction was associated with approximately 15 percent of the decline in productivity that occurred in the decade of the seventies (Carlson 1981:17–20).

Research and development is not only an important force behind changes in productivity but also a substantial item in the international trade activity of the United States. Such items as aircraft, chemicals, machinery, and scientific instruments all rely heavily on R and D and all are responsible for a notable trade balance. Industries that rely heavily on R and D are also important exporters of technology.

Currently, R and D receives preferential treatment because monies spent for labor and materials are treated as expenses and deducted from income in which the expenditures occur. Other countries have similar provisions and also offer even greater incentives. As a result, U.S. firms are forced into a less competitive position. The ratio of civilian R and D spending to GNP in the United States is about equal to that in the United Kingdom but lower than in West Germany and in Japan.

To spur productivity and growth in GNP as well to as enhance the international competitiveness of U.S. firms, George Carlson (1981:17–20), then an economist in the Treasury's Office of Tax Analysis, recommended that a tax credit on wages and equipment be used if policymakers decided to encourage further expenditures on R and D. Although there are problems with the definition and identification of eligible investment associated with tax credit, Carlson believes it would be relatively neutral in its effect within the R and D sector. It would proportionately decrease cost, regardless of the length of time of the undertaking or the combination of current and capital expenditures used.

The revenue impact on the Treasury of such a measure would depend on exactly how it was planned, but it would probably be marginal. Privately funded R and D is now running at about $30 billion a year. A 10-percent tax credit could cost approximately $3.0 billion.

Investment incentives and effective tax rates

Businesses have normally used the allowance for the wearing out of assets as a means to build up capital reserves for replacing plant and equipment. This practice worked reasonably well during periods of little or no inflation; but with the rapid rise of prices during the past fifteen years, companies have had to write off their assets on the basis of original or historical costs rather than of current replacement costs. As a result, they have been unable to recover the real cost of their investments, and their effective rate as contrasted with the statutory corporation income tax rate has been appreciably higher (Modahl 1980:26).

The effective tax rate is defined simply as the share of nominal income from an investment that the Treasury takes in taxes. It is the product of many factors but most notably the following: the statutory tax rate, depreciation rules, the investment tax credit, the rate of inflation, and the rate at which income-producing assets wear out (Siegfried 1974:245–59) (Fiekowsky 1978:1–33). If the deduction for depreciation matched perfectly the amount and time pattern over which the capital wore out, the effective rate of taxation on the asset would equal the normal, statutory 46-percent rate of taxation.

The effective rate of taxation declines and is lower than 46 percent if the depreciation allowances and investment tax credit exceed the actual decline in the value of the asset. These deductions have had an important impact because, according to congressional tax experts, the effective tax rate has been averaging around 20 percent (Merry 1981a:33). Harvard economist Dale Jorgenson estimates that the effective tax rate on corporation income climbed from 13.5 percent in 1977 to 25 percent by early 1981. He attributes this stunning rise almost entirely to a combination of the doubling of inflation and interest rates. Together, he notes they have significantly eroded the value of depreciation allowances (Jackson and Jonas 1981:28). Additional discussion of the relationship between the corporation income tax and inflation appears in Chapter 7.

Rate reduction and incentives

There is little doubt that a reduction in the corporate tax rate would have a salutary effect on capital formation. Lawrence Summers investigated the effect of cutting the levy on corporate income and concluded that relatively small reductions would have substantial positive effects on investment. Moreover, according to his research, a tax reduction announced by government today, but effective sometime in the future, would have a greater impact on capital formation in the short run than an immediate cut in the rate (Rossana 1981:16).

The reason for this seeming anomaly is connected with the complicated effects of accelerated depreciation. The value of depreciation allowances are larger for higher tax rates and would be less after a reduction in rates. Businesses, realizing that rates are going to fall in the future, would, where feasible, step up their purchases of plant equipment to take advantage of the larger depreciation expenses available before the tax cut.

Summers notes that the policy of announcing future tax cuts has the advantage of preventing an immediate tax loss to the Treasury. He concludes that in the long run, there is no difference in the effects on capital formation between all immediate and delayed tax reduction (Rossana 1981:16–17). Table 6.4 shows short-run differences and long-run similarities between the two policies.

In another study, Roger H. Gordon and Burton G. Malkiel (1981:178) estimated the efficiency gain resulting from a marginal reduction in the corporation income tax rate. Their findings revealed that the gain is approximately 40

Table 6.4. *A corporate tax reduction from 48 percent to 40 percent stimulates investment sharply*

Year	Percent increases in investment from:	
	Immediate tax reduction	Preannounced tax reduction, implemented in year 4
1	7.1%	9.5%
2	7.2	10.8
3	8.5	12.2
4	7.3	8.5
5	8.6	8.6
10	9.0	10.3
15	10.5	10.5
20	10.8	10.8
50	14.7	14.7

Source: Lawrence H. Summers, "Tax Policy and Corporate Investment," paper presented at a conference on "The Supply-Side Effects of Economic Policy," Washington University and the Federal Reserve Bank of St. Louis, October 24–25, 1980, as reproduced in Robert J. Rossana, "Structuring Corporate Taxes for a More Productive Economy," *Business Review,* Federal Reserve Bank of Philadelphia, January/February 1981, p. 17.

percent larger than the revenue loss. The private sector bears the high cost of $2.40 on the last dollar of the corporation income tax. This loss is composed of $1.00 of lost income paid in taxes and $1.40 in increased inefficiency. These estimates do not include the distortion imposed on savings decisions that, if included, would further increase the estimate for inefficiency.

On the basis of their extensive research, Gordon and Malkiel (1981:178) note that the corporate income tax is either more expensive to administer than other federal levies, in which case it should probably be cut, or is justified because it is more equitable than other alternatives. Another possible rationalization for the tax is that marginal government spending, which is financed by the levy, could be more than twice as valuable as marginal expenditures in the private sector.

Gordon and Malkiel (1981:178–9) also state that reducing corporate rates would leave unaltered the relationship between personal income and personal tax obligations, and therefore "would not affect the degree to which the tax law approximates either a consumption or comprehensive income tax." The authors conclude that large efficiency gains appear achievable from a reduction in the tax rate on corporate income. However, there may be some cost in tax equity. They do warn that since the measure of excess burden falls as the square of the distortion, larger changes in the rate will not make the efficiency gains look so favorable.

Current and future status of investment incentives

Members of the U.S. Congress finally began to realize in the late 1970s that at least some of the lack of economic growth was due to various government policies. Prominent among these policies were the hodge-podge tax provisions surrounding business investment and corporate income.

The capital cost recovery act

After extensive hearings, the Capital Cost Recovery Act was introduced to Congress in 1979. This proposed legislation, known as the 10–5–3 bill, was designed to speed up depreciation allowances. Its name stems from its provisions that would shorten the time over which certain business assets could be depreciated for tax purposes. Most buildings could be depreciated over ten years, three times faster than the then current allowance. Equipment could be depreciated in five years instead of ten, and investment in cars and light trucks could be written off in three years.

The objectives of the bill were to reduce taxes and increase the rates of return on plant and equipment, thereby increasing investment, productivity, and output. Estimates of the effect of the proposed legislation were quite different. From an expenditure of approximately $231 billion in 1978, the econometric model of Data Resources revealed that 10–5–3 would raise investment in plant and equipment by approximately $21 billion by 1984. The Congressional Research Service, which used different assumptions, estimated the increase to be about $18 billion. Norman Ture, then a private economic consultant and specialist in taxation, predicted that outlays for plant and equipment would rise by $76 billion by 1984 (Pierson 1980:48).

The main attribute of 10–5–3 was its presumed salutary effect on capital formation that, in turn, would raise productivity and real output. Any increase in real output would, ceteris paribus, exert downward pressure on inflation. Another advantage of the bill was that it would have simplified the complex asset depreciation range legislation that Congress passed in 1971 (Halverson 1979a:11). That law, with its many rules and regulations, formed the basis for depreciation practices for tax purposes throughout the decade of the seventies.

Several key organizations, including the National Federation of Independent Business (representing smaller businesses), the U.S. Chamber of Commerce, the Business Roundtable, and the National Association of Manufacturers, were instrumental in the drive to permit more rapid depreciation for capital equipment (Halverson 1979a:11). Senator Lloyd Bentsen, chairman of the Joint Economic Committee, backed the passing of 10–5–3, as did more than half the members of the House of Representatives. It received bi-partisan support from both Senate and House committee members (Halverson 1979b:15), as well as from a solid block of senators (Halverson 1979a:11).

Martin Feldstein (1979c), the president of the National Bureau of Economic Research, and Rudolph Penner of the American Enterprise Institute each agreed that the impact of the inflation on corporate taxes was a very serious problem. Each also favored a formal scheme of indexation for handling the issue of depreciation. Under this plan, businesses would have been able to increase the nominal value of their capital in line with inflation by using the appropriate price deflators constructed by the Commerce Department. Depreciation would then have been calculated on the marked-up and more realistic values of plant and equipment ("The Huge Stakes . . ." 1979:124).

The Capital Cost Recovery Bill would not have been able to handle appreciable changes in the rate of inflation. Feldstein's (1979c) research showed that for each one percentage point decline in the general level of prices, effective capital costs would decline by 1 to 2 percent, compared with an indexed scheme. Conversely, increases in inflation would have exacerbated the problem of understated depreciation, the very problem Congress was trying to resolve. Nevertheless, since 10–5–3 would have yielded results quite similar to the effect of indexation in 1979, both Feldstein and Penner supported passage of the bill by Congress ("The Huge Stakes . . ." 1979:124).

The then Federal Reserve Board chairman, G. William Miller, supported the idea of sharply increased depreciation rates in July of 1979. Three months later, as secretary of Treasury and a leading member of President Carter's cabinet, he strongly opposed 10–5–3 on the grounds that it would cut in half the revenue obtained from the corporation income tax. This reduction, he argued, would increase the federal deficit, cause the government to increase its borrowing from the public, and "crowd out" private investment. The conclusion seemed to be that reducing taxes on capital information and increasing the rate of return would not, in the final analysis, cause investment to increase (Pierson 1980:48). It is interesting to note that Data Resources estimated revenue losses at about $11 billion, far lower than Treasury's predictably huge estimate ("The Huge Stakes . . ." 1979:125).

Although Norman Ture estimated that more rapid depreciation allowances would stimulate enough saving to prevent any crowding out, critics pointed out several drawbacks to 10–5–3 (Pierson 1980:48). One criticism centered around a little publicized provision that would have permitted nearly half the construction costs of certain nonresidential buildings to be written off in three years. Another was the lack of any provisions to require periodic review of depreciation schedules. Should the rate of inflation dip much below 10 percent, 10–5–3 would have provided unrealistically high writeoffs. Moreover, the Capital Cost Recovery Bill did not really offer much help to ailing steel firms and other basic industries that were suffering from inadequate earnings on their existing capital ("Updating Depreciation" 1979:144).

Another reason the business community did not overwhelmingly support 10–5–3 was its alleged unneutrality within the private sector. Some analysts noted that it would distort the flow of capital such that some industries, which devoted a high proportion of assets to research and development, would have received relatively small benefits because R and D expenditures were not depreciated but expensed entirely on an annual basis. In addition, some of the most rapidly growing and competitive U.S. industries, such as electronics and aerospace, already had fast depreciation schedules and would benefit utility industries would have had more credits than they could have used, and they would have much preferred a general reduction in the corporation income tax rate ("The Key . . ." 1979:85). The chorus of critics of 10–5–3 became notably larger by the spring of 1980. Supporters of the aerospace, electronics, and computer industries, where the useful life of capital equipment can be extemely short, publicized their views within and out of government. Out of the controversy and discussion within the business community came a new and important point. Although more rapid depreciation allowances would improve the current cash flow position of a company, 10–5–3 would have had very little effect on the earnings per share of businesses. Young, high technology firms were discovering that the ratio of earnings per share was a critical factor when going to the capital markets to raise equity funds, and availability of capital was and is the most important limiting factor on the growth of these dynamic firms (Modahl 1980:26).

Sufficient doubts about 10–5–3 caused Ronald Reagan to withdraw his endorsement during the political campaign in the autumn of 1980, although he remained sympathetic to the idea of liberalizing depreciation allowances to encourage investment ("Paring Personal Taxes . . ." 1980:68).

In the spring of 1981, despite rapid inflation and much continuing support in Congress for liberalized depreciation allowances, depreciation policy was the same as it had been in 1971. Companies could depreciate their capital over the estimated useful life of each asset. This procedure often involved lengthy haggling and bargaining with the Treasury and did not permit a business to depreciate fully its investment after an allowance had been made for the inroads of inflation. As a result, the corporation tax was partially a tax against capital and served to decrease the country's capital stock.

The accelerated cost recovery system: This environment formed the backdrop for President Reagan's depreciation proposal, which was merely a variation of 10–5–3. His plan, called the Accelerated Cost Recovery System (ACRS), recommended eliminating the useful life concept. In its place, the administration proposed five new time categories for depreciation: eighteen years for most residential rental structures; fifteen years for low-income housing and certain nonresidential buildings; ten years for factories, retail stores, and warehouses; five years for most machinery and equipment; and three years for trucks, cars, and equipment used for research and development (Merry 1981a:33). In addition, his plan would liberalize the investment tax credit that firms take ("Reagan's Go-for-Broke Package" 1981:22–3).

The forecast of the revenue impact of ACRS was very large. Administration officials predicted an increase in corporate tax revenues of only $8 billion from the 1980 level. Total corporate taxes adjusted for inflation would fall substantially, at the same time the planned federal budget would be rising from $520 billion to $940 billion in 1986. The government made no secret of its desire to cut corporation income taxes substantially. In fact, Norman Ture, former treasury undersecretary for Tax and Economic Affairs, stated, "There's a huge philosophical sentiment to get the corporate tax out of the system" (Jackson and Jonas 1981:28). He stated that, in addition to ACRS, direct reduction in corporation income tax rates was on the administration's agenda. Moreover, the administration's package also contained provisions for the liberalized treatment of dividends as well as tax incentives for research and development.

Investment incentive plans would definitely move the tax system closer to the point at which there would be no corporation income tax. Nevertheless, Ture manifested misgivings over corporate tax strategy when he noted that it would be better not to do it gradually. He noted that the Reagan administration intended to investigate the integration of corporate and personal income taxes with the goal of eliminating the double taxation of corporate profits (Jackson and Joans 1981:28).

Most of the business community supported the President's Accelerated Cost Recovery System, although some lobbyists pushed to increase their share of total proposed tax cuts. But since ACRS was but a modification of 19–5–3, it was not surprising that those industries that had little income and, therefore, little or no tax liability did not see the administration's proposal as helpful. Auto producers, steel, railroads, and airlines all fell into this capital hungry but low profit category.

Criticism of ACRS was similar to that leveled against 19–5–3. Some analysts saw a marked breach of the neutrality maxim in ACRS because they believed that its depreciation provisions would channel investment capital away from some kinds of assets and into others (Merry 1981a:33). Managers of financially healthy companies underlined the point that the benefits of ACRS would be distributed arbitrarily, and Representative Dan Rostenkowski, chairman of the powerful House Ways and Means Committee, stated that the president's program favored such long-lasting assets as oil pipelines over such short-lived assets as auto factory tools (Merry 1981b:3).

Congress has been moving toward more liberalization of taxes on business enterprises since 1979, when several key members, desirous of increasing prductivity and the international competitiveness of the economy, took up the cause and recommended the reduction of the tax burden on firms. Despite criticism of the flaws in ACRS, Congress cut business taxes by increasing depreciation allowances when it made the Accelerated Cost Recovery System part of the tax law in August of 1981.

In a curious reversal of the tax legislation of 1981, Congress passed the Tax Equity and Fiscal Responsibility Act of 1982 (TEFRA). This law formed the basis for both personal and business taxation from 1983 to 1986. In addition to increased excise and social security taxes, deductions from gross income were decreased, and many of the tax reductions on businesses afforded by the 1981 tax law were reversed. The investment tax credit on capital expenditures were reduced, and deductions that companies would claim for depreciating assets were tightened. Moreover, several corporate tax preferences were reduced by 15 percent (U.S. Department of Treasury 1982:9).

CHAPTER 7

The corporation income tax and inflation

To understand the effect of inflation on corporations, it is necessary to understand the impact on the firm's income of traditional accounting practices together with the tax code. Inflation changes the prices of the items an enterprise buys and sells, thereby affecting costs and revenues, income, and the effective tax base. In addition, the use of the convention of historical cost accounting has a very important impact on business tax liabilities.

Introduction

There is almost universal agreement that the historical cost method of accounting significantly increases nominal profits during periods of inflation. Profits are higher than what they would be if all of a firm's costs and receipts were expressed in similar and constant prices (Mathews 1975:338).

Martin Feldstein (1979b:57) has discovered that the effective tax rates on capital income of various kinds increased substantially during the inflationary decade of the seventies. The reason was not due to increases in the statutory rates of taxation but to the mismeasurement of capital income. Mismeasurement occurs during inflation because of two main features in the present U.S. tax code: depreciation allowances on structures and equipment permitted by the government are based on the original or historical costs of the capital rather than the current replacement costs; and inventories are valued at current prices, and nominal or paper profits that accrue because of this practice are subject to the corporate income tax.

Depreciation allowances

The government permits businesses to deduct allowances for the wearing out of plant and equipment from revenues when computing tax liabilities. The law mandates that these deductions be based on not only the original cost but also the expected life of the capital. The rules of the Internal Revenue Service actually allow for a shorter taxable period than the useful service of capital goods. Consequently, when there is no inflation, a firm can realize a real gain in the present value of its cash flow. On the other hand, when the general level of prices is rising, allowances for the wearing out of plant and equipment

Table 7.1. *The present value of statutory straight-line depreciation allowances relative to the present value of price-level-adjusted depreciation allowances*

Inflation rate	Ten-year equipment[a]	Thirty-year structure[a]
0%	109%[b]	111%[b]
2	100	88
4	93	73
6	87	61
8	82	53

[a] Statutory lifetimes.
[b] The entries in the table are ratios of the present value of the statutory allowances and their price-level-adjusted alternatives. The real after-tax discount rate is 3 percent.
Source: Based on Richard Kopcke, "Are Stocks a Bargain?," *New England Economic Review,* May/June 1979, as reported by Marcelle Arak in, "Inflation and Stock Values, Is Our Tax Structure the Villain?," *Quarterly Review,* Federal Reserve Bank of New York, Winter 1980–81, p. 7.

that are based on historical rather than replacement costs understate the true value of the depreciating capital.

The higher the rate of inflation, the smaller the present value of real depreciation allowances. If, for example, the inflation rate is 8 percent, a business is allowed to deduct only 82 percent of the replacement value of capital equipment with a statutory life of ten years, and only 53 percent of a thirty-year structure. Table 7.1 shows other alternatives.

Tables 7.2 and 7.3 present different views of the problem and dramatically illustrate the relationship between inflation and depreciation allowances and their impact on a corporation's taxable income, after-tax cash flow, and internal rate of return. Assume that a firm is considering the purchase of capital equipment that costs $300,000 and has an expected life of five years. Managers of the enterprise calculate and predict that the cash income before taxes will average approximately $100,000 each years. For simplicity, corporate taxes are assumed to be 50 percent.

Column 2 of Table 7.2 shows the pre-tax annual cash flow that would be earned by the new equipment; column 3 the untaxed cash receipts that are allowable, straight-line depreciation deductions; column 4 taxable income; column 5 corporate taxes to be paid; and column 6 the after-tax cash flow the enterprise would realize on its investment. The internal rate of return, which is simpler than net present value to use for comparative purposes, is estimated to be 10.4 percent.

Table 7.2. *Depreciation, taxable income, and cash flow with zero inflation*

(1) End of year	(2) Net cash receipts	(3) Untaxed cash[a] receipts	(4) Taxable[b] income	(5) Taxes[c] paid	(6) After-tax[d] cash flow
1	$100,000	$60,000	$40,000	$20,000	$80,000
2	100,000	60,000	40,000	20,000	80,000
3	100,000	60,000	40,000	20,000	80,000
4	100,000	60,000	40,000	20,000	80,000
5	100,000	60,000	40,000	20,000	80,000

[a] Depreciation deduction, which is cash on hand but with no immediate claim against it.
[b] Column (2) minus column (3).
[c] Column (4) multiplied by the assumed tax rate of 50 percent.
[d] Column (1) minus column (5).
Source: John A. Tatom and James E. Turley, "Inflation and Taxes: Disincentives for Capital Formation," *Review,* Federal Reserve Bank of St. Louis, January 1978, p. 3.

Table 7.3 is similar to Table 7.2 in all respects except that the rate of inflation is assumed to be 10 percent. This difference affects the calculations of the return on investment by increasing the pre-tax cash receipts in column 2 and decreasing the real after-tax cash flow in column 6. Of crucial importance is the fact that the $60,000 per year allowable deduction for depreciation remains unchanged as prices increase. As a result, taxable income and tax liabilities increase more rapidly than inflation, even though pre-tax cash receipts rise at the rate of inflation. Consequently, the real purchasing power of the after-tax cash flow declines, and this deduction is reflected in a fall in the rate of return to 6.9 percent from 10.4 percent in the zero inflation example.

In comparing the two cases, it is clear that government policy that disallows inflationary adjustments in depreciation causes the present value of future, real depreciation deductions to decline and a firm's net cost of investment in plant and equipment to rise. The Treasury's requirement of using historic costs to calculate depreciation not only reduces the corporation's rate of return but also increases uncertainty because the future pattern of inflation cannot be predicted. Consequently, future depreciation allowances, taxable income, tax liability, and after-tax cash flow all become uncertain. Other things equal, the government's explicit pro-inflation policy will have adverse effects on investment behavior, the capital–labor ratio, real wages, the growth in GNP, and real per capita income.

Inventory profits

Under the U.S. tax code, a firm's inventory profits are subject to income taxation. Profits from the sale of inventory or stocks on hand can occur for

Table 7.3. *Depreciation, taxable income, and cash flow with 10 percent inflation*

(1) End of year	(2) Net cash[a] receipts	(3) Untaxed cash[b] receipts	(4) Taxable[c] income	(5) Taxes[d] paid	(6) After-tax real[e] cash flow
1	$110,000	$60,000	$ 50,000	$25,000	$77,273
2	121,000	60,000	61,000	30,500	74,793
3	133,100	60,000	73,100	36,550	72,539
4	146,410	60,000	86,410	43,205	70,490
5	161,051	60,000	101,054	50,526	68,628

[a]This column is equal to the noninflated cash receipts in Table 7.2 adjusted for the 10-percent rate of inflation, compounded annually.
[b]Depreciation deduction, which is cash on hand but with no immediate claim against it.
[c]Column (2) minus column (3).
[d]Column (4) multiplied by the assumed tax rate of 50 percent.
[e]Column (2) minus column (5), but adjusted for the 10-percent rate of inflation, compounded annually.
Source: John A. Tatom and James E. Turley, "Inflation and Taxes: Disincentives for Capital Formation," *Review,* Federal Reserve Bank of St. Louis, January 1978, p. 5.

two reasons. If there is a relative change in prices favoring a specific enterprise, the real value of its stock of goods has increased. If, on the other hand, there is a rise in the general level of prices, then the increase in the value of the inventory is nominal and not real; but the inflated value is subject to taxation.

Companies that practice *last-in-first-out* or LIFO method of accounting typically manifest small inventory profits. In the more traditional *first-in-first-out* or FIFO method, the oldest item of stock is assumed to be the first sold. Since the elapsed time in inventory for a given item is shorter under LIFO, FIFO accounting yields higher nominal profits during inflation; the more rapid the inflation, the higher the paper profits.

Given this strong incentive to adopt the LIFO method of accounting, it is a rather remarkable fact that a large proportion of inventories in the United States are still calculated on a FIFO basis, even after a decade and a half of notable inflation. In an environment of generally rising prices, switching from FIFO to LIFO will cause reported pre-tax profits to decline; post-tax profits, adjusted for inflation, will rise. Regardless of the accounting practice used, the tax on inflated or what has been called spurious inventory profits (Tideman and Tucker 1976:43) is a tax on capital, and it has a depressing effect on the investment in stocks of goods.

Economic effects of inflation

Tables 7.2 and 7.3 and the accompanying text demonstrate how the process of inflation together with current tax law reduces the net real rate of return on plant and equipment. These factors work to depress business demand for new investment. That is, for any given real market rate of return, firms will desire less investment funding than previously.

The market for investment funds

At the same time, the rise in the general level of prices together with inflation-induced taxation exert an adverse effect on acquiring funds for capital formation. Tatom and Turley (1978:5–8) and Feldstein, Green, and Sheshinski (1978:S53–S70) in two separate studies show that taxation of income derived from capital is based on nominal rather than real returns (Nowotny 1980:1031–2). Inflation increases personal taxes by increasing the taxable base and is compounded by the progressive nature of the individual income tax structure. Inflation causes tax bracket creep whereby individuals are pushed into higher rates of taxation even though their real income remains constant.

These characteristics of the system reduce the real income of those who derive revenue from sources of capital. Consequently, individuals who supply equity and bond financing must be compensated for any anticipated loss in real income, and then aforementioned authors have demonstrated that this will require a higher real rate of return than the preinflationary period. The effect of rising prices together with the taxes on investment income is to decrease the supply of funds for investment (Tatom and Turley 1978:5–8). The new market equilibrium, real rate of return will be determined by the shapes and magnitudes of the changes in the demand and supply of funds for investment; but because both demand and supply decrease, the amount of funds for capital formation is unambiguously reduced. Partial equilibrium analysis leads to the usual sequence of events that entails declining investment with a concomitant fall in the capital-to-labor ratio and real wages.

A general equilibrium approach would require investigation of the disposition of the tax funds collected from capital income. Public spending on government capital projects would partially counteract the decline in real wages and economic development. If the tax monies are used mainly to redistribute income, there would be very little mitigation of the depressing effects on capital formation and the growth in real incomes.

The impact of inflation and taxes on shares

Marcelle Arak (1980–81:5) has analyzed the effect of a change in the expected rate of inflation on equity share values. He notes how inflation reduces the after-tax real income of shareholders because taxes are levied on nominal capital gains, nominal inventory profits, and nominal corporate income (because of the reduction in the real value of depreciation allowances). Counterbalancing these factors is the positive rise in prices that reduces the real value of the debts of the enterprise.

Arak's (1980–81:7) calculations, which are based on an assumed four percentage point rise in the expected inflation rate, reveal the following: the tax on inventory profits causes a 5.4 percent reduction in the value of shares; the capital gains tax is responsible for an additional decline of 5.3 percent in equity value; and the largest fall of 10.9 percent is due to the tax on understated depreciation allowances. The effect of inflation and of the tax code on debt is responsible for a 4.8 percent increase in the equity value of corporations. The new impact of all four of these factors reveals a 16.8 percent reduction in the value of shares.

Arak's (1980–81:7) estimate of the expected rate of inflation in the United States during the decade of the seventies was 6 percent. He calculates that this figure coupled with the tax structure caused a 25-percent fall in real share prices.

Nonneutrality of inflation and the debt–equity ratio

A general rise in prices always diminishes the real value of debt because it can be repaid in money that has depreciated in value. This encourages firms to satisfy a larger portion of their capital requirements by borrowing. Moreover, although nominal interest rates rise during inflation, tax law treats interest as a deductible expense before calculating taxable income, whereas dividends are fully taxable. It is likely that after-tax interest costs of firms will decline, creating an incentive for them to issue fewer shares and raise more capital through debt finance (Tideman and Tucker 1976:37–8). Alan Auerbach (1981:421) has demonstrated in a formal way that the likely effect of inflation is to make equity a more expensive source of funds and debt cheaper.

The noneutrality of inflation and taxes will probably affect portfolio composition as well as debt to equity ratios. The corporation's tilt toward borrowing is inefficient because risk is allocated between bondholders and shareholders differently than would be the case without the current structure of taxes. In addition, as noted, tax policy that exempts interest and taxes profits not only encourages greater gearing of leverage but also increases the risk of corporate bankruptcy (Tideman and Tucker 1976:38).

Inflation-induced tax distortion and the required rate of return

Because investments differ in durability and, therefore, in patterns of depreciation, inflation distorts corporation income. Inflation, together with taxation, distort and increase the required rates of return on capital. T. Nicolaus Tideman and Donald P. Tucker (1976:40) have made a detailed study in which they posit different rates of inflation. They then examine the impact of inflation taxation on different types of investment, ranging from equipment and inventory to longer-lived structures.

They discovered that even if there were no general increases in the price level, the U.S. tax structure differentially affects the real returns to capital. Inflation exacerbates this unneutrality of tax system, although, surprisingly, a few inequalities in the rates of return among different types of investment are increased (Tideman and Tucker 1976:40). These differentials imply substantial distortion in the allocation of capital among alternative firms, industries, and sectors in the economy (Feldstein and Summers 1979:460–8).

Other allocational effects of inflation taxation

Rising prices and the antiquated U.S. tax structure cause a misallocation of labor and capital in the economy. This induced inefficiency occurs because the cost of labor is expressed in current prices and deducted from current receipts when calculating taxable income; however, the cost of plant, equipment, and, in many cases, inventories are deductible only if original rather than replacement costs are used. As noted, the use of relatively low original or historic costs, which existed before a rise in prices, does not permit full allowance for the replacement of plant and equipment, understates true costs, and overstates income so that the corporate tax becomes a levy against capital. This bias against investment influences firms to use relatively more labor and less capital.

Previous references have mentioned the importance of the capital-to-labor ratio to growth in GNP and real per capita income. In the decade of the 1970s, a unique combination of circumstances led to a reduction in the ratio. Emerging social changes encouraged the entrance of unprecedented large numbers of women into the labor market. The female labor force participation rate increased from 43.3 in 1970 to 51.6 in 1980. In addition, individuals born during the baby boom following World War II entered the labor market. The labor force grew from approximately 83 million to 105 million workers during the decade of the seventies.

At the same time, government inflation and tax policy encouraged the substitution of labor for capital. The result of these forces was to drive down the capital-to-labor ratio, causing laborers to be less productive because they had less capital with which to work. Statistics show a marked reduction in productivity during the decade.

Another interesting circumstance engendered by inflation taxation is the creation of incentives for two or more enterprises to merge their operations. Tax benefits are available when the general level of prices rise and a firm's accounting practices cause its dollar but not replacement value of inventories to increase appreciably. If the business plans to liquidate a substantial portion of its stocks, the large paper profit arising from selling at the difference between current and preinflation prices will subject the firm to correspondingly large corporate taxes (Tideman and Tucker 1976:40).

A second firm may be induced to purchase the enterprise contemplating liquidation of inventory. The acquiring firm is permitted to value the inventory at current prices and incur a much lower tax liability than the liquidating enterprise. Moreover, the selling firm owes no tax on the accounting profits generated by the sale of its stocks. In addition, any gains by shareholders of the liquidating firm will be taxed at the long-term capital gains rate of taxation (Tideman and Tucker 1976:40).

A more subtle force pushing companies toward more mergers and higher industry concentration ratios becomes more apparent when the combined effect of high marginal rates of taxation and inflation are analyzed. Between 1973 and 1978, it was estimated that this combined figure for the highest federal tax bracket was 132 percent. These kinds of rates caused the withdrawal of some six million investors from the equity market, and, as a result, the share value of many corporations was actually less than book value (Gilder 1981:176).

This divergence in value encouraged many managers and boards of directors to follow a policy of buying the equipment and structures of firms whose equity value may have been temporarily below the real replacement value of its capital assets. The risk, time, and cost of constructing new capital could be circumvented by purchasing the assets of the millions of owners who then turned to tax shelters and to collecting paintings, gold, diamonds, and Swiss francs (Gilder 1981:176). For a more detailed discussion of this kind of behavior see Chapter 5.

One further distorting effect of inflation taxation should be mentioned. It arises in business enterprises that use LIFO rather than FIFO accounting procedures. Unlike the case with FIFO, inventories manifest practically no inflationary gains when an enterprise uses the last-in-first-out method of financial record keeping. The firm is taxed, however, on the difference between the replacement costs of its depreciable assets and the Internal Revenue Service allowance for the wearing out of plant and equipment, the latter valued at original or preinflation costs. The effect of inflation in combination with tax law is to influence the firm to carry larger stocks and use less other capital than would be the case in an economy with stable prices (Tideman and Tucker 1976:35).

Inflation and effective tax rates on capital income

It is possible to measure empirically the impact of the mismeasurement of income, due to inflation and the use of historical cost accounting, on the

Table 7.4. *Inflation and effective rates of corporate income taxes*

Year	Increase in consumer price index	Effective rate of tax	Statutory rate of tax
1968	4.7%	54%	48%
1969	6.1	60	48
1970	5.5	65	48
1971	3.4	62	48
1972	3.4	58	48
1973	8.8	64	48
1974	12.2	96	48
1975	7.0	73	48
1976	4.8	67	48
1977	6.8	66	48

Source: "Truth in Taxation," *The Wall Street Journal,* August 23, 1979, p. 22. Reprinted by permission of *The Wall Street Journal,* © Dow Jones & Company, Inc. 1979. All Rights Reserved.

effective rates of taxation. Using official data from the Bureau of Economic Analysis of the United States Department of Commerce, *The Wall Street Journal* conducted a study in 1979 that demonstrated how inflation substantially increased reported current profits and effective or real rates of taxation. The latter are calculated by dividing inflation-adjusted profits by corporation tax liabilities.

Federal, state, and local corporate profit tax liability equaled $52.4 billion in 1974, and the Commerce Department's inflation-adjusted corporate profit figure for the same year was $54.8 billion. The division of these two numbers yields an effective tax rate of 96 percent ("Effective Tax Rates" 1979:18). Data in Table 7.4 reveal that effective corporate tax rates ranged from a low of 54 percent in 1968 to 96 percent in 1974, when inflation reached its highest peak during the period analyzed ("Truth in Taxation" 1979:22). there is a positive though less than perfect correlation between the price index and real tax rates.

Tideman and Tucker (1976:48–54) have analyzed Department of Treasury data from a representative sample of corporate balance sheet and income statements in an effort to estimate the extent to which corporate tax liabilities are inflated by rising prices and current accounting practices. They show that tax liabilities would be substantially lower if adjustments were made to allow for inflation. When a steady 10-percent rate of inflation is assumed, tax over-payments as a percent of actual 1972 tax liabilities ranged from 7 percent in mining to 233 percent in railroads. The only category in the twenty groups studied with an underpayment was the service industry. The average overpayment for all nonfinancial industries was 25 percent.

In a study made in 1980, Price Waterhouse and Company (1980:1–25) analyzed the effect of adjusting inventories and depreciation on sales, dividends, net return on assets, earnings, and share prices for 157 large industrial companies and 58 firms in finance, retailing, transportation, and utilities (all selected from the 1979 *Fortune Directory*). Firms with losses were excluded. The report used the new inflation accounting procedures promulgated by the Financial Accounting Standards Board.

Under these recently approved rules, companies calculate the effect of rising prices by using two different procedures. The constant dollars method uses the consumer price index to allow for the nominal changes in inventory and depreciation costs. The current cost accounting procedure eschews use of the rather general adjustment afforded by the consumer price index and adjusts for the changing prices of the specific assets a company owns.

The broad conclusions of the report were revealing and startling. Inflation-adjusted profits for the majority of industries studied ranged from 40 to 70 percent lower than reported profits, the latter based on traditional, original, or historical cost accounting practices. Constant dollar income for the transportation group equaled 56 percent of reported profits; for utilities, it was only 31 percent. Calculations of real tax rates revealed burdens that were from 15 to 25 percentage points higher than statutory rates. Several industries were paying out twice the amount in dividends than nominal and reported figures showed. The dividend payout for retailers was 300 percent of profits that had been adjusted for rising prices. It was more than 500 percent for utilities. In effect, these two industries are paying dividends out of capital, and the substantial reduction in their share prices reflect this behavior.

As might be expected from these kinds of figures, real rates of return are generally from 30 to 50 percent below the distorted values that historical cost accounting yields. An exception to this pattern are financial companies that have no inventories and little fixed capital to depreciate. For this group, the historic and constant dollar accounting procedures produce virtually the same rates of return at 14 and 13 percent. No figure was reported for the current cost method of adjustment. More typical are the rates of return in the transportation sector, which are 16, 5, and 2 percent respectively. Table 7.5 presents a summary of the Price Waterhouse findings.

Feldstein and Summers (1979:445–70) have made the most detailed examination of the effect of inflation-induced taxation on the corporate sector. Their study is notable for two major contributions. The first is the comprehensive treatment of all capital income generated by the corporate sector. In addition to corporate profit tax burdens, Feldstein and Summers study the effect of taxes on the income earned by the suppliers of capital to corporations.

Table 7.5. *The effects of inflation on the corporate sector, 1979*

Industry	Income[a]			Effective tax rate[b]		
	Historical basis	Constant dollar	Current cost	Historical basis	Constant dollar	Current cost
Industrial	100%	60%	63%	⁻39%	53%	53%
Financial	100	95	NR[c]	28	28	NR
Retailing	100	42	NR	42	68	NR
Transport	100	56	30	30	44	50
Utilities	100	31	17	34	62	78
	Return on net assets[d]			Dividend payout ratio[e]		
Industrial	17%	8%	8%	33%	65%	66%
Financial	14	13	NR	32	35	NR
Retailing	16	5	NR	31	299	NR
Transport	16	5	2	29	42	72
Utilities	10	4	2	76	543	521

[a]Ratio of income from continuing operations as reported on a constant dollar and current cost basis to that reported in the historical financial statements.
[b]Taxes as a proportion of historical, constant dollar and current cost basis of income.
[c]Percentage return on net assets on historical, constant dollar, and current cost basis.
[d]Percentage return on net assets on historical, constant dollar, and current cost bases.
[e]Percentage of income paid as cash dividends on historical, constant dollar, and current cost bases.
Source: Disclosure of the Effects of Inflation: An Analysis, Price Waterhouse and Company, New York, May 1980, pp. 2–3.

Their second contribution is the explicit treatment of corporate debt. They note that it has been implied in the literature that the saving in corporate taxes that arises from the exclusion of real gains on debt issued by companies during inflation is sufficient to offset the extra taxes that are occasioned by the mismeasurement of income, depreciation, and inventory profits. To obtain an empirical and reliable answer on the issue, Feldstein and Summers (1979:445–8) traced the income created by companies through to the ultimate recipients. They found that the inflated excess tax paid on interest received by individual and institutional lenders from debtor corporations was slightly greater than the tax saving of the corporate borrowers. As a result, they concluded that the real gains and losses on interest could be safely ignored when evaluating the effect of inflation-induced taxation of capital income generated by the corporate sector.

Calculations by Feldstein and Summers (1979:445, 458) showed that the combination of rising prices and unindexed tax laws caused the tax burden for the corporate sector to be increased by more than $32 billion in 1977, the last year in their study. This extra inflation tax represented 54.3 percent of the

Table 7.6. *Effective tax rates and extra taxes on corporate source income due to inflation, 1954–1977*

Year	Inflation rate	Extra tax (billions)	Extra tax as a percent of corp. income tax	Effective rate of taxation
1954	−0.5%	$ 1.9	12.2%	63.5%
1955	0.4	2.9	14.4	61.9
1956	2.9	4.7	23.4	68.4
1957	3.0	4.6	24.1	68.5
1958	1.8	3.5	21.6	67.0
1959	1.5	3.5	16.9	62.8
1960	1.5	3.4	17.7	62.8
1961	0.7	2.5	12.8	62.2
1962	1.2	2.4	11.6	57.1
1963	1.6	2.8	12.3	57.1
1964	1.2	2.6	10.8	53.3
1965	1.9	3.4	12.5	52.5
1966	3.4	4.6	15.6	53.9
1967	3.0	4.9	17.7	54.2
1968	4.7	7.5	22.3	60.8
1969	6.1	11.4	34.2	66.0
1970	5.5	10.9	39.3	67.8
1971	3.4	9.8	32.8	62.3
1972	3.4	9.9	29.5	58.0
1973	8.8	22.7	57.3	70.0
1974	12.2	40.6	95.1	94.9
1975	7.0	27.2	66.6	69.3
1976	4.8	27.2	56.5	64.9
1977	6.8	32.3	54.3	66.3

Source: Martin Feldstein and Lawrence Summers, "Inflation and the Taxation of Capital Income in the Corporate Sector," *National Tax Journal,* December 1979, pp. 458–61.

year's corporate income tax liabilities. Total additional taxes on corporate capital during the decade 1968–77 amounted to almost $200 billion. In 1974, which was the year of the highest rate of inflation, extra taxes on corporate-produced income were 95 percent of the corporate income tax. Other comparisons can be made by inspecting Table 7.6.

Feldstein and Summers (1979:461) have also calculated the effective tax rate on capital income that has its source in the nonfinancial corporate sector. This figure averaged 63.6 percent during the 1954–77 period analyzed but rose markedly during the high inflation experienced in the mid-1970s. The real rate of taxation, displayed in column 4 of Table 7.5, reached its peak of over 94 percent in 1974. In 1981, the government took in taxes 75 percent of all income generated by corporations. The residual of 25 percent left to investors has in recent years yielded an after-tax rate of return of 2.6 percent (Feldstein 1981:24). Current real rates of taxation are higher than they were in the 1950s, and this trend indicates that inflationary pressures have been sufficiently powerful to more than compensate for the introduction of investment tax credits, liberalization of rules on depreciation, and outright reductions in statutory rate of taxation (Feldstein and Summers 1979:460).

William E. Cullison (1980:15) has added a further dimension to the Feldstein and Summers study by including and analyzing data on the foreign operations of U.S. firms for the years 1965–75. Incorporating into the analysis both foreign source income and tax credits claimed for foreign taxes paid reduces the effective tax rate in the relatively high inflation years. The rate drops from 94.9 to 82.4 percent in 1974, from 69.3 to 63.3 in 1975, and from 70.0 to 68.8 percent in 1973. In all other years, the real rate of taxation increased by one to two percentage points.

Foreign experience

The effect of inflation on recipients of corporate source income is not unique to the United States. The Mathews Committee (1975:347–56) reports a wealth of data that shows how the effect of rising prices and tax policy regarding depreciation and inventory allowances have eroded the financial position of Australian firms. The committee also cites evidence that shows the profits of industrial and commercial companies in the United Kingdom more than doubled between 1963 and 1973, but after-tax profits were only about one-third of their 1963 level.

In an independently conducted study covering the years 1954–76, Professor G. H. Lawson (n.d.:1–13; 1978:61) of the University of Manchester Business School came to conclusions about the effect of inflation tax rules and accounting practices on the United Kingdom business sector that were amazingly similar to those of Feldstein and Summers. He found that the overstatement of profit averaged 81 percent over the years, reaching 134 percent in 1974.

The rate of return on equity averaged 2.5 percent per annum during the twenty-three-year period, but from 1965 to 1976 it averaged a negative 2.7 percent. Despite these low and negative figures, United Kingdom manufacturing companies consistently paid out dividends in excess of their earnings, and the resulting deficits were financed with bank loans. In effect, companies substituted debt for equity with a consequent increase in financial instability and risk of bankruptcy. Moreover, gear or leverage ratios were about five times higher than the period 1954–64, and the index of real share values, which stood at 363 in 1965, had dropped to 184 in January 1978.

At the company level, 64 percent of the profits were taken in taxes by the government. A total of 24 percent of earnings was paid out in interest and subject to individual and institutional taxation. The remaining residual of 12 percent was available for payment to shareholders; and to the extent that these funds were distributed, they were taxable at individual and company rates.

The effective tax rate on United Kingdom companies averaged 71 percent between 1954 and 1975 and actually exceeded 100 percent in three years. The effective tax rate on equity earnings during the same period averaged 83 percent and exceeded 100 percent in six years. The real tax rate on income created by companies is not known because the tax on recipients of the interest paid out by firms for the use of borrowed funds has not been calculated. That sum would have to be added to the tax on company income and the tax on dividends to derive the total effective tax rate on capital income generated by companies.

Robert Coen (1978:1–33) derived results from his study for the Treasury Department that are somewhat at odds with the work of Feldstein and Summers, Cullison, and Lawson. His estimates of annual depreciation flows reflect the economic life of capital. Therefore, both the actual service life of an asset and the loss of efficiency as it ages are incorporated into his figures.

Coen (1978:21) notes that the business community often complains that the tax allowances the Internal Revenue Service permits to be calculated on a historical cost basis do not permit full replacement of assets during inflationary periods. He points out, however that if firms are allowed to write off capital more rapidly than it is actually wearing out, some of the criticism of business is blunted.

The research of Coen (1978:26) shows the actual tax depreciation allowances for manufacturing companies in the United States were not large enough to replace capital in the early post–World War II era, but due to liberalization of the tax code, depreciation allowed by the Treasury was more than adequate from about 1960 to 1971. Moreover, if the law had required companies to use the actual service life of assets and to depreciate them at historical costs in order to calculate tax liabilities, tax allowances would not have been sufficient to cover capital replacement requirements.

On the other hand, if firms had been permitted to adjust capital costs for inflation, Coen (1978:26) concludes that tax allowances would have been extremely generous. This conclusion and others must remain tentative, for, as Coen notes, they rest "on a very special set of assumptions" that he considers with the year 1971, which is just before the onset of the substantial inflationary pressures that have plagued business performance for more than a decade.

Alleviation of inflation-induced taxation

The Mathews Committee (1975:357) notes that the issue of inflation, taxation, and financial instability of the business sector is worldwide. Even though the problem is pervasive, it has imperfect but reasonable and practical solutions.

Depreciation allowances

Although there are many variations on the central theme, there are two basic approaches to the depreciation question. The first method would entail either a very rapid or immediate deduction of investment expenditures from current income. The second alternative would adjust the cost basis of depreciating capital. Costs would be reconciled with inflation by using some type of price index.

Both methods would largely compensate for the lower present value of depreciation deduction due to inflation. Though there are proponents of immediate deduction, Martin Feldstein (1979b:58; 1979c:1–25) offers two cogent reasons for choosing the second alternative. He believes that very rapid depreciation would be viewed as a tax subsidy, and official figures would show a relatively low effective rate of taxation. As a result, political pressure would inhibit any further reduction in the real effective rate. Feldstein also argues that very rapid depreciation would distort incentives and cause a mis-allocation of capital among different types of firms and industries.

Three practical methods can be used to measure price changes:

1. the use of a broad measure of the rise in the general level of prices, such as the consumer price index;
2. the application of an index of only capital goods; and
3. the use of particular pertinent indices to be applied to different types of assets, such as, buildings, tools, equipment, trucks, and cars.

All prices do not rise at the same time so the alternative methods would generate different effects on profits and tax liabilities. The Financial Accounting Standards Board decreed that all large firms use the first or third method in reporting the results of operations in 1979, and both methods for 1980 and subsequent years. An examination of Table 7.5 shows substantial differences for some industries as the result of using alternative methods. Nevertheless, the probability is very high that any one of the three ways of adjusting for inflation would more accurately depict the true financial status of a firm when compared with the use of the historical cost method.

Inventory/stock allowances

Tideman and Tucker (1976:42–3) note that in order to approach the elimi-nation of tax-related distortion in incentives as well as the distribution of income, spurious inventory profits must also be eliminated. Taxing normal gains on inventories amounts to taxation of capital. It is a capital problem for all nonfinancial corporations but especially for those holding large inventories, such as retailing, petroleum, forestry, and metals industries.

Inflated inventory profits did not become a serious problem until the rate of inflation exceeded 3 percent in the late 1960s. In their work at the National Bureau of Economic Research, Feldstein and Summers (1979:460–8) found that the overstatement of profits averaged less than $1 billion a year between 1954 and 1967, but in 1968 the figure jumped to $3.4 billion. From then until 1977, overstated inventory profits on which federal, state, and local taxes were paid amounted to $125 billion.

There are several ways of adjusting the value of inventories to mitigate the impact of inflation, but because of the great diversity among businesses, there is no perfect way to handle the problem. The simplest and least costly method was advocated by the Mathews Committee (1975:569–70). It recommended adjusting the nominal value of stocks by revaluing the opening inventory, using the prices of closing stocks. This proposal would be easier to apply in practice than LIFO procedures because it involves "fewer calculations and the maintenance of less complicated records . . . ," especially important considerations for both large and small businesses.

Concluding remarks on inflation and taxation

The United States has been devoting about 6 percent of GNP for net investment, less than half the average figure for major industrial countries. Moreover, much of U.S. net private investment is channeled into housing and inventories, leaving less than 3 percent of GNP for increasing plant and equipment. Between the second half of the 1960s and 1970s, spending on new plant and equipment dropped by 40 percent (Feldstein 1981:24).

Corporate profits as a proportion of national income have decreased steadily from 14 percent in 1965 to 8.5 percent in 1980. This reduction of profits as a share of income is the principal reason total corporate taxes have declined during recent years. These figures do not mean that the tax has become capricious or less onerous. In fact, despite rate reductions, the introduction of tax credits, and the liberalization of depreciation allowances, inflation has boosted the effective rate of tax to record levels.

A rising price level inflates dividends and drives individuals into higher tax brackets even though real income remains constant or falls. Inflation also overstates the income of capital because it reduces the present value of allowances for depreciation and increases the cost of replacing inventories, both of which are based on past noninflated costs rather than on current costs. Due to the mismeasurement of depreciation deductions alone, the 1979 profits of nonfinancial corporations were overstated by more than $50 billion, and tax liabilities were $20 billion, or 40 percent higher than they would have been had depreciation allowances been indexed. Inflation-induced taxation caused the effective rate of taxation to average about 69 percent between 1970 and 1977; the rate was about 75 percent in 1981 (Feldstein 1981:24).

Under current depreciation rules, there is a marked variation in tax burdens among industries. The Price Waterhouse study (1980:3–25) reports effective tax rates ranging from 28 percent in the financial sector to 78 percent in utilities. Work at the National Bureau of Economic Research shows that additional taxation due to inflation is responsible for less than 25 percent of total taxes paid in some industries and 100 percent of tax liabilities in others (Feldstein and Summers 1979:468).

Feldstein (1979a:22–3) has demonstrated that with moderate inflation rates and discount rates, an acceleration depreciation schedule that provides a five-year life for equipment and a ten-year life for structures can largely correct for rising prices and capricious tax effects. If inflation is outside the range of 4 to 12 percent, and the real discount rate outside 4 to 7 percent, then indexation is a clearly superior means of correcting the measurement of depreciation allowances. He notes, however, that the search for a neutral depreciation rule is futile because different industries and firms have varied leverage or gearing rations of debt and equity as well as diverse kinds of plant and equipment (Feldstein 1981:24).

Adjusting for inflation in the business sector implies a noticeable reduction in revenue to government as well as a redistribution of the tax load. It is also vitally important because it will encourage capital formation, economic growth, rising real wages, and a modicum of downward pressure on the price level.

Summary and conclusion

The corporation income tax has few advocates. Other than its revenue productivity and the fact that it exists it has little to recommend it and much to indict it.

The issue of shifting and incidence is not yet settled. New theoretical research and improved empirical techniques promise to advance our understanding of how the corporate levy works. Answers to questions about shifting and incidence are mandatory if we are to know the effect of the tax on the distribution of income. Currently, it is not known which income class in the population bears what particular amount of the tax. En ante, it might best be described as a random tax and, therefore, as capricious and inefficient.

If all or most of the tax is borne by shareholders, double taxation of income is created by corporations. To mitigate the possible effects of double taxation, various methods of integrating the personal and corporation income taxes have been proposed. All of them are complicated and fraught with administrative and other practical difficulties. There is little chance of implementing even practical integration proposals in the near future. Should policy makers wish to ameliorate some of the negative effects of the present tax on income produced by corporations, they could create various tax preferences. For example, all or some portion of dividend income, on which a tax of 46 percent has already been paid, could be exempted from personal income taxation.

Special investment tax incentives are effective in spurring specific types of capital expenditures. Ceteris paribus, they raise the net rate of return on capital and lower the effective rate of taxation. In a period of little or no inflation, tax incentives are not neutral among alternative investments and, therefore, cause distortions in the allocation of scarce capital funds. For policy makers wishing to achieve certain goals, nonneutrality may be an attribute of tax incentives schemes.

The most important problem associated with the corporation income tax in the United States and in many industrially advanced countries is its strong negative effect on capital formation and economic growth when there is a substantial amount of inflation. A rising price level erodes the purchasing power of the dollar. Current financial reports, which combine figures on capital expenditures, depreciation, and inventories in the dollars of 1965, 1974, and 1981, for example, are commingling different currencies to measure costs and income. It is clear that in using 1981 dollars, which are worth little more than thirty cents of the 1965 currency, firms cannot recover their replacement costs.

The consequences for many firms of inflation-induced taxation have been increased debt financing, a growing risk of financial failure, falling equity earnings, and an inherent inability to generate sufficient profits to retain capital. Such industries as retailing and utilities, which have been subject to effective tax rates of approximately 70 percent and have been paying out 300 to 500 percent of their income in dividends, are approaching crises.

The Mathews Committee (1975:339) notes that one criterion for judging a tax system is its compatibility "with the maintenance of financial stability in the business sector, with continuity of business investment and operations, in short with business survival." Strong evidence now indicates that the corporation income tax does not meet this criterion.

Changes in the tax treatment of corporations are mandatory for the long-run survival of private sector production. Perhaps eliminating the levy would be the wisest course. Irving Kristol, (1980:28), Norman Ture (Jackson and Jonas 1981:28), Martin Feldstein (1981:24), and Lester Thurow (1981:97–101), voices from the political right, center, and left, have all recommended its demise.

CHAPTER 8

Social security payroll taxes

The United States payroll tax began under authorization of the Social Security Act of 1935. This law established two important social programs: one for retirement benefits and the other for unemployment compensation. Each has exerted a powerful influence on the economy, but social security is the largest and most pervasive of the two programs.

Several programs now comprise what is popularly known as social security. The original statute was designed strictly to provide retirement benefits to workers covered by the law and was called old age insurance (OAI). By 1939, Congress had changed the law to provide survivor benefits, and the system became known as OASI. When disability benefits were added in 1954, the program was immediately renamed OASDI. The last major functional expansion came in 1965 with the adoption of medicare and, predictably, the social security program became known as old age survivors, disability, and health insurance or OASDHI (Social Security Administration 1982a:1–20). Today, it is the largest government program in the United States.

Early history

Weaver (1982:58–124) has written an excellent history of social security, in which she relates its controversial beginning. The program was started partly in response to the depressed economic conditions of the 1930s. Savings that had been set aside for retirement were lost in the economic turmoil of the times; unemployment was at an unprecedented high level; and middle-aged workers were hard pressed to provide for their immediate families, without the added burden of providing for their aged parents. In addition, several proposed alternative retirement schemes, such as the Townsend Plan, were receiving growing interest, sympathy, and public support from voters.

Acceptance of the idea of government insurance was far from unanimous. The demand for social security had not crystallized. Congressional opponents of the Roosevelt administration's bill made many efforts to introduce elements of competition into the process and provision of old-age security. At the same time, members of the President's Committee on Economic Security, bureaucrats, and other social insurance advocates, the potential public suppliers of the service, were very active and effective in selling the idea of compulsory public social insurance. In fact, when President Roosevelt made it clear to Congress that it had an all-or-nothing choice, his bill or none, it soon became law.

Despite this legislative success, the Social Security Board, which had responsibility for organizing and administering the program, soon faced funding, political, and constitutional problems. Perhaps the most serious threat centered on the constitutionality of the Social Security Act.

Because of precedents and previous interpretations by the Supreme Court, constitutional lawyers, bureaucrats, politicians, and other interested parties believed that the act might be declared unconstitutional if the court viewed social security as an insurance scheme. Consequently, the government's public relations experts instructed social security bureaucrats to play down the use of insurance terms when discussing the act. This constraint proved to be a distinct disadvantage because political acceptance rested to a considerable extent on the notion that social security was an insurance system.

Pessimism regarding the Supreme Court's position on the Social Security Act was well placed. Seven out of nine of President Roosevelt's New Deal acts that had been passed by Congress were ruled unconstitutional in 1935 and the early part of 1936. However, after his inauguration in 1937, President Roosevelt launched an unprecedented attack against the Supreme Court, which culminated in a plan to expand the Court's membership and pack it with individuals politically sympathetic to the goals of the Roosevelt administration. This attack and political pressure had the desired effects. On May 24, 1937, the Court validated all parts of the Social Security Act

The original intent of Congress was to finance the social security program on a fully funded basis. This method requires taxes to be saved and invested in a trust fund that would become large enough to guarantee all benefit obligations. Such a fully funded scheme would be similar to private insurance plans (Ferrara 1982:5–6).

Full funding of social security was altered by major changes in the law in 1939. The effect of these changes was to combine and incorporate two conflicting goals into the program. The idea of individual equity, whereby workers would receive a fair rate of return on their contributions, was abandoned and replaced by a strong welfare element, as exemplified by the large redistribution of funds within the system. Individual equity was replaced by what has become known as social adequacy and a pay-as-you-go system of financing (Munnell 1977:5–7).

Despite the abandonment of the insurance principle in 1939, government officials and publications continued to sell the program by using terms associated with the private insurance industry. As one critic notes, use of the word *contributions* instead of taxes implies a voluntary payment (Friedman 1977:26). In addition, the so-called trust funds of social security do not accumulate funds to pay benefits later. Unlike private trust funds, they are much too small to fulfill this function. Moreover, despite the opposite impression given by social security publications, workers do not finance their own benefits. Workers now in the labor force are not "building protection for themselves and their families under the social security program." Rather, they are paying taxes to finance benefits to individuals who no longer work. Finally, as indicated by the effect of the 1939 amendments, the relationship between taxes paid and benefits received is very tenuous.

Pervasiveness of social security

Currently, nine of ten workers in the United States pay social security taxes. Between 35 and 40 million individuals, or about one of every six persons in the country, receive monthly social security checks. In 1982, there were more than 24 million individuals sixty-five and over (nearly all of the country's older population) who also had health insurance under medicare. In addition, another 3 million disabled people under sixty-five also had medicare protection. Nearly every family in the United States had a stake in the social security program (Social Security Administration 1982b:5).

Mechanics of the tax

Information in Table 8.1 shows the taxable earnings base and actual tax rates since the inception of the program. The maximum tax increased from $30 on a covered earnings base of $3,000 in 1937 to $2,792 on a base of $39,600 in 1985. The tax rate on employees, which began at 1 percent, is scheduled to be 7.15 percent from 1986 to 1989 and 7.65 percent for 1990 and later. Self-employed individuals who paid 9.9 percent in 1985 are scheduled to pay 10 percent in 1986.

The wage and salary base subject to taxation is scheduled to increase automatically beyond $39,600 during the next several years to keep pace with increases in wage levels. Because of poor planning and the stagnating economy, these scheduled increases in rates and the tax base will have to be revised upward in order to provide sufficient funds to keep the program afloat.

As noted in Table 8.1, employers pay a tax per employee equal to that paid by the workers. This feature means that the total social security tax will be more than 14 percent between 1985 and 1989. Nearly all economists believe that the employer tax is actually borne by the workers, so that they actually pay a tax of more than 14 percent on their earnings. Further analysis of this question appears later in this chapter.

Cash benefits, taxes, and number of individuals receiving benefits

Table 8.2 indicates that cash payments under OASDHI rose from about $24 million in 1940 to $113.5 billion in fiscal 1980. Taxes for just the old-age and survivors part of the social security program increased from about $550 million to $95 billion during the same period, but cash benefits were nearly $98 billion in 1980. Cash benefits exceeded tax revenues for the ten years preceding 1984.

One reason for the discrepancy between receipts and cash benefits paid out is Congressional generosity. Table 8.3 shows the benefit increases in Social Security since 1939, automatic increases in benefits that are tied to the consumer price index.

Despite the many changes in the system during the years, OASDHI is still primarily a social program that provides benefits to retired workers and their families. To be eligible for cash benefits, individuals must meet certain requirements. Workers must have been employed in a job covered by the social security program, and they must have paid social security taxes for a sufficient number of years.

The amount of benefits received depends, among other things, on the amount of income earned and the amount of taxes paid into the system. Workers who have paid the maximum tax receive larger benefits than those who have paid a smaller amount of taxes. The benefit schedule, however, is sometimes described as progressive because lower income workers receive in benefits a higher proportion of the taxes they paid than do higher income earners. In fact, many employees who have had below average earnings can retire and have a higher standard of living than they did when they were still in the labor force.

The financing problem

For purposes of analysis, it is the current vogue to divide the financial problems of the social security system into at least two distinct periods – the near-term crisis and the long-run problem. The immediate challenge is that funds required to cover the expenditures of the old-age and survivors program are anticipated to fall short by $150 to $200 billion between now and 1990. In fact, the OASI program was forced to borrow $4 billion from the disability fund in the autumn of 1982 to cover retirement checks through the end of the year, and another $13 billion by the end of December to help pay benefits through June 1983 ("Social Security Forced . . ." 1982:8A).

Factors that have pushed the social security program toward bankruptcy include low national rates of saving, investment, and production, and high

Table 8.1. *Earnings base and actual tax rate*

Beginning	Annual earnings base	Tax rate (percent) Employer and employee, each					Tax rate (percent) Self-employed				
		Total	OASI	DI	HI	Maximum tax	Total	OASI	DI	HI	Maximum tax
1937	$ 3,000	1.0	1.0			$ 30.00					
1950	3,000	1.5	1.5			45.00					
1951	3,600	1.5	1.5			54.00		2.25			$ 81.00
1954	3,600	2.0	2.0			72.00	3.0	3.0			108.00
1955	4,200	2.0	2.0			84.00	3.0	3.0			126.00
1957	4,200	2.25	2.0	0.25		94.50	3.375	3.0	.375		141.75
1959	4,800	2.5	2.25	.25		120.00	3.75	3.375	.375		180.00
1960	4,800	3.0	2.75	.25		144.00	4.5	4.125	.375		216.00
1962	4,800	3.125	2.875	.25		150.00	4.7	4.325	.375		225.60
1963	4,800	3.625	3.375	.25		174.00	5.4	5.025	.375		259.20
1966	6,600	4.2	3.5	.35	0.35	277.20	6.15	5.275	.525	0.35	405.90
1967	6,600	4.4	3.55	.35	.5	290.40	6.4	5.375	.525	.5	422.40
1968	7,800	4.4	3.325	.475	.6	343.20	6.4	5.0875	.7125	.4	499.20
1969	7,800	4.8	3.725	.475	.6	374.40	6.9	5.5875	.7125	.6	538.20
1970	7,800	4.8	3.65	.55	.6	374.40	6.9	5.475	.825	.6	538.20
1971	7,800	5.2	4.05	.55	.6	405.60	7.5	6.075	.825	.6	585.00
1972	9,000	5.2	4.05	.55	.6	468.00	7.5	6.075	.825	.6	675.00

Year										
1973	10,800	5.85	4.3	.55	1.0	631.80	8.0	6.205	.795	1.0	864.00
1974	13,200	5.85	4.375	.575	.9	772.20	7.9	6.185	.815	.9	1,042.80
1975	14,100	5.85	4.375	.575	.9	824.85	7.9	6.185	.815	.9	1,113.90
1976	15,300	5.85	4.375	.575	.9	895.05	7.9	6.185	.815	.9	1,208.70
1977	16,500	5.85	4.375	.575	.9	965.25	7.9	6.185	.815	.9	1,303.50
1978	17,700	6.05	4.275	.775	1.0	1,070.85	8.1	6.010	1.090	1.0	1,433.70
1979	22,900	6.13	4.33	.750	1.05	1,403.77	8.1	6.010	1.040	1.05	1,854.90
1980	25,900	6.13	4.33	.750	1.05	1,587.67	8.1	6.010	1.040	1.05	2,097.90
1981	29,700	6.65	4.525	.825	1.30	1,722.35	9.3	6.7625	1.2375	1.30	2,762.10
1982	32,400	6.70	4.575	.825	1.30	2,170.80	9.35	6.8125	1.2375	1.30	3,029.40
1983	35,700	6.70				2,392.00	11.3				4,034.10
1984	37,500	7.00				2,625.00	14.0				5,250.00
1985	39,600	7.05				2,791.80	14.1				5,583.60
1986–7	42,000	7.15				3,003.00	14.3				6,006.00

Sources: *History of Social Security*, U.S. Department of Health and Human Services, SSA Publication No. 05–1011, USGPO, October 1981, pp. 3–4; and SSA Publication No. 05-10035, January 1985, pp. 29–30.

Table 8.2. *Selected data for OASDHI and OASI*
(in millions of dollars)

Fiscal year	OASDHI cash benefits	OASI taxes	OASI cash receipts	OASI number of recipients
1940	$ 24	$ 550	$ 16	222,488
1945	248	1,310	240	1,288,107
1950	928	2,106	727	3,477,243
1955	4,855	5,087	4,333	7,960,616
1960	11,080	9,843	10,270	14,157,138
1965	18,094	15,857	15,226	19,127,716
1970	31,570	29,955	26,267	23,563,634
1971	36,865	31,915	31,101	24,361,500
1972	41,275	35,711	34,541	25,204,542
1973	51,130	41,318	42,170	26,309,163
1974	58,194	48,455	47,849	26,941,483
1975	66,586	56,017	54,839	27,732,311
1976	75,332	59,555	62,140	28,399,725
1977	84,264	68,895	71,270	29,228,350
1978	92,531	74,047	78,524	29,718,195
1979	103,974	84,358	87,592	30,347,848
1980	120,272	97,688	100,615	30,936,668
1981	128,741	119,016	119,413	31,580,097
1982	155,699	124,246	134,655	31,866,946
1983	166,902	130,506	148,024	32,271,893

Source: Social Security Bulletin, December 1980, vol. 43, no. 12, pp. 36–45, and February 1985, vol. 48, no. 2, p. 33.

rates of unemployment. These economic variables have been responsible for a stagnating economy that finds it increasingly difficult to finance the relatively heavy expenditures of the social security system. Moreover, the system has been tied so intricately to changes in the economy that both benefits and taxes are overly sensitive and vulnerable to uncontrollable economic and demographic variables.

The long-run problems with the system center on its structure together with demographic factors. When the postwar baby boom generation reaches retirement age after the turn of the century, the ratio of the number of workers paying taxes to support retirees will be at an all-time low. It is estimated that between now and the year 2030, the ratio of the number of tax-paying workers to pensioners will drop from 3.2 to 2.0. Assuming constant benefits, payroll taxes on workers will have to double in order to maintain currently legislated benefits. Although the predicted ratio of two tax-paying workers to one retiree may seem low, current ratios in Germany and Italy are already 2.2 and 1.4, respectively (Chickering and Rosa 1982:3).

Table 8.3. *OASI benefit increase since 1939*

Year	Percentage increase
1950	77.0%
1952	12.5
1954	13.0
1959	7.0
1965	7.0
1968	13.0
1970	15.0
1971	10.0
1972	20.0
1974	11.0
1975	8.0
1976	6.4
1977	5.9
1978	6.5
1979	9.9
1980	14.3
1981	11.2

Source: Social Security Administration, *History of Social Security,* U.S. Department of Health and Human Services, SSA Publication No. 1011, U.S.G.P.O., October 1981, p. 2.

These various near- and long-term factors are discussed at greater length in the following sections.

Pay-as-you-go financing

As noted in the discussion of the history of social security, the government program does not function like private insurance. Private premiums are invested on behalf of the worker sufficient to finance a pension when the individual retires. Social security taxes, however, are not invested on behalf of the worker. There is no fund or saving that earns a return for the worker. In fact, the taxes paid by today's working individual are immediately given to those who are retired. Current taxes are used to pay current benefits, hence the phrase *pay-as-you-go.* Social security is a giant intergenerational transfer scheme that takes funds from relatively younger workers and gives them to older nonworkers.

The political decision to use a pay-as-you-go system is largely responsible for the precarious position of the social security program. It permitted politicians continually to add attractive features to the program over the years while largely postponing major costs until some unknown future time.

The strategy of selling social security by using insurance terms proved very successful. The program has grown enormously over the years, and many new features have been added to the original law.

The year 1939 saw the law expanded so that benefits would be paid to dependents of retirees and to survivors of deceased employees. Cash payments were authorized for husbands of insured workers in 1950, and six years later disability insurance was added for individuals who became unable to work due to sickness or injury. The retirement age was lowered for women in 1956 and for men in 1961. Beneficiaries could now retire at sixty-two but with slightly reduced net monthly benefits. In 1965, benefits were added for some divorced spouses as well as for full-time students aged eighteen to twenty-one. Congress added benefits for dependent grandchildren in 1972 (Social Security Administration 1982a:1–20). Politicians increased benefits by 40 percent between 1971 and 1973 ("Archer Traces . . ." 1981:3).

Congress also made revolutionary changes in 1972, when it authorized the linking of increases in benefits with increases in the consumer price index so they would automatically rise together. To help pay for increased benefits, Congress also tied the wage base that forms the basis of taxation to a wage index, which historically had been increasing and was expected to continue to rise.

Congressmen and bureaucrats hoped that as average wages rose, a larger proportion of the total payroll would generate increased social security taxes ("Your Stake . . ." 1981:506). Unfortunately for the financial viability of the program, the growth in real wages turned negative and remained so for the next decade (Capra, Skaperdas, and Kubarych 1982:4).

Social security and the redistribution of income

The idea that social security payments should be based on need rather than on the amount a worker contributes to the system has been fostered since 1939. Consequently, as noted, the program has been saddled with the two separate objectives of providing retirement income and redistributing income. The attempt to fulfill the redistributive function has been largely responsible for the program's financial woes. This is due in part to the fact that the rate of return on the taxes paid by retirees has had little relation to normal market rates of return. The first beneficiary of social security, for example, paid a total of $22 in taxes but received approximately $20,000 in benefits ("Your Stake . . ." 1981:504).

The benefit formula governing the amount retirees receive has been characterized as progressive because higher paid employees receive a smaller proportion of their preretirement income than do lower paid employees. In 1981, the formula was constructed to give retiring individuals who had earned the minimum wage each working year about 68 percent of their gross annual wages. An average wage earner received 54 percent, and individuals who earned the maximum taxable wage received about one-third of their preretirement income.

Many lower wage workers have a higher standard of living after retirement than when they were working because social security income until recently carried no tax liability or other payroll deductions (Feldstein 1977:92–3). In 1982, an average sixty-five-year-old retiree recovered his entire lifetime social security tax paid within nine months of retiring (Capra et al. 1982:1–2, 8). Yet, he or his wife will continue to draw benefits for an additional twenty-five years. It is apparent that the financial structure of the social security system is fundamentally flawed. As presently designed, average retirees both now and in the future can expect to receive benefits that, by any measure, far exceed the taxes paid during their working years.

Table 8.4 emphasizes these points and shows the lifetime social security profile of new retirees at age sixty-five in January 1982. If they had earned the maximum taxable income and had paid the maximum tax possible, the total taxes paid during their working lifetimes amount to $11,346. For retirees whose incomes equaled average wages covered by social security, total taxes paid equal only $7,209.

The long run under alternative assumptions

The Social Security Administration has made several long-run projections about the retirement and disability systems based on optimistic, intermediate, and pessimistic assumptions about the economy. Under the intermediate assumptions, which at this time appear to be somewhat optimistic, the tax rate required to avoid a long-term deficit (given the scheduled tax rates) does not take effect until 2015. However, as illustrated in Table 8.5, the pessimistic set of assumptions, which at present appear to be too pessimistic, indicate that the combined retirement and disability programs will be in deficit for the next seventy-five years. The true position may lie somewhere between these two extremes.

There is little question that indexing benefits to the consumer price index, declining labor productivity, and high rates of unemployment have had a deleterious effect on social security finances. As we have noted, however, the fundamental long-term problem with the system centers around the fact that the benefits of retirees are enormously large and out of proportion when compared to their lifetime contributions.

A retiring individual reaching sixty-five in 1982, for example, who earned average wages from 1937 through 1981, would have paid in during a working lifetime a total of $7,209 in social security taxes. These contributions entitle

Table 8.4. *Lifetime employee contributions to old age and survivors insurance by calendar year, new retiree aged 65 in January 1962*

Year	Tax rate employee only (percent)	Maximum taxable income (dollars)	Maximum tax possible (dollars)	Average wages in covered employment (dollars)	Tax for average wage earner (dollars)
1937	1.000	3,000.00	30.00	1,137.96	11.38
1938	1.000	3,000.00	30.00	1,053.24	10.53
1939	1.000	3,000.00	30.00	1,142.36	11.42
1940	1.000	3,000.00	30.00	1,195.00	11.95
1941	1.000	3,000.00	30.00	1,276.04	12.76
1942	1.000	3,000.00	30.00	1,454.28	14.54
1943	1.000	3,000.00	30.00	1,713.52	17.14
1944	1.000	3,000.00	30.00	1,936.32	19.36
1945	1.000	3,000.00	30.00	2,021.40	20.21
1946	1.000	3,000.00	30.00	1,891.76	18.92
1947	1.000	3,000.00	30.00	2,175.32	21.75
1948	1.000	3,000.00	30.00	2,361.64	23.62
1949	1.000	3,000.00	30.00	2,483.20	24.83
1950	1.500	3,000.00	45.00	2,543.96	38.16
1951	1.500	3,600.00	54.00	2,799.16	41.99
1952	1.500	3,600.00	54.00	2,973.32	44.60
1953	1.500	3,600.00	54.00	3,139.44	47.09
1954	2.000	3,600.00	72.00	3,156.64	63.11
1955	2.000	4,200.00	84.00	3,301.44	66.03
1956	2.000	4,200.00	84.00	3,532.36	70.65
1957	2.000	4,200.00	84.00	3,641.72	72.83
1958	2.000	4,200.00	84.00	3,673.80	73.48
1959	2.250	4,800.00	108.00	3,855.80	86.76
1960	2.750	4,800.00	132.00	4,007.12	110.20
1961	2.750	4,800.00	132.00	4,086.76	112.39
1962	2.875	4,800.00	138.00	4,291.40	123.38
1963	3.375	4,800.00	162.00	4,396.64	148.39
1964	3.375	4,800.00	162.00	4,576.32	154.45
1965	3.375	4,800.00	162.00	4,658.72	157.23
1966	3.500	6,600.00	231.00	4,938.36	172.84
1967	3.550	6,600.00	234.30	5,213.44	185.08
1968	3.325	7,800.00	259.35	5,571.16	185.26
1969	3.725	7,800.00	290.55	5,893.76	219.54
1970	3.650	7,800.00	284.70	6,186.24	225.80
1971	4.050	7,800.00	315.90	6,497.06	263.13
1972	4.050	9,000.00	364.50	7,133.80	288.92
1973	4.300	10,800.00	464.40	7,580.16	325.95
1974	4.375	13,200.00	577.50	6,030.76	351.35
1975	4.375	14,100.00	616.88	8,630.92	377.60
1976	4.375	15,300.00	669.38	9,226.48	403.66
1977	4.375	16,500.00	721.88	9,779.44	427.85
1978	4.275	17,700.00	756.67	10,556.03	451.27

Table 8.4. *(cont.)*

Year	Tax rate employee only (percent)	Maximum taxable income (dollars)	Maximum tax possible (dollars)	Average wages in covered employment (dollars)	Tax for average wage earner (dollars)
1979	4.330	22,900.00	991.57	11,479.46	497.06
1980	4.520	25,900.00	1,170.68	12,513.46	565.61
1981	4.700	29,700.00	1,395.90	13,594.27	638.93
Total			11,346.16		7,209.00

Source: James R. Capra, Peter D. Skaperdas, and Roger M. Kubarych, "Social Security, An Analysis of Its Problems," *FRBNY Quarterly Review,* Autumn, 1982, p. 6.

Table 8.5. *Long-term projections of cost rates for retirement and disability programs by calendar year: in percent*

Year	Cost rate:[a] intermediate	Cost rate:[a] pessimistic	Scheduled tax rate
1985	11.70	12.40	11.4
1990	11.64	12.85	12.4
1995	11.42	12.97	12.4
2000	11.03	12.82	12.4
2005	10.95	12.97	12.4
2010	11.53	13.92	12.4
2015	12.82	15.76	12.4
2020	14.44	18.17	12.4
2025	15.97	20.70	12.4
2030	16.83	22.63	12.4
2035	17.02	23.94	12.4
2060	16.81	28.49	12.4

[a]The cost rate is defined as annual outlays as a percentage of taxable payroll, or the tax rate needed to avoid a deficit.
Source: James R. Capra, Peter D. Skaperdas, and Roger M. Kubarych, "Social Security, An Analysis of Its Problems," *FRBNY Quarterly Review,* Autumn 1982, p. 6.

the retiree an initial benefit of $535 per month ($803 if the individual had a nonworking spouse). As a result, the retiree recovers his entire lifetime social security taxes in thirteen months (in only eight months if married). Table 8.6 shows these and other measures of social security retirement costs and benefits.

Table 8.6. *Measures of social security retirement costs and benefits*

Retiree	Time it takes retirees to recover their lifetime contributions	
	Average wage earner	Maximum wage earner
	1982 retiree	1982 retiree
Single retiree (or married with a working spouse)	13 months	16 months
Married with nonworking spouse	9 months	11 months
	2010 Retiree	2010 Retiree
Single retiree (or married with a working spouse)	23 months	34 months
Married with nonworking spouse	16 months	23 months

Other measures of social security retirement costs and benefits[a]

Measure	1982 retiree	2010 retiree
Time to recover lifetime contribution (employer–employee taxes)	2 years 2 months	3 years 10 months
Time to recover lifetime contributions (employer–employee taxes) plus interest	5 years 4 months	12 years 5 months
Ratio of present value of benefits to contributions with interest	2.7	1.3

[a] Estimates computed using the Social Security Administration's intermediate economic and demographic assumptions for a sixty-five-year-old retiree with average lifetime earnings, who is single or has a working spouse who qualifies for benefits based on her own earnings record.
Source: James R. Capra, Peter D. Skaperdas, and Roger Kubarych, ''Social Security, An Analysis of Its Problems,'' *FRBNY Quarterly Review,* Autumn 1982, p. 8.

The bottom half of Table 8.6 has been adjusted to allow for three factors. First, because the workers' taxes could have been earning interest, a simple straight accumulation of taxes paid underestimates the retirees' lifetime contribution to the system. Secondly, future benefits need to be discounted in order to obtain their present value. Finally, it is assumed that the social security taxes paid by employees are actually borne by the employees.

Capra, Skaperdas, and Kubaryck (1982:8) found after making these various adjustments that the ratio of the present value of benefits to contributions (including earned interest) equalled 2.7 for the 1982 retiree. The figure was greater than one even for the individual who retires in 2010. A figure greater than one means that benefits exceed the value of contributions and that the social security system is providing a subsidy. Consequently, the current structure of benefits and taxes will have to be altered if the present system is to be retained in the long run.

Summary of major financial problems

Several factors have combined to endanger the financial basis of the social security system. One of the most important was the transformation of the program from an insurance to a welfare system. Benefits legislated by politicians exceed taxes paid by individuals. Today's retirees will receive several times more in retirement checks than they paid in taxes. Exacerbating this problem is the fact that earlier retirement and greater longevity have increased the average retirement period by about 35 percent since 1935 ("Saving Social . . ." 1983:16A).

Demographic changes also have had and will continue to have important effects. The ratio of current workers who support current retirees has decreased from sixteen to one in 1950 to three to one today. It is predicted to decrease further as we enter the next century.

Cost-of-living adjustments (COLAS), which are tied to the consumer price index rather than to a wage index, have also weakened the financial structure of social security. Real wages that were the basis for social security taxes declined slightly during the 1970 decade, whereas the retiree benefits adjusted for inflation climbed by 50 percent. Part of the explanation of this boon to recipients was the overindexing of benefits (Munnell 1977: Ch.3). Congress has now remedied this problem.

Low national rates of growth in saving, investment, and production have contributed heavily to the financial crisis. Moreover, the social security system has through legislation become overly sensitive to general economic behavior, especially in recessions, when unemployment increases, leave many millions of workers no longer paying social security taxes.

In summary, it is fair to say that economic and demographic factors have combined with ill-advised legislation to place the social security system in near-term and long-run financial jeopardy.

Some economic effects of social security

The social security program has two important, potential economic effects on individuals and the economy. The first is its effect on employment and the supply of labor, and the second is its impact on the volume of savings. Each factor is important for the continued economic growth and health of the economy.

Employment and the supply of labor

Social security payroll taxes are levied on employees and employers. In 1984, the combined tax rate was 14 percent on the first $35,700 of employees' earnings for a total of $4,998 in social security taxes. Most economists agree, however, that splitting the tax equally in this way has little bearing on the impact of the tax. If the supply of labor is inelastic, workers bear the combined tax rate of 14 percent. Economists believe that the supply of labor, at least for men, is quite inelastic so that they tend to bear all or most of the burden of the combined tax. When the supply of labor is less inelastic, a tax wedge develops between what the employer is willing to pay a worker and what that worker receives. Because the worker receives less than he or she earns (by the amount of the tax), less labor will be offered in the market.

This tendency to reduce the quantity of labor may be counterbalanced if workers do not view the social security tax as a decrease in real income but merely postponed income to be received later in the form of retirement benefits. This point should not be overemphasized because the courts have ruled that workers do not have property rights to the social security taxes they have paid to the government. Moreover, because of the capriciousness of the social security program, working wives whose incomes are less than their husbands' incomes receive no benefits for the taxes they have paid. They obviously do not believe that their present reduction in incomes due to social security taxes will be compensated by future benefits.

It seems rational to conclude that the combined employer-employee tax is borne largely by workers. Moreover, it appears that on net balance, a tax on employment, much like other taxes, tends to inhibit the amount of the service or commodity supplied. It is pertinent to note that a study conducted by the Congressional Budget Office (1978) estimated that the 1977 increases in payroll taxes reduced employment in the United States by about 500,000 workers, and estimates of the job loss caused by the 1983 increase in social security taxes range between 1 and 2.2 million (Bandow 1983:30). There is little doubt that payroll taxes produce a welfare cost by distorting the labor-leisure choice of workers, but social security taxes are scheduled to rise for the rest of the 1980s.

Another distorting effect on the labor supply is caused by the social security earnings test. Workers between the ages of sixty-two and seventy face an earnings tax with a zero rate up to a certain level of income (Congress periodically increases this level slightly), 50 percent over a succeeding set of incomes with a marginal rate of zero above a specified level. For example, in 1983, beneficiaries between sixty-five and sixty-nine lost $1 in benefits for each $2 earned above $6,600. As Peter Germanis (1983:9) has noted, the earnings test tax along with social security taxes and federal and state income taxes make these older workers one of the most heavily taxed groups in the country.

Workers in this age group are faced with the choice of retiring completely, continuing to work full time and face heavy taxation, or finding a part-time job where the income earned is sufficiently small to prevent them from being pushed into the 50-percent tax bracket. The earnings test has implications that are exceptionally complicated, but it seems reasonable to conclude that it reduces the amount and quality of the supply of labor.

Another way that social security can decrease the labor supply is through early retirement. In accordance with social security formulas, low income retired workers receive benefits that are quite large in relation to previous earned wages and salaries. In addition, because benefits are not subject to income taxes, some low income workers actually realize higher net incomes in retirement than when they were working. Middle and higher income earners receive substantially smaller pensions than previous earnings, with the result that early retirement is much less attractive to them.

Henry Aaron (1982:62), former commissioner and expert on the social security system, believes that the program probably creates incentives for individuals to work until sixty-five. He notes that benefits are based on the earnings history of individuals and that benefits on a given earnings history are actually raised for each year workers defer drawing benefits.

Alan Blinder, Roger Gordon, and Donald Wise (1981:475) claim that the rules governing social security result in a wage subsidy for individuals who continue to work between the ages of sixty-two and sixty-five. There is some disagreement in the literature on this point (Burkauser and Turner 1981:467–72), but there is no disagreement over the fact that a large and increasing number of individuals have been retiring between the ages sixty-two to sixty-four (Aaron 1982:61, 64).

There may, of course, be a variety of reasons to explain this phenomenon. As Aaron (1982:64) notes, it may reflect a drastic decline in health or work opportunities in this crucial age bracket. It might also reflect the growing average wealth of this cohort.

Michael Boskin and Michael Hurd (1981:2–3) believe that the structure of social security benefits has exerted a powerful influence on retirement decisions. They base their conclusion on empirical work covering the period 1969 through 1973, when the real level of benefits increased markedly. As they note, this period provides a close approximation to a natural or social experiment.

The results of Hurd and Boskin's (1981:1–38) work, in which they control for such factors as health, wages, age of spouse, and private wealth, indicate that the large changes in social security benefits in the early 1970s had substantial short-run effects on speeding up early retirement and reducing the labor force participation for individuals between sixty and sixty-four. Benefit increases caused a drop of approximately 8 percent in the participation rates of this age group.

Social security and savings

Martin Feldstein (1974:905–26) was the first economist to perform system-atic econometric work on the relationship between social security, savings, and the nation's supply of capital. The theoretical basis for this research rests on the life-cycle model of household consumption and saving. Theory yields results that, unfortunately, work in opposite directions. Consequently, unam-biguous conclusions about the relationship between savings and social secu-rity cannot be made on the basis of theory alone.

The first effect has a contractionary impact on savings because workers view social security taxes as a substitute for retirement savings. As a result, workers reduce the amount they would have saved for retirement by approx-imately the amount of social security taxes they pay.

An opposing effect centers on the point that social security induces earlier retirement. Retirees then must increase private savings during their working lives to provide for the longer period they will spend in retirement.

Complicating the analysis is the fact that the social security program is a pay-as-you-go, unfunded system that makes intergenerational transfer pay-ments from younger workers to older retirees. Robert Barro (1974:1095–117) and others (Kochin 1974:385–94) have pointed out that private inter-generational gifts from older individuals to their children and others could cancel and offset the effect of the social security transfers, and there would be no net effect on savings.

Since the answers to the issues posed here cannot be deduced from theory alone, researchers have had to resort to empirical analysis of the effect of social security on savings. This is exactly what Feldstein (1974:905–26) attempted to do in his seminal article on the subject. His early statistical work supported the notion that social security's first effect on savings was dominant and, as a result, reduced household savings by between 40 and 50 percent and total private savings, including corporate savings by between 32 and 42 per-cent. Later work by Feldstein and Pellechio (1977) and associates tends to support these general ideas and estimates.

Feldstein's research on social security and saving has been the target of intense criticism; the objections to his work are of several different types. One theoretical issue centers on the applicability of the life-cycle model to the case at hand. Robert Myers (1975), Joseph Pechman et al. (1968), James Schulz et al. (1974), Peter Diamond (1977), and Henry Aaron (1982) have expressed doubts about the usefulness of this model in analyzing long-run household decisions about consumption, saving, and social security.

There is merit in their criticism, many individuals do not plan how they will consume their income and wealth over their expected lifetime. Feldstein answers this criticism by agreeing that although some individuals make absolutely no provision for their consumption during the retirement years, this irrational saving behavior is neither universal nor typical (Feldstein and Pellechio 1977:3–4). Cross-sectional econometric evidence does not support the view that such irrationality is prevalent.

As briefly noted, Robert Barro (1974:1095–117) and several other scholars (Kochin 1974:385–94) have proposed a theoretical argument stating that the social security program will have little or no effect on household saving. There are two aspects to this view. The first states that social security replaces what children would voluntarily spend to support their retired parents. The second view holds that current workers will increase their planned bequests to their children in order to offset the extra tax burden their children will have to bear under social security. To accomplish this goal, workers will have to save more during their working lives. It is possible for this increased saving for bequests to approximate the reduction in saving due to the promised benefits workers will receive when they retire. Under these special conditions, the conclusion is that social security does not appreciably alter the amount of personal savings.

Since history shows that economic progress boosts the real income of each succeeding generation higher than that of its parents, Feldstein and Pellechio (1977:36–7) do not believe there will be massive intergenerational private transfers. Moreover, the net worth of today's average older couple will not permit extensive or sizeable bequests. They conclude with the help of data that for the general population there are neither substantial bequests nor widespread support of retirees by their children. As a practical matter, the evidence suggests that the Barro effect is relatively unimportant.

Alicia Munnell (1976:1013–32) is responsible for the theoretical development of the *retirement effect*. Munnell shows that social security induces workers to retire early. Because they will live longer under retirement conditions, she theorizes that such workers will actually increase saving during their working years in order to reach and maintain their desired consumption levels over longer periods of time after retirement. The data tend to support this idea with respect to what Munnell calls private retirement savings, which interestingly excludes the value of such assets as stocks, bonds, and residential real estate. Feldstein (1979d), on the other hand, in using the same data found a substantial negative effect on total personal saving. Later work by Munnell tends to confirm the general Feldstein position that social security has a depressing effect on savings (Weaver 1982:238).

Despite the many different studies Feldstein has conducted, considerable controversy exists about the size and direction of his estimates of the effect of the social security program on the supply of household savings. The most damaging criticism came from Dean Leimer and Selig D. Lesnoy (1980, 1982:606–42), who discovered a programming error in Feldstein's work that was responsible for significantly overstating his results. Their research indicated that the 1930–74 data Feldstein used resulted in no effect on personal savings from social security (Zucker 1980:25).

Feldstein responded by constructing a new econometric model with additional data for the years 1975 and 1976; he derived results similar to his original estimates. He still contends that social security is responsible for reducing private saving by nearly 40 percent. Leimer and Lesnoy's model covering 1930–77 generates results that do not support the idea that social security has reduced personal saving ("The New NBER . . ." 1980:95–6).

Researchers have discovered why different investigators can obtain such diverse results on the issue of social security's effect on saving. One factor has become known in the literature as the social security wealth variable (the future net benefits workers will receive on retirement). This variable is particularly slippery because it is very difficult to assess today how workers evaluate the benefits they will receive years from now when they retire.

Alternate ways of calculating this variable yield alternative answers with respect to the effect of social security on personal saving. Leimer and Lesnoy (1980, 1982:606–42) used a number of different, generally accepted techniques about forming expectations and applied them to future social security benefits. They demonstrated that one could obtain almost any result desired.

Alan Auerbach and Laurence Kotlikoff (1981:35) conclude that a number of specification problems associated with social security econometric models can easily lead to highly unstable coefficients and the rejection of the notion that social security decreases household saving, even if it were actually true. Their work suggests "that virtually any social security time series coefficient, negative, zero, or positive, is potentially consistent with the life cycle hypothesis." A careful later study by Owen Evans (1982:1–10) respecifies the social security–savings model and concludes that there is tentative evidence for the proposition that the social security program increases consumption and decreases personal saving.

Assessment of the time series evidence on the issue of social security and saving is at best nebulous. The question cannot be settled on theoretical grounds, and much better data are required before further econometric experimentation is apt to prove successful.

Feldstein (1980:7) has graciously admitted the programming error Leimer and Lesnoy discovered in his time series, but he emphasizes that the results of his microeconomic household, cross-sectional and cross-country research remain virtually unchanged. These studies do support the hypothesis that social security has been responsible for depressing private saving (Feldstein and Pellechio 1977). However, part of Aaron's (1982:45–50) survey shows that other work directly and indirectly casts doubt on results generated from cross-sectional analysis. Moreover, although Feldstein's work comparing the effect of social security on savings in various countries supports his general contention that savings are depressed, other international research is at this time inconclusive. Some studies support and others negate the Feldstein hypothesis. In an extensive cross-country analysis, Robert Barro and Glen McDonald (1979:275–89) conclude that the data available are not rich enough to yield statistically valid conclusions on the effect of social security programs on household savings.

It is worth noting here that Owen Evans (1982:8–10) has tried an entirely different approach in an effort to assess the effect of social security on savings. He has argued on the basis of his econometric work that U.S. transfer programs, which include social security and comprise a substantial part of total transfers, may have decreased personal saving by redistributing wealth from people in higher income brackets to individuals and households that have higher than average propensities to consume. His econometric tests indicate that the propensity to consume transfer payments is about unity.

Evans' approach has the advantage of being much simpler in both form and structure than previous work in this area. On the other hand, much more empirical analysis is required before anything more than the most tentative conclusions can be entertained.

Summary of economic effects

Economists generally agree that employees bear both the employer and employee share of social security taxes. There is also considerable agreement that the tax decreases the volume of employment offered in the market. Moreover, the social security earnings tax distorts the supply of labor and, together with other taxes, causes older workers between sixty-five and sixty-nine to be one of the highest taxed groups in the country.

The question of the effect of social security on the magnitude and direction of personal savings cannot be answered by theory alone. Much controversy surrounds all the empirical work, and no definite answers exist at this time.

It is not known whether social security causes workers to decrease or increase saving. A known factor is that a shift from a pay-as-you-go government program to a mandatory private system of retirement will generate substantial savings that will be invested in the nation's capital stock (Ferrara 1982:113–33). Increases in physical and human capital will, in turn, increase real wages and economic growth over the long run.

Proposals to alter the system

The plethora of specific suggestions to alter the social security system range from short-run patchwork suggestions to fundamental changes. The most prominent suggestions in the literature are discussed here. Some are more politically feasible than others.

Altering the cost-of-living allowance (COLA)

Several ways of changing the manner in which retirement benefit COLAs are used to protect retirees from inflation have been suggested. One change would substitute the newly created 1983 consumer price index for the old one. The new index places much less weight on the cost of housing. Because many retired individuals and couples own their homes, this change would not work great hardships on the elderly population, although it would reduce monthly benefits checks.

Due to changes in the law and the use of the old CPI, real incomes of retirees increased by about 50 percent during the 1970s, whereas real wages of workers who were paying the taxes to support retirees fell slightly. Due to this unforeseen outcome, it has been suggested further that benefits be indexed by some fraction of the CPI. The figure of 60 percent is prominently mentioned.

Another recommendation calls for indexing benefits in accordance with an average wage index adjusted for changes in productivity. Workers responsible for increases in productivity would earn and receive these gains; at the same time, retirees would receive protection against inflation. Moreover, the social security fund would not only save money, but also its status and level would be less sensitive and vulnerable to the economic fluctuations of the economy.

Use of the general fund

The report of the 1979 Advisory Council on Social Security recommended unanimously that sole reliance on payroll taxes should be dropped. Members of the council suggested that hospital insurance programs be financed entirely by portions of personal and corporation income taxes. The council also recommended that payments from general revenue be made to the social security trust funds during times of high unemployment when social security tax collections decline substantially (*Social Security Bulletin* 1980:11).

Use of the value-added tax (VAT)

Tax experts Gerhard Brannon (1979:17–20) and Lester Thurow (1982:26) have come out strongly in favor of using the value-added tax (VAT) to supplement revenues and maintain the current level of benefits in the retirement program. Brannon does not see substantial differential efficiency or equity effects if the VAT is substituted for part of the payroll tax. Both Thurow and Brannon favor the use of a consumption-type tax to help maintain the financial viability of the social security system. As Thurow notes, individuals would be paying for benefits in accordance with what they consumed or took out of GNP, rather than with what they contributed through their labor.

In contrast to the Brannon–Thurow position, the 1979 Advisory Council on Social Security voted unanimously to reject the use of a VAT to finance social security (*Social Security Bulletin* 1980:11).

Proposals for fundamental reform

James Buchanan (1968:386–95) and Buchanan and Colin Campbell (1966:14) were among the first to advocate fundamental reform of the social security system. In the final analysis, their plan, proposed in 1966, envisaged a voluntary and actuarily sound system. Stripped of its welfare aspects, the government program could then compete with private insurance and other financial institutions. Among other benefits, this competition would encourage efficiency and keep downward pressure on costs.

Other proposals followed the publication of the Buchanan–Campbell plan. J. Pechman, H. Aaron, and M. Taussig (1968) produced a major study for The Brookings Institution that recommended separating the insurance and welfare aspects contained in the social security program. The welfare elements would be financed by general revenue funds; but the retirement program benefits, also financed from general revenue, would be related directly to the income earned by individuals during their working lives.

Alicia Munnell (1977) also recommended the separation of retirement and welfare benefits. Unlike the Pechman–Aaron–Taussig proposal, she advocated continued use of payroll taxes to finance the benefits of retirees. Supplementary security income designed to achieve social adequacy goals would be financed from the general revenue fund. One result would be a reduction in payroll tax rates with a concomitant required increase in general revenues.

A more recent plan promulgated by the Department of Health and Human Resources (then HEW) proposed a double-decker benefit system. Under this alternative, all aged and disabled individuals, whether they ever held a job, would be eligible to receive a Tier I grant of a standard amount. Individuals who had worked in jobs covered by social security would receive Tier II benefits equal to a constant proportion of their average earnings (Van de Water 1979:13–16).

Other prominent alternatives include Martin Feldstein's (1975:75–95) and the Boskin–Shoven–Kotlikoff (Boskin et al. 1982:13) plans. Each proposal represents a fundamental change in the social security system, but each maintains the central role of government in the provision of retirement benefits.

The Feldstein proposal for reform

Martin Feldstein's (1975:75–95) work on the social security system has been concerned mainly with its effect on the economy's rate of saving. His research indicates that the social security program has had an adverse effect on individual and national saving and economic growth.

As a result, Feldstein advocates the separation of the insurance and welfare portions into distinct government programs. The latter would be financed with money from the general revenue fund, but retirement would be based on private insurance principles. Mandatory social security tax payments would be deposited into a large government trust fund that would ultimately be fully funded. Workers' taxes would thus be saved, earn interest, and finance retirement benefits.

These funds would be used to retire gradually the enormous outstanding government debt as well as purchase private debt. Private sellers of these instruments could then invest in the private sector, which would increase the capital stock and real incomes. Feldstein's plan avoids the discouraging aspects on saving of the present pay-as-you-go social security system.

Although benefits would not be increased beyond those already embedded in the law, tax rates would be increased substantially in the short run. Higher current taxes would permit lower taxes on the present younger generation sometime in the future because the interest earned by the large reserve fund could be used to finance a portion of future benefits.

As with most government programs, there would be gainers and losers under the Feldstein proposal. Recall that the early retirees of the present system received much more in benefits than they paid in social security taxes. To a lesser extent, today's retirees still get back four to five times what they have contributed to social security (Boskin 1980b:16). Each succeeding generation has, through intergenerational transfer payments from workers to retirees, been paying these unearned windfall gains to retirees.

Feldstein's proposals would ultimately stop this chain letter effect, but the burden of paying for these past, unearned windfall gains would rest with the current, older working population. Along with all others in the system, they would be subject to the higher tax rate, but their benefits would not increase on retirement as a result; the lower tax rates that would be operative in the future as the trust fund earned more and more interest would apply only to younger workers who have not yet retired. Moreover, younger workers may realize higher lifetime incomes due to the higher rate of saving and investment engendered by the effects of the trust fund. Browning and Browning (1978:180) estimate roughly that workers aged fifty and above would probably be worse off under the Feldstein proposal. As they point out, the exact age would depend on the magnitude of the higher tax rate, how long it would remain in effect, and the rate of return on the new investment encouraged by the growing trust fund.

The Boskin–Shoven–Kotlikoff plan

This plan addresses the long-term problems of social security. It would be implemented over the long run and would gradually phase out most welfare and redistributive effects of the current system. It would also scale down scheduled future benefits embedded in the present law. Consequently, the much higher payroll taxes that will be required in the next century could be avoided.

The keystone of the plan is the creation of what Michael Boskin, John Shoven, and Laurence Kotlikoff (BSK) call personal security accounts, or PSAs. These accounts would be treated as if families were purchasing insurance with their own and their employers' social security taxes.

Families over age fifty-five would be unaffected and subject to the provisions of the current law, but all younger households would receive PSA credits equal to the value of the contributions they have made into the system plus a 2 percent real rate of interest. Each dollar of credit would provide actuarily determined, inflation-indexed benefits for old-age spouse-survivor, child-survivor, and health insurance ("Social Security: Personal . . ." 1983:1–2).

Each participant under the BSK plan would receive an annual accounting from the system that would show the value of the accumulated benefits. This kind of information would facilitate sound planning for retirement, including household decisions about personal savings and purchasing private insurance.

Implementation of PSAs would gradually phase out the welfare aspect of the current social security system. Moreover, BSK believe that the slow elimination of unaccrued benefits for successively younger families diffuses the "burden of social security's long-term financial crisis fairly across young and middle-aged Americans ("Social Security: Personal . . ." 1983:1)

Other provisions in the BSK plan include:

1. Universal coverage of all private and government workers;
2. Elimination of the earnings test for all participants;
3. Benefits would be indexed, but on the basis of new 1983 consumer price index;
4. Old-age annuity payments would remain tax free, thus preserving the idea of providing benefits on an actuarial basis; and
5. PSA credits would be designed to protect those with modest incomes and to assist families with children.

Boskin, Shoven, and Kotlikoff believe their plan would accomplish the following:

1. Slowly eliminate the inequities and inefficiencies in the present social security system;
2. Provide a sound financial insurance system that will guarantee participants' future benefits;
3. Gradually transform and integrate the present system into a program that is based on the principles of private insurance and capital markets;
4. Virtually eliminate the uncertainty surrounding the present program by providing each participant an annual financial accounting that explicitly states the benefits registered in the individual's PSA account; and finally and importantly
5. Provide for a cash reserve sufficient to protect social security benefits during periods of short-run economic fluctuations.

There is little doubt that the basic structure of social security is in need of reform. Some critics believe that nothing short of making the retirement system private will protect the younger and middle-aged workers of today. Under current law, younger workers' rates of return on their social security taxes will be far lower than what private market plans can offer (Ferrara 1982:149–56).

Professor Friedman's retirement plan

Professor Friedman (1977:25–29) has a strong antipathy to the forced governmental provision of a retirement system because it infringes on the freedom of individuals to make their own choices and plans. He also objects to the gross misrepresentations that politicians and bureaucrats have perpetrated about the social security program. Moreover, he deplores the system's negative effect on saving, capital accumulation, and employment as well as the capricious benefits provided by the law. In addition, Friedman believes that the payroll tax is exceptionally regressive and that lower income workers are treated unfairly because most of them begin working and paying social security at a relatively young age. Importantly, lower income workers have a shorter life span and draw benefits for shorter periods of time than their more affluent contemporaries (Browning and Browning 1978:173).

To nullify these disadvantages, Professor Friedman proposes to phase out gradually the present regimen in favor of a purely voluntary system of insurance. Welfare payments for the elderly poor would be financed by general revenues.

Friedman's transition period would permit current retirees to continue receiving their existing benefits. Individuals nearing retirement would receive substantial pensions but less than if the present system were perpetuated. Middle-aged workers would continue to pay taxes but receive smaller pensions.

Younger workers would receive no government benefits, but tax rates would fall appreciably as retirees died and ceased drawing benefits.

This proposal would encourage private saving and capital accumulation as workers would have to make arrangements for retirement with insurance companies and other financial institutions. The Friedman proposal would have some of the same beneficiary effects as Feldstein's, but the big losers would be middle-aged workers and perhaps younger workers. The latter's position would depend to a fair degree on the rate of growth in real incomes generated by the increases in saving and capital stock. Current retirees and future generations would be the big gainers.

The Heritage Foundation solution

The essential points of this proposal are: ("Heritage Offers . . ." 1982:1, 4)

1. Social security benefits for those individuals already retired or nearing retirement will be maintained.
2. The Social Security Administration shall establish an individual account for each person in the system. Individuals would receive an annual statement indicating how much they and their employers have paid into the program and an estimate of expected benefits on retirement.
3. The conflicting goals of welfare and insurance embedded in the present program shall be gradually separated. A mandatory savings plan would be introduced to finance an actuarily fair retirement annuity. Welfare aspects of the present program would be transferred to a means-tested system and financed by the general fund.
4. Retirement provisions and the purchase of life, disability, and old-age life insurance could be handled by the Social Security Administration or privately through the use of such institutions as individual retirement accounts. Individuals could choose either public or private provision of these services.
5. Participation in either the private or public system would be mandatory.
6. Lastly, general revenues would be used to bridge the gap between the present pay-as-you-go system and the fully funded program.

The Ferrara plan

Ferrara's (1982:114–15) plan contains certain similarities to the Heritage proposal. The welfare and insurance functions of social security would be split apart. An improved Supplementary Security Income Program with its means test would be used to fulfill the welfare function.

Retirement and insurance functions would be handled exclusively through private markets. Individuals would have their own saving and insurance accounts in their own individual retirement accounts (IRAs). The IRAs would include survivor, disability, and old-age health insurance.

Ferrara (1982:149–56) shows under alternative assumptions that high, average, and low (minimum wage) income earners would be substantially better off financially under this proposal than under government-run social security. For example, single individuals who begin work at eighteen and never earn more than the minimum wage (all figures in this example are in 1980 dollars) would, at real rate of return of 4.5 percent, retire at sixty-five with $18,400 per year. This figure compares with the $6,700 per annum that the social security system would provide.

Another advantage of the Ferrara (1982:115) plan is that it would provide instantaneous vesting and portability rights, regardless of how many different locations and jobs a worker holds. This point is important because the courts have ruled that participants in the present social system do not have property rights to the funds they have contributed to the system.

The Ferrara (1982:102) plan would be phased in over several years. Support of current retirees would come partly from some of the resulting benefits of the plan that younger individuals would experience. Ferrara believes his plan would increase and create new wealth, some of which could be devoted to paying off some liabilities of the current system. Some of the funding to cover the costs during the transition phase from the pay-as-you-go to an individually funded system would have to be squeezed from the general fund. Ferrara also mentions that the sale of unused, surplus federal property might be used to help defray transition costs.

Congressional attempts to save social security

Although economists had criticized the financial structure underlying social security from the inception of the program, it was not until the early 1970s that politicians and others began to understand that a pay-as-you-go system can be fraught with many problems. Nevertheless, after several years of debate, Congress passed a new social security law in 1977 that was to solve the financial problem for years into the next century. The solution consisted mainly of raising taxes and tax rates on employees, employers, and the self-employed while leaving benefit schedules virtually untouched.

By 1980, it was clear that both the short- and long-run financial viability of the social security program was in deep trouble. The newly elected Reagan administration made an attempt at reform, but the political reaction was so strong that the President quickly dropped the initiative and appointed a National Commission on Social Security Reform to deal with the problem.

After much public discussion, debate, politicking, and handwringing, Congress adopted many of the commission's recommendations in the spring of 1983 and passed another law designed to save social security. Members of both political parties once again believe they have solved the monetary problems of social security. Lawmakers in both the Senate and House of Representatives say their new law will ensure the financial health of social security for seventy-five years or more (Merry 1983:3).

Major provisions of the 1983 law

The new law boosts and accelerates payroll taxes on employers and employees. By 1990, the combined rate will be 15.3 percent. Taxes on the self-employed have also been raised. The tax base against which the rate is levied is unknown but presumably it will be higher than the 1985 figure of $39,600. The tax base rises automatically with average wages. It is estimated that the increases in rates will generate an additional $40 billion for the trust funds during the rest of the 1980s.

The new law for the first time imposes taxes on social security benefits. They will be collected by the Treasury through the income tax, but the revenue will be credited to the social security trust funds.

Benefits are subject to tax if half of the benefits together with other income, including tax free income, exceed a base amount of $25,000 for individuals and $32,000 for joint returns. These amounts are written into the law in nominal terms, and there is no allowance for erosion in the value of the dollar and tax base due to inflation.

Changes in benefits

The cost-of-living adjustment that has been applied each July will now be delayed until January, and future changes will be made each January. It is estimated that the system will be saved about $40 billion through the remainder of the decade. Interestingly, cost-of-living changes of less than 3 percent prohibited by the old law are permitted under the 1983 Act.

The new law changes and reduces the social security benefits gained by people who spent most of their lives in non–social security employment. These individuals are for the most part federal employees, who are sometimes referred to as double dippers because they also receive even more generous benefits than social security provides. It is estimated that this proposal will save the system nearly $300 million by 1990.

Benefits could also be affected by the new stabilizer feature which is designed to prevent the depletion of the trust funds when inflation rises more rapidly than wages. If these funds drop below a 15-percent reserve between 1985 and 1988, the cost-of-living adjustments would be limited to the change in the consumer price index or workers' average wages, whichever is lower. In 1989 and thereafter, the trigger would be a 20-percent reserve. Should fund reserves exceed 32 percent of the amount required for a year, beneficiaries would receive an extra cost-of-living adjustment.

The new social security bill, which was signed into law by President Reagan on April 21, 1983, decreases the constraints on how much money can be earned during retirement. The old law mandated that for every $2 of earnings above $6,600 earned by a retiree less than seventy years old, benefits must be reduced by $1 or a marginal tax rate of 50 percent. Under the new law, benefits are reduced by $1 for every $3 over the base amount of $6,600, but the base amount is in nominal terms and there is no provision to adjust it for inflation. Consequently, the real value of the base will continue to fall with inflation, and the effective tax rate will continue to increase over the years.

For individuals who delay retirement beyond sixty-five, a bonus in benefits of an extra 3 percent for each year of full-time work through the age of seventy-one will be paid. The bonus increases by a quarter of a percentage point starting in 1990 and rises to a limit of 8 percent per year in 2009.

Other provisions of the 1983 law

Beginning in 1984, all new federal employees were required to join the social security system. Moreover, congressional and judicial employees, members of Congress, federal judges, the vice-president, and the president, as well as some 3,000 top political appointees must also become part of the system. Current government bureaucrats will continue to enjoy their own existing and more liberal retirement benefits.

In addition, all employees of nonprofit organizations are compelled to participate in the social security program. Importantly, employees of state and local governments who are currently covered are prohibited from withdrawing from the system. This provision is particularly important because the number of employees in state and local governments who have withdrawn and petitioned to withdraw from the system has grown dramatically during recent years. Some 75,955 state and local employees opted out of the social security system in 1980, and an additional 104,506 had plans to leave in 1981. Moreover, nearly 900 nonprofit organizations have threatened to leave ("Getting Out" 1981:16). These requirements regarding federal, state, and local government employees will increase trust fund revenue by approximately $22 billion by 1990. Later, when these individuals become eligible for retirement, they will actually draw down on the trust fund.

Nevertheless, if the country is to keep its compulsory social security program, a case can be made that federal workers should be gradually brought into the program. Dr. Rita Ricardo-Campbell (1984:24) makes the telling point that equity demands universal coverage because benefits are, to a significant extent, welfare benefits.

Perhaps the most important new provision with a long-term implication is the increase in the qualifiable age for retirement. The new law raises the retirement age from sixty-five to sixty-seven in stages beginning in 2003. The age for full retirement benefits will rise to exactly sixty-six in 2003 and continue slowly rising to sixty-seven in 2027. Workers born after 1938, but before the end of World War II, will be affected slightly. The baby boom generation born after the war will be most affected. One nonfiscal rationalization for these provisions is that individuals are living longer than their fathers and mothers. Curiously, the age for early retirement will remain at sixty-two, but the penalty for early retirement will rise from 20 to 30 percent (Merry 1983:3).

Evaluation of the 1983 law

None of the ideas generated in the previously mentioned proposals for reform was adopted by Congress. The tension and schism between the retirement and redistribution functions remain and will continue to plague the social security program. Congress produced a Band-Aid rather than fundamental reform.

The basic economic effects of social security on the economy were largely ignored. Higher and accelerated employment taxes will, ceteris paribus, inhibit economic growth. The price of labor will be higher, and output, saving, and capital accumulation slower. A relatively lower growth rate will inhibit not only saving but also the social security tax base itself. In addition, it will have negative effects on the collection of other taxes, thereby increasing the deficit and perhaps putting upward pressure on interest rates.

Taxing benefits, as the new law does, will exacerbate these unwanted economic effects. It is estimated that in the beginning these taxes will reduce benefits for only about 10 percent of OASDI beneficiaries (Germanis 1983:9). However, these individuals are precisely those that do save and provide funds for the investment market.

Paul Roberts (1983:26) has calculated that taxing benefits above certain thresholds, as the 1983 law provides, will increase the marginal rate of taxation on the private pension and investment income of middle and upper income retirees from 50 to 77 percent. It will, for example, place a retired couple with a $36,000 income in the same marginal tax bracket as a married working couple with an income of $175,000. He also notes that those social security recipients who continue to work and earn income in excess of the social security earnings limitation, which was $6,600 in 1985, will face a combined marginal tax in excess of 100 percent.

Roberts (1983:26) concludes correctly that once individuals who are making financial plans for retirement realize that their marginal rates on private retirement income in excess of the thresholds set by the new law will exceed 50 percent, their rate of saving will decrease. The effects of this 1983 provision are to encourage individuals to become more dependent on social security and to exacerbate the long-run financial problems of the system. Moreover, the various threshold amounts that determine taxability are stated in nominal terms. Inflation will immediately introduce a bracket creep so that more and more less well-off couples will be subject to relatively high marginal tax rates on their retirement income.

Another important aspect of the new law is its indifference to the rate of return on the taxes that today's and tomorrow's younger workers now pay and will pay. No attempt to spread the burden is built into the system due to the excessively high, nonactuarial returns paid to retirees during the past forty years of the program. Although compelled to join and pay taxes to the system, these individuals could obtain much higher real rates of return by investing their funds in the private sector.

The new law not only disregards Professor Friedman's criticism, but it also exacerbates the problem. Poorer workers who start their lifetime work earlier, who normally do not graduate from colleges or universities, and who start paying social security taxes sooner, on average die before their more prosperous cohorts. As a result, they do not receive benefits for as long a period as their colleagues of the same age. Under the 1983 law, these poorer workers will have to work to age sixty-seven, which means they will be paying taxes for an even longer period of time but receiving benefits for an even shorter time.

Finally, very little was done to solve the medicare problem of social security. Although a study by the Congressional Budget Office (1978) suggests that the medicare fund will be insolvent by 1987, congressional action was confined to constraining payments to hospitals for various types of hospital treatment. It has been estimated that the saving from this provision will approach $20 billion by 1988. It is possible that this amount will avoid the short-term deficit, but with the number and medical costs of senior citizens growing inexorably, the medicare problem will have to be attacked again, and soon.

Summary

The social security program will continue to survive, but its costs are high. Congress needs to address the special problem associated with the unfair treatment of women as well as the problems of low income earners who on average have historically had shorter life spans. In addition, higher and accelerated taxes on employees, employers, and the self-employed, as well as new taxes on social security benefits, will all have adverse effects on the economy. Finally, the failure of Congress to separate the retirement function of social security from the welfare function of society will continue to plague the system.

CHAPTER 9

The value added tax

Introduction

The value added tax (VAT), a relatively new type of tax, is a major form of taxation in Europe. In addition to the European Economic Community (EEC), which now requires its members to have such a levy, Finland, Norway, and Sweden all have value added taxes. Most of the Latin American countries also use a VAT.

The rapid ascendancy of the VAT in so many countries has contributed to a growing interest in its possible use in the United States, and a lively debate has emerged between proponents and opponents. Advocates first proposed it as a replacement for all or part of the tax on corporation income. President Nixon proposed the VAT as a way of reducing property taxes used to finance local schools (Strout 1978:5). Richard W. Lindholm, an economist and perhaps the leading proponent of the VAT, suggested that its chief advantage would be to boost exports and thereby help solve balance of payments problems (Halverson 1979c:11). It has also been considered as a principle source for additional income to finance rapidly expanding government expenditures and more recently as a means of alleviating the rising burden of social security and income taxes (Long 1978:7), as well as the national debt.

Characteristics of the VAT

The VAT is a general tax applied at each point of exchange of goods or services, from primary production to final consumption. It is levied on the difference between the sale price of the goods or services to which the tax is applied and the cost of goods and services bought for use in production. All European VATs are similar in design. Those of the Common Market countries were developed or modified in conformity with EEC directives, and the Scandinavian countries followed closely, differing mainly in the use of a single rate instead of several. The Latin American countries, on the other hand, restrict deductibility of taxes on producers' goods much more severely, partly to avoid any incentive for excessive capital investment.

200

Origins of the value added tax

The VAT originated with F. Von Siemens, German industrialist and advisor to his government, who proposed in 1918 that the VAT replace the established German multistage turnover tax (Hafer and Trebing 1980:6). T. S. Adams, an American economist, independently devised a form of the VAT at about the same time and recommended that the United States government use it (Lindholm 1970:1178). The Shoup tax mission to Japan recommended use of the VAT, and in 1950 the Japanese Diet adopted it for use by local governments (Lindholm 1976:42). Adoption and use by a national government had to wait until 1954, when France introduced it to replace its system of turnover taxes (McLure 1972:60).

Value added taxation received its biggest boost in 1962, when the Neumark Committee recommended it be used as the standard form of sales tax in the Common Market countries. A decade later, all EEC countries including the United Kingdom had adopted the tax. Since the late 1960s, use of the tax has spread to the less developed countries. Table 9.1 presents a summary of the countries that use the VAT (Due 1976:65).

Types of value added taxes

The most comprehensive class of value added taxation is the gross product type. With this kind, firms are not permitted to deduct the purchase price of capital goods when calculating their tax base. Moreover, they are not allowed to deduct the depreciation of existing capital. The tax base at each stage of production includes wages, rent, interest, profits, and depreciation. Using national income accounting terminology and ignoring the government and foreign sectors, the tax base is equal to the sum of consumption and gross investment or GNP.

In the income-type VAT, business enterprises are allowed to deduct capital depreciation before calculating tax liabilities. The tax base is defined as consumption plus net investment, or GNP minus depreciation, which is equal to net national product.

The most common form of value added taxation exempts not only depreciation but also plant and equipment. Since all capital is excluded, the tax base corresponds to the output of consumer goods or, equivalently, to the income earned by all factors in producing consumption goods.

Deriving the value added

Table 9.2 illustrates how the value added to a product by different firms at various stages in the production process can be derived. Four producers each

Table 9.1. *Countries having value added taxation*

Country	Year introduced	Basic rate
EEC countries		
France	1954	20%[a]
Denmark	1967	15
Germany, Federal Republic of	1968	11[a]
Netherlands	1969	16[a]
Luxembourg	1970	10[a]
Belgium	1971	18[a]
Ireland	1972	6[a]
Italy	1973	6[a]
United Kingdom	1973	8
Other European countries		
Sweden	1969	18
Norway	1970	20
Austria	1973	16
Latin America		
Brazil	1967	16[a]
Uruguay	1968	10
Ecuador	1970	4[a]
Costa Rica	1971	8
Honduras	1971	3
Bolivia	1973	5
Chile	1974	20
Argentina	1975	25[a]
Panama	1975	5
Colombia	1975	15[a]
Mexico	1980	10
Middle East		
Israel	1978	8
Africa[b]		
Tunisia	1955	17.8
Ivory Coast	1960	10[a]
Morocco	1961	14[a]
Senegal	1966	10[a]
Malagasy Republic	1969	13.6[a]
Algeria	—	25[a]
Far East		
Korea	1977	10

[a] In addition to the basic rates shown, these countries have other rates for various items and processes.
[b] Limited mainly to the manufacturing sector.
Sources: Sijbren Cnossen, *Excise System,* The Johns Hopkins University Press, Baltimore, 1977, pp. 18–21; Alan Tait, "Is the Introduction of a Value-Added Tax Inflationary?" *Finance and Development,* June 1981, pp. 38–42.

Table 9.2. *Deriving the value added of bread*

Stage of production	Receipts	Value added
1 (wheat)		
Farmer $.20	= $.20	.20
2 (flour)		
Miller .20 + .10	= .30	.10 or (.30 − .20 = .10)
3 (bread)		
Baker .20 + .10 + .17	= .47	.17 or (.47 − .30 = .17)
4 (services)		
Retailer .20 + .10 + .17 + .08	= .55	.08 or (.55 − .47 = .08)
Sales price to the consumer	.55	
Total value added		$.55

contribute something that adds utility to the loaf of bread being produced. The miller buys wheat from the farmer at a price of twenty cents and, after milling the wheat, sells the flour to a baker for thirty cents. Because two-thirds of the price the baker pays represents the farmer's receipts, ten cents of the miller's selling price of thirty cents is the value the miller adds to the wheat during the processing of wheat into flour.

The baker converts the flour into bread and sells it to the retail store for forty-seven cents, and because the cost of the flour was thirty cents, the baker has contributed the difference of seventeen cents. The retailer adds eight cents of value to the bread by taking delivery at a cost of forty-seven cents, stocking, protecting, and pricing it, and receiving payment of fifty-five cents from the consumer at the place of business. The retail price to the consumer is the sum of the value added to the product by each producer at each stage of production.

Methods of calculating the VAT

There are three principal alternative ways to derive tax liabilities. The addition method specifies that a firm's tax base is the sum of its payments to the factors of production. The subtraction way of calculating the amount of revenue owed to the government involves deducting the cost of production from the firm's sales receipts. With the third or credit method, the business derives its gross tax liability by applying the pertinent statutory rate or rates to total sales. From this figure, it deducts the amount of tax already paid on the purchase of inputs.

The tax credit method offers several advantages over the other two approaches. For most firms, it makes compliance an easier task. It also facilitates cross-auditing. In addition, the tax credit method emphasizes the consumption aspects of the tax and diminishes the danger of pyramiding because it requires separate itemization of the tax on all transactions between firms and encourages firms to regard the levy as an element distinct from the selling price of goods and services.

Scope of the tax

The advocates of value added taxation generally assume that the scope of the levy would be limited to business enterprises. Probably the most difficult problem in designing the VAT is the question of what to include in the definition of business. Indeed, this definition varies from one country to another. For example, the United States Department of Commerce defines business as "all organizations which produce goods and services for sale at a price intended at least to approximate costs of production" (Sullivan 1966:191). It includes all private, profit-making enterprises, mutual financial institutions, cooperatives, and nonprofit businesses.

The VAT applies to all of these businesses, but exclusions and exemptions of certain activities are made in practice. Government may reduce the tax base by granting exemptions for the benefit of special industries as well as the administration of the levy. Similarly, the existence and realization of capital gains raises the question of whether they should be taxed. In terms of the general intent of consumption taxation, the answer would appear to be negative because capital gains do not reflect consumption expenditures. With regard to secondhand goods, it can be argued that if their prices reflect the tax originally paid on them, they should not be taxed again. But as a practical administrative matter, it is much simpler to include them. In addition, taxing secondhand goods discourages the converting of new goods into used ones for tax purposes.

Incidence and equity

It is helpful to distinguish between the statutory and economic incidence of a levy. This distinction is often made regarding sales taxes. Although its legal liability is imposed on the retailer, the sales tax is usually assumed to be passed on largely to the individual who purchases goods and services from the retailer. This forward shifting increases the prices of retailer goods and reduces the consumer's purchasing power. In this case, the economic incidence of the tax differs from the statutory liability, because the former takes into account both the final resting point of the tax and its economic effects on consumers.

The analysis of incidence suggests that the VAT, in its usual consumption form, might best be regarded as a sales tax because the burden is distributed largely in relation to consumer spending. The VAT, like other sales taxes, is classified as an indirect tax because it is paid by business firms to the government and shifted mainly to the consumers of products, rather than being collected directly by the government from the consumers.

A principal equity concern of the VAT regards the relative burden it imposes on individuals with different amounts of income and wealth. Opponents of the VAT allege that it is regressive because it taxes consumption, and they believe lower income individuals spend a larger proportion of their incomes on consumption goods than do higher income individuals. VAT proponents state that the validity of this argument depends on several unsettled issues. One is that the analysis of regressiveness ignores the benefit side of fiscal policy; that is, the net benefits derived from government spending or transfer payments are not taken into account. Another issue is that the alleged regressiveness of the tax could be alleviated by adjustments to the income tax rate and/or by special tax credits. Finally, when individuals' tax burdens are compared with their permanent rather than annual income, consumption taxes may not be regressive but proportional (Davies 1980:204–7). In the final analysis, the degree of desirable regressivity or progressivity of a newly regarded tax should not be evaluated in isolation but considered along with the present impact of existing patterns of taxes and expenditures.

Neutrality of the VAT

A tax is neutral when all economic decisions are unaffected by the levy. For practical purposes, no tax can be considered completely neutral. Although all taxes alter economic behavior to some degree, certain taxes can be judged superior on efficiency grounds.

Proponents of VAT claim it would achieve superior allocational efficiency. A tax on each firm's value added can be thought of as a proportional tax on the firm's use of the factors of production. If each firm combines all its factors in the most efficient fashion, resources are moved into their most productive use. Proponents conclude, therefore, that a uniform VAT on all firms imposes the same proportional tax cost and is neutral toward the choice of production methods or the use of productive resources.

In practice, however, the tax is likely to end up being less neutral than its theoretical construction. Critics claim that political necessity requires that the tax be applied with numerous exemptions. They define political necessity as a concept that contains certain categories, such as food, clothing, housing, and medicine. In addition to narrowing the overall tax base of the VAT, numerous exemptions would erode the neutrality of the tax and distort the allocation of resources.

It should be noted that the VAT, like the personal income and payroll taxes, is not neutral with regard to an individual's choice between leisure and labor or market and nonmarket activities, such as those performed in the home, for charitable organizations, and in the underground economy. On the other hand, it is now known from recent research on the integration of corporate and personal income taxes that the corporate levy distorts the consumption choices of individuals, as well as financial and production decisions of firms. The weight of evidence and argument leads to the conclusion that replacing the corporate profits levy with the VAT would improve the allocation of resources (McLure 1980b:311–12).

Price effects

Analysts generally agree that adoption of the VAT, per se, would lead to higher prices. The central question is, however, what would happen to prices if, as is proposed in the United States, the VAT were substituted for other taxes.

Charles McLure (1980b:315) argues that reductions in the personal income tax are not likely to lead to falling prices, so that replacing it with a VAT would probably result in a net increase in prices. He notes that a cut in the corporate profits tax would be reflected in lower prices, so there would be virtually no price effect if a VAT were substituted for the corporate levy. McLure concludes that replacing the payroll tax with the VAT would likely produce effects midway between the results he predicts for personal and corporate taxes. He reasons that reduction in the half of the payroll tax that is paid by the employer would allow prices to fall; but reduction in the half employees pay would not be reflected in a change in prices.

These conclusions are based partly on the belief that the corporate profits tax is borne by all owners of capital. This position has been argued persuasively by A. C. Harberger, C. McLure, D. Fullerton, J. Shoven, J. Whalley and others, and, although consensus appears to be growing for this view within the profession, agreement is far from unanimous.

Alan Tait (1981:38–42), assistant director in the Fiscal Affairs Department at the International Monetary Fund, studied the introduction of the VAT in thirty-one countries in an attempt to discover the effect on the general level of prices. His statistical and other evidence indicated that the VAT had no effect on the rate of change in prices in twelve countries, and little or no effect in nine additional countries. Among the many variables operating, he found that the tax could have contributed to higher prices in four countries. In six (or 19 percent) of the countries analyzed, Tait found that the VAT was associated with a once-and-for-all shift in prices. He concluded that it is quite possible to adopt a VAT without shifting or increasing the rate of change in the price level.

International trade and finance effects

Proponents of the VAT believe it will improve the volume of exports and the balance of payments for countries that adopt the levy. They argue that its adaptability to General Agreement on Trade and Tariff (GATT) rules, which allow rebates of the tax on exports but full taxation of imports, will permit United States exports to be priced more competitively ("Is There a VAT . . ." 1978:2–3).

This argument has appeal if the VAT replaces the kind of tax that is followed by downward pressure on prices once it is removed. If, as discussed in the previous section on price effects, the corporate profits levy is replaced by a VAT, exports will at first become more competitive. As time passes, the competitive edge is likely to be blunted by changes in the exchange rate, which will adjust as the result of tax-induced increases in the balance of payments. The net result of these various changes will be a stronger currency for the exporting country (McLure 1980b:316).

Administrative costs

The cost of administration is another criterion for evaluating the merits of a tax. The initial administrative costs of introducing a VAT would be relatively high.

Perhaps the most important factor affecting the cost of using a VAT is the degree of complexity of the tax. The use of multiple rates and numerous exemptions, in contrast to the single uniform rate, would raise administrative costs. Another cost consideration is whether the levy is designed to replace part of an existing tax or used as a supplementary source of government revenue. If the VAT replaces only part of an existing tax or is merely added to the present system, administrative cost savings may be negligible. In fact, adding a VAT may increase the current cost of the government's tax-collecting apparatus.

Summary of VAT characteristics

The VAT is a levy on the value that a firm adds to products and services. It is a multistage tax applied to each level of production and distribution. The tax base for any given firm is the difference between its total taxable sales and its total taxable purchases of goods and services from outside sources. Viewed another way, the tax base can be conceived as the sum of the firm's payments for wages, rent, interest, and profits.

The common method of calculating the tax is to apply the tax rate on the firm's sales and subtract credits equal to the tax on all the goods and services purchased from other firms. With the consumption type of VAT, tax credits on capital assets are deducted in full when invoiced.

Because of political, social, economic, and administrative realities, the concept of a single tax rate is often modified by exemptions and multiple rates. These modifications can simplify some aspects of tax collection, especially for small firms. They can also lighten the tax burden on specified consumer purchases, such as food and medicine. In other respects, they create additional complexities in calculating and applying the tax, as well as introducing more allocational distortions into the economy.

VAT proposals in the United States

The idea of a value added tax has existed in the United States for more than sixty years. The state of Michigan actually adopted and used a form of the tax for almost fifteen years. It was discarded in favor of a progressive system of personal and corporate income taxes and then reintroduced in 1976. Congressmen have introduced bills for a national value added tax on three separate occasions, but there was scant support for such legislation until 1979.

Historical background

The value added tax was first suggested for use in the United States by T. S. Adams in 1921. It was immediately introduced into Congress by an amendment to the Revenue Act of 1921 by Senator Reed Smoot (Hafer and Trebing 1980:6). In 1932 and 1933, researchers at The Brookings Institution recommended that the states of Alabama and Iowa adopt value added taxes. Writing in 1940, Professor Paul Studenski, noted tax theorist, concluded that the VAT was the ideal business tax. His conclusion was based on the notion that the tax is neutral because the return to each factor of production, wages, rent, interest, and profits bears the same proportionate tax burden (Lindholm 1976:41–2).

Studenski's support of VAT, together with that of T. S. Adams, led to the introduction of a bill in the Senate by Senator Joseph O'Mahoney in 1940. It proposed that the federal government adopt the VAT (Lindholm 1976:42). Congress did not approve the bill, and, except for the Michigan experience, the issue of value added taxation remained rather dormant until 1966. At that time, the influential Committee for Economic Development (1966) recommended a VAT in lieu of increasing the corporate income tax. The committee also believed that the VAT would encourage savings by taxing consumption.

The following year, the West Virginia legislature considered a VAT but rejected it by a narrow margin. At the same time, the Citizen's Advisory Tax

Structure Task Force recommended to the governor that the state of California adopt a VAT to replace both property taxes and part of the state's levy against corporate income. In the summer of 1970, the President's Task Force on Business Taxation recommended that if substantial additional federal revenues .were desired, government eschew increases in personal and corporate income taxes in favor of value added or some other form of indirect taxation (McLure 1973:96). Two years later, at the president's request, the Advisory Commission on Intergovernmental Relations completed a thorough study of the VAT (Lindholm 1976:43–4).

Nothing concrete emerged from this flurry of activity between 1966 and 1972. No legislation was enacted, and interest in value added taxation in the United States abated until the latter part of the decade.

The Tax Restructuring Act of 1979

By the late 1970s, even legislators realized that the United States economy was in deep trouble. It was overregulated, stagnant, and wracked by double-digit inflation. Productivity and saving were falling, and capital formation was negligible. Average real income was actually falling.

The president and his staff, enamored with the idea of redistributing incomes and armed with outdated macroeconomic policies, never came to grips with the fundamental problems that plagued the economy. In fact, the administration's regulatory, fiscal, and monetary policies clearly exacerbated the economy's problems (Blinder 1981).

This brief, bleak picture of the economy formed the backdrop for congressional investigation and proposals for action. In an unusual and ironic switch, Congress proved to be far ahead of the executive branch in perceiving the basic problem and formulating policies to regenerate the economy.

Senator Long opts for VAT

The chairmen of the two most important finance committees in Congress reached agreement in 1978 on the need to restructure incentives in order to encourage capital formation, efficiency, and economic growth. Senator Russell Long (1978:6), then chairman of the Senate Finance Committee, opened public discussion of the value added tax when he proposed that it be substituted for income and social security taxes. In an important speech before the Tulane Tax Seminar in New Orleans on November 30, 1978, he noted that the punitive rates of taxation on income created by corporations had reached 84 percent. Senator Long urged abandoning use of the income tax to effect wholesale redistribution of income and wealth because high rates of taxation were discouraging work and investment.

The corporation profits tax discourages saving because it reduces the rewards for saving. It also takes most of its yield from individuals with a relatively high propensity to save, precisely those people who would otherwise make funds available for capital formation. There is little doubt that replacing the corporate tax with a VAT would have strong, positive effects on capital formation, the capital-to-labor ratio, and real wages (McLure 1980b:310).

Senator Long (1978:7) also recommended that revenues from the VAT replace those from social security taxes. The effect of such a substitution is not clear. Some analysts believe that at least part of the payroll levy is a tax on employment that inhibits the hiring of workers, adds to business costs, and reduces the output of goods and services. Researchers also contend that social security taxes alter the relative price of leisure and work, inducing workers to decrease their supply of labor (Hafer and Trebing 1980:7); but, as previously noted, the VAT is not neutral between leisure and labor.

Substituting value added taxes for the payroll levy is not apt to have much impact on saving and capital formation in the long run. Income generated by capital is not subject to social security taxes. On the other hand, under the VAT, income that is saved or invested is not taxable until spent for consumption.

Senator Long's address at the Tulane Tax Seminar generated enormous interest in value added taxation in the United States. All the major newspapers, news magazines, and television news broadcasts carried stories about the tax. The principal negative reaction came from the Carter administration ("Blumenthal Says . . ." 1979:7). Charles Schultze, then chairman of the President's Council of Economic Advisors, noted that "a sales or value added tax goes right into the consumer price index," which, in turn, "leads through cost-of-living allowances to higher wages and still higher prices." Treasury Secretary Michael Blumenthal said he was not unsympathetic, but it was clear that the administration was cool toward a VAT. Some critics opposed the levy because the huge revenues produced could be used to finance unneeded programs, it would be difficult to administer, and it could preempt state and local taxes (Tate 1979:5A). Other opponents labeled the VAT unfair because it could be regressive (Kraus 1979:22; Pierson 1980:48). Additional reaction ranged from healthy skepticism to warm acceptance (Fritchey 1979:5A; Halverson 1979c:11).

Chairman Ullman's proposal: The general response to the suggested use of a VAT convinced both Senator Long and Representative Ullman, chairman of the House Ways and Means Committee, to hold hearings on proposed legislation. In September 1979, in a speech at a tax conference sponsored by the United States Chamber of Commerce, Mr. Ullman outlined in detail his plan to restructure the entire federal tax structure. Initial reaction was favorable

("Plan to Shift . . ." 1979:1, 6) and induced Mr. Ullman to introduce the Tax Restructuring Act the following month ("Ullman Introduces . . ." 1979:3).

The Ullman (1980:52–5) act would restructure the tax system to promote growth in investment and productivity. Total tax reductions were predicted to equal $130 billion on a calendar year basis. Net proceeds from the VAT imposed by the bill were to match the $130 billion tax reduction.

The social security tax rate, which was then 6.13 percent and scheduled to increase to 6.65 percent in 1981, would be reduced to 4.5 percent, saving employees and employers approximately $52 billion. There would be comparable rate reductions for the self-employed.

The individual income tax would be cut by approximately $50 billion in 1981, and $42 billion of this sum would be concentrated in the middle income tax brackets. To further encourage capital formation, the maximum tax rate on investment income would be reduced to 50 percent, matching the rate on wages and salaries. At the same time, there would be more generous credits and increased benefit payments to the working poor and welfare recipients.

The bill would also permit the creation of special savings accounts into which individuals could deposit up to $1,000 per year, and the earnings on the principal would not be taxable until withdrawn. To encourage further savings and investment, limits on individual retirement accounts (IRAs) would be increased to $2,000 per year, and new limited IRAs would be permitted for those not qualified for the old IRAs. Interest earned on these accounts would not be taxed until withdrawn at retirement. Similarly, dividend reinvestment plans would permit up to $1,500 per year to be reinvested and free of taxes until withdrawn.

Business taxes would be reduced by about $28 billion per year by cutting the top rate on corporate income from 46 to 36 percent and by widening the brackets and lowering the rates on corporate profits subject to less than the maximum rate. New investment would be encouraged further by permitting more rapid depreciation schedules for the wearing out of plant and equipment and by liberalizing the tax credit on assets with a useful life of three or more years.

The unique feature of the bill would impose the VAT at each stage of the production and distribution process, including the retail stage. The tax would generally be 10 percent of the value of property or services and would be included in the price that a business charges its customers. Each business in the production and distribution chain would receive a credit for the VAT previously paid on its purchases of property and services from other businesses (including purchases of plant and equipment). Thus, each business would pay a net tax equal to 10 percent of the value it adds to the product, and the total tax paid with respect to sales to customers would be 10 percent of the retail value of the product.

To avoid narrowing the VAT base, special rules or special tax rates would be limited except where considered absolutely essential. Food, medical care, and residential housing would be taxed at only a 5-percent rate at the retail level. Transactions of charities, public and private nonprofit educational institutions, mass transit, and nonretail sales by farmers and fishermen would be given a zero rate, which means there would be no tax but the taxpayer would receive applicable VAT credits. Governments and nonprofit organizations other than charities would be exempt from the VAT; they would pay no tax and get no credit. The bill provided special rules for real property, interest transactions, and insurance companies. Also, businesses that have sales of property and services below $10,000 per year could elect to be exempt from the VAT.

The VAT would be imposed on imports. Exports would be zero rated to permit a rebate of the VAT previously paid for goods and services associated with the export. In another provision of the bill, the social security tax reductions would be funded directly from value added tax receipts and not from income tax revenues.

Economic growth and the VAT

The principal reason Representative Ullman and Senator Long supported the Tax Restructuring Act of 1979 was its heavy emphasis on measures designed to regenerate the economy. They believed that replacing parts of the social security, personal, and corporate income taxes with the VAT would substantially increase the rate of economic growth.

Advocates noted that European countries using the VAT experienced rapid economic growth by relying more heavily on indirect taxes than did the United States. However, one is unlikely to reach acceptable conclusions about the role of tax systems in economic growth without having some idea of the relationship between fiscal variables and the growth process.

According to O. Eckstein and V. Tanzi (1961:268), tax policy and tax systems can affect economic growth in at least five ways. First, the automatic response of revenue to economic growth, together with expenditure trends, helps determine the level of aggregate demand. Second, the level of surplus or deficit of the budget adds or subtracts from the supply of saving. Third, the general character of the tax system influences the total rate of saving and investment. Fourth, specific structural characteristics influence both total savings and investment. Finally, specific policy measures that change the tax rates or the nature of the taxes themselves can influence growth, either by design or by accident.

A shift to a VAT would be conducive to a higher rate of saving because the proposed reduction of the corporate income tax would increase after-tax corporate profits, which would, in turn, be reflected in higher retained earnings and/or dividends. The marginal propensity to save out of dividends is normally higher than it is from other sources of income.

Increased saving, is of course, no advantage unless matched by increased investment. An important problem with the current U.S. economy, however, is that there are insufficient savings to channel into investment due largely to ill-advised government policies. Moreover, it is often argued that the business income tax, as a tax on profits, discourages risk taking because it is paid by efficient and profitable firms, not by their less efficient and unprofitable competitors. The VAT, on the other hand, as a tax on consumption, would be more or less neutral concerning risk taking. Therefore, from the standpoint of an efficient allocation of investment, substituting a VAT for the corporate income tax would lead to a greater internal generation of capital and dividends in profitable industries in which returns are high and, at the same time, to withdrawal of capital from the declining sectors.

The fate of the Tax Restructuring Act

Analysts generally agreed that the Tax Restructuring Act would reallocate resources from consumption toward investment. Economists at Data Resources Incorporated estimated that the Ullman bill would increase real expenditures on plant and equipment by 6.1 percent by 1985. Analysts at Evans Econometrics Incorporated put the increase in investment at 1.5 percent per year (Pierson 1980:48). Few individuals doubted the potential of the Tax Restructuring Act to promote economic growth.

At the same time, there were many competing ideas on how to change the tax code to regenerate the economy. One leading proposal was the 10–5–3 rapid depreciation bill that would reduce taxes on capital assets by permitting faster write-offs for buildings, equipment, trucks, and automobiles.

The least radical of the various tax alternatives making the rounds in Congress was Senator Bentsen's small savers bill, which would exclude from taxable income up to $200 received in interest and dividends for individuals and $400 for couples. Revenue estimators predicted that the cost to the Treasury would be between $2 billion and $3 billion annually, but estimates of the effect on savings ranged from imperceptible by Treasury officials to $4 billion by the United States League of Savings Associations (Pierson 1980:48).

Another competing tax program making the rounds in Congress was the Kemp–Roth bill. Its immediate aim was to counteract inflation-induced tax bracket creep by a straight across-the-board, 10-percent tax cut for three successive years.

The Tax Restructuring Act was the most massive and radical of all the alternatives to which Congress gave serious consideration. Mr. Ullman stated that his package of tax reductions and increases would be the largest adjustment in United States taxation since 1913, the year the individual tax was passed into law. His bill had many critics. The Treasury opposed it, as did the sponsors of the other aforementioned programs. Newly appointed Treasury Secretary William Miller contended that replacing part of individual income and social security taxes with a VAT would make the entire federal tax structure significantly less progressive. Liberal reformers opposed the Ullman bill, 10–5–3, the small savers bill, and Kemp–Roth on the grounds that they would be unfair to the poor because higher income recipients would benefit more from the tax reductions (Pierson 1980:48).

An important feature of the Tax Restructuring Act was the partial rather than full replacement of income and social security taxes. This characteristic lead to another serious criticism. It was feared that this new, very productive VAT would lead to further growth in an already rapidly expanding government (McLure 1980b:317). According to a Tax Foundation study, a consumption type VAT would produce about $11 billion for each one percentage point of its rate ("VAT . . ." 1979:3). As critics noted, this relatively invisible and painless source of large revenue might prove to be an exceedingly attractive source of funds for new spending programs. Moreover, after enactment of a VAT, it was easy to imagine Congress returning corporate and individual income rates to higher levels.

Senator Long (1978:7) had foreseen this possibility in his Tulane address, but Representative Ullman had not included any provisions that addressed this problem, which led to apprehension in the business community and other quarters. In response to criticism, Mr. Ullman introduced the Tax Restructuring Act of 1980, which included a provision that would limit total government spending to a fixed percentage of the gross national product. To diffuse the faultfinding of liberal reformers, he also proposed that food, shelter, medical care, and government services be exempt from the VAT (McLure 1980b:302).

The newly proposed features in the Tax Reconstruction Act of 1980 reduced estimated revenue from the VAT from $130 billion to $115 billion. It also blunted the charge that it was a regressive tax. Nevertheless, criticism and competition from alternative tax proposals were so large that the Ullman bill never came to a vote.

The VAT and the retail sales tax

Some opponents of the VAT have argued that if a tax on sales is to be adopted by the central government, then a retail sales tax is preferable. The VAT and a retail sales levy are both sales taxes, and, because each has virtually the same tax base, the economic effects would be similar. Moreover, a uniform tax rate for the two levies would produce about the same amount of revenue.

Both taxes are equally neutral with regard to methods and techniques of production.

In addition, the two forms of taxation have the following similarities: both have about the same international effects; both impinge about equally on that part of the country's tax base traditionally reserved for state and local governments; and either levy can be made as visible or as hidden to the consumer as desired by legislators and tax bureaucrats.

It is claimed that there would be less evasion under the VAT, but experience does not support this statement. The VAT is prevalent in Europe, where avoidance of taxes has been developed to a high art (Beman 1979:18). Tax experts claim that individuals in France and Italy annually evade billions of VAT dollars. In fact, an Italian Senate investigation revealed that Italians hide about $24 billion dollars in transactions from tax authorities using false invoices, underbilling, and fake sales receipts. These frauds cost the government $2.4 billion in VAT payments, or about 25 percent of total receipts of the value added tax. France also has a thriving underground economy in which only cash is accepted as payment for services. Recent evidence shows that Argentinians cope with triple-digit inflation and the VAT by using false invoices, receipts, and understated output records (Martin 1981:1, 18). It would appear that the VAT is not immune from evasion.

Critics make a strong case for using a retail sales tax if more indirect taxation is to be used. There is a wealth of experience at hand because businessmen and consumers are quite familiar with state and local retail sales taxes.

Summary and conclusion

Value added taxation represents a relatively new technique for calculating taxes on the output of economic enterprises. Experience in countries that have adopted a VAT shows that it is never levied in its pure form. For administrative, equity, and political reasons, changes and exemptions are made when implementing the tax. Consequently, the tax begins to lose its neutral characteristics. On the other hand, there is virtually unanimous agreement that a VAT would encourage saving and investment and promote economic growth.

The introduction of a VAT would necessarily increase the operating costs of the Internal Revenue Service by requiring new services and additional personnel. Furthermore, because both exemptions and differential tax rates are almost certain to be included in the structure of the VAT, there would be an additional increase in administrative costs.

The VAT would increase business compliance costs because it would require a new tax form and new accounting entries for collections and credits. Even with one uniform rate, the cost of administering the VAT would be relatively high. According to one estimate, collecting the levy in the United Kingdom costs companies approximately $1 billion a year, or about 12 percent of what the government receives from the tax. Government and consumer costs must, of course, be added to business costs to obtain the total cost of collection to society.

Proponents list several advantages of the VAT. It would:

1.   be based on consumption, and thus provide a relatively stable revenue base;
2.   be relatively neutral in its economic effects;
3.   encourage savings;
4.   have a large revenue potential. Each one percentage point in the rate would produce about $11 billion in revenue; and
5.   help balance the rapidly rising, progressive tax bracket creep of the individual income tax.

Opponents list several disadvantages of the VAT. It would:

6.   lead to excessive government spending and waste;
7.   be harmful to new and marginal business activities;
8.   exacerbate inflationary pressures;
9.   be regressive in its pure form;
10. be a tax hidden from the consumer because it would be incorporated into the price of goods and services; and
11. conflict with retail sales taxes on which state and local governments rely.

Despite several attempts to introduce a VAT in the United States, none has been adopted at the federal level. One reason often stated is that virtually all the economic effects of a VAT are likely to be shared by a retail sales tax. Therefore, if it is decided that the federal government should impose a broad-based consumption tax, it does not necessarily follow that a VAT is the best alternative. Administrative considerations and the familiarity with the retail approach suggest that the retail sales tax may be preferable to the VAT as a route toward taxation of consumption. For most economists, the expenditure tax would be superior to both types of sales tax.

CHAPTER 10

The sales tax

Introduction

The sales tax, after the federal income tax, is probably the tax most familiar to the American taxpayer. Most consumers confront retail sales taxation on a daily basis and give it little thought. It is simply a part of the shopper's life. The sales tax has an obvious meaning to consumer and economist alike; it is a tax, generally ad valorem, on the transfer of commodities and services, usually at the retail level. An ad valorem tax is one in which the product bears a uniform percentage of the purchase price.

The sales tax is not necessarily a single-stage tax. It can be levied at any number of points in the production and distribution process. In reality, the sales tax is often a combination of a turnover tax and a single-stage tax (Morgan 1964:7). Although the sales tax base can vary considerably, the sales tax is not an excise tax that is a specific selective levy (Due 1957:3). Normally, the sales tax applies to a general category of goods (e.g., all retail commodities), with any exemptions made explicit. Although the sales levy is very similar in economic effect to the business occupation tax, it can be distinguished by legislative intent. The sales tax is implicitly or explicitly made with the intent that the levy will be passed forward to the purchaser, whereas the gross receipts occupation tax is on business per se for the privilege of doing business (Due 1971:2).

The most common form of the sales tax is the levy on retail sales. Difficulty in precisely defining the sales tax is enhanced by the problem associated with clearly understanding what is meant by retail sale. Purchases from one business to another are not usually considered by the economist or layman to be retail sales, but most state sales tax statutes consider a retail sale any sale in which the buyer does not intend to resell the purchased item.

It is virtually impossible to give a precise definition of a retail sales tax. Legislators give retail sales taxes many different names, and the levies take many different forms. Nevertheless, the definition of a retail sale, particularly as it applies to business, is important insofar as economic effect is concerned because a sales tax can be both a tax on consumption and investment. Intelligent arguments for and against a retail sales tax must keep this fact in mind.

217

Significance

Because of the federal system of government in the United States, the states directly provide many public services. As a result, much of revenue-raising responsibility rests with the states. However, the states have, as a practical matter, relatively limited revenue sources. Aside from the sales tax, the only other important nonincome taxes available to the states are business excise levies, taxes on liquor and cigarettes, and severance taxes (Due 1971:4). The retail sales tax is the most significant source of state tax revenue. In calendar year 1983, the various sales taxes provided $116 billion to all United States governments (*Quarterly Summary* 1984:1).

Sales taxes are of limited significance at the federal level of government. In 1983, they produced just over 7 percent of total federal revenue. All federal excise and sales taxes are selective, that is, they are imposed on specific products (e.g., tobacco, alcohol, gasoline, and telephone services), usually at the manufacturer's level, rather than on a wide range of retail commodities.

Development and history

The sales tax in the United States was a grass-roots phenomenon that grew out of American experimentation. John F. Due (1971:1–2) writes, "It was influenced very little by experience with sales taxation in other countries and represented the first significant use of sales taxes at the retail level in the world." The American ancestor to the sales tax was the business occupation tax, distinguished from the modern sales tax by legislative intent. The business occupation tax is a levy on business and not intended to be passed forward to the purchaser, as is true of the sales tax.

The first, modern state retail sales tax was legislated in Mississippi in the early 1930s, when that state changed its business occupation levy to a sales tax. This change took place by eliminating most of the levy's multistage application and raising the tax rate to 2 percent from a fractional figure. Because Mississippi's new tax was so successful as a revenue raiser, other states soon passed sales tax legislation. In the years 1933–8, twenty-six states (including Hawaii) imposed the tax, although five of those states allowed it to expire after one or two years (Due 1971:5).

One important factor largely explains the introduction and rapid spread of the sales tax. The economic depression of the 1930s reduced state revenues from other taxes at the same time that expenditures for relief needs were increasing and state participation in federal programs requiring some state revenue was increasing. Thus, the sales tax with its low rate, large yield, and easy collection became very attractive to financially strapped states (Due 1971:2–5).

Just as economic depression helped to begin the spread of a new state revenue source, prosperity inhibited the spread of the state sales tax. But following World War II, new demands were made for state expenditures, particularly for education. Other available revenue sources could not fully accommodate the new demands. State officials were generally wary of raising the income tax for fear of driving out business and meeting popular resistance. Moreover, the property tax remained almost entirely a local government revenue source. Consequently, in 1947, a slow trend began toward renewal or adoption of the sales tax. By the beginning of 1983, a total of forty-five states and the District of Columbia used a sales tax.

Structure and characteristics of the sales tax

There are three types of sales taxes: vendor, consumer, and hybrid. Although the types differ in structure, particularly by the legal basis of imposition, all three operate with basic uniformity.

A vendor tax is a levy on the privilege of engaging in business as a retailer. In this sense, the vendor tax is very similar in structure to the gross receipts business occupation tax. J. F. Due (1971:25) reasonably calls vendor taxes sales taxes because the legislative intent at the time of enactment was probably for the tax to be passed onto the purchaser, even though such an act is not required by the law. Legislative intent is very clear in some states that require shifting insofar as possible.

Several states employ what can be called a consumer sales tax, that is, a levy imposed on a retail sale. The measure of liability is the selling price rather than gross receipts, as in the case of vendor and business occupation taxes. All of the consumer tax states require separate quotation of the tax and prohibit retailers from advertising that they are absorbing the burden of the tax.

In some states, the sales tax is a hybrid tax because it contains features of both the vendor and consumer levies. Legal responsibility for the tax lies with the vendor, although the seller is required to collect the tax from the consumer.

Many years of experience with all three types of sales taxes operating in the United States have shown that all three work satisfactorily. If there is a major advantage in one type, it is in the vendor tax because full legal responsibility for payment is clear and undivided (Due 1971:26).

Stages of imposition

The sales tax can be imposed at one or more stages in the distribution and production process. The policy choices are two: a single-stage or multiple-stage sales tax. A multiple stage tax is a turnover tax that involves every stage of production at a low percentage of each production sale, regardless of the value added. Thus, the total tax liability of a product, as a percentage of the final selling price, depends on the number of transactions entered in the production process. A single-stage sales tax is levied at only one stage in the production or distribution process (e.g., manufacturer or retail level).

There are several disadvantages and only one advantage to the multiple-stage tax. This form of the sales tax produces serious economic distortions among business firms in terms of tax burden as a function of the number of sales transactions taxed per firm. A turnover tax can also create serious import–export problems.

In practice, the turnover tax is not applied in pure form but characterized by rate differentiation, which greatly increases administrative costs. Because of the importance of the number of transactions leading to the final retail sale, the turnover tax leads to nonuniformity in consumer burden. The only advantage of a multiple-stage sales tax is that it can obtain a given revenue at a lower average tax rate. This factor may be a political concern when high tax rates are considered undesirable by the citizenry. The United States has never used a turnover tax.

The advantage of a single-stage sales tax is that all the disadvantages of the multiple-stage levy are avoided. A disadvantage of the single-stage tax, when compared with the multiple-stage levy, is that it requires a higher rate to obtain a given sum of money. Moreover, one group of firms must face the entire burden of dealing with the tax (Due 1957:358).

Once the decision is made to employ a single-stage tax, then a collection stage must be selected. There are three possible collection stages: the manufacturing, wholesale, or retail level. The best choice for the stage of imposition depends essentially on the desired coverage of the sales tax.

If the coverage is to be general and wide, then a retail sales tax is preferable because a uniform ad valorem rate can then be imposed. With an equal rate, ad valorem manufacturer sales tax, discrimination and resource allocation distortion will result at the retail level because the ratio of retail to manufacturer's prices differs among products (Musgrave and Musgrave 1976:329). When a general sales tax is desired, a tax imposed at the wholesale level creates the same undesirable effects as the manufacturer sales levy. Given a choice for a general sales tax, the retail base is clearly preferable.

If a sales tax is to be selective, that is, levied on a specific group of products (as with federal sales taxes in the United States), then the best stage for imposition is not clear. If a specific product is to be taxed, then differentiation from similar products must be possible. The appropriate stage of collection is then unique to the product in question. If a nonretail tax is deemed more appropriate, then whether a manufacturer or wholesaler is more preferable is even less clear because neither form has overwhelming advantages.

Forms

Most sales taxes in the United States are purely retail sales taxes, and the general nature of most sales taxes makes an ad valorem form attractive. The alternative to an ad valorem form, a specific or unit tax, suffers from efficiency disadvantages. Because a unit tax is a tax on the quantity of sales rather than on the value of sales (as with an ad valorem levy), the producer may be induced to make inefficient adjustments to the unit in which the product is sold. Also, a unit tax is not tied to inflation (as prices rise, the tax per unit remains the same) and, thus, is not as reliable a source of revenue during inflationary periods. The sales tax base can take one of three forms: a levy on consumption only, on consumption plus investment, or on all turnover. Most sales taxes in the United States attempt to be consumption based. Most state and local sales taxes in the United States are retail in nature and take an ad valorem form.

Exclusions and exemptions from sales taxes

A general sales tax attempts comprehensive coverage of consumption. In practice, however, the wide base of a truly general consumption tax is narrowed by legislative exclusions and exemptions.

Sales not subject to a tax can be divided into two categories. The first category consists of those sales excluded from the definition of taxable sales, that is, certain goods purchased for business rather than personal use. The second category includes consumption goods that are specifically exempted from taxation by legislative act. In this survey, exceptions to sales taxation of producers' goods are called exclusions; all exceptions to the taxation of consumer goods are called exemptions.

Exclusions

Many retail sales are made from one business to another. One estimate of the business portion of the sales tax as a percentage of total sales tax yield is between 15 and 25 percent, defying the widely held belief that the sales tax is purely a consumer tax (Morgan 1964:20–7). This fairly high yield is a reflection of the failure of policymakers to take into account the economic rationale of not taxing capital goods that are to be used in future production. Legislative realization of the evils of multiple-stage taxation, however, is found in the exclusion of producers' goods from sales taxes in some jurisdictions.

Some states employ what can be called a direct use rule. That is, materials and goods that are directly dispensed in the process of production are excluded from taxation. Some examples of excluded items are fuel, electricity, cleaning agents, and grease and oil used in machines. The importance of the direct use rule is that it increases the number of exclusions that are used as components in the production of a final good. A true consumption-based sales tax is more closely approximated.

Among producers' goods that are excluded are the following:

1. In nearly all states, sales for resale are excluded without specific exemption.
2. About two-thirds of the states exclude some items with a direct use rule.
3. All states using a direct use rule that provides for the general exemption of producer goods also exclude industrial fuels (except Wisconsin).
4. Industrial power is fully taxed in several states. In the other states, industrial power is partially or fully excluded.
5. Machinery was generally taxed in the earlier days of sales taxation. On economic grounds, exclusion of capital is clearly warranted, and there has been a trend toward the exclusion of machines.
6. The treatment of agricultural goods varies widely. Over half the states exclude from tax the sales of livestock feed, fertilizer, and seed to those persons engaged in the production of farm goods for sale. Farm livestock sold by individual farmers is never taxed, and the sale of livestock by commercial dealers is rarely taxed. Insecticides sold for farm use or for producing food are excluded from tax by most states that exempt feed, seed, and fertilizer. Paralleling the trend with regard to industrial machinery, farm machinery, which at one time was almost universally taxed, is increasingly being excluded.

Exemptions of consumer goods

The second category of goods for which special exemption is made are those that fit the definition of taxable sale but are specifically exempted for political, administrative, or social reasons. The social benefits of any exemption must be weighed carefully against the three general economic costs of exemption. First, the tax base is eroded and revenue is reduced. Second, exemption results in a relocation of resources and in consumer excess burden because consumers shift from taxed to untaxed goods and, in the process, lose satisfaction. At the same time, government receives no additional revenue. Third, administration, audit, and compliance become more difficult and costly.

Although the sales tax coverage of commodities is relatively broad in most states, there are several major exemptions. Because an alleged objection to a sales tax is that it is regressive, many states exempt food in one way or another. Two general approaches are used to provide relief to low income families.

First, in fifteen states, all or almost all food is exempted from the sales tax. Second, some states offer a credit against income taxes representing tax paid on certain necessities.

Other important exemptions include household fuel, utility service, drugs and medicine, and clothing. A few states exempt newspapers, other periodicals, and books.

A major exemption is for goods subject to special excises. Even though an argument exists supporting such an exemption, there is little justification for it. This unfortunate exemption is discussed in more detail later in this chapter.

Some exemptions are made by class of vendor or purchaser. For example, twenty-three states and the District of Columbia exempt purchases by all charitable, religious, and educational institutions, and nonprofit hospitals of items bought for their own use and consumption. Also, if a state uses a tax that the courts consider to rest on the consumer, then because of constitutional reasons the state cannot tax sales to the federal government.

Exemptions are usually made for noneconomic reasons and at the cost of narrowing the taxable base of consumer goods. Exclusion of producers' goods is economically justified and done to promote a truly single-state retail sales tax on consumer goods.

Sales taxation of services

Most sales taxes are confined to tangible property even though there is no fundamental justification for the exemption of such intangible goods as services. J. F. Due (1971:86–7) offers several basic reasons for including services in the base for sales taxation. First, expenditure on services and the purchase of goods are both consumer expenditures that satisfy wants in a similar manner.

Secondly, when services are taxed, greater revenue is gained from a given tax rate. For example, Iowa extended its tax to include a wide range of services and in so doing increased its tax yield by about 12 percent. Moreover, the expansion of the tax base through the inclusion of services avoids adverse effects, such as the loss of business to out-of-state firms because of a tax rate hike.

Thirdly, because expenditures on services may tend to rise as income rises, the broad taxation of services may push the distribution of the sales tax burden toward progressivity rather than regressivity.

However, D. G. Davies (1970:138–46) finds that taxation of utility services, housing services, and medical care makes the tax more regressive. The most progressive effect on taxing services comes from the taxation of insurance. However, Davies's general conclusion is that taxing services has little impact on the distribution pattern.

Another advantage of taxing services is that administration is simplified.

Vendors (e.g., repair shops) who previously had to distinguish between sales and services no longer have to do so. An excess burden would also be avoided for those vendors.

Which services should be taxed? It is rather obvious that services of employees should not be taxed because double taxation would result, a tax on final retail sales and a tax on factor services or incomes. Daniel C. Morgan, Jr. (1964:122) offers a general guide for selecting services to be taxed. He would include all services sold at retail for personal satisfaction. Although a general tax on services purchased by consumers is advisable, it is not yet widely found in practice.

In the early days of the first sales taxes, only the sale of tangible personal property was taxed. This made the system relatively simple, and it conformed to the widely held belief that a tax on service is a tax on labor. With increased revenue demands, the administrative difficulties caused by the failure to tax services, and the realization that equity justifies the taxation of services as well as of tangible products, there has been a transition toward the taxing of services; but change has been slow.

Local government sales taxes

Just as the state sales tax was a product of economic difficulty and the need for more revenue, so was the municipal sales tax. In 1934, the City of New York enacted the first municipal sales tax in North America. The 2-percent levy was part of a program to finance unemployment relief. With the passing of the depression, the city sales tax remained. By 1955, the tax rate was 3 percent and the tax yielded $312 million, more than any state sales tax except Michigan or California. The tax yielded about 27 percent of total city tax revenue (Due 1957:315).

A key development that made the effective use of a municipal sales tax possible was the 1950 introduction of a state-administered local sales tax in Mississippi. State involvement in administration goes hand in hand with the state authorization by constitution or statute that is needed for a local government sales tax. By January 1971, local governments in twenty-three states and the District of Columbia had levied a sales tax. Of 153 municipalities with a population of 100,000 or more, 72 were obtaining revenue from sales taxes (Mikesell 1971:266–7). Recent data show that the sales tax produced about 14 percent of total tax revenue for all local governments and a little more than 26 percent for all municipalities. Now, nearly 4,000 local governments use a sales tax.

There are problems associated with a local sales tax, the most troublesome one being the shifts in purchasing that result from rate differentials between jurisdictions. The move away from local administration of local sales taxes should help this situation.

Use taxes

To avoid revenue losses due to out-of-state purchasing, all states using sales taxes impose use taxes on the initial use of goods purchased outside of the state but brought into the state for use. In terms of collection, the use tax is the weakest part of the system of sales and use taxes. It is difficult to prevent revenue leakage on mail order sales made by firms that do not operate retail stores in the home jurisdiction. However, states generally offer credit for sales tax paid in other states and try to eliminate discrimination against interstate commerce.

State tax administration is operated through a tax or revenue department headed by a commissioner or director appointed by the governor and who serves at the governor's discretion. Administration of sales taxes is rarely the direct responsibility of an elected official.

Every state with a sales tax has some kind of system for registering vendors. Collection of the tax and tax liability of the vendor are determined by a system that either requires the payment of the tax on each individual sale or collects tax on the basis of periodic returns, usually monthly or quarterly. The latter system is preferable and more popular. Most states have an audit system to check on delinquency and the amount of tax paid.

Evaluation of the sales tax

The economist as scientist can state with some authority, regarding standards for evaluating the sales tax, that the structure of the tax should not create such market distortions as the misallocation of resources, disturbance of distribution channels, and loss of productivity efficiency. Moreover, the administration of the tax should be managed in an optimal manner. Beyond these two important points, the economist can make the general observation that the tax structure should be designed to promote goals determined by society and embodied in legislation made by elected policymakers.

Economic effects

The analysis of the sales tax in practice indicates that the levy in the United States does not tax a true consumption base, nor does it tax a base of consumption plus investment. Although most tangible consumer goods and many new business investment goods are included in the base, most services are not taxed, and many values are taxed more than once in the production–distribution process. If the sales tax is intended to be a uniform tax on consumer expenditures, then evaluation of current practice reveals that the intention has not been fulfilled.

The objections to multiple-stage sales taxation have been set forth. The importance of excluding producers' goods from sales taxation has also been noted. If the sales tax is to be general and widely applied, then the best form of a single-stage tax in terms of economic effects is a retail levy with the exclusion of most producers' goods.

Like other forms of taxation, the sales tax creates a disincentive on work effort. Prices of consumption goods are often raised and, thus, the real wage is reduced. Unless wage earners suffer from money illusion, disincentive effects will result (Musgrave and Musgrave 1976:485). As is discussed later, however, the sales tax disincentive effects may be less than those created by an income tax.

The real economic costs of a sales tax go beyond the loss of consumer expenditure power, disincentive effects, and the costs of administration. The vendor's cost to meet compliance requirements must also be taken into account. These costs take the form of additional bookkeeping, clerical, and computer time. Although many studies have ignored these costs, one conducted under the sponsorship of the Ohio State University's Bureau of Business Research concluded that the average cost of compliance was 3.93 percent of tax liability (Due 1971:313).

Advantages

An advantage of the sales tax is that it avoids the adverse effects on economic incentives created by a progressive income tax. The sales tax does not affect the earnings from new capital equipment as does the income tax, which lessens both the supply of capital available for expansion and the incentive to expand. The income tax may also adversely affect work effort more so than the sales tax. However, such a claim must be stated with caution because comparison must be made between taxes of equal yield, and that is difficult to do in this case.

A second advantage of the retail sales tax is that it is easier to administer than an income tax (Due 1957:31). The costs of administration and compliance, taken together, are relatively low. Moreover, as the history of the retail sales tax demonstrates, the low-rate tax has been a very successful source of revenue for the states and local governments that have adopted it.

Finally, although the retail sales tax is sometimes overlooked by the consumer, it still remains an evident form of taxation. This is an advantage in that it tends to emphasize the public accountability of politicians.

Disadvantages

The most popular argument made against the sales tax is one of equity. It is alleged that the sales tax is regressive because it places a relatively greater burden on consumers who spend a higher percentage of their incomes on taxable goods, in other words, the poor. Modern research, however, indicates that many sales taxes are either roughly proportional or progressive (Davies 1960b, 1980).

A second argument is that the sales tax in practice contains a host of minor defects that result in economic distortions, inequities, complicated adminis- tration, and unnecessary loss of revenue. A few examples of such defects are:

1. motor vehicles are taxed at lower rates than other goods;
2. some states fail to tax rentals of tangible personal property, which is an illogical exemption; and
3. club dues usually go untaxed and represent an attractive item for tax base expansion.

Each of these practices introduces economic distortions into the system.

J. F. Due (1957:386–7) does not consider the sales tax an ideal form of taxation in practice; but even if it must be considered second best, minor defects in structure could be eliminated and the major adverse effects miti- gated with changes in the laws.

Proposals for reform of the sales tax

There are two pressing needs for reform. First, sales from one business to another should be excluded whenever administratively possible. Second, ser- vices performed for households should be taxed, with very few exceptions. One justifiable exception is permanent housing rentals, which should not be taxed in order to avoid discrimination in favor of consumers using owner- occupied housing.

Morgan (1964:120) offers three guidelines for reform of a consumption- based sales tax that serve as tests against which all calls for special exceptions must be compared:

1. Tax only consumption expenditure items.
2. Tax all consumption expenditure.
3. Tax only sales to final (nonbusiness) consumers.

The mistakes of the original sales tax laws need to be redressed, even at the cost of opposing special interest groups.

In jurisdictions where regressivity is a problem, a program of credit against income tax, which permits a subsistence level of expenditure free from taxa- tion, will mitigate this difficulty. The credit can take many different forms in practice. Seven states and the District of Columbia use a credit program. A credit against income tax is very effective for eliminating regressivity at the lower end of the income scale and making the tax more progressive over a wide range of incomes. There are some administrative problems associated with the credit, such as providing a net refund to the very poor, but discrimination and unnecessary loss of revenue are essentially eliminated (Musgrave and Musgrave 1976:331–3).

Unjustifiable exemptions should be repealed. Perhaps the most regrettable exemptions are on goods that face special excises (e.g., cigarettes, liquor, and gasoline). The intent of the exemption is to avoid double taxation, but it makes little economic sense. If placing an excise on a good is justifiable before a sales tax is introduced, it would appear unjustifiable to reduce the relative burden of the excise by exempting it from the sales tax. Moreover, audit of and compliance with the sales tax are made more complicated with the exemption of goods facing special excises.

The sales taxation of farm purchases is generally difficult to solve. Taxing agricultural items equivalent to materials used in manufacturing, which are not normally taxed, is discriminatory, and taxing expensive machine equipment is contrary to the guideline of taxing only sales to final (nonbusiness) consumers. Farming is as much a business as is manufacturing and demands the same treatment. But because farmers are not registered vendors, exclusion by the usual certificate techniques is not possible. To help resolve this difficult problem, J. F. Due (1971:64) recommends exempting various economic inputs in the agricultural area.

Finally, change should occur in the area of local government sales taxation. At the least, standards need to be established calling for state administration, a uniform base of state and local taxes, and liability on location of vendor. A more radical approach would eliminate local sales taxes, raise the state tax rate, and distribute the revenues to local governments on the basis of population, per capita income, or some other standard of distribution. With the latter approach to reform, local government autonomy would be compromised, but this cost must be weighed against the costs of local administration of local taxes, economic distortions resulting in sharp rate differentials between localities, and increased overall administrative costs due to two layers of administration and compliance.

CHAPTER 11

State taxes

The state–local sector is the most dynamic and experimental in the use of taxes in our federal system. Since World War II, state–local tax revenues have grown more rapidly than those of the federal government. Furthermore, these governments have led the way in trying out such diverse revenue devices as lotteries, user fees, and constitutional limits on the level of taxation (Courant, Gramlich, and Rubenfeld 1980:8–20).

Reasons for growth in state–local taxes

There are several reasons for the relative growth of the state–local government sector of the economy. These factors help account for an increasing decentralization of financial affairs in federal countries since the end of World War II. A discussion of several of the factors pushing up state–local taxes follows (Davies 1977:65–82):

1. State–local governments in a federally structured country are originally assigned and tend to keep a wide variety of government functions that require resources for their fulfillment. The important areas of education, highways, health, welfare, and fire and police protection illustrate important responsibilities that are often assigned to state–local governments by constitutional authority. State–local jurisdictions will grow more rapidly than central governments if the income elasticity of demand for their services increases more rapidly than it does for federal programs. This factor has been operative in most countries since the end of World War II. Large increases in population and its density have fostered strong and increasing demands for precisely those goods and services that state–local governments provide.

2. A second factor that suggests the possibility of increasing fiscal decentralization is the so-called Baumol effect. W. J. Baumol observes (1967:415–26) that state–local governments, unlike the private sector, are little affected by technological change. He cites primary and secondary education as an illustration of an activity that has been little affected by technology. One teacher is still used for an average classroom of students. The minor changes that have affected the education of school-age children have not appreciably altered the pupil-to-teacher ratio. At the same time, there have been large increases of output and productivity in the private sector of the economy. If

there is mobility of individuals in labor markets, the salaries of state–local public servants will increase in line with salaries in the private sector, at the same time that the proportion of public servants in the work force is growing. Society will, therefore, need to devote an increasing share of its resources to state–local functions that are largely unaffected by changes in technology. Otherwise the level of state–local government services will decline.

3.   A third reason that may cause fiscal decentralization is related to the issue of efficiency. It is sometimes alleged that political or other nonmerit factors are more important in the recruitment of state–local personnel than is the case with federal employees. In addition, it is said that state–local employees are normally not as highly trained, as capable, or as efficient as their counterparts in the federal government. Although only a hypothesis, if these statements are found to be empirically verified, then appreciably more workers will be required to obtain a given level of state–local output. The increased payroll costs will be an important factor behind the growing financial importance of noncentral governments.

4.   The exportation of taxes from one state or local unit to the residents of another government enhances the possibility that these jurisdictions will grow relative to the federal government. Since nonresidents are helping to finance State A's expenditures, A's programs and services are a bargain to its citizen taxpayers. The cost of the services is lower to the citizen taxpayers of A as a result of the tax exportation, and, consequently, citizens will take more of these services. If the citizens of each jurisdiction reason in a similar way, the total taxes and expenditures for all state and local governments taken together will grow more rapidly than the expenditures of governments that are not affected by this factor. Ceteris paribus, one may expect that as government activity increases, public expenditure growth rates will be higher for state–local than for federal levels of government (McLure 1967:49–77).

5.   Another reason that may account for growth in the relative importance of state–local governments is the increasing self-awareness of minority groups within countries. The demands for public services are likely to be stable and somewhat alike within a country with a homogeneous population, but countries containing a diverse population may find the reverse true. The disenchantment of ethnic, radical, and other groups with the federal government has led such groups to petition smaller units of government to meet their demands for a variety of services. The votes of minority groups weigh more heavily in smaller units of government, where the total numbers of voters are less than in the nation as a whole. We can observe the phenomenon of increasing political power being exercised within lower levels of government by New Australians in Australia; French Canadians in Canada, Blacks, Indians, Puerto Ricans, Southeast Asians, and Mexican Americans in the United States; and various minorities in Great Britain and other parts of Europe.

6. One last factor should be noted in the list of plausible reasons the process of fiscal decentralization may be expected to increase. As Geoffrey Brennan (1975) notes, ''If a tax system is reasonably progressive to start with, and imposes a marginal tax rate at the top end which approaches (or is equal to) that which is considered to be the highest feasible one, it is virtually inevitable that additional expenditures are financed in a less progressive way than existing expenditures are, and that the progression of the income tax should decline with increasing revenue demands.'' As this process of decreasing progression continues, federal financing of public projects becomes less attractive relative to state–local financing. The tax–price bargain provided to low income earners through the progressive federal income tax becomes less of a bargain, and, ceteris paribus, state–local jurisdictions become more important as providers of social output. Even if a federal government violates the constraint on the marginal rate of taxation and increases its tax rates, for example, from 0 to 5 percent on the lowest income class and from 50 to 55 percent on the highest income class, such a tax is only proportional at the margin. Although the overall tax structure remains progressive after the change in rates, the federal tax system is less progressive than previously. As a result, the tax–price bargain or federally provided service is made less attractive to many citizen voters.

Suppose further that an increase in government expenditures is financed by inflation rather than by an increase in discretionary tax rates. Although the effect is capricious and not as certain as the effect of a change in tax rates, under these circumstances most individuals will find that their nominal incomes increase. In the absence of indexation, they will be subject to higher tax rates, even though their pre-tax real incomes may be declining. Once again, the tax–price bargain of federally provided goods and services is made less attractive to many taxpaying consumers.

Table 11.1 shows the ratio of state–local taxes to total government taxes. The data indicate that the long-run trend of these taxes has been rising. Additional analysis also indicates that the elasticity of state–local taxes with respect to GNP is greater than the elasticity of total taxes to GNP. State–local taxation has truly been a growth industry (Bahl 1980).

Features of state–local taxes

Two features that characterize our state–local tax structure are its relative stability in revenue over time and the mild progressivity in the burden of the system. States rely largely on personal income and retail sales taxes, whereas local governments depend heavily on property taxes. Modern research recognizes that these levies are roughly proportional or mildly progressive. Researchers also find that states are becoming more susceptible to the busi-

Table 11.1. *Ratio of provincial–state–local taxes to total governmental taxes*

Year	Australia[a]	United States[b]	United States[c]	Canada[c]	West Germany[b]	Switzerland[b]
1947			.240	.232	.236	
1948		.269	.258	.282		
1949	.118	.316	.297	.309		
1950	.126	.277	.265	.310		
1951	.109	.243	.235	.274	.410	
1952	.120	.247	.242	.259	.399	
1953	.125	.255	.248	.263	.405	.512
1954	.135	.288	.277	.286	.403	
1955	.142	.281	.270	.291	.402	.508
1956	.145	.289	.276	.291	.418	.476
1957	.151	.297	.281	.324	.439	.536
1958	.157	.319	.301	.356	.443	.484
1959	.182	.348	.295	.349	.453	.524
1960	.174	.325	.300	.352	.470	.503
1961	.164	.337	.310	.364	.475	.527
1962	.176	.338	.309	.407	.471	.505
1963	.186	.339	.308	.417	.463	.530
1964	.185	.360	.328	.410	.561	.501
1965	.175	.360	.327	.422	.452	.531
1966	.173	.399	.318	.419	.442	.514
1967	.180	.371	.325	.433	.444	.548
1968	.179	.361	.321	.439	.451	.536
1969	.180	.362	.320	.431	.455	.553
1970	.174	.398	.349	.441	.448	.546
1971	.165	.423	.366	.440	.449	.562
1972	.190	.420	.363	.441	.488	.552
1973	.213	.420	.353	.439	.478	.592
1974	.203	.391	.391	.412	.489	.595
1975	.199	.417	.349	.424	.477	.622
1976	.206	.406	.341	.426	.482	.591
1977	.202	.414	.361	.488	.486	.599
1978	.203	.414	.352	.509	.483	.584
1979	.201	.398	.335	.500		
1980	.194	.394	.333	.491		
1981[d]		.382	.357	.463		

[a] Australia has no separate social security tax.
[b] Excludes social security contributions.
[c] Includes social security contributions.
[d] Through the third quarter of the year.
Sources: Commonwealth Bureau of Census and Statistics and Australian Bureau of Statistics, Australian National Accounts, National Income and Expenditure, various years; U.S. Depart-

ness cycle as they increase their reliance on income taxes. Consequently, this tax has added an element of increased instability in revenue production over recent years (White 1983:103–14).

Ironically, it is precisely during this recent trend that state governments have relied increasingly on economic growth rather than legislated increases in rates for additional revenue. The Advisory Commission on Intergovernmental Relations (ACIR) has found that more than half the increase in revenues between 1968 and 1970 was due to legislative action, but by 1975–77 the figure had dropped to less than one-fourth (Gold 1983:9). Moreover, during 1978, 1979, and 1980, thirty-two states reduced their taxes on sales or personal income. The largest number of reductions occurred in 1979 following the enactment and impact of Proposition 13 (Gold 1983:9).

Proposition 13

The most recent dramatic fiscal event affecting state and local taxation was the taxpayer revolt, which started with the 1978 passage of Proposition 13 in California. This change in California's constitution severely limited the ability of local governments to increase property taxes. Since that time, many local jurisdictions and nineteen states have instituted statutory or constitutional limitations on expenditures or revenues. Table 11.2 clearly indicates the impact of the revolt on expenditures and employment.

At the same time, forty-three state legislatures considered tax bills in 1983 that would have increased revenue by more than $12 billion annually. The reasons for this activity in the face of the tax revolt are complex, but a major factor is the economic recession, which has had the effect of depressing revenue while putting upward pressure on spending, especially social expenditures. Moreover, the federal government has been decreasing its rate of aid to states. Federal aid as a proportion of total state revenue declined from 24.8 percent in 1970 to 23.3 percent in 1982 (Gold 1983:8).

Table 11.3 shows the national totals of tax revenues for all levels of government, by type of tax, for 1985 and prior periods. The data for the last twelve-month period shows state–local governments collecting about 44 percent of total United States taxes and the central government making up the balance with 56 percent of total taxes levied.

ment of Commerce, The National Income and Product Accounts of the United States, 1929–65, and Survey of Current Business, various years; Dominion Bureau of Statistics, Canada, National Accounts, Income and Expenditure 1926–56, National Accounts and Expenditures by Quarter, 1947–61, and National Accounts and Expenditures, various quarters; United Nations, Yearbook of National Accounts Statistics, 1969 and 1972; OECD, Revenue Statistics of OECD Member Countries, 1965–1971; and OECD, National Account Statistics, various years.

Table 11.2. *The tax revolt's effect on state–local expenditures and employment: state–local expenditure and personnel growth before and after proposition 13*

	Average annual percent increase or decrease (−)			
	Per capita expenditures (adjusted for inflation)		Public employment (per 1000 population)	
State and region	1957–1978	1978–1981	1957–1978	1978–1981
United States Total	4.40%	0.54%	2.7%	−1.1%
New England				
Connecticut	2.85	0.52	2.2	1.2
Maine	4.66	−1.12	2.6	−0.1
Massachusetts	4.03	−0.10	2.0	−0.5
New Hampshire	3.43	1.12	2.4	−0.9
Rhode Island	5.17	2.08	2.9	−0.6
Vermont	4.49	−1.39	2.9	−0.7
Mideast				
Delaware	4.63	2.30	3.4	−0.7
Dist. of Columbia	7.12	−1.31	5.0	−0.8
Maryland	4.86	−1.39	3.6	−2.2
New Jersey	4.68	1.15	3.0	0.0
New York	4.89	0.24	1.9	1.6
Pennsylvania	4.93	−0.82	2.8	−0.6
Great Lakes				
Illinois	4.49	0.97	2.7	−0.6
Indiana	3.56	2.88	2.6	−0.2
Michigan	4.30	0.40	2.7	−3.2
Ohio	4.16	0.71	2.5	−0.2
Wisconsin	4.44	1.90	3.0	−0.1
Plains				
Iowa	4.22	0.65	2.6	−0.7
Kansas	3.55	1.97	2.5	0.3
Minnesota	4.51	1.53	2.6	−0.2
Missouri	3.85	3.05	2.9	−0.4
Nebraska	4.68	0.60	3.1	−0.7
North Dakota	3.85	2.44	2.7	0.4
South Dakota	3.75	1.18	2.7	−0.8
Southeast				
Alabama	4.69	0.48	3.2	−1.1
Arkansas	4.89	1.48	2.9	0.2
Florida	3.90	−1.10	2.4	−3.9
Georgia	4.68	1.46	3.4	−1.4
Kentucky	5.34	−1.56	3.1	−1.9
Louisiana	3.37	3.22	2.4	−1.0
Mississippi	5.40	1.41	3.2	−0.4
North Carolina	5.03	0.50	3.5	−0.3
South Carolina	5.11	1.72	3.8	−3.6

Table 11.2. (*cont.*)

| | Average annual percent increase or decrease (−) | | | |
| State and region | Per capita expenditures (adjusted for inflation) | | Public employment (per 1000 population) | |
	1957–1978	1978–1981	1957–1978	1978–1981
Tennessee	5.23	−0.41	3.0	−1.1
Virginia	5.07	1.67	3.6	−2.7
West Virginia	5.72	0.55	3.8	−0.6
Southwest				
Arizona	3.88	−0.01	3.3	−4.1
New Mexico	3.64	3.59	3.0	1.1
Oklahoma	3.12	3.99	2.5	1.4
Texas	4.09	1.22	3.1	−1.5
Rocky Mountain				
Colorado	3.71	−0.42	2.9	−3.5
Idaho	3.96	−1.34	3.0	−2.1
Montana	4.05	−1.34	3.0	−2.1
Utah	4.18	0.36	2.7	−3.9
Wyoming	4.08	6.41	2.4	2.2
Far West				
California	4.11	−0.73	1.8	−2.2
Nevada	3.16	−0.99	2.7	−6.2
Oregon	4.48	0.23	2.5	−2.2
Washington	3.91	1.84	2.2	−3.1
Alaska	10.14	14.54	6.2	3.5
Hawaii	4.99	−3.76	2.3	−1.6

Source: Advisory Commission on Intergovernmental Relations, *Significant Features of Fiscal Federalism, 1981–82 Edition,* ACIR, Washington, April 1983, p. 2.

From the twelve-month period following Proposition 13 (June 1978–9) to the year ending in June 1984, total taxes of all levels of government rose from about $514 to $726 billion, or 41 percent. Interestingly, state and local governments, which felt the full impact of these tax constraining propositions, saw their tax revenue increase by nearly 58 percent; federal government levies rose by 27 percent (*Quarterly Summary* 1983:7; 1984:5).

Sources of state revenue

The structure of state taxes has changed markedly during the past eighty-five years. Property and excise taxes provided almost all of the states' revenues at the turn of the century. Presently, general sales, income, and taxes associated

Table 11.3. *National totals of federal, state and local tax revenue, by level of government and by type of tax: second quarter of 1985 and prior periods (Millions of dollars. Data not adjusted for seasonal variations.)*

| Period | Total | Level of tax-imposing government | | Indiv. income | Corp. net income | Property | General sales, gross receipts, customs | Motor fuel sales | Tobacco product sales | Alcoholic beverage sales | All other |
		Federal	State and local								
Quarters											
1985:2nd	217,375	127,049	90,326	110,300	27,094	21,542	24,712	6,441	2,048	2,091	23,147
1st	193,789	105,080	88,709	94,572	17,134	27,851	24,056	6,283	2,640	2,037	19,216
1984:4th	196,152	106,369	89,783	94,096	17,156	32,734	23,615	6,263	1,849	2,106	18,333
3rd	187,697	110,763	76,934	96,238	18,372	21,565	22,754	6,037	2,359	2,207	18,165
2nd	197,176	112,868	84,308	94,501	26,633	20,213	23,241	5,704	2,236	2,172	22,476
1st	175,399	93,351	82,048	85,914	13,090	25,831	22,135	5,707	2,193	2,136	18,393
1983:4th	181,163	97,847	83,316	86,940	15,191	31,355	20,901	6,015	2,249	2,050	16,462
3rd	171,996	101,826	70,170	90,885	13,134	20,290	20,219	5,465	2,455	2,358	17,190
2nd	177,379	103,272	74,107	89,770	19,108	18,597	19,931	4,021	2,226	2,079	21,647
1st	159,011	88,050	70,961	83,957	8,534	22,604	18,255	3,759	1,935	2,058	17,909
1982:4th	162,664	88,075	74,589	81,769	9,527	28,894	17,807	3,856	1,724	2,099	16,988
3rd	160,277	97,994	62,283	90,296	10,003	17,861	17,142	4,023	1,779	2,204	16,969
2nd	186,621	116,568	70,053	97,673	23,774	18,768	17,928	3,925	1,662	2,109	20,782
1st	159,593	92,655	66,938	79,346	14,217	20,958	17,732	3,745	1,574	1,930	20,091
1981:4th	169,755	97,908	71,847	82,744	15,084	28,185	17,333	3,910	1,668	2,116	18,715
3rd	163,087	105,042	58,045	88,793	14,917	15,591	16,795	3,862	1,720	2,304	19,105
2nd	190,526	125,974	64,552	96,282	31,148	15,642	16,735	3,547	1,706	2,082	23,366
1st	147,762	85,898	61,864	70,990	15,013	18,934	16,392	3,550	1,539	2,064	19,280
1980:4th	153,400	88,800	64,600	76,939	14,419	25,071	15,412	3,795	1,672	2,008	14,084
3rd	143,533	91,392	52,141	76,881	15,131	14,571	14,726	3,637	1,647	2,254	14,686

Source: Quarterly Summary of Federal, State and Local Tax Revenue, Bureau of the Census, U.S. Department of Commerce, December, 1985, p. 5.

with trucks and automobiles are the major sources of revenue. The property tax is now almost exclusively in the domain of local governments.

Table 11.4 shows the national totals of state and local tax revenue by level of government for 1985 and prior periods. Comparisons can be made between and among taxes, as well as over time. The data indicate that state and local governments raised approximately $333 billion in 1984. States collected 61 percent of the total and local governments about $127 billion (the remaining 39 percent). The figures show that although general sales taxes exceed personal income taxes, combined income taxes on individuals and corporations are the most important source of revenue to states. Motor fuel and motor vehicle taxes are a distant third in the ranking (*Quarterly Summary* 1985:7).

Income taxes

Although not a state at the time, Hawaii adopted individual and corporate income taxes in 1901. This action apparently had no effect on the various states. It was not until 1911, when Wisconsin passed both individual and corporate tax laws, that the modern state movement toward this method of taxation really began (Pechman 1977:249).

Most state personal income tax laws are similar to the federal income tax. States have continued to move toward uniformity with federal definitions. They allow deductions and personal exemptions, and they also withhold taxes at the sources. The major difference between federal and state income taxes is that the rate structure of the former is much higher and more progressive. Because of interstate competition, states tend to use appreciably lower statutory rates than the central government.

Today, forty-one states have general income taxes, and nearly thirty-five hundred local governments employ the personal income tax. Five states use a flat rate and thirty-six have progressive rate structures. Statutory rates of taxation range from a low of 1 percent in several states to a high of 13.5 percent; New Mexico has the highest number of tax brackets at nineteen (ACIR 1983:49–53).

The personal income tax recently has been the most rapidly rising major tax for most states, but in terms of total revenue, the general sales tax is still the leader nationwide. Much of the growth in income tax revenue has been due to inflation, which has automatically pushed taxpayers into higher and higher brackets.

Although the statutory progression in state rates is less steep than the federal structure, ten states have adopted various forms of indexation. Indexation, combined with the recession of 1982, has placed several of these states under severe fiscal pressure. At the same time, indexing has tended to vitiate the distorting effects of inflation on tax structures.

Table 11.4. *National totals of state and local tax revenue, by level of government and by type of tax: second quarter of 1985 and prior periods (Millions of dollars. Data not adjusted for seasonal variations.)*

Period	Total	Level of tax-imposing government		Indiv. income	Corp. net income	Property	General sales and gross receipts	Motor fuel sales	Tobacco product sales	Alcoholic beverage sales	Motor licenses	All other
		State	Local									
Quarters												
1985: 2nd	90,326	61,566	28,760	20,323	6,221	21,542	21,807	3,390	1,133	860	2,389	12,661
1st	88,709	53,515	35,194	17,697	4,185	27,851	21,103	3,348	1,038	798	2,134	10,555
1984: 4th	89,783	50,073	39,710	16,626	3,566	32,734	20,536	3,385	1,123	829	1,716	9,268
3rd	76,934	48,680	28,254	16,479	3,617	21,565	19,446	3,359	1,126	776	1,750	8,816
2nd	84,308	58,165	26,143	18,776	5,943	20,213	20,236	3,187	1,109	831	2,096	11,917
1st	82,048	49,239	32,809	16,948	3,497	25,831	19,528	3,120	1,037	777	2,069	9,241
1983: 4th	83,316	45,748	37,568	15,436	3,334	31,355	18,358	3,083	1,101	800	1,532	8,317
3rd	70,170	43,474	26,696	14,727	2,897	20,290	17,642	3,163	1,093	724	1,593	8,041
2nd	74,107	49,864	24,243	15,573	4,609	18,597	17,627	2,846	1,089	793	1,996	10,977
1st	70,961	42,325	28,636	13,604	3,271	22,604	16,519	2,597	933	727	1,853	8,853
1982: 4th	74,589	40,239	34,350	13,539	2,504	28,894	15,697	2,711	1,085	737	1,426	7,996
3rd	62,283	38,821	23,462	12,850	2,835	17,861	14,932	2,758	1,094	713	1,487	7,753

2nd	70,053	46,076	23,977	14,152	4,641	18,768	15,751	2,688	1,050	756	1,892	10,355
1st	66,938	40,243	26,695	12,302	3,541	20,958	15,559	2,519	985	703	1,889	8,482
1981:4th	71,847	38,462	33,385	12,644	2,854	28,185	14,976	2,688	1,015	748	1,317	7,420
3rd	58,045	37,383	20,662	11,857	2,936	15,591	14,451	2,654	1,038	678	1,377	7,463
2nd	64,552	44,005	20,547	13,398	4,974	16,642	14,662	2,463	1,068	740	1,707	9,898
1st	61,864	37,739	24,125	10,985	3,705	18,934	14,518	2,424	933	696	1,866	7,803
1980:4th	64,600	34,960	29,640	11,213	2,745	25,071	13,560	2,535	1,014	677	1,200	6,585
3rd	52,141	33,084	19,057	10,645	2,744	14,571	12,775	2,424	1,015	654	1,253	6,060
2nd	57,099	39,385	17,715	11,687	4,897	13,754	12,936	2,397	998	668	1,527	8,236
1st	56,479	35,253	21,226	10,059	3,404	16,658	13,863	2,405	928	671	1,906	6,585
1979:4th	59,461	32,241	27,220	10,331	2,673	23,008	12,756	2,583	955	642	1,134	5,379
3rd	48,357	30,602	17,755	9,696	2,507	14,028	12,022	2,443	983	619	1,065	4,994

Source: Quarterly Summary of Federal, State, and Local Tax Revenue, Bureau of the Census, U.S. Department of Commerce, December 1985, p. 7.

Sales and excise taxation

Sales levies are among the oldest taxes used by governments. Evidence indicates that these taxes were levied more than five thousand years ago in both Egypt and China.

Sales or consumption taxes are normally considered indirect taxes because they are collected from businesses when goods are produced or sold. The actual burden of the tax may not rest on the producer; it could be borne by consumers or suppliers to manufacturers, or some combination of all these parties. Specific economic data concerning the elasticity of the demand and supply of final consumption goods and intermediate and raw materials must be known before definite conclusions can be reached about who actually bears the burden of sales taxes.

State sales taxes apply to a wide range of commodities and services, although a proportionately greater amount of goods rather than services have been subjected to sales taxation. Moreover, the base of state sales taxes appears to be diminishing as more and more jurisdictions increase the number of exemptions. Steven Gold points out that eleven states exempted food from taxation between 1971 and 1981. A total of twenty-seven states exempt food from the tax base. Thirteen states have also passed exemptions for medicine, and twenty-one have excluded residential fuels, such as natural gas and electricity, from the tax base (Gold 1983:12–13).

As of 1985, forty-five states had general sales taxes and nearly four thousand local governments used this source of revenue. Rates at the state level ranged from a low of 3 percent in several states to a high of 6 percent in Minnesota, New Jersey, Pennsylvania, and Rhode Island. These four states, however, exempt both food and drugs. Due to the pressures and fears of intrastate competition or constraints by state legislatures, local sales tax rates are generally much lower than those of the states (ACIR 1983:49–53).

Sales taxes are of great importance to state governments. Table 11.4 shows that the sales tax is the single most important source of income to state revenue systems. It is also a relatively stable source of income compared to personal and corporate income taxes. Although all of these taxes are sensitive to the business cycle, income tax revenues fluctuate more widely over time. This kind of behavior places much stress on the budgetary process and much pressure on state legislatures, especially during recessionary periods.

Excise taxes

Excise taxes are sales taxes on specific commodities. The most important of these to states are levies on motor fuel, tobacco products, and alcoholic beverages. Traditionally, the excise tax has been specified in terms of units of output, such as the number of gallons of gasoline or number of cigarettes. In inflationary periods, these specific-type taxes are very insensitive in normal terms but quite sensitive in real terms because price does not enter into calculating the tax liability. For example, despite increases in the rate of taxation, the average cigarette tax decreased from 48.7 to 29.9 percent between 1954 and 1981 (Gold 1983:14).

As a result, several states have changed their laws and adopted ad valorem or percentages-of-price taxes in place of formerly specific excise taxes. S. Gold (1983:13) reports that twelve states have, in effect, switched their gasoline taxes from specific to ad valorem levies.

Excise taxes are not general and can be avoided. However, these levies are usually placed on goods with relatively inelastic demands. The economic effect is generally a relative rise in price but a rather insensitive response in quantity bought. Consequently, excise taxes are more easily passed forward to the consumer than most taxes.

The economic effects of sales taxes are discussed in Chapter 10, as is the controversial issue of the burden of the sales tax. Despite this issue, sales taxes have been quite popular with the states, due no doubt primarily to the large amount and stability of tax collections.

State corporation income taxes

The first modern version of the state corporation income tax was adopted by Wisconsin in 1911, the same year it adopted the individual income levy (Maxwell and Aronson 1977:115). By 1985, only Nevada, Texas, Washington, and Wyoming did not have corporation income taxes. Revenue from the tax has grown steadily for the states, but its upward trend was broken temporarily by the recession of 1981–2. Nevertheless, tax collections in 1983 amounted to $14.1 billion, or a little less than 8 percent of the total of all state tax revenue (*Quarterly Summary* 1984:13,16).

The most difficult problem associated with the corporate income tax revolves around the allocation of the interstate income earned by one or more corporations in one or more states (Ratliff 1962:Ch. 5). Despite the fact that some states have, until recently, been slowly adopting the federal definition of a tax base, much diversity remains among the states. The varying provisions in different states increase the cost of compliance for business firms and no doubt contribute to inequities and noncompliance in some cases.

The state corporation income tax is an administrative jungle for both business and tax authorities. Not much has changed since a report of a U.S. House of Representatives judiciary subcommittee noted that the system of state corporation income taxations "reaches farther and farther to impose smaller and smaller liabilities on more and more companies. It is the picture of a system which calls upon tax administrators to enforce the unenforceable and the tax-payer to comply with the uncompliable'' (Maxwell and Aronson 1977:124). Moreover, the states' different methods of allocating, apportioning, and calculating the basis of taxation greatly complicate the determination of the incidence of state corporation income taxes.

This system became even more unmanageable as a result of the federal government's Economic Recovery Tax Act of 1981 (ERTA). With a goal of increasing investment and economic growth, ERTA appreciably increased the federal corporate income tax depreciation allowances, which would substantially reduce the revenue from this levy. The states responded to ERTA in such a way as to protect state corporate tax collections and, incidentally, vitiate the positive economic effects that the federal government wanted to encourage.

In late 1981 and 1982, more than half the states with corporation income taxes passed laws that blunted the effect of the accelerated depreciation provided by ERTA. Some states retained their pre-1981 rules; others permitted only a fraction of the new federal depreciation rates to become oeprative, whereas several states actually raised their tax rates on corporations. The new costs of compliance per se to multistate businesses increased appreciably.

Economic effects: The economic effects of the corporation tax are covered in Chapters 6 and 7. To reiterate briefly, many economists believe this tax fails on both equity and efficiency grounds and that is has been detrimental to the long-term growth of the country. Martin Feldstein and James Poterba (1980:2–3) have found that state and local taxes, including the corporate income tax, reduce the return to capital of nonfinancial corporations by almost 2 percentage points or 16 percent of pre-tax returns.

The state corporate income tax sometimes double taxes corporate income, always double taxes dividends, and is very costly to administer. Moreover, this is little doubt that it distorts the geographical allocation of investment. Its only salvation appears to be that it is politically popular. This position is probably based to some extent on the erroneous opinion that corporation taxes are borne by corporations and not by individuals.

State death and gift taxes

As with the income tax, states entered the death tax field on a permanent basis before the federal government. Fewer than ten states used these taxes before the turn of the century; but by 1916, forty-two of the then forty-eight states had adopted some form of death taxes (Maxwell and Aronson 1977:128).

The wealth of dead individuals can be taxed in two different ways. One method is the estate tax and the other is the inheritance tax. The estate tax is, in some ways, less complicated than the inheritance tax because the base of the estate tax is the entire value of the assets of the deceased at the time of death. The federal government uses the estate tax and, in practice, allows some deductions from the tax base for wealth bequeathed to the surviving spouse and to charities. The tax rate structure is progressive.

A few states use the estate tax and apply progressive rates, but most states use inheritance taxes, which are levies against various living individuals who are beneficiaries receiving part of the estate. Because there are different classes of beneficiaries, it is a more complicated tax.

States also collect gift taxes. These taxes were originally designed mainly to inhibit the transfer of wealth to avoid death duties. Now, however, the federal government also levies a similar tax at higher rates, and state gift taxes are of little consequence.

The federal government allows death taxes paid to state governments to be credited against the federal estate tax, but the amount of this credit is relatively small. Federal provisions in estate statutes not only have reduced interstate competition to lower death taxes but also have encouraged states to pass death tax laws because the state taxes due (up to the amount of federal credit) would actually go to the United States Treasury in the absence of state laws. Only Nevada has no death duties (Gardner 1978:327).

State death and gift taxes are relatively unimportant revenue producers. In 1982, these levies produced about $2.3 billion for the forty-nine states with death tax laws, and this sum represented a little more than 1 percent of total state government receipts (ACIR 1983:27,31).

Economic effects: The economic effects of death taxes are varied and not entirely certain. Due and Friedlaender (1973:346–47) argue that because the tax is to be collected from an individual's estate sometime in the future, resultant decisions about work and leisure are likely to have less effect on economic behavior than income taxes. This argument is plausible, but more empirical research needs to be done on the issue.

Death taxes tend to increase the demand for liquidity and, thus, shift investment into more conservative ventures. The necessity of having money to pay death taxes encourages wealthy individuals to alter portfolios so they are more liquid. At the same time, beneficiaries may be encouraged to save more from this source of wealth than most alternatives. The Friedman permanent income hypothesis holds that all transitory income will be saved. Although not necessarily agreeing with this position, Due and Friedlaender believe that the marginal propensity to save out of transitory income is relatively high. Consequently, death taxes, which are levies on a type of transitory income, will reduce savings to a greater extent than will alternative taxes.

Death duties affect the lifetime consumption and saving patterns of individuals, but the net effect cannot be theoretically determined. If individuals wish to leave a certain amount to their heirs, they will have to save more than the targeted amount because of impending estate or inheritance taxes. Alternatively, knowing that a large part of one's wealth will go to the government at death might encourage one to consume more and leave less. This is both an individual and empirical issue, and careful econometric analysis is necessary to sort out and derive the net effect of the opposing forces.

The main justification presented in favor of death taxes appears to be the belief that such duties take wealth from richer individuals and redistribute it to those who are less wealthy. Since wealth is more unevenly distributed than income, progressive death duties can be more effective than income taxes in redistributing money. One effect of this possibility, however, has been the development of the death tax avoidance industry. These firms use the country's higher priced and more talented lawyers to help the very wealthy escape death taxes through various legal but extremely complicated schemes.

State severance taxes and tax exporting

Because of the tax actions of several western states and provinces in Canada, severance taxation and the exporting of taxes have become very interesting if not volatile fiscal subjects. The United State Supreme Court has handed down several recent rulings on severance taxes (McLure 1981a:1–37).

Tax exporting refers to the shifting of the burden of a tax from the residents on one jurisdiction to another one (McLure 1980a:257–62). Severance taxes are those applied to oil and minerals as they are removed (severed) from the ground. This class of economic goods is a possible candidate for tax exportation because most of the oil, gas, or minerals found in one state will be sold and consumed in other states.

Michigan imposed the first state severance tax in 1846. Currently, twenty-nine states have special taxes on minerals. The courts normally consider severance taxes as excise levies. As a result, they are not normally treated as property taxes and bear none of the constraints associated with taxes on property (Stinson 1977:7).

A pure severance tax is levied against the amount of the commodity produced. This factor greatly simplifies the administration of the tax because tax authorities need know only how many tons or barrels producers are manufacturing. Some states now apply a percentage tax rate to the value of the product extracted, and this practice has been subjected to sharp criticism by those states unendowed with these resources (Levy 1981:1–3).

Producing states take the position that the severance tax is needed to provide funds for the public facilities required to support the areas in which there is rapid energy development. Some proponents also argue that the tax assures

Table 11.5. *Severance tax revenue*

State	Percent of national severance tax revenue 1981	Percent of the state's total tax revenue		
		1981	1975	1970
Texas	34.5	26.9	18.3	14.2
Alaska	18.3	50.5	14.4	12.5
Louisiana	12.8	29.1	35.6	29.3
Oklahoma	9.4	26.9	14.5	10.1
New Mexico	5.1	27.4	13.4	13.3
Wyoming	2.2	19.4	11.8	5.0
Montana	1.6	21.3	6.3	3.7
North Dakota	1.6	22.8	2.6	2.6

Source: Steven D. Gold, "Recent Developments in State Finances," *National Tax Journal,* 36, No. 1, March 1983, p. 14.

a revenue cushion for the period following depletion of the energy resources.

Opponents of severance taxes believe that it drains income from energy-poor states; that resource-owning states do in fact export their taxes to energy-using states. They also claim that these taxes permit resource states to reduce business taxes, thus attracting businesses and a tax base from other areas, which further facilitates the transfer of wealth away from energy-poor states.

There is no question that severance taxation is gaining in importance. Revenues have increased from less than a billion dollars in 1973 to $3.7 billion in 1980. Although coal manifested the highest rate of growth, it comprises only about 9 percent of the total revenue. Oil and gas severance revenues comprise the bulk of the total revenue from this source of taxation (Levy 1981:2–3).

As indicated by the data in Table 11.5, revenue from the severance tax is highly concentrated among a few states. Approximately 75 percent of the total national severance tax revenue is collected by just four states – Texas, Alaska, Louisiana, and Oklahoma. Table 11.5 also shows the enormous impact of the increase in energy prices during the 1970s on the finances of the severance-taxing states.

One crucial question associated with the issue of severance taxation is, Who really pays the tax? Is the tax actually exported to users of energy in other states? Unfortunately, this is a very difficult question to answer. Opponents of the tax naturally claim that the tax is passed on to consumers in states without energy resources. Economists generally believe this would happen only if substitutes for the petroleum or coal were not available. Because foreign sources are available, the workings of the market probably prevent the passing through to consumers of severance taxes. This probably applies more to petroleum than to coal because foreign coal producers are not now competitive with United States producers.

Another economic effect of severance taxes is to restrict somewhat the use of the ore deposit. This result occurs because the tax is a constant dollar amount per ton mined or extracted. The profit-maximizing firm will produce only up to the point at which marginal cost, inclusive of tax, will equal market price. Consequently, some deposits where the costs of extraction without tax are less than the anticipated market price are not in fact exploited (Stinson 1977:8).

It is unfortunate that the founding fathers of the country did not allocate this source of revenue to the central government. As Charles McLure (1981b:4) points out, a well-thought-out constitution would provide that the central government obtain the rents from natural resources. Taxes from this source could then be used to increase the formation of capital or to replace other taxes that distort economic choices. McLure adds that sound policy would, of course, require all the social costs associated with extracting and processing minerals to be subtracted before deriving net economic rents.

States will no doubt continue to levy severance taxes. But policy makers need to be aware that the distributional effects of these taxes are quite complicated. It is more likely that the owners of resources, wherever they reside, will bear the burden of the tax rather than consumers in resource-poor states.

The lottery as a source of public finance

One of the older but less savory sources of public finance is the lottery. Earlier government lotteries date back to Imperial Rome. They reappeared in Europe during the fifteenth century, becoming quite common on both the continent and in England by the seventeenth century. Proceeds were used for financing such public projects as Westminster Bridge and parts of the British Museum library. Today France, Germany, Sweden, the United Kingdom (Holloway 1983:39–41) and many Latin American countries run some form of governmental lottery.

In colonial America, thirteen colonies used the lottery as a form of voluntary taxation. The first modern case in the United States began in New Hampshire in 1964 (Watson 1973:4). Since then thirteen additional states have established state-run public lotteries, and fifteen more states are in the process of introducing this system of gambling (American Legislative Exchange Council 1982:3).

Objectives of state government lotteries: The prime objective of a lottery is to raise money to fund government projects. Often, the money is earmarked for

Table 11.6. *State revenue from lotteries, 1981*
(millions of dollars)

State	Revenue	State	Revenue
Connecticut	$ 57.6	New Hampshire	$ 4.0
Delaware	5.6	New Jersey	149.0
Illinois	86.0	New York	102.7
Maine	1.1	Ohio	110.1
Maryland	185.0	Pennsylvania	152.0
Massachusetts	70.0	Rhode Island	12.9
Michigan	215.0	Vermont	.5

Source: American Legislative Exchange Council, "Option Three: State Lotteries," *The State Factor,* Washington, D.C., January 1982, p. 3.

education or aid to the elderly. Many of these spending programs tend to promote income redistribution from higher to lower income groups.

A secondary objective of some lotteries is to compete with the illegal numbers games in the hope of driving these competitors out of business. In general, this objective has not been fulfilled, in part because the state lottery payoffs are not attractive enough to stifle competition.

Lottery revenues: The first projections of lottery revenues to the states were exaggerated. Vermont and New York soon found that the state's take was well below expectations. The poor revenue performance of the lotteries was due in part to poor planning. The design of the early systems did not tap the proper market. Not until New Jersey adopted the lottery, and demonstrated proper lottery designs to other states, did revenues equal or exceed expectations. The New Jersey planners provided more convenient marketing locations, lower priced tickets, and weekly and, later, daily payoffs. Consequently, revenues soared. Sales exceeded projections by more than 200 percent in the first year of operations (Watson 1973:6).

Table 11.6 shows the 1981 annual revenue for the fourteen states that had at least a full year of experience with the lottery. The amounts range all the way from a half million dollars in Vermont to $215 million in Michigan. The total revenue for all lottery sales was nearly $1.2 billion.

Lottery costs: Early estimates of costs in New Hampshire averaged about thirty cents for each dollar of net revenue ("The Economic Case . . ." 1975:67). In New Jersey, the costs were approximately thirty-eight cents for every dollar in revenue collected. As in the case of New Hampshire, these figures were much higher than the state's cost of collecting broad-based taxes. State costs, however, do not include the substantial expenses taxpayers incur in paying taxes. More recent cost estimates indicate that states have learned how to reduce expenses. After start-up costs of from $750,000 to $1.5 million, states now average a maximum of 15 percent of the total lottery revenue for administration (American Legislative Exchange Council 1982:4).

Burden of lottery expenditures: Opponents of the lottery as a vehicle of public finance have claimed that public lottery expenditures are regressive. In an early study, Roger E. Brinner of Harvard University concluded that low income groups in Massachusetts spend a much higher percentage of their income to buy lottery tickets than do higher income groups ("The Economic Case . . ." 1975:67).

A more recent study of New York and New Jersey lottery and nonlottery players disclosed that ticket purchasers are drawn heavily from the middle income group. Moreover, the proportion of low income earners who did not buy tickets did not differ significantly from other higher income classes (Watson 1973:10). A 1981 analysis of lottery players indicates that the majority of lottery players have incomes that range from $18,000 to $56,000. Those individuals whose incomes range from $5,700 to $18,000 constitute only about 15 percent of those who purchase lottery tickets. Approximately 5 percent of the players earn in excess of $56,000 (American Legislative Exchange Council 1982:3).

The impact of taxes on economic growth

The tax revolt of 1978 spawned a new spate of studies on the relationship between state taxes and economic growth. Robert J. Genetski and Young D. Chin (1978:1–4) published one of the first and more influential of these articles in late 1978. Through the use of statistical analysis, they were able to derive several specific conclusions.

They found that between the years 1964 and 1976, the economic growth of a specific state relative to the average economic growth in all the states were not directly related to the level of its state and local government tax burden. However, they discovered that a given state's rise in income was loosely associated with a change in the state's relative tax load. Those jurisdictions that manifested greater than average increases in the tax burden tended to display below average rates of growth. On the other hand, states with less than average growth in the tax burden revealed above average growth in state income.

Genetski and Chin's most powerful conclusions came when they lagged the effects of tax changes by three years. Allowing three years for economic forces to adjust to changes in taxes revealed a strong negative relationship between an above average rise in the tax burden and a below average increase in state income. Moreover, their analysis showed a strong and significant correlation between less than average upward movement in state taxes and above average economic growth.

The Genetski–Chin study was followed by a report on the relationship between state taxes and economic growth by the Joint Economic Committee (1981:34) of the U.S. Congress. After an extensive analysis of the data, the Committee concluded that, in the 1970s, states with the most rapid economic growth not only had significantly less increase in their income taxes but also that the pattern of their distribution in income taxes was less progressive than states with slow rates of growth. States with patterns of rapid growth rates eschewed increasing reliance on income and property taxes and, instead, relied more heavily on sales taxation, which tends to encourage saving and capital formation. The JEC reports that states that experience relative declines in their total tax burdens grow significantly faster than those that increase the relative burden of taxation. Moreover, every increase in state tax rates causes an incremental decline in economic growth.

In a more recent study of the relationship between state tax changes and state economic growth, Jeffrey Goettman (1982:48) produced findings that were similar to those of the Genetski–Chin and JEC reports. An important feature of his analysis was the consistency of his results. Low tax states grew faster in the 1970s than high tax states for all the various tax measures he used to analyze the basic relationship. Regression analysis strongly supported the notion that a significant negative correlation exists between changes in tax burdens and variations in state economic growth.

More specifically, Goettman (1982:21–31) found that high growth states increase their total state tax burden by less than the national average. On the other hand, low growth states boost their tax loads by more than the national state average. States with greater than average rates of growth increase their income tax burden at a significantly lower rate relative to states that experience below average changes in state income. High growth states also increase the use of income taxes as a percentage of total taxes notably less than the national average, whereas the opposite relationship holds for low growth states. Similar results hold for the state corporation tax.

Interestingly, but not surprisingly, high growth states finance expenditures by relying relatively more heavily on consumption taxes than the national average for all states. Low growth states finance their expenditures by relying relatively less on sales taxes than the average state (Goettman 1982:37). These results tend to support the incentive economists who believe that sales taxes inhibit economic growth less than income taxes, because under consumption levies saving is left untaxed. Consequently, investment is encouraged, productivity increases, and real wages and incomes increase.

In a report released in 1983, L. Jay Helms (1983:1–19) used sophisticated econometric analysis to study the effect of state and local taxes on economic growth. He pooled time series and cross-section data to estimate his model.

Helms concluded that a state's pattern of taxation significantly affects its ability to attract, keep, and foster businesses. But he also found that taxes cannot be analyzed in isolation. When revenues are used to provide services that are valued relatively highly by businesses and their employees, a state may actually encourage economic activity through its expenditure policy. On the other hand, Helms found that rising tax rates significantly reduce economic growth when additional revenue is spent on transfer payments.

Helms concluded that the effects of the pattern of taxation on a state's economy depend importantly on the use of the additional tax revenues. When they are allocated to such traditional public services as highways, education, public health, and safety, the positive effect on economic decisions may more than offset the disincentive effects of the increased taxes. When the additional tax revenues are used to redistribute incomes, the possibility of interstate migration means that states will pay a higher price for using redistributive tax and expenditure policies than will the federal government.

CHAPTER 12

Local government taxes

Introduction

Much of government's work gets done at the local level. This fact is reflected in both the structure and sheer numbers of local jurisdictions. Table 12.1 shows the numbers and dynamic character of local governments. The most dramatic change during the twenty years tabulated in the table is the decrease in the number of school districts from nearly thirty-five thousand in 1962 to only fifteen thousand in 1982. This shift reflects the strong move toward consolidation of schools, especially in rural and suburban areas.

The other marked change in the structure of local jurisdictions is the rapid rise of special districts. Special districts are independent, limited-purpose governmental units that have substantial fiscal and administrative independence from general-purpose local jurisdictions, such as counties and municipalities. Most special district governments are created to fulfill a single function, although a few are authorized to provide two or more public services ("Special Purpose . . ." 1982:3).

Table 12.2 shows both the number and type of functions performed by the nearly twenty-nine thousand special district governments in the United States during 1982. Natural resources is the largest single category. These jurisdictions perform such varied functions as drainage, flood control, irrigation, and soil and water conservation. The other functions are for the most part self-explanatory. The list does, however, give a feeling for the richness and diversity of the public services that are financed through taxes and fees.

The next several sections of this chapter examine the various means of funding the differing types of local government. The first and most important tax of local governments is the property levy.

The property tax

The property tax has long been a significant source of income for state and local governments. Though its relative importance has declined since the early 1900s, mostly due to expansion of other state taxes, it still represents the largest source of revenue to local governments (Maxwell and Aronson

251

Table 12.1. *Number of governmental units in the United States total by level of government by state, 1982 selected years 1942–1982*

Year	All govern- ment units	Countries	Munici- palities	Townships and towns	School districts	Special districts
		A. Total units				
1942	155,116	3,050	16,220	18,919	108,579	8,299
1952	116,807	3,052	16,807	17,202	67,355	12,340
1957	102,392	3,050	17,215	17,198	50,454	14,424
1962	91,237	3,043	18,000	17,142	34,678	18,323
1967	81,299	3,049	18,048	17,105	21,782	21,264
1972	78,269	3,044	18,517	16,991	15,781	23,885
1977	79,913	3,042	18,862	16,822	15,174	25,962
1982	82,688	3,041	19,083	16,748	15,032	28,733

Source: U.S. Department of Commerce *1982 Census of Governments,* Bureau of Census, Washington, D.C., 1982 and other years.

1977:134). One of its most important functions is to provide funds for school districts.

Property taxation in the United States has had many critics. However, despite staunch criticism on both equity and efficiency grounds, only minor changes have been made over the years.

The tax base

During the nineteenth century, the property tax base generally included all property, and each jurisdiction used a uniform rate. Properties owned by the government and by religious, charitable, and educational institutions were exempt. Both real and personal property comprised the tax base. Personal property was divided between tangible and intangible property. Problems of duplication arose with this system, however, since intangible property was often representative of real property. Intangibles are, for the most part, no longer subject to this tax.

Today, the property tax base is much more narrow. It is mainly a tax on real estate, business equipment, and inventories. It varies across the United States, with approximately sixty-six thousand governments having the authority to impose it, many with overlapping jurisdictions (Aaron 1975:6). Almost 90 percent of assessed property is residential, with tangible personal property comprising most of the balance (Maxwell and Aronson 1977:149). Household items are not usually taxed because the effective administration and monitoring of the tax is costly.

Table 12.2. *Special district governments by function: 1982*

Function	Number	Percent
Total	18,733	100.0
Single-function districts:		
Natural resources	6,276	21.8
Fire protection	4,567	15.9
Housing and community development	3,308	11.5
Water supply	2,696	9.4
Sewerage	1,617	5.6
Cemeteries	1,582	5.5
Educational buildings	965	3.4
Parks and recreation	928	3.2
Hospitals	777	2.7
Libraries	642	2.2
Highways	595	2.1
Health	455	1.6
Airports	361	1.3
Other	1,457	5.1
Multiple-function districts	2.507	8.7

Source: U.S. Department of Commerce *1982 Census of Governments,* Bureau of Census, Washington, D.C., 1982 and other years.

Assessment

The most serious problem associated with the property tax is inaccurate assessment. Though most state laws demand an assessment close or equal to actual value, property is commonly assessed well below its full market value. Statistical studies show that the larger the divergence between assessed and market values, the larger the deviation from the average assessment. As a result, inequities are introduced into property taxation. The lack of a standard also prevents an individual from comparing assessments, or even from being aware that one's assessment is not average. Because the assessment will be below market value, a citizen is unlikely to question or ask for a review of the assessment.

Other problems stem from underevaluation because property assessments are often used for purposes other than taxation. These figures are also used as determinants of shares in state grants. Policy decisions on debt and tax rates are also often associated with property assessments. The impact, therefore, is felt in a wide variety of areas. Attempts by state governments to equalize assessments have been largely ineffective, and wide dispersion of assessment values has continued to occur among and within local areas.

Cost of administration: Costs can vary greatly with the system used. Unfortunately, an equitable system may not necessarily be cost effective. In general, cities that have lowered the amount of on-site inspection have succeeded in lowering costs, even if assessment/sales ratios and assessments are checked and reevaluated annually. The use of computers has decreased costs and improved statistical estimates while maintaining appraisal principles (Peterson et al. 1973:105).

Appeals: A procedure of appeal is an important part of the tax system because it is designed to protect taxpayers from widely dispersed assessment values. However, few property owners actually use the appeal. Those who do tend to be large investors who have enough to gain from reassessment to cover the costs of time involved (Peterson et al. 1973:105). Also, because assessment values are determined fair or unfair by comparing them to similar assets, the appeal only remedies individual inequities and not general, systematic biases.

Breakdown of sources of tax revenue

Although available government data do not include a breakdown of the property tax impact among various sectors of the economy, estimates can be made from information provided. Relative differences among nonfarm business tax payments exist, both in reference to industry capital output ratios and taxes as a proportion of wealth. Industries that are capital intensive and, thus, tend to have high capital output ratios have high property taxes in terms of output and income measures. Differences in tax payments as a proportion of capital seem to be mainly affected by location of activities. Activities in urban areas are taxed more highly as opposed to those in lower rate areas (Netzer 1966:23).

Varying methods of taxation also account for differences among industries. Assessment by a state agency is usually much closer to full value than that done locally, leading to generally higher assessments. Personal property is normally taxed at lower rates than real property, so those industries with large amounts of personal property ownership relative to real property have lower rates of taxation. On the basis of net output or income, the property tax is also not neutral among industries. Effective rates for manufacturing and services are low, but they are highly variable in the mining industry. Farmers, on the other hand, pay high taxes relative to farm income and product and low taxes relative to value of capital employed (Netzer 1966:26–8).

Taxes on housing are another component of the property tax. The tax on housing, when considered as an excise tax and independently of benefits, is one of the highest of the consumption taxes. This levy also comprises a significant amount of the total money spent on housing in terms of homeowners' and renters' payments. However, further analysis shows that individuals who actually make the payments are not necessarily those bearing the burden of the tax, but simply its initial impact.

The incidence of the property tax

Recent research has brought about a whole new outlook on the incidence of property taxes. The conclusions drawn from the new analyses are important in that they point toward new directions in public policy decisions and property tax modifications. Under the traditional view, property tax incidence theory was approached in the same manner for a given locality and for the entire nation. Using this approach, analysts believed the property tax on structures was regressive, with the burden of the tax being borne in proportion to a consumer's use of these buildings. The tax on land, with land supply held constant, was borne by landowners and thought to be progressive.

The new view does not see the traditional approach as a correct analysis for the nation as a whole. Instead, the property tax is considered as one cost factor in using the taxed commodities. Because all goods are not taxed by the same amount, investors will tend to shift their holdings from heavily to lightly taxed goods. The adjustments made by the owners of these goods will reduce overall rates of return. All owners of capital bear the property tax, which makes it a progressive tax.

The traditional view

Taxes on land: To determine the incidence of the tax on land, the simple competitive model is used, with land being a fixed commodity and with ownership diffused. Using this case, no owner can raise his price without losing his customers or the users. The landowner must bear the tax. The present landowner, however, bears only the increase in the property tax that has occurred since he purchased the property. This conclusion holds true because current property taxes are accounted for in the prices of land purchased. Increased taxes on land will reduce return relative to other assets, causing land prices to fall. Moreover, because the taxes are determined by the value of the land, the tax liability decreases as land values fall.

Taxes on structures: Structures, unlike land, are not fixed. Over a period of time, an increase in property taxes will decrease investment in new and standing structures. Therefore, the number and quality of structures will be lower and the prices higher than they otherwise would have been. Adjustments will continue until rental income rises to its former level. The rent on structures is then equal to the rental cost of total capital invested in them plus property taxes. Using this theory, the tax burden would be borne by individuals according to their ownership of taxed structures.

Studies done on the incidence of residential and nonresidential property taxes have found them to be highly regressive for low income families and moderately regressive for middle income families. Benefits derived from expenditures were also found to be regressive, compounding this effect. Netzer (1966:41–3) describes a chart showing nonresidential property taxes as a percentage of income as a U-shaped curve, at first falling as income rises and then rising for the highest groups.

Under the assumptions of the traditional view of the property levy, in which occupants of property bear the tax, residential property taxes have been found to be highly regressive. Two explanations have been offered for this regressiveness. One theory is that homes of lower market value are assessed at a greater percentage of market value than are higher priced homes. Another explanation is that expenditures on housing are not very income elastic, with low income families spending a higher proportion of their income on housing.

The new view

Perhaps the best description of the new view, developed largely by Mieszkowski (1972:73–96), is condensed as follows. The new view sees the property tax as being borne by all owners of capital. The redistribution process is described as taking place through three phases:

1. a uniform tax imposed on all property;
2. the redistribution of the tax through differentials in locational and industrial tax rates; and
3. the impact on the supply of land and capital in after-tax rents and rates of return.

A uniform tax on land and capital goods would be borne by the owners because, assuming that supplies of land and capital are fixed, no means would be available to avoid the tax. The tax would not change prices but instead would decrease rates of return of owners by the amount of the tax. However, the property tax is not uniform, resulting in adjustment of ownership of the property affected by the tax. One major consequence of this fact is that investors will shift ownership from taxed assets to goods or areas less heavily taxed. Withdrawal from the more heavily taxed goods or areas will tend to make these goods scarcer, thereby increasing their value and before-tax rates of return. These adjustments move the variables toward an equilibrium at which rates of return after taxes tend toward equality (Aaron 1975:40).

The property tax policy of a local government, therefore, plays a role in demand for land in the area, with high taxes discouraging ownership. If supplies are fixed, then prices are unaffected. Under this situation, a tax would reduce the owner's income and distribute it to the general public. However, supply is not necessarily fixed because governments and private parties are involved in annexation and landfill decisions.

When tax rates vary across jurisdictions and among industries, payments made to other factors of production will also be affected. High taxation in some areas and on some uses causes the amount of available capital goods to decline. Workers will have less capital at their disposal with which to work and so their real wage rates will decline. Because labor is rarely perfectly mobile, workers living in higher tax areas tend to earn lower wages. Both workers and owners of capital assets have an incentive to move from the area, and this movement will eventually drive down land values and rents.

When considering the impact of variations in tax rates, three kinds of differences are important. The first is variations in tax rates among jurisdictions within a given metropolitan area. Because owners have difficulty shifting a higher rate on to consumers when it occurs in such a limited area, the major impact of the tax will be on land values. Consequently, higher than average tax rates decrease the attractiveness and land price of a given area. To the extent that consumers are restricted to housing in a certain area, the costs of high taxes may be partially borne by the consumer (Aaron 1975:44).

Variations in tax rates among metropolitan areas and states differ significantly. Some results of this dispersion are tax-induced changes in real wages and in the prices of goods and services that compete only within the area. High taxes tend to increase prices of goods and decrease real wages.

Tax rates that vary between land and capital used by industries act as excise taxes on consumer goods. Because property taxes are generally positively correlated with income across states and regions, it indicates that these effects make the property tax more progressive or less regressive.

Joseph Pechman and Benjamin Okner (1974:59) have estimated the distribution of the property tax under various assumptions. One estimate assumes that the property tax is borne in proportion to property income. The other estimate assumes that the tax is borne only by the land owners. Both distributions show the tax to be regressive in nature in the two lowest income classes and progressive in the middle and upper income groups. However, these estimates are based on annual income and underestimate progressivity, especially in the lower income groups. In any case, when the property tax results in a reduction in capital income, the tax is, on balance, progressive in nature.

Table 12.3 does not consider excise tax effects of the property tax. It has been shown, however, that excise tax effects increase the progressive nature

Table 12.3. *Alternative estimates of effective property tax rates, by adjusted family income class, 1966*

Adjusted family income class	Assumption regarding property tax on land	
	Borne in proportion to property income in general	Borne by landowners
(thousands of dollars)	(percent)	(percent)
0–3	2.5	2.4
3–5	2.7	2.8
5–10	2.0	2.2
10–15	1.7	1.9
15–20	2.0	2.2
20–25	2.6	2.8
25–30	3.7	3.7
30–50	4.5	4.4
50–100	6.2	6.1
100–500	8.2	7.8
500–1,000	9.6	8.8
1,000 and over	10.1	8.7

Source: Joseph Pechman and Benjamin Okner, *Who Bears the Tax Burden?* The Brookings Institution, 1974, Table 4–8, p. 59, and Pechman and Okner, unpublished estimates. See Henry J. Aaron, *Who Pays the Property Tax?* Washington, D.C.: The Brookings Institution, 1975, p. 47.

of the tax. The importance of the effects on consumers of heavily taxed industries' products is diminished with the following explanation. Some businesses subject to heavy taxes will be able to pass these forward through higher prices and some will not. The same conclusions hold for lower taxes and reductions in prices. Firms that dominate national or local markets will generally be more successful in passing the taxes forward to consumers than those who face more competition. Because the effects vary widely, and because consumers buy a wide variety of products, the consumer will be buying products where some prices are higher, some lower, and others are unchanged due to property taxes. As a result, there are compensating effects as some of the prices tend to balance out. Consequently, the property tax burden on consumers is less important than would be supposed.

Another possible result of the reduction of the rate of return on capital through property taxes is that it may change the relative supply of capital and labor available. Aaron (1975:49) concludes that if the property tax causes less saving and capital stock than would exist if the same revenues were raised by an alternative tax, total production and real wages per worker will be lower and the rate of capital return higher. Economic theory helps in predicting these effects, but no empirical estimates have been derived as to their size. Without this information, it is difficult to determine whether these theoretical predictions would naturally affect policymaking decisions.

The new view of property taxation assumes that owners of real property are attempting to maximize long-run profits and that owners are free from external constraints. Although the general validity of the new view is unaffected by various extraneous conditions, situations still remain in which the traditional view is more applicable. Examples of such situations are when rent control is in effect or when rents are set collusively. These restrictions make the incidence of the tax fall on renters, with benefits from lower taxes going to owners of the rental property.

Both the traditional and new views of property tax incidence can be used to determine effects of change in property tax policy. When considering local changes, the traditional view is useful because it looks at changes in an isolated setting. With more national questions, the new view might serve better because it looks at changes in the aggregate. However, it should be kept in mind that the question of the incidence of the property tax is not fully resolved. Additional theoretical and empirical work needs to be done before strong policy implications can be formulated.

Economic effects

Most revenue from the property tax comes from the housing, business structure, and business equipment components of the base. As a result, an overall effect of the property tax is to shift investment from these physical assets to human development, with most property tax revenue going toward education and human services. This reallocation of resources is generally not counterproductive because the return on investment in education is about the same as that in physical capital. Another major effect of the property tax is the substitution away from taxed real property toward other inputs by some firms, leading to a reallocation of resources among industries. The effects of the tax are complicated, however, and some cases must be examined individually.

Land

Very high property taxes can be placed on land without really changing its quantity in any real sense. A tax increase, though, often makes owners reevaluate their investment in the land. Reducing returns on land, therefore, may not reduce its quantity, but may reduce its usefulness to the economy as a whole depending on the action of owners (Harris 1967:34).

Business

The effects of the property tax on business stem mostly from the fact that it is an unneutral tax that does not apply to all inputs. Labor is the obvious example of an exempted input. The property tax affects capital intensive industries to a much larger degree than labor intensive industries. This result is muted to an extent by the effect of payroll taxes. Nevertheless, where the substitution of labor for real property is not feasible, some industries have been penalized by the tax. An example of this effect is the decline of the railroad industry, which was accelerated by heavy property taxation that their transportation competitors escaped (Netzer 1966:73).

Differences in rates of taxation occur both among and within locations. Differences within a jurisdiction can cause unusual dispersion of capital investments, industries, and the labor force in a metropolitan area and lead to local inequities. Interregional differences in business taxation often result when areas attempt to offer special breaks or inducements to attract industry. Though this strategy might seem reasonable, little actual evidence has been found that such a policy is successful in the industrial development of an area (Groves 1967:23).

Housing

The property tax on housing creates an excise tax higher than that on other uses of personal income. To help offset this outcome, the tax system provides exemptions and incentives to invest in personal housing. For example, imputed rent on housing is not taxed, and interest paid on mortgages is deductable as are property taxes. The effect on this tax offset, however, is not necessarily equal among income groups. Although property tax payments are about proportional to gross rental value of housing overall, income tax advantages increase proportionally with family gross income. Consequently, tax incentives to owner-occupied housing are much more relevant for wealthier families.

Demand effects: Since the demand for housing is relatively inelastic, the property tax causes little substitution of other goods for housing consumption. However, the property levy does have the effect of changing the demand for quality in housing. One example of this is the shift from rented to owner-occupied housing. This movement has occurred in spite of rising property taxes and is probably due to the tax advantages. Another possible explanation is that the majority of new housing has been built in the suburbs, and it is here that taxpayers can clearly see the benefits gained through the tax. Housing consumers in the cities, many of them renters, generally find it much more difficult to make this connection.

Another inelastic effect on the demand for housing is the construction of smaller rooms. In the construction industry, efficient use of resources dictates building larger units and rooms, but the property tax encourages the construction of smaller units. Due to the higher price of housing, people purchase smaller quantities than before. Fewer resources will be used by the housing industry, leading to an excess burden over the initial cost of the tax, one that does not generate revenue for government purposes.

Effects on improvements: The effects of the property tax on household improvements are not the same for all types of neighborhoods. For analytic purposes, neighborhoods can be divided into three types: blighted, downward transitional, and upward transitional. In blighted neighborhoods, some investors avoid the problem of relatively high property taxes simply by not paying them.

Large tax liabilities greatly limit cash flow from a housing investment. This result leads to depressed market prices for the property. Unable to sell the properties at a good price, owners often let them deteriorate. If the tax rates were equalized among city neighborhoods by lowering the taxes on such buildings, owners could sell at a higher price, and perhaps individuals better able to manage the investment could take their place.

Investors in a deteriorating neighborhood are greatly concerned with future market conditions. Equalization of tax rates could help the situation by improving these expectations. Small investors rely on assessed value to determine the market value of their property. When assessment is done infrequently in a downward transitional neighborhood, owners may be unaware of the declining value of their property. When owners finally do realize the situation, the result can be panic selling of property in a given neighborhood, or loss of confidence in the property by current owners (who experience a large decline in assessed value). More frequent assessments that follow the trend of market values would eliminate the shock of drastic changes in assessed values.

The greatest impact against improvements due to property taxes occurs in upward transitional neighborhoods. The level of taxation may be high enough to make people leave the area. It is the marginal effect of taxation, however, that really works against improvements. Rates of return are greatly lowered when property upgrading is subject to increased taxes. This effect is felt the most where improvements are taxes at high rates. Because the potential for large housing projects exists in upward transitional neighborhoods, and because these investments are very sensitive to tax rates, property tax policy in these areas plays a crucial role in their development.

Cities

There is concern as to the effect the property tax has on investment in city real estate. Overall property tax rates in cities are high compared to other areas. As a result, there is an incentive to locate in areas outside a city and also to invest in assets other than real estate. Surveys of tax rates in cities display a great deal of nonuniformity among various classes of property. In some cases, the effective tax rate on multi-unit family housing and commercial property is significantly higher than that on single family homes. In other cities, the opposite situation is found. This lack of uniformity is largely due to the assessment methods used when determining tax value. Finding standards to determine market value is difficult, especially because of the wide variety of property in the cities and the infrequent sales. Although some of these discrepencies are unconsciously due to assessment techniques, other cities deliberately taxed multiple family and business property at higher rates than single family homes. Some businesses cannot easily relocate to another city to avoid high taxation (utilities, newspapers, and banks). This immobility can raise city tax revenues without provoking public reaction.

Heavy taxation of multifamily dwellings also occurs when the property tax is viewed as a benefit tax. In this case, number of households rather than assessed value could be a factor in defending heavier taxation. Another justification for lighter taxing of single family homes that they can then compete with suburban housing.

The property tax also appears to inhibit renewal attempts within the cities. One way to avoid this problem is to provide tax exemptions on selected projects, and programs doing this have been implemented in some areas.

Appraisal of current system

Though many inequities of the system have been discussed, the property tax in the aggregate has been successful in raising revenues and allowing for growth of local public expenditure. The existence of the property tax also tends to increase investment in human capital, with funds diverted from some lower return, physical capital investments. Among the structural advantages in the present system is its sensitive response to small incremental changes in rates. This factor makes the system flexible in its application, with small changes easy to implement. In this manner, local governments can concentrate first on expenditures and then derive necessary tax rates. The present system also provides local governments with a means of raising funds while preserving local autonomy. Keeping administration and assessments a part of local government helps maintain the basic tie between community income levels and property tax liabilities.

Administrative problems: Most criticisms surrounding the property tax deal with its administrative problems. A major reason that the property tax is difficult to administer is that it is based on a process of valuation that is subject to human judgment. Basic problems resulting from assessment methods include assessment of heterogenous property within a given jurisdiction at wide variations of market value; both systematic and unsystematic differential treatment of various types of property, and variation of assessment methods among jurisdictions. These factors are important because assessment values are often used for other purposes, such as state aid and other programs.

When assessments are deliberately reduced for specific taxed properties, intentional inequalities exist. Communities may do this to encourage a firm to locate or stay in the area because of the benefits it brings. Property taxes within residential areas have also been changed in order to keep desirable residents in the community. Not all of these concessions are given at the initiative of local officials. Firms often apply considerable pressure to communities to gain tax adjustments, especially in areas in which tax rates are high.

Though it may seem equitable and beneficial to vary the effective tax rates according to consumption of public services, in practice, variable rates would very likely subject the system to informal and perhaps illegal negotiations. It would also add to the system's complexity. Giving certain tax breaks to homeowners is also objectionable; the end results are capital grants to homeowners, in terms of increased property values, and a heavier burden through reduced property values on those people not qualified for the tax breaks.

Unintentional inequalities are a result of the shortcomings of assessment methods. Improved administration to combat this is often costly. Generally, the greater the amount an area spends on administration, the fewer inequalities that exist (Aaron 1975: 62–3). Therefore, due to budget constraints, the cost of removing further inequalities from a system must be justified by the benefits of equity gained in doing so.

Elasticity of the property tax

It is difficult to analyze the elasticity of the property tax in the usual sense for several reasons. Its nominal or tax-assessed values and economic base or market values do not vary proportionally. Moreover, governments can alter expected revenues through two means: adjustments of the assessments or the nominal tax rates. Finally, the property tax revenue requirements are determined by the annual budget less income received from other sources. Despite these complications, conclusions drawn from a variety of studies show that the property tax has the ability to raise large amounts of revenue with small increases in nominal tax rates. This result is what makes the property tax such a popular source of local funds, a characteristic that may be unfortunate for taxpayers if administrative problems are not corrected.

Administrative reforms

Some progress has been made in improving administration of the property tax. The Advisory Commission on Intergovernmental Relations (ACIR) (1974:3) has targeted four basic areas for property tax reform. They are legitimacy, procedures, technical proficiency, and compassion.

Legitimacy: This area is concerned with legalizing assessment practices currently in operation. This point recognizes the problem of the differences between state laws regarding assessment and the actual procedures used. There are several ways to rectify this difference, and the ACIR's suggestions include statewide, full value assessment and appraisal; statewide, full value appraisal and uniform functional assessment; and statewide, full value assessment and locally set assessment levels. Each system has a number of advantages and disadvantages; however, the ACIR (1974:6–12) firmly recommends using 100 percent appraisal as a good foundation for a consistent system of property taxation.

Procedures: Another area in need of reform is the information provided to taxpayers regarding rates and procedures of the system, that is, the openness of the property tax. Attempts are being made to take the mystery out of the property tax; one step toward this goal is the increasing use of a full disclosure policy. A good full disclosure policy contains basically four parts: state studies of annual local assessment ratios, publication of these studies, use of these studies as evidence in taxpayer appeals, and a tolerance zone within which the assessment must fall to prohibit appeal (Shannon 1967:104). Areas using full disclosure list all basic information used to calculate the tax on the tax bill, along with some comparative information to give citizens an idea of the fairness of their taxed amount. Taxpayers should also have ready access to information on the system of appeal and any possible tax exemptions.

Although the idea of a full disclosure policy is generally well received, there have been some political obstacles to its implementation. Some policymakers are not eager to publish ratio studies on all districts within a state because this might lead to actions to equalize these ratios and to certain political repercussions.

Technical proficiency: Another way in which property tax administration can be improved is through increasing the technical proficiency of the assessors.

Efforts have been made to raise professional standards and skills of assessors, including better instructional materials and education assistance funds for personnel. The increasing use of computers has improved efficiency in administration and allowed for more frequent and accurate assessment adjustments.

Compassion: The last targeted area of reform, called compassion, focuses on tax relief to people overburdened by the property tax. Perhaps the most common form of a tax relief program is the circuit breaker. It was first introduced in 1964, and now as many as twenty-four states have circuit breaker programs. Just as electrical circuit breakers protect against overloads, these programs are designed to provide protection from excess taxes, usually calculated as an amount over a certain percentage of household income.

Circuit breakers are state tax relief programs, usually run in coordination with the state income tax. Although the principle of the program remains the same, each state has set up its own program guidelines to target particular needs. Coverage among the states varies; some programs are restricted to senior citizen homeowners, others to both senior citizen homeowners and renters, and some to all property taxpayers alike. The states also vary in their determination of what constitutes excess property taxes. Most states use one of two approaches, either the threshold or sliding scale formulas. When using the threshold approach, excessive taxes are taxes above a fixed percentage of household income. Based on the ability to pay, it tends to make residential property tax progressive over a range of incomes.

The sliding scale approach rebates a set percentage of property tax paid to eligible taxpayers within given income classes, with rebate percentages decreasing as income increases. This system maintains tax differentials among jurisdictions and differently valued homes and prevents taxpayers' share of costs from being zero, so that decisions concerning proposed increases will be considered in a responsible manner (ACIR 1974:1–9).

Advantages cited for circuit breakers include lower costs, inclusion of both renters and homeowners, and legal simplicity compared with alternative tax relief programs. The program is under criticism, however, partly on the grounds that circuit breakers tend to subsidize people who spend a large proportion of their income on housing and those with fluctuating incomes. Moreover, under the new view of property taxation, the tax is progressive. Thus, a tax relief system is not justified.

Although administration of the property tax has improved, it still has not reached an acceptable level of efficiency and equity. Because the property tax is the principal source of local revenues and the instrument that helps local autonomy, its improvement is an important problem that still needs much attention.

Other sources of local revenue

Property taxes have been and are the most important source of revenue for all local governments, including municipalities, counties, school districts, townships, and special districts. Nevertheless, local governments continually look for additional sources of revenue. When a jurisdiction relies almost entirely on property taxes for financing spending programs, property owners often oppose certain bond issues that will finance benefits the property owners calculate to be worth less than the property taxes they would have to pay. Consequently, local officials seek alternative sources of revenue in order to broaden the tax base and increase the potential support for community programs. In that way, a superior correspondence between benefits received and taxes paid can be achieved.

The local government tax base has broadened appreciably during the past twenty-five years. In 1957, the property tax provided almost 87 percent of all local government tax revenue; by 1982, that figure had decreased to 76 percent. Municipalities, counties, and special districts were the most successful in broadening their tax base, whereas school districts and townships still collected 96 and 94 percent, respectively, of their total taxes with the property levy in 1982 (ACIR 1983:34).

Sales and gross receipts taxes

All local governments increased their sales taxes as a share of total taxes from about 7 to 13 percent between 1957 and 1982. This substantial increase occurred despite the fact that many local governments do not have the authority to levy sales and gross receipts taxes. Other communities that have the power to impose these taxes have resisted adopting them, believing they would inhibit economic development in their areas by putting the jurisdiction at a disadvantage in a attracting commercial and industrial investment, as well as residential housing.

Nevertheless, nearly four thousand communities now use sales taxes. Naturally, urban and commercial centers benefit more from commodity taxation than do rural areas. Municipalities now collect more than 26 percent of their total tax revenues with the sales tax, a figure far higher than for any other type of local government (ACIR 1983:34).

Most local sales taxes are either administered or controlled by state authorities. Frequently, states collect sales taxes and share a portion with local governments. Cities often piggyback the state tax by adding .05 or 1 percent to the state tax rate.

Local sales taxes have generally worked well, especially where the host state requires uniform rates among the various local taxing jurisdictions. Standard rates prevent differentials among municipalities, protecting merchants from tax rate competition.

Local sales taxes do broaden the tax base and serve to involve more than just property owners in the total budgetary process. Local sales taxes also cause individuals who do not live in the municipality, but shop, work, and use the public facilities of the community, to help pay for cleaner streets, police protection, lighting, and other locally provided services.

Income taxes

All types of local governments except special districts use income taxes. The income levy has been the most rapidly growing local tax during the past twenty-five years. In 1957, local income taxes accounted for only a little more than 1 percent of all revenue, but by 1982, income tax revenues had increased by nearly 500 percent.

A serious problem associated with municipal income taxes involves the potential competition of nontaxed adjacent areas. Imposing an income tax may drive city employers to the suburbs and cause potential businesses to locate in surrounding nontaxed areas in order to avoid the increased cost of hiring labor. It is assumed here that employees are aware of real net take-home pay in their calculations of where and how long they choose to work. This incentive to employer outmigration tends to keep tax rates low if not completely inhibit the adoption of local income taxes.

Another potential problem with income taxes is the relative instability of revenue to government. The elasticity or sensitivity of income tax yields to changes in income is greater than unity. This means that a 10-percent decrease in community income is accompanied by a greater than 10-percent fall in income tax revenues. The decline in government receipts normally occurs just when the demands on government for welfare and other social services are increasing. By way of comparison, it is generally believed that property tax values and sales have an elasticity close to unity, so that revenues do not fall faster than the incomes of residents. They are more stable sources of government revenue.

The costs of administering income taxes can vary greatly among local governments located in different states. Where there is centralized state administration, and this is now the norm, costs of administration tend to be very low. Moreover, some problems involving the allocation of resources are muted somewhat when the tax base and rate are identical for all taxing governments within a state.

As with any local tax, there have been problems with the income tax; but, like the sales tax, it has proved to be a useful complement to the property levy. It has been especially attractive in states in which there has been centralized control and administration. Income taxes broaden the local tax base, cause nonproperty owners to help support local government services, and provide substantial amounts of revenue, especially to relatively wealthy communities.

User costs and fees

One of the most rapidly rising and increasingly important sources of local government public finance is the use of fees and user costs. This movement to the use of prices to finance and supply government goods and services was enhanced in 1978 by the passage of California's Proposition 13 and similar legislation in other states. However, the use of user costs was on the rise before that time.

Rationale

The rationale for charging fees for certain goods and services that governments provide is easy to understand. Goods that have primarily private characteristics, that is, those that satisfy the desires mainly of an individual and can be excluded from use by others (unless paid for) are prime candidates for user charges.

On the other hand, it would be difficult and costly to exclude the benefits of national defense from an individual living in the United States once those goods and services were built and put to use protecting the country. Consequently, governments must compel individuals to pay taxes for these collective type goods rather than permit citizens to choose whether they would like to pay a price for a desired quantity of national defense.

Although elements of collectiveness exist in some goods and services provided by local jurisdictions, private characteristics dominate the vast majority of these goods. Examples of some of these products and services are electric power, gas distribution, water supply, and sewer service. Governments now charge fees for the use of such various recreational facilities as golf courses, swimming pools, municipal and county beaches, parks, tennis courts, and arboreta. Moreover, pricing is currently used in refuse collection, ambulance and bus service, government cemeteries, museums, and libraries. Clearly there is a wide range of items for which local governments can and do charge user fees. Table 12.4 presents a more complete picture of the items that are now priced by cities.

Advantages of user fees

Prices in the private economy serve to determine what and how much shall be produced and the quality of the goods made, and to ration the available but

Table 12.4. *Examples of the fees and charges employed by cities*

Commercial	*Transportation (other than*
Exhibition fees	*mass transit)*
City market charges	Airport fees
Auditorium and conference	Bridge and ferry tolls
center charges	Dockage and wharfage fees
Additional police traffic	Parking fees
control fees	Tow-in and storage charges
Occupational license fees	
	Other
Education	Library charges
School lunch charges	Museum charges and sales
Book and uniform charges	Animal shelter fees
Tuition for adult and other	Trash collection charges
continuing education	Landfill use charges
	Street cut repair fees
Health and related services	Dangerous tree removal fees
Clinic charges	Sanitation permits and fees
Hospital charges	
Ambulance fees	*Public utilities*
Licenses for health facilities	Water service charges
	Electricity charges
Housing	Gas charges
Public housing rental	Mass transit fares
Urban renewal charges	Taxi licensing
Recreation (illustrative)	
Golf course fees	
Tennis fees	
Swimming pool charges	
Ski registration	
Municipal athletics	
Sailing and canoeing	
Park entrance fees	
Camping permits	

Source: Selma J. Mushkin, "The Case for User Fees," *Taxing and Spending,* April 1, 1979, p. 18.

limited supply of goods and services among the competing buyers. By emulating the private market, government can perform these same functions and achieve certain advantages associated with the private sector (Mushkin 1979:16–19).

Prices or user fees tend to adjust the amount and quality of government services to real citizen demand. If fees are not charged, government officials have no accurate measure of the strength of demand for a service. If something worthwhile is free, individuals will take more and more of it. Demand becomes artificially inflated.

Moreover, the voting mechanism is at best a crude caricature of the market and a very imperfect substitute when it comes to fulfilling the economic functions that market pricing performs. The majority tend to obtain what they desire, whereas the minority often lose out. Yet all individuals are compelled to pay for the governmentally provided goods through the payment of taxes.

User fees delineate more clearly the signals that consumers transmit to government. User charges permit citizens to choose both the quantity and type of goods and services desired. They feed valuable information from consumers to government producers. Consequently, efficiency in resource allocation and production is enhanced, and public management is improved. Waste tends to be minimized.

Equity

Interestingly, the use of prices in the public sector may actually improve the equity rating of government in many situations. User fees rest on the premise that people who benefit from a government service should pay for it, and people who do not benefit should not be compelled to pay. Many of the "free" services now provided by government are paid for by taxes on all income groups, but, in many cases, it is the middle and upper income classes who receive the bulk of the benefits from these governmentally provided goods and services. Several items come to mind: tennis courts, golf courses, higher education, ski lodges and slopes, park facilities, airport facilities for private planes, docks for boats, and conference facilities.

It should be noted that equity can be improved by introducing a system of impure fees. Lower income groups could benefit by integrating a sliding scale of fees into a general pricing system. In that way, lower prices could be charged for various items that would loom large in a low income budget. Some items, such as vaccinations for children, might even have a negative price.

One final posssble advantage of employing user costs should be mentioned. Migration of individuals due to government policy would be reduced if some fees were adopted in lieu of high taxes. Outmigration of middle and upper income groups to the suburbs from central cities that have high taxes due to problems associated with poverty, pollution, crime, and congestion would be inhibited if charging for services were instituted. The incentive to move because of paying high taxes that benefit others would be blunted.

Conclusion

Local governments have exercised much ingenuity in diversifying their revenue systems. In addition to local sales, gross receipts, and income taxes, local jurisdictions have increased revenues by using gasoline and parking taxes, license and permit fees, and user fees for many goods and services. Moreover, local governments have been successful in attracting grants from both the federal and state governments. The property tax remains, however, the bulwark of local public finance.

CHAPTER 13

The distribution of tax burdens

Incidence studies seek to determine who actually pays how much in taxes (Break 1974:119–237). Two objects of research on incidence are to determine whether the tax structure of a country has had an effect on the distribution of income and to ascertain if the tax structure is equitable as perceived by the majority of voters. To help find the answers to these questions, researchers study the vertical equity of taxes. Unlike the rule of horizontal equity, which implies that individuals in like economic circumstances should be taxed similarly, vertical equity is concerned with the distribution of taxes between and among different income classes.

Most governments, societies, and countries either explicitly or implicitly use individual or household income as a measure of the economic well-being of the taxpaying unit. Vertical equity in taxation is concerned with the relationship between taxes paid and the income of the taxpayer. Even though a rich individual's tax bill is larger than that of a less wealthy person, if the tax as a proportion of income is lower than that of the person with a smaller income, the levy is characterized as a regressive tax. If the ratio of taxation is constant for all individuals, regardless of the level of income, it is proportional tax. Finally, if the share of income a person pays in taxes increases as income increases, it is a progressive tax.

Although the choice is no longer as clear cut as it was a decade ago, many citizens in industrialized democracies appear to favor a progressive tax as the most equitable kind. This preference by electorates, if it still is a preference, is purely subjective. Economists are unable to defend or attack taxes and tax structure on equity grounds.

Statistical and theoretical problems of tax incidence studies

A researcher faces several difficulties when studying the incidence of taxes. They can best be characterized as statistical and theoretical problems.

The first problem of most tax incidence studies is that they rest in part on surveys of consumer household budgets. Because all consumers are not questioned, the results of these surveys are subject to sampling errors. Perhaps a more important source of difficulty is the fact that those householders questioned must remember, for example, how much money was spent and what items were purchased over the relevant time period. Even with accurate written records, which the average consumer does not keep, the statistics gathered are subject to error.

Fortunately, most householders have a fairly accurate estimate of their income. In addition, income and payroll taxes withheld by employers are normally identifiable and known. Unfortunately, the impact of annual tax liabilities associated with company or corporate incomes, and of such direct taxes as sales taxes and excise duties, is not known precisely by the consumer. In such instances, the researcher must make estimates, which are subject to error.

Estimation is particularly difficult in the case of corporation taxes, because economists have not developed a satisfactory theoretical basis for analyzing the incidence of these levies. Some analysts believe that company taxes are borne only by the company owners, whereas others think that company taxes are passed on entirely to the consumers of the company's products or to its employees or suppliers of factor services. Still others believe that portions of the tax are borne by owners, consumers, and workers. None of these positions is implausible in individual cases. The revealed pattern of incidence, however, depends significantly on which of these various assumptions is adopted.

A similar problem occurs with property taxation. Until relatively recently, almost all tax experts believed that property taxes were regressive. Now H. J. Aaron (1975:18–55, 92–6), a highly respected economist and public finance specialist, has argued that these levies are progressive.

Compounding the statistical difficulties already mentioned is the fact that budget and income surveys normally consist of annual data. The Taxation Review (Aspery) Committee (1974:29–30) notes that "it is tempting with annual statistics to argue as if families in each income group are there all their lives, which of course is not the case."

The lowest income class in almost any budget study nearly always has an average propensity to consume that is greater than unity; often it is greater than two. When a household can spend twice its annual income on consumption, the concept of annual income is obviously not a useful indicator of the economic well-being of that household.

For individuals and households in the present to consume more than their current income, the relationship between their past income and consumption must have been such that positive saving enabled the accumulation of assets that can now be run down. Alternatively, there must be an expectation that future income will exceed consumption (so that liabilities can be incurred currently). The decision to reduce assets or incur liabilities stems from an attempt to stabilize one's consumption over the lifetime of a household (Davies 1961:585).

Normally, it is younger individuals who can incur liabilities in the present in order to consume; older citizens can liquidate past savings in order to consume more than their current annual incomes permit.

Annual income figures tend to understate the long-run incomes of current low income earners. At the same time, they tend to overstate the lifetime incomes of individuals who currently receive high incomes.

This proposition holds because current low income recipients consist, in a large measure, of very young and old retired persons. The remaining lifetime average incomes of young individuals will be higher than their relatively low current incomes. Old and retired workers, who have passed their peak earning years, will have had previous earnings that averaged more than their relatively low or zero incomes. On the other hand, high income earners are, on average, between fifty and fifty-five years of age and at their peak lifetime incomes. Their average lifetime incomes will be less than their current high incomes.

Reliance on annual figures, therefore, tends to overstate the average rate of tax that current lower income recipients pay on their lifetime incomes and to understate the rate of tax of the higher income earners. This conclusion follows from the fact that the rate of taxation is derived by dividing the amount of tax paid by the individual's or household's annual income. As a result, the incidence of tax or the tax structure appears more regressive or less progressive than it actually is in almost all incidence studies (Davies 1963:410–15; 1980:204–7).

Incidence and long-run equity can best be measured by comparing different individuals' ratios of lifetime taxes paid to lifetime income earned, but this information is not available. Probably the next best solution is to use income concepts that have a longer time horizon than one year. Irving Fisher's concept of income and Milton Friedman's notion of permanent income have been used with some success (Davies 1959:72–8; 1960b:987–95; 1971:187–9), but the need for a longer time horizon in incidence studies has only recently been recognized in the literature.

Compounding the problems already mentioned are the basic criticism recently made against the methodology of tax incidence research. L. Thurow (1975:185–94), in his brilliant review of several Brookings essays, notes that the fundamental difficulty with tax incidence studies is that they are empirically formidable and theoretically impossible. As Thurow acknowledges, every tax has three major effects. First, it withdraws income from individuals and the economy. Second, through multipliers and other devices, it generates macroeconomic effects. Finally, a tax helps to pay for government expenditures. The problem for the researcher studying the incidence of a tax is to hold constant the expenditure and macroeconomic effects while analyzing the impact of the tax on real income. This is an extraordinarily difficult task. Thurow argues convincingly that our current techniques for discovering the incidence of taxes are seriously flawed.

In his wide-ranging assessment of the methodology of incidence studies, L. DeWulf (1975:96–104) has also criticized the many empirical investigations that public finance scholars have completed. His reservations are similar to those of Thurow. He contends that the present state of incidence theory is such that no clear conclusions can be reached and empirical studies yield only very approximate results.

Despite the pertinent warnings of Thurow and DeWulf, it is worthwhile examining the latest efforts of scholars engaged in incidence studies. The results are presented in a quantitative format, but the statistical and theoretical problems just discussed should prevent the reader from interpreting the data too literally. There is an unfortunate and unfounded air of precision about the results of incidence research. These estimates are at best very general impressions of reality.

Empirical results of research on tax incidence

This section presents estimates of federal, state–local, and total tax rates by income class for the United States. We shall examine the figures from each of two separate studies.

United States taxes as a proportion of income

The most ambitious tax incidence study of any country is the one completed by J. Pechman and B. Okner (1974) on the United States. It is based on what they call the MERGE file. To alleviate deficiencies in the raw material that formed the basis for previous research on tax incidence, Pechman and Okner combined information on thirty thousand families and single persons included in the 1967 Survey of Economic Opportunity (conducted by the Census Bureau for the U.S. Office of Economic Opportunity) with a file containing information from ninety thousand federal, individual income tax returns filed for the year 1966.

Pechman and Okner provide the reader with eight different sets of assumptions about the tax shifting process, each one illustrating a plausible but different approach to the incidence of the tax structure. We shall deal only with what they call variants 1C and 3B. The assumptions of variant 1C produce the most progressive looking tax structure; those of 3B generate the least progressive system. The assumptions associated with the other variants yield a pattern of tax incidence that falls between those of variants 1C and 3B.

The assumptions behind variant 1C are:

1. individual income taxes are not shifted;
2. sales and excise taxes are paid by consumers;

Table 13.1. *United States taxes as percent of income, 1966*

Income range $ per annum	Variant 1C[a]			Variant 3B[b]		
	Federal	State local	Total	Federal	State local	Total
0–3,000	8.8	9.8	18.7	14.1	14.1	28.1
3,000–5,000	11.9	8.5	20.4	14.6	10.6	25.3
5,000–10,000	15.4	7.2	22.6	17.0	8.9	25.9
10,000–15,000	16.3	6.5	22.8	17.5	8.0	25.5
15,000–20,000	16.7	6.5	23.2	17.7	7.6	25.3
20,000–25,000	17.1	6.9	24.0	17.8	7.4	25.1
25,000–30,000	17.4	7.7	25.1	17.2	7.1	24.3
30,000–50,000	18.2	8.2	26.4	17.7	6.7	24.4
50,000–100,000	21.8	9.7	31.5	20.1	6.3	26.4
100,000–500,000	30.0	11.9	41.8	24.4	6.0	30.3
500,000–1,000,000	34.6	13.3	48.0	25.2	5.1	30.3
1,000,000 and over	35.5	13.8	49.3	24.8	4.2	29.0
Total	17.6	7.6	25.2	17.9	8.0	25.9

[a] Variant 1C assumes that corporation income and property fall on owners of property.
[b] Variant 3B assumes that half of the corporation income tax and all taxes on improved property are passed forward to consumers.
Source: J. A. Pechman and B. A. Okner, *Who Bears the Tax Burden?* The Brookings Institution, Washington, D.C., 1974, p. 62.

3. corporation taxes and property taxes fall on owners;
4. payroll taxes are borne by employees;
5. income consists of wages, interest, dividends, rents, royalties, accrued capital gains, and transfer payments; and
6. annual income for the one year is an accurate reflection of the economic position or well-being of a household.

The use of these assumptions and the necessary statistical manipulations produce the results recorded on the left side of Table 13.1 (under the heading Variant 1C). Tax rates rise continuously from the lowest to the highest income group. State–local rates of taxation are regressive through the lower income ranges but progressive from the $5,000 to the $1,000,000 and over income classes. The average rate of taxation for all residents was just over 25 percent. The rate of state–local taxation averaged 7.6 percent and that for the federal government was 17.6 percent, or about two and one-third times the rate for subnational jurisdictions.

As mentioned, the assumptions associated with Pechman and Okner's variant 3B produce the least progressive tax structure of the eight variants they construct. Variant 3B reflects the following differences from variant 1C:

1. half the corporation income tax is assumed to be passed on to consumers;
2. property taxes on land are borne by landowners only and not by
   recipients of property income in general;
3. taxes on improved property (dwellings, etc.) are shifted to consumers; and
4. half the payroll tax on employers is passed forward to consumers.

These differences in assumptions are responsible for the significant differences recorded between the left and right sides of Table 13.1. The second set
of estimates of average tax rates suggests that federal rates are only mildly
progressive, state–local figures are regressive throughout the entire income
range, and finally that the pattern of total rates of taxation is U-shaped.

The U-shaped pattern of effective ratios means that the tax structure is
regressive in the lower ranges of income, proportional in the middle ranges,
and rather sharply progressive at the higher end of the income scale. It is not
unusual to observe that the lowest income class or two has a higher taxation
rate than succeeding middle income households. In some twenty-two countries that DeWulf (1975:111–14) surveys, twelve reveal that the tax structure
is regressive between the lowest and next-to-lowest income group.

The purported relatively high tax rate for the lowest income class is due
partly to the underlying assumptions about tax shifting. However, probably
the most important influence is the previously noted tendency for annual income
to underestimate significantly the economic position of most households located
in the lowest income class.

Budget studies repeatedly show that consumption expenditures for the lowest income group range from 150 to 350 percent of annual mean income.
Although the economic well-being of the average household in the lowest
income class cannot, by any stretch of the imagination, be characterized as
affluent, it is much stronger than its annual income suggests. The high estimate of the effective tax rate for this group is largely illusory.

In relation to the figures in Table 13.1 and those following, it should be
emphasized that the average tax rate calculated for a given income range hides
both large and small differences among individual households. Moreover, the
dispersion around the average effective tax rate increases as the average income
of the particular group increases.

Pechman and Okner (1974:71–82) report interesting discoveries that do not
depend crucially on the differences in incidence assumptions they make. They
find that homeowners pay lower taxes than renters, urban residents pay lower
taxes than people living in rural areas, and single people pay higher taxes than
married couples. Families that have the major portion of their income from
transfer payments have the lowest rate of tax, and households that derive large
incomes from property pay the highest effective tax rates.

One conclusion is particularly noteworthy. Pechman and Okner (1974:38) find that, no matter which of their various sets of assumptions on incidence they use, income from capital bears a much heavier tax load than income from labor. If corporation income taxes and property taxes are assumed to be taxes on capital, the average rate of tax on capital is calculated at 33 percent, compared to an average effective rate of about 17.5 percent for labor.

Even if corporation income and property taxes are assumed to be paid in whole or in part by consumers, capital is subject to a significantly higher tax rate than labor. The eight different sets of assumptions yield a mean tax rate of about 25 percent on capital and 17 percent on labor. For a society that relies primarily on increases in capital to create job opportunities and rising real per capita incomes, these are sobering statistics.

The statistics completed by Pechman and Okner (1974:81) also reveal that sales and excise taxes are proportional or very mildly progressive. Under the assumptions of both variants 1C and 3B, the tax rate on consumption increases as income rises, beginning with the very lowest population decile in the income distribution and continuing through the first several population deciles.

This interesting general tendency, first reported by the author (Davies 1959:72–8; 1960b:987–95), is due partly to the fact that the very lowest income recipients have been eliminated from the analysis. When Pechman and Okner (1974:67–8) arrange their data by population deciles of the income distribution rather than by income classes, they explicitly modify their assumption (which underlies figures in Table 13.1) that the annual income for any given year accurately reflects the economic well-being of a household or individual. They correctly justify eliminating the very lowest income recipients from consideration by noting that "annual incomes in the first five percentiles are not representative of the income of such units over a long period."

As indicated in an earlier section in this Chapter, entitled Statistical and Theoretical Problems of Tax Incidence Studies, cogent reasons can also be observed for readjusting downward the relatively high incomes reported in any given year. Individuals ordinarily begin their lifetime income cycle at young ages with relatively low incomes, see their incomes peak when they are approximately fifty years old, and experience falling incomes during the last working decade of life and near zero incomes during retirement. The probability is extremely high that a household experiencing large earnings in a given year had considerably lower income before that year and will earn lower income during some time period after that year. The current year income overestimates the true long-run economic position of this household. In relation to that year's high income, tax rates paid are made to appear lower than warranted. As a consequence, the upper end of the tax structure seems to be less progressive or more regressive than it actually is if the economic well-being of taxpayers is measured accurately.

Pechman and Okner (1974:54) agree that high annual incomes, like very low annual incomes, vary substantially, "but, at these levels, the effect of income variability on the effective rates of consumption and property taxes is likely to be small because the ratio of consumption and housing expenditures to income is small." It should be emphasized, however, that scholars use income not only to help calculate tax liabilities but also to measure the economic position of taxpayers. In the final analysis, it is the ratio of taxes paid to income that yields the rate of taxation for the various households and income classes. If the income concept adopted overestimates the economic position of a household, the resultant tax rate will appear to be larger than it is.

Pechman and Okner (1974:5–6) reach the general conclusion that the United States tax structure is virtually proportional or only slightly progressive for most households. On the average, federal and state–local taxes amounted to about 25 percent of income. There is not much variation from this average for households and individuals in the range of incomes between $2000 and $30,000, a range that encompasses approximately 87 percent of all family units. Table 13.1 shows that above the income level of $30,000, tax rates become sharply progressive under the assumptions of variant 1C but only mildly so under variant 3B. Under the most progressive set of assumptions, taxes reduce inequality as measured by the Gini coefficient by less than 5 percent.

The Browning–Johnson tax burden study

Edgar K. Browning and William R. Johnson (1979) completed a more recent study of tax burdens in the United States. Their work is based on data collected by the U.S. Census Bureau from a representative sample of households.

In making estimates of the United States tax burden, Browning and Johnson (1979:5) make the following assumptions:

1. individual income taxes are not significantly shifted;
2. corporation and property taxes fall on all owners of capital;
3. employee and employer payroll taxes are borne by employees;
4. the burden of sales taxes rests on factors of production; and
5. income consists of money income, income-in-kind (e.g., food stamps), imputed rental income from owner-occupied residences, and accrued capital gains.

The authors also make alternative assumptions about the degree of competition in the economy. One set of burden estimates assumes a competitive economy; another set is based on noncompetitive incidence assumptions. There is, however, little difference in the two sets of estimates.

Table 13.2. *Average tax rates by income decile (percent)*

Income decile	Type of tax				
	Sales and excise	Payroll	Income	Property and corporation income	Combined
1	2.3%	3.3%	0.7%	5.5%	11.7%
2	2.6	3.9	1.8	4.2	12.5
3	3.4	5.4	3.0	4.5	16.3
4	4.1	6.9	4.7	4.4	20.2
5	4.7	8.0	6.4	4.1	23.2
6	5.0	8.5	8.1	3.9	25.5
7	5.2	8.2	9.5	3.8	26.7
8	5.3	7.9	10.8	4.1	28.1
9	5.3	7.2	12.2	5.3	30.0
10	5.5	3.8	13.6	15.4	38.3
Top 1 percent	5.6	1.1	12.4	28.8	47.9
All deciles	4.9	6.2	10.0	7.9	29.1

Source: Edgar K. Browning and William R. Johnson, *The Distribution of the Tax Burden,* American Enterprise Institute, Washington, D.C., 1979, p. 51.

Major findings: The major findings of the Browning–Johnson research are summarized in Table 13.2. Household income is ranked from the lowest 10 percent or first decile to the highest or tenth decile. The most striking feature is the highly progressive nature of the U.S. tax structure. The average rate of taxation of the combined federal, state, and local tax systems rises continuously and significantly from 11.7 percent in the lowest decile to 38.3 percent in the highest 10 percent of households. It doubles over the first five deciles and then increases less rapidly over the next five deciles. The sharpest increase in tax rates, however, occurs between the highest and next highest deciles. Although the average tax rate for the whole population is approximately 29 percent, the top 1 percent of households have a combined rate of nearly 50 percent.

Income taxes manifest the highest degree of progressivity of the four major groups of taxes, although, interestingly, the top 1 percent of households have an effective rate (12.4 percent) that is slightly below that of the highest decile (13.6 percent). Sales and excise taxes show progressivity throughout the ten deciles. The tenth decile has a rate just about double the lowest 10 percent of households. Property and corporation income taxes display a very definite U-shaped pattern of rates. The top 10 percent of households have rates that are about 300 percent higher than any other decile; the top 1 percent bear an average rate nearly twice that of the tenth decile and more than 500 percent

Table 13.3. *Average tax rates by income class (percent)*

Income (thousands of dollars)	Number of households (millions)	Type of tax				
		Sales and excise	Payroll	Income	Property and corporation income	Combined
0–5	7.58	2.3%	3.3%	0.7%	5.5%	11.7%
5–10	14.37	3.0	4.7	2.4	4.4	14.5
10–15	13.65	4.3	7.3	5.3	4.2	21.0
15–20	11.93	5.0	8.4	8.0	4.0	25.3
20–25	9.06	5.2	8.2	9.9	3.9	27.1
25–30	6.59	5.3	7.7	11.2	4.5	28.8
30–40	6.52	5.3	7.1	12.6	5.4	30.4
40–50	2.92	5.4	5.9	13.8	7.8	32.9
50–100	2.76	5.5	3.7	14.4	13.5	37.0
100+	0.69	5.6	1.1	12.4	28.9	48.0

Source: Edgar K. Browning and William R. Johnson, *The Distribution of the Tax Burden,* American Enterprise Institute, Washington, D.C., 1979, p. 53.

higher than any other decile. The payroll tax reveals a picture opposite that of property and corporation income levies. Its pattern can be described as an upside down U. This behavior partly reflects the fact that there is an upper limit of income that is subject to payroll taxes.

Table 13.3 reveals the same type of information contained in Table 13.2. The principal difference is that households are categorized by dollar income, rather than having household income divided into deciles.

The general patterns observed in Table 13.2 are again present. The higher the income group, the higher the average rate of taxation. The overall structure is markedly progressive. The highest income class pays rates that are more than 400 percent higher than the lowest income group, and the medium taxpayer pays a combined rate that is approximately two and a half times that of the lowest income classification. The lower 50 percent of the households face income tax rates that range from .7 percent to about 8 percent. The upper 50 percent pay average rates that range from 9.9 to a little more than 14 percent.

This structure of rates, along with the distribution of households by income size, is compatible with a Tax Foundation (1985:1) study that found that the top 50 percent of income earners pay 93 percent of the federal income tax bill, whereas the bottom 50 percent bear 7 percent of the income taxes collected. The top 10 percent pay about 50 percent of the bill. Moreover, this sharp degree of progression is on the rise, as Table 13.4 illustrates.

Table 13.5 shows that for all taxes combined, the upper 50 percent of the

Table 13.4. *Federal income taxes paid by high and low income taxpayers 1975 and 1983*

Adjusted gross income class	Income level		Percent of tax paid		Average tax	
	1975	1983	1975	1983	1975	1983
Highest 10%	$23,425 or more	$41,501 or more	48.6	50.3	$7,367	$14,419
Highest 25%	15,895 or more	27,806 or more	66.4	73.4	4,359	8,420
Highest 50%	8,930 or more	14,888 or more	92.9	93.1	2,815	5,339
Lowest 50%	8,929 or less	14,887 or less	7.1	6.9	214	386
Lowest 25%	4,044 or less	6,882 or less	.4	.6	22	72
Lowest 10%	1,525 or less	2,723 or less	nil	nil	2	12

Source: Monthly Tax Features, Tax Foundation, Washington, D.C., May 1985, 1.

Table 13.5. *Share of total tax paid by decile (percent)*

Income decile	Type of tax				
	Sales and excise	Payroll	Income	Property and corporation income	Combined
1	0.7%	0.8%	0.1%	1.0%	0.6%
2	1.6	2.0	0.6	1.7	1.4
3	3.0	3.8	1.3	2.5	2.5
4	4.7	6.3	2.7	3.2	3.9
5	6.6	9.1	4.5	3.7	5.6
6	8.6	11.6	6.9	4.3	7.5
7	10.6	13.5	9.6	5.0	9.4
8	13.1	15.7	13.3	6.5	11.9
9	16.9	18.2	19.1	10.6	16.2
10	34.2	19.0	42.0	61.5	40.9
All deciles	100.0	100.0	100.0	100.0	100.0

Source: Edgar K. Browning and William R. Johnson, *The Distribution of the Tax Burden,* American Enterprise Institute, Washington, D.C., 1979, p. 58.

taxpayers pay 86 percent of the total tax load, whereas the lower half pays the balance of 14 percent. Browning and Johnson's figures on the income tax differ somewhat from the Tax Foundation's estimates, partly because they include state and local as well as federal data on this levy.

Browning and Johnson also calculate the average rate of taxation for the four major federal levies. These are shown in Table 13.6. Excise and personal income taxes are progressive. The corporation income tax is progressive from

Table 13.6. *Average rates of federal taxes (percent)*

| Income decile | Type of tax | | | | |
	Excise	Payroll	Income	Corporation income	Combined
1	0.7%	3.3%	0.6%	2.4%	7.0%
2	0.8	3.9	1.6	1.9	8.1
3	1.0	5.4	2.6	2.0	11.1
4	1.2	6.9	4.0	1.9	14.2
5	1.5	8.0	5.5	1.8	16.7
6	1.5	8.5	6.9	1.7	18.6
7	1.6	8.2	8.1	1.7	19.5
8	1.6	7.9	9.1	1.8	20.4
9	1.6	7.2	10.2	2.4	21.4
10	1.7	3.8	11.6	6.8	23.9
All deciles	1.4	6.2	8.5	3.6	19.8

Source: Edgar K. Browning and William R. Johnson, *The Distribution of the Tax Burden,* American Enterprise Institute, Washington, D.C., 1979, p. 63.

the first through sixth deciles, but turns regressive because of the upper limit of income to which social security rates may be applied. Overall, the rate rises from 7 percent to about 24 percent between the lowest and highest deciles of household income.

Table 13.7 shows the average rates of taxation for the major taxes employed by state and local governments. The pattern of the combined property and corporation income tax is once again U-shaped, although the highest decile bears a rate almost three times that of the first or lowest decile. The income, sales, and excise levies are progressive. Their weight in the combined total is such that the overall state–local tax system in the United States is progressive.

This finding is at odds with the Pechman–Okner study, mainly because Browning and Johnson do not treat sales taxes as consumer levies but, rather, as taxes on factors of income. This feature, along with Browning and Johnson's broad definition of income, helps explain the overall difference in tax burdens that exists between these two major studies.

It is sometimes alleged that federal taxes are much more progressive than state–local tax structures. Indeed, Pechman and Okner find that state–local systems are primarily regressive. Browning and Johnson's (1979:64) findings do show a difference between the two tax systems, but they are both progressive, and the contrast between them is moderate. As they point out, the top decile tax rate in the central government system is approximately 3.4 times the lowest rate, whereas the comparable figure for the state–local tax structure

Table 13.7. *Average rates of state and local taxes (percent)*

Income decile	Type of tax			
	Sales and excise	Income	Property and corporation income	Combined
1	1.6%	0.1%	3.1%	4.7%
2	1.8	0.2	2.3	4.4
3	2.4	0.4	2.5	5.2
4	2.9	0.7	2.5	6.0
5	3.2	0.9	2.3	6.5
6	3.5	1.2	2.2	6.9
7	3.6	1.4	2.1	7.1
8	3.7	1.7	2.3	7.7
9	3.7	2.0	2.9	8.6
10	3.8	2.0	8.6	14.4
All deciles	3.5	1.5	4.3	9.3

Source: Edgar K. Browning and William R. Johnson, *The Distribution of the Tax Burden,* American Enterprise Institute, Washington, D.C., 1979, p. 64.

is 3.1. These crude figures hide some important differences, but the similarities between the systems are marked.

A final caveat

At the beginning of this chapter, we warn that tax incidence studies, at least of entire tax systems, rest on very tenuous theoretical foundations. The warning needs to be repeated and emphasized. It is easy to fall prey to the sense of security and objectivity that quantification seems to bring to investigations. A false sense of precision is often introduced where it is not warranted.

Yet, the correct use of statistical techniques is often precisely the safeguard required to put quantitative results in their proper perspective. Perhaps this is what Professor Thurow (1975:191) had in mind when he commented on the considerable contribution made by Pechman and Okner. He observed that, given the reported statistical dispersion in results within each income class, the pattern of effective rates of taxation reported in Table 13.1 is neither interesting nor important. The variance within each income class "is much larger than the variance across income classes. The tax system is both progressive and regressive."

CHAPTER 14

Status of U.S. taxes and policy

How do U.S. taxes and policy stack up against the various criteria for a sound and effective tax system enumerated in Chapter 1? The answer is not encouraging.

By the mid-1980s, the chorus of critics of the tax structure had grown enormously. As Pechman (1982:145) notes, there is an almost universal demand for tax revisions and tax reduction. The reason for this state of affairs is the intense and near universal dissatisfaction with the way taxes actually work in practice. They fail to a significant degree to meet the principles of a good tax. Chapters 1, 2, 3, 5, 6, 7, and 8 chronical a long list of important and critical defects in the federal tax structure.

Despite the recent legislation authorizing the indexing of the individual income tax, the tax system as a whole has not been able to cope effectively with the capricious and counterproductive effects of inflation. Moreover, there is danger that this partial indexing of the system will be repealed by a Congress deeply concerned over unprecedentedly high and continuing budget deficits.

Other serious defects embedded in the tax structure include the existence of a socially unproductive tax shelter industry; the extreme complexity of the system with the concurrent growth of the tax preparation and avoidance industry; the inequitable and inefficient marriage, payroll, capital gains, and individual and corporate income taxes; and the high cost of administering these levies. Perhaps more important is their built-in bias against saving, investment, and work effort, and, at the same time, their encouragement of consumption, leisure, and the evasion of taxes through illegal activity in the large and growing underground economy.

Prospects for reform

It is unlikely that the United States tax structure will be improved significantly in the near term. Congressional tax and finance committees are at present virtual prisoners of highly organized, well-financed, single issue, special interest groups. Because of the nature of modern representative government, these powerful organizations exert influence on tax laws far in excess of their small size. Taxpayers remain rationally ignorant of tax matters because the cost to the average taxpayer in terms of the time, money, and effort needed to fight well-organized, narrow, special interest groups greatly exceeds the benefits of their opposing the tax privileges requested by and granted to a given lobby. These factors are exactly why the federal income tax base is constantly being eroded and becoming ever more capricious in its effects on Americans.

Nevertheless, tax reform is a recurrent theme in the United States. A time comes when the situation becomes so imperfect that a growing recognition of the need for basic change becomes apparent. That time is imminent because tax scholars, lawyers, business and financial executives, and many legislators now recognize the desirability of fundamental improvement in the federal revenue system. Moreover, the public at large is beginning to share this view. Economists and others would do well to recognize, however, that the barrier to effective tax reform and policy is more a political than economic problem.

Michael Graetz (1983:267) touches on this issue when he notes that the politics of tax policy in 1983 are quite different from those in 1969. He observes that power has become much more diffuse in Congress, and the Political Action Committees (PACs) have enormous influence over the direction of campaign financing. David Broder (1985:4D) notes that approximately 600 PACs gave $12.5 million in campaign contributions in 1974. A decade later, 4000 PACs gave candidates more than $100 million. This remarkable difference represents a 700 percent increase in donations.

John Witte (1985a:18–19) has made a strong argument that representative democracy harbors deep institutional defects that now generate failures in tax policy. The over-representation of special-interest tax groups and the behavior of the rationally ignorant individual taxpayer-voter dictates that decisions on tax policy need for the most part to be insulated from congressional politics.

Witte's (1985a:17) careful research traces the history of the income tax in the United States and shows clearly the results of the increasing democratization of the tax policy process in Congress that began in the early 1970s. His analysis centers on the rate of increase in tax expenditures (loopholes) that normally increase benefits to some select group of individuals. Tax expenditures generally decrease the tax base, increase the complexity of the tax code and tax regulations, weaken horizontal equity by the introduction and expansion of "tax breaks" to select groups or individuals, and exacerbate market distortions and economic inefficiencies.

The many changes in the early 1970s in congressional rules that further democratized the House of Representatives weakened the power of the Committee on Ways and Means and its chairman. Witte (1985a:5) notes that following these changes, the number of modifications in tax expenditures adopted by Congress skyrocketed. These expenditure changes averaged about six per year between 1946 and 1969. During the early 1970s and post-Watergate era, they averaged about seventeen a year, an increase of more than 175 percent.

Most changes in tax expenditures increase the benefits to special interests. In the period prior to congressional reforms, expanded benefits represented about 52.5 percent of the modifications in tax expenditures. Since 1970 that figure has increased to 64 percent. Between 1946 and 1969, approximately 43 percent of the changes tightened up provisions while only 4.5 percent had a neutral impact. Figures for the period after 1970 shows that only about 26 percent of the modifications in tax expenditures represented reduced benefits (Witte 1985:17).

Witte (1985a:18–19) concludes with much evidence to support his position that the tax problem is rooted in flawed institutional arrangements that permit excessive, virtually unconstrained representation of a plethora of narrow special interests. Meaningful reform, something beyond a multitude of political trades, under present political institutions essentially is doomed to failure.

A survey of econometric studies on tax rates and capital gains

In addition to the cross-sectional analysis cited in the text, Feldstein and Slemrod (1978c:134) have used time series analysis to study the lock-in effect and its impact on government revenue. They compared the two years before the 1969 Act that increased taxes with the two years most recently available. Realized gains increased by 18 percent during this period for individuals with income less than $100,000. Investors with incomes between $100,000 and $500,000, and those in excess of $500,000 whose tax rates were more substantially affected by the 1969 law, realized gains decreased by 12 percent and 35 percent, respectively. The time series data support the idea of sensitivity developed in their massive NBER cross-sectional study (Feldstein 1978b:508).

Feldstein and Slemrod (1978c:134) conclude that under high rates of taxation unrealized gains remain locked into portfolios. Lowering tax rates would unlock them and permit a substantially higher volume of trading in assets, which would not only make investors better off but also make Treasury richer in the process, at least in the short run (Feldstein 1979b:55).

Otto Eckstein, the president of Data Resources, Inc., agrees with the NBER finding. He notes that investors in the top tax bracket "don't sell stock and don't take their capital gains" (Zucker 1978:24). Researchers at Data Resources, who analyzed a series of tax proposals, estimated that if the tax on capital gains were totally eliminated, federal tax receipts would decline by $5.1 billion in 1978 but then rise by approximately $38 billion during the next five years ("Footnotes to the Above" 1978:20).

It is interesting to note that Congress drafted and approved a law in the spring of 1984 that decreased the holding period for long-term tax eligibility from twelve to six months for individual taxpayers. This action was based on the belief that the lock-in effect, with its adverse effect on capital market efficiency, would be reduced. Such a change will reduce effective rates of taxation and increase the number of sales of capital assets.

Chase Econometrics Associates has pointed to other positive economic effects that would flow from a cut in taxes on capital gains. After analyzing a proposal set forth in 1978 by Senator Hansen and Congressman Steiger, which set the precedent for the actual tax reduction in capital gains taxation, Chase researchers concluded that decreasing the top rate on capital gains from approximately 50 to 25 percent would have such a positive effect on economic growth that the government budget deficit would be reduced. They estimated that an additional 440,000 jobs would be created by 1985, and that the government deficit would be $16 billion less than what it would be if the Hansen–Steiger tax cut bill were not adopted and tax rates were left unaltered ("Footnotes to the Above" 1978:20).

Criticism of research on the revenue sensitivity of tax reduction

Economists other than those at Treasury disagree with the findings of the NBER, Data Resources, and Chase Econometrics. Joseph Pechman of The Brookings Institution is skeptical of their econometric results. He agrees that a reduction in rates will unlock portfolios but does not believe that investors are as sensitive to changes in the tax rates as the Feldstein and Slemrod results indicate. Pechman does not believe that there can be a Laffer effect in the current practice of taxing capital gains whereby tax receipts would actually increase as Congress reduces rates (Zucker 1978:24).

One criticism against the NBER results emanated from John Yinger (1978:428), a staff member of the President's Council of Economic Advisers, on the eve of Senate debate on the 1978 Tax Act and after the House of Representatives voted against President Carter's position on taxation by reporting out a bill that cut taxes on capital gains. Yinger made three principal objections to the research done at the National Bureau of Economic Research.

The first criticism was that Feldstein et al. failed to take into account the possibility that a taxpayer, at the time he or she wished to sell assets, might use tax shelters and deductions to reduce the marginal levy on earned income and, therefore, decrease the rate to be applied to capital gains (Yinger 1978:428). If the practice Yinger envisaged were significant, there would be little or no lock-in effect because an investor could virtually escape paying large amounts of taxes on capital gains.

The implication of this reasoning is that high rates of taxation levied on capital gains do not inhibit the selling of assets nor cause Treasury to lose revenue. Yinger's point is that there is not likely to be, as the NBER researchers assume, a one-way causal relationship between changing tax rates, the independent variable, and the realization of gains, the dependent variable.

There is also an objection in the staff paper of the Council of Economic Advisers to the use by NBER economists of cross-sectional data as a base for extrapolating trends overtime. In addition, Yinger (1978:428) states that Feldstein et al. do not consider the revenue effect that lowering capital gains tax rates would have on the policies of companies regarding dividend distribution. Yinger argues that if the recommendations of the NBER studies were adopted, investors would be encouraged to turn over and sell assets more often, thereby realizing gains more frequently. However, lower tax rates on capital gains create the incentive for individuals to exchange shares that carry a history of large dividend payouts for securities with anticipated large gains. He concludes that because the tax rate on dividends is higher than that on capital gains, Treasury's revenue loss on dividends may more than offset the increase in receipts from the taxation of gains.

Feldstein's defense of sensitivity research

Feldstein (1978b:507–8) turns aside Yinger's criticisms. He agrees that some investors are able to lower their tax rate on capital gains with the use of tax shelters and deductions in the year they wish to sell assets to realize gains, but he is confident that this kind of behavior has little impact on the total pattern of variation in the rates among taxpayers. As a result, he believes that distortion in the NBER estimates from this factor is likely to be small.

In answer to Yinger's objections to drawing historical inferences from cross-sectional analyses, Feldstein points to the corroborating evidence in a previously cited paper that used time series evidence to analyze the relationship between the lock-in effect and taxes on capital gains. He believes this work clearly supports the massive cross-sectional study completed at the National Bureau of Economic Research.

Feldstein concedes the third criticism in the CEA staff report that lowering tax rates on capital gains may cause investors to switch from shares with a record of high dividends paid to stocks with high anticipated gains. He states that any loss in revenue to Treasury as a result of such switching will occur only in the short run. He also reasons that a temporary reduction in the growth of taxable dividends, together with such factors as growth in corporate earnings and increases in share prices, will lead to long-run growth of companies. Under these circumstances, a reduction in the capital gains tax may eventually be responsible for the growth in taxable dividends, with a consequent rise in revenue from this source (Feldstein 1978b:507–8; Feldstein, Slemrod, and Yitzhaki 1980:777–91).

Further criticism and advancement of sensitivity research

Using a pooled, time series/cross section sample, Gerald Auten and Charles Clotfelter (1982:613–32) conducted a careful study of the elasticity of capital gains realization with respect to marginal tax rates. Their approach allows them to differentiate between transitory and permanent tax effects. This factor is important because some changes in realizations are due to taxpayers choosing the timing of their sales to take advantage of fluctuations in their incomes rather than changes in the marginal tax rates per se.

Further criticism and advancement of sensitivity research

Auten and Clotfelter (1982:613–32) introduce several independent variables in their econometric work to control for transitory and permanent income, as well as several other factors. Moreover, unlike Feldstein et al., they examine realizations from all sources of capital and not just from the sale of shares. In addition, they have a smaller number of high income taxpayers in their panel of taxpayers so that their results are probably more representative of the behavior of moderate income households.

Their results indicate that permanent reductions in capital gains tax rates significantly increase realizations of long-term capital gains. Auten and Clotfelter (1982:613–32) conclude, however, that their estimates, unlike those of Feldstein et al., do not provide strong support for the notion that tax rate deductions will actually increase tax revenues for the Treasury.

Minarik's model

Building from the latest version of the capital gains model of the Feldstein research team, Joseph Minarik (1981:241–77) produced a critical and imaginative econometric analysis of capital gains realizations. He introduces weighting techniques into the estimating equations and, following an early paper by Auten and Clotfelter, incorporates additional independent variables in an attempt to control for transitory influences on the marginal rates taxation.

An important consequence of these procedures is the production of appreciably lower elasticity estimates on the sensitivity of sales or realizations of capital to changes in tax rates than those of the Feldstein team. The elasticity for all income classes together is -0.79, which means that, on average, shareholders would increase their realizations of gains but by a smaller percentage than a reduction in the capital gains tax. Minarik's two highest dividend income classes of $20,000–$50,000 and $50,000 and over each have elasticities in excess of unity, although the former's figure is only -1.08 causing realizations to increase just slightly more than a cut in tax rates. Elasticity for the $50,000 and over dividend income group is -1.27. Tax revenues would, therefore, increase following a reduction in the tax rate for the highest income class (Minarek 1981:262–63).

It is clear that despite the use of the latest econometric techniques, there are substantial differences in the results of various investigators. James Wetzler (1981:280–81), who has been critical of all empirical work done on the elasticity of realizations with respect to tax rates, believes the problem with these statistical investigations lies in the undeveloped theory of capital gains behavior. He suggests more work on the theory of investor's holding periods and the exact relationship between these periods and realizations. Once the relevant theory is straightened out, empirical results should begin to converge around common estimates. Nevertheless, modeling capital gains behavior is an extremely complicated exercise. One must conclude, at least for now, that we are not sure exactly what the revenue effects are of a cut in capital gains tax rates.

References

Aaron, H. 1975. *Who Pays the Property Tax?* Washington, D.C.: The Brookings Institution.

(ed.) 1976. *Inflation and the Income Tax.* Washington, D.C.: The Brookings Institution.

1981. *The Value Added Tax.* Washington, D.C.: The Brookings Institution.

1982. *Economic Effects of Social Security.* Washington, D.C.: The Brookings Institution.

Aaron, H. and M. Boskin (eds.) 1980. *The Economics of Taxation.* Washington, D.C.: The Brookings Institution.

"Administration Deficit Projection." 1984. *The Wall Street Journal* December 3:3.

Advisory Commission on Intergovernmental Relations 1974. *The Property Tax in a Changing Environment.* Washington, D.C.: ACIR.

1980. *Changing Public Attitudes on Governments and Taxes.* Washington, D.C.: ACIR.

1981. *Interstate Tax Competition.* Washington, D.C.: ACIR.

1983. *Significant Features of Fiscal Federalism.* Washington, D.C.: ACIR.

American Legislative Exchange Council 1982. "Option Three: State Lotteries," *The State Factor* January:3–4.

Anderson, H. et al. 1981. "Putting Reaganomics to the Test," *Newsweek* June 15:29.

Anderson, M. 1978. "The Roller-Coaster Income Tax," *The Public Interest* Winter: 17–28.

Ando, A. and F. Modigliani 1963. "The Life Cycle Hypothesis of Saving," *American Economic Review* 53:55–84.

1964. "The Life Cycle Hypothesis of Saving, Correction," *American Economic Review* 54:111–13.

Andrews, W. 1974. "A Consumption-Type or Cash Flow Personal Income Tax," *Harvard Law Review* 87:April:11:13–88.

Arak, M. 1980–81. "Inflation and Stock Values," *Federal Reserve Bank of New York Quarterly Review* 5:Winter:3–13.

"Archer Traces Roots of Problems in Social Security Trust Fund." 1981. *Monthly Tax Features* (Tax Foundation) 25:May:3.

Atkinson, A. and N. Stern 1980. "Taxation and Incentives in the UK," *Lloyds Bank Review* April:43–51.

Auerbach, A. 1981. "Inflation and the Tax Treatment of Firm Behavior," *American Economic Review* 71:419–23.

Auerbach, A. and L. Kotlikoff 1981. "An Examination of Empirical Tests of Social Security and Savings," NBER Working Paper No. 730.

293

294   References

Auerbach, A. and L. Summers 1979. *The Investment Tax Credit: An Evaluation.* NBER Working Paper No. 404.

Auten, G. and C. Clotfelter 1982. "Permanent vs. Transitory Tax Effects and the Realization of Capital Gains," *Quarterly Journal of Economics* 96:613–32.

Bahl, R. 1980. "State and Local Government Finances and the Changing National Economy," in *Special Study on Economic Change* 7. Joint Economic Committee, Washington, D.C.: USGPO.

   1984. *Financing State and Local Government in the 1980s.* New York: Oxford University Press.

Bailey, H. 1969. "Capital Gains and Income Taxation," in A. Harberger and H. Bailey (eds.), *The Taxation of Income from Capital.* Washington, D.C.: The Brookings Institution.

Ballentine, J. 1977. "Non-Profit Maximizing Behavior and the Short-Run Incidence of the Corporation Income," *Journal of Public Economics* 7:135–46.

Bandow, Doug 1983. "The Faulty Foundations of Social Security," *The Wall Street Journal* April 25:30.

Barro, R. 1974. "Are Government Bonds Net Wealth?" *Journal of Political Economy* 82:1095–1117.

Barro, R. and G. McDonald 1979. "Social Security and Consumer Spending in an International Cross Section," *Journal of Public Economics* 12:275–89.

Bartlett, B. 1978. *National Review* October 27:1334.

Baumol, W. 1965. *Economic Theory and Operations Analysis.* Englewood Cliffs, N.J.: Prentice-Hall.

   1967. "Macroeconomics of Unbalanced Growth," *American Economic Review* 57:415–26.

Beenstock, M. 1979. "Taxation and Incentives in the UK," *Lloyds Bank Review* October:9.

Beman, L. (ed.) 1979. "An Invisible VAT Would Hinder Tax Evasion," *Business Week* October 1:18.

"Better Taxes." 1983. *The Economist* September 17:13–20.

Bennett, J. and M. Johnson 1979. "The Political Economy of Federal Government Paperwork," *Policy Review* Winter:27–43.

Bhatia, K. 1972. "Capital Gains and the Aggregate Consumption Function," *American Economic Review* 62:866–79.

Blinder, A. 1981. *Economic Policy and the Great Stagflation.* New York: Academic Press.

Blinder, A., R. Gordon, and D. Wise 1981. "Rhetoric and Reality in Social Security Analysis – A Rejoinder," *National Tax Journal* 34:473–8.

Blume, M., J. Crockett, and I. Friend 1974. "Stock Ownership in the United States: Characteristics and Trends," *Survey of Current Business* 54:November 1974:16–40.

"Blumenthal Says Value Added Tax Idea Deserves Full Airing by Congress." 1979. *The Wall Street Journal* February 6:7.

Blumstein, M. 1984. "Why Timing is Everything for Investors' Tax-Planning," *New York Times* March 4:Section 12, 22, 28.

"Boom in Coin and Token Collecting." 1980. *The Canberra Times* February 24:17.

Boskin, M. 1975a. "Efficiency Aspects of the Differential Tax Treatment of Market and Household Economic Activity," *Journal of Public Economics* 4:1–25.

1975b. "Notes on the Treatment of Capital," mimeo, National Bureau of Economic Research, Stanford:1–7.

1978a. "Agenda for Tax Reform," in M. Boskin (ed.), *Federal Tax Reform*. San Francisco: Institute for Contemporary Studies.

1978b. "Taxation, Saving, and the Rate of Interest," *Journal of Political Economy* 86:S3–S27.

1978c. "Is Heavy Taxation of Capital Socially Desirable?" *Tax Review* 40: October: 43–6.

1979. "Tax Treatment of the Family," *The NBER Reporter* Winter:5.

1980a. "Comments," in J. Pechman (ed.), *What Should Be Taxed: Income or Expenditure?* Washington, D.C.: The Brookings Institution.

1980b. "On the Future of Social Security," *Stanford Alumni Almanac* January:16.

Boskin, M. and M. Hurd 1981. "Social Security and Retirement," *The NBER Digest* August/September:2–3.

Boskin, M. and L. Lau 1978. "Taxation and Aggregate Supply: Preliminary Estimates," *1978 Compendium of Tax Research*. Office of Tax Analysis, U.S. Treasury, Washington, D.C.: USGPO.

Boskin, M. and E. Sheshinski 1979. *Optimal Treatment of the Family: Married Couples*. Working Paper No. 368. Boston: National Bureau of Economic Research.

Boskin, M. and J. Shoven 1980. "Issues in the Taxation of Capital Income in the United States," *American Economic Review* 70:164–70.

Boskin, M., J. Shoven, and L. Kotlikoff 1982. "A Way to Save Social Security," *Business Week* November 8:13.

Bradford, D. 1980a. "The Case for a Personal Consumption Tax," in J. Pechman (ed.), *What Should Be Taxed: Income or Expenditure?* Washington, D.C.: The Brookings Institution.

1980b. "Tax Neutrality and the Investment Tax Credit," in H. Aaron and M. Boskin (eds.), *The Economics of Taxation*. Washington, D.C.: The Brookings Institution.

Bradley, B. 1985. *The Fair Tax*. New York: Pocket Books.

Brannon, G. 1971. *The Federal Reserve System*. New York: General Learning Press.

1979. "Value-Added Tax and the Financing of Social Security," *Tax Review* May:17–20.

Brazier, H. 1980. "Income Tax Treatment of the Family," in H. Aaron and M. Boskin (eds.), *The Economics of Taxation*. Washington, D.C.: The Brookings Institution.

Break, G. 1974. "The Incidence and Economic Effects of Taxation," in *The Economics of Public Finance*. Washington, D.C.: The Brookings Institution.

1983. *State and Local Finance*. Madison: University of Wisconsin Press.

Break, G. and J. Pechman 1975. *Federal Tax Reform*. Washington, D.C.: The Brookings Institution.

Brennan, G. 1975. "On Indexing the Personal Income Tax Rate Schedule." Department of Accounting and Public Finance, Australian National University. Unpublished manuscript.

Brimmer, R. and S. Brooks 1981. "Stock Prices," in H. Aaron and J. Pechman (eds.), *How Taxes Affect Economic Behavior*. Washington, D.C.: The Brookings Institution.

"Britain, the Case for Tax Reform." 1983. *The Economist* September 17:19–24.

Broder, D. 1985. "A Bitter Meal Prepared for the Senate," *The Durham Morning Herald*.

Brown, C. V. and P. M. Jackson 1979. *Public Sector Economics*. Oxford: Martin Robinson and Co.

Browning, E. and J. Browning 1978. *Public Finance and the Price System*. New York: Macmillan Co.

Browning, E. and W. Johnson 1979. *The Distribution of the Tax Burden*. Washington, D.C.: American Enterprise Institute.

Buchanan, J. 1968. "Social Insurance in a Growing Economy: A Proposal for Radical Reform," *National Tax Journal* 21:386–95.

Buchanan, J. and C. Campbell 1966. "Voluntary Social Security," *The Wall Street Journal* December 20:14.

Bulkeley, W. and L. Richert 1979. "Venture Capital Is Plentiful Once More, Partly Due to Change in Capital Gains Tax," *The Wall Street Journal*, June 15:42.

Burkauser, R. and J. Turner 1981. "Can Twenty-Five Million Americans Be Wrong? – A Response to Blinder, Gordon, and Wise," *National Tax Journal* 34:467–72.

Cain, G. and H. Watts 1973. "Toward a Summary and Synthesis of the Evidence," in Cain and Watts (eds.), *Income Maintenance and Labor Supply*. Chicago: Rand McNally.

Canto, V., D. Joines, and R. Webb 1979. "Empirical Evidence on the Effects of Taxes on Economic Activity," *Proceedings of the Business and Economic Statistics Section*. American Statistical Association.

Capra, J., P. Skaperdas, and R. Kubarych 1982. "Social Security: An Analysis of Its Problems," *Quarterly Review*, Federal Reserve Bank of New York Autumn:4.

Carlson, G. 1981. "The Role of Tax Policy in Encouraging Research and Development," *Tax Review* May:17–20.

Carnes, N. 1978. "Tax Cut Brings Better Economy to Puerto Rico," *Durham Morning Herald* December 17:9C.

Chickering, A. and J-J Rosa 1982. "The Social Security Problem: We've Got Company," *The Letter* 8:3.

Christian, E. 1977. *Integrating the Corporate Tax, Methods, Motivations and Effects*. Washington, D.C.: American Enterprise Institute.

Citibank 1977. "How Inflation Creates Wealth for the IRS," *Monthly Economic Letter* September:12–14.

Clotfelter, C. 1982a. "Tax Cut Meets Bracket Creep: The Rise and Fall of Marginal Tax Rates." Duke University, Department of Economics. Mimeo.

1982b. "Tax Evasion and Tax Rates: An Analysis of Individual Returns." Duke University, Department of Economics Working Paper No. 82–1.

1985. *Federal Tax Policy and Charitable Giving*. Chicago: University of Chicago Press.

Cnossen, S. 1973. *Excise Systems: A Global Study of the Selective Taxation of Goods and Services*. Baltimore: The Johns Hopkins University Press.

Coen, R. 1978. "Depreciation, Profits, and Rates of Return in Manufacturing Industries," *Office of Tax Analysis Papers* vol. 1, paper no. 3. Washington, D.C.: Department of the Treasury.

Committee for Economic Development 1966. *A Better Balance in Federal Taxes in Business.* New York: CED.

Committee on Ways and Means, U.S. Congress 1978. *Tax Reduction.* Washington, D.C.: USGPO.

Congressional Budget Office 1978. *Aggregate Economic Effects of Changes in Social Security Taxes.* Washington, D.C.: USGPO.

1980. *Indexing the Individual Income Tax for Inflation.* Washington, D.C.: USGPO.

Congressional Record 1977. Vol. 123, no. 119, July 14.

1978. Vol. 124, no. 6, January 26.

Cook, L. 1978. "Capital Gains Tax a Problem for Many Elderly Americans," *Durham Morning Herald* July 29:12A.

Council of Economic Advisors 1981. *Economic Report of the President.* Washington, D.C.: USGPO.

1984. *Economic Report of the President.* Washington, D.C.: USGPO.

Courant, P., E. Gramlich, and D. Rubenfeld 1980. "Why Voters Support Tax Limitation Amendments: The Michigan Case," *National Tax Journal* 33:8–20.

Cullison, W. 1980. "Trends in Federal Taxation Since 1950," *Economic Review.* Federal Reserve Bank of Richmond May/June.

David, M. 1968. *Alternative Approaches to Capital Gains.* Washington, D.C.: The Brookings Institution.

David, M., H. Groves, R. Miller, and E. Wiegner 1970. "Optimal Choices for an Averaging System . . . ," *National Tax Journal* 23:275–95.

Davies, D. 1959. "An Empirical Test of Sales Tax Regressivity," *Journal of Political Economy* 67:72–8.

1960a. "Relative Burden of Sales Taxation: A Statistical Analysis of California Data," *The American Journal of Economics and Sociology* 19:April:289–95.

1960b. "Progressiveness of a Sales Tax in Relation to Various Income Bases," *American Economic Review* 50:987–95.

1961. "Commodity Taxation and Equity," *The Journal of Finance* 16:581–90.

1963. "A Further Reappraisal of Sales Taxation," *National Tax Journal* 16:410–15.

1970. "Significance of Taxation of Services for the Pattern of Distribution of Tax Burden by Income Class," *Sixty-Second Annual Proceedings of the National Tax Association:*138–46.

1971. "Clothing Exemptions and Sales Tax Regressivity," *American Economic Review* 61:187–9.

1976. *International Comparison of Tax Structures in Federal and Unitary Countries.* Canberra: Australian National University Press.

1977. "An Analysis of Fiscal Centralization, Decentralization, and the Pattern of Federal and State–Local Taxes," in R. Mathews (ed.), *State and Local Taxation.* Canberra: Australian National University Press.

1980. "The Measurement of Tax Progressivity, Comment," *American Economic Review* 70:204–7.

298   **References**

Day, P. 1980. "Borrowing Blitz in Nation of Savers Sparks Rethink by Keynesian Holdouts," *The Australian* February 29:11.

DeFina, R. 1980. "Increasing Personal Saving: Can Consumption Taxes Help?" *Federal Reserve Bank of New York Quarterly Review* 5:Autumn:21–7.

DeWulf, L. 1975. "Fiscal Incidence Studies in Developing Countries: Survey and Critique," *IMF Staff Papers* March:61–131.

Diamond, P. 1977. "A Framework for Social Security Analysis," *Journal of Public Economics* 8:275–98.

Diamond, P. and J. Mirrlees 1978. "A Model of Social Insurance with Variable Retirement," *Journal of Public Economics* 10:295–336.

Dreyfus Corporation 1981. "The Infla-Tax Treadmill," *Letter from the Lion* Winter:2.

Due, J. 1957. *Sales Taxation.* Urbana: University of Illinois Press.

1971. *State and Local Sales Taxation: Structure and Administration.* Chicago: Public Administration Service.

1976. "Value Added Taxation in Developing Economics," in N. Wang (ed.), *Taxation and Development.* New York: Praeger.

Due, J. and A. Friedlaender 1973. *Government Finance.* Homewood, Ill.: Richard D. Irwin.

Eckstein, O. 1979. "Statement before the Subcommittee on Taxation and Debt Management," in A. Laffer and J. Seymour (eds.), *The Economics of the Tax Revolt: A Reader.* New York: Harcourt Brace Jovanovich.

Eckstein, O. and V. Tanzi 1961. "Comparison of European and United States Tax Structures and Growth Implications," in *The Role of Direct and Indirect Taxes in the Federal Revenue System.* Princeton, N.J.: Princeton University Press.

"The Economic Case against State-Run Gambling." 1975. *Business Week* August 4:67–8.

"Economic Diary." 1985. *Business Week* October:24.

"Effective Tax Rates." 1979. *The Wall Street Journal* August 30:18.

Eisner, R. and M. Nadiri 1968. "On Investment Behavior and Neoclassical Theory," *The Review of Economics and Statistics* 45:369–82.

Evans, M. 1978. "Taxes, Inflation, and the Rich," *The Wall Street Journal* August 7:10.

1980. "The Bankruptcy of Keynesian Econometric Models," *Challenge* January–February:13–19.

Evans, O. 1982. "Social Security and Household Saving in the United States: A Reexamination," IMF Fiscal Affairs Department Memorandum 82/75.

Feenberg, D. 1981. "Alternative Tax Treatments of the Family," *The NBER Digest* April:1–2.

Feenberg, D. and H. Rosen 1980. *Alternative Tax Treatments of the Family: Simulation Methodology and Results.* Working Paper no. 497. Boston: National Bureau of Economic Research.

Feldstein, M. 1973. "Tax Incentives, Corporate Saving, and Capital Accumulation in the United States," *Journal of Public Economics* 2:159–71.

1974. "Social Security, Induced Retirement, and Aggregate Capital Accumulation," *Journal of Political Economy* 82:905–26.

1975. "Toward a Reform of Social Security," *The Public Interest* Summer:75–95.

1976a. "Taxing Consumption," *The New Republic* January 28:14–17.

1976b. "The Social Security Fund and National Capital Accumulation," *Funding Pensions: Issues and Implications for Financial Markets*. Boston: Federal Reserve Bank of Boston.

1977. "Facing the Social Security Crisis," *The Public Interest* Spring:88–100.

1978a. "The Welfare Costs of Capital Income Taxes," *Journal of Political Economy* 86:S29–S51.

1978b. "The Appropriate Taxation of Capital Gains," *Tax Notes* 10:October:507–8.

1978c. "Do Private Pensions Increase National Saving?" *Journal of Public Economics* 10:277–93.

1979a. "Three Treats to Our Standard of Living," *The Wall Street Journal* June 14:15.

1979b. "Adjusting Tax Rules for Inflation–Capital Gains and Capital Income," 40: *Tax Review* January:55.

1979c. "Adjusting Depreciation in an Inflationary Economy: Indexing versus Acceleration," NBER Working Paper No. 395.

1979d. "The Effect of Social Security on Private Saving: the Time Series Evidence," NBER Working Paper No. 314.

1979e. "International Differences in Social Security and Saving," NBER Working Paper No. 355; also in 1980, *Journal of Public Economics* 14:225–44.

1980. "Social Security's Impact," *Business Week* October 13:7.

1981. "Reviving Business Investment," *The Wall Street Journal* June 19:24.

Feldstein, M. and D. Frisch 1977. "Corporate Tax Integration: The Estimated Effects on Capital Accumulation and Tax Distribution of Two Integration Proposals," *National Tax Journal* 30:37–52.

Feldstein, M., J. Green, and E. Sheshinski 1978. "Inflation and Taxes in a Growing Economy with Debt and Equity Finance," *Journal of Political Economy* 86:S53–S70.

Feldstein, M. and A. Pellechio 1977. "Social Security and Household Wealth Accumulation: New Microeconomic Evidence," NBER Working Paper No. 206.

Feldstein, M. and J. Poterba 1980. "The Impact of State and Local Taxes on Corporate Capital," *The NBER Digest* November/December:2–3.

Feldstein, M. and J. Slemrod 1978a. "Inflation and the Excess Taxation of Capital Gains on Corporate Stock," *National Tax Journal* 31:107–18.

1978b. "How Inflation Distorts the Taxation of Capital Gains," *Harvard Business Review* 56:September–October:21–2.

1978c. "The Lock-in-Effect of the Capital Gains Tax: Some Time Series Evidence," 10: *Tax Notes* August:134.

Feldstein, M., J. Slemrod, and S. Yitzhaki 1980. "The Effects of Taxation on the Selling of Corporate Stock and the Realization of Capital Gains," *Quarterly Journal of Economics* 94:777–91.

Feldstein, M. and L. Summers 1979. "Inflation and the Taxation of Capital Income in the Corporate Sector," *National Tax Journal* 32:445–70.

Feldstein, M. and S. Yitzhaki 1978. "The Effects of the Capital Gains Tax on the Selling and Switching of Common Stock," *Journal of Public Economics* 9:17–36.

Fellner, W., K. Clarkson, and J. Moore 1975. *Correcting Taxes for Inflation.* Washington, D.C.: American Enterprise Institute.

Ferrara, P. 1982. *Social Security: Averting the Crisis.* Washington: Cato Institute.

Fiekowsky, S. 1978. "Pitfalls in the Computation of Effective Tax Rates Paid by Corporations," *Office of Tax Analysis Papers.* Washington, D.C.: U.S. Department of the Treasury.

First Chicago Bank 1979. "Profits and Investment: Fact and Fiction," *World Report* March/April:7.

1980. "The Debate over Cutting Taxes," *World Report* July–August:2.

Flanagan, W. 1980. "Your Money Matters," *Wall Street Journal* July 7:28.

"Footnotes to the Above." 1978. *The Wall Street Journal* May 8:20.

"The 40% Solution." 1980. *The Wall Street Journal* October 21:34.

Fredland, J., J. Gray, and E. Sunley, Jr. 1968. "The Six Month Holding Period for Capital Gains," *National Tax Journal* 21:467–78.

Friedman, M. 1977. "Payroll Taxes, No; General Revenues, Yes," in M. Boskin (ed.), *The Crisis in Social Security.* San Francisco: Institute for Contemporary Studies.

Friend, I. and C. Lieberman 1975. "Short-Run Asset Effects on Household Saving and Consumption: The Cross-Section Evidence," *American Economic Review* 65:624–33.

Fritchey, C. 1979. "Value Added Tax Idea Still Alive," *The Durham Morning Herald* October 16:5A.

Fuerbringer, J. 1984. "Only Small Tax Changes Are on This Year's Agenda," *New York Times* Section 12, March 4:37.

Fullerton, D. 1980. "On the Possibility of an Inverse Relationship Between Tax Rates and Government Revenues," NBER Working Paper No. 467.

Fullerton, D., J. Shoven, and J. Whalley 1978. "General Equilibrium Analysis of U.S. Taxation Policy," in *1978 Compendium of Tax Research.* Office of Tax Analysis, Washington, D.C.: U.S. Department of the Treasury.

Gardner, W. 1978. *Government Finance.* Englewood Cliffs, N.J.: Prentice-Hall.

Genetski, R. and Y. Chin 1978. *The Impact of State and Local Taxes on Economic Growth.* Chicago: Harris Economic Research Office Service, Harris Bank.

Germanis, P. 1983. "For $168 Billion Only a Band-Aid for Social Security," *The Heritage Foundation Backgrounder* February 25:9.

"Getting Out." 1981. *The Wall Street Journal* January 7:16.

Gilder, G. 1981. *Wealth and Poverty.* New York: Basic Books.

Goettman, J. 1982. *State Tax Changes and State Economic Growth in the Seventies: A Supply Sides Study.* Department of Economics, Duke University. Unpublished manuscript.

Gold, S. 1983. "Recent Developments in State Finances," *National Tax Journal* 36:1–29.

Goode, R. 1951. *The Corporate Income Tax.* New York: Wiley.

1964. *The Individual Income Tax*. Washington, D.C.: The Brookings Institution.

1976. *The Individual Income Tax*. Washington, D.C.: The Brookings Institution.

1980. "The Superiority of the Income Tax," in J. Pechman (ed.), *What Should Be Taxed: Income or Expenditure?* Washington, D.C.: The Brookings Institution.

Gordon, R. and D. Bradford 1980. "Taxation and the Stock Market Valuation of Capital Gains and Dividends," *Journal of Public Economics* 14:109–36.

Gordon, R. and B. Malkiel 1981. "Corporate Finance," in H. Aaron and J. Pechman (eds.), *How Taxes Affect Economic Behavior*. Washington, D.C.: The Brookings Institution.

Graetz, M. 1980. "Expenditure Tax Design," in J. Pechman (ed.), *What Should Be Taxed: Income or Expenditure?* Washington, D.C.: The Brookings Institution.

1983. "To Praise the Estate Tax, Not to Bury It," *The Yale Law Review* 93:259–86.

Green, J. 1978. "Taxation of Capital Gains," in M. Boskin (ed.), *Federal Tax Reform*. San Francisco: Institute for Contemporary Studies.

Greytak, D. and R. McHugh 1978. "Inflation and the Individual Tax," *Southern Economic Journal* 45:168–80.

Groves, H. 1946. *Postwar Taxation and Economic Progress*. New York: McGraw-Hill.

1964. *Financing Government*. New York: Holt, Rinehart, and Winston.

1967. "Property Tax – Effects and Limitations," in *The Property Tax: Problems and Potentials*. Princeton, N.J.: Tax Institute of America.

Guilder, G. 1979. "Taxes Here and Abroad," *The Wall Street Journal* November 9:22.

Gwartney, J. and R. Stroup 1980. *Economics: Private and Public Choice*. New York: Academic Press.

Hafer, R. and M. Trebing 1980. "The Value Added Tax – A Review," *Review*, Federal Reserve Bank of St. Louis January:6.

Haig, R. M. 1959. "The Concept of Income – Economic and Legal Aspects," in R. A. Musgrave and Carl S. Shoup (eds.), *Readings in the Economics of Taxation*. Homewood, Ill.: Richard D. Irwin.

Hall, R. 1969. "Consumption Taxes Versus Income Taxes: Implications for Economic Growth," *Sixty-First Annual Conference on Taxation*. Columbus, Oh.: National Tax Association.

Hall, R. and D. Jorgenson 1967. "Tax Policy and Investment Behavior," *American Economic Review* 57:391–414.

Hall, R. and A. Rabushka 1983. *Low Tax, Simple Tax, Flat Tax*. New York: McGraw-Hill.

Halverson, G. 1979a. "Downturn May Hurt Drive for Faster Tax Write-Offs," *The Christian Science Monitor* October 26:11.

1979b. "Congress Mulls Plan for Faster Depreciation," *The Christian Science Monitor* July 10:15.

1979c. "Revenue-Hungry Congress Eyes Value Added Tax," *The Christian Science Monitor* March 7:11.

Hamilton, M. 1984. "IRAs: Good for the Taxpayers, But Not for the Economy," *The Washington Post National Weekly Edition* April 16:18.

Harberger, A. 1962. "The Incidence of the Corporation Income Tax," *Journal of Political Economy* 70:215–40.

1964. "The Measurement of Waste," *The American Economic Review* May:58–76; reprinted in A. Harberger 1974, *Taxation and Welfare*. Boston: Little, Brown and Company.

1980. "Tax Neutrality in Investment Incentives," in H. Aaron and M. Boskin (eds.), *The Economics of Taxation*. Washington, D.C.: The Brookings Institution.

Harris, M. 1980. "Making Money in Antiquities," *The Bulletin* (Australia) February 26:64–7.

Harris, C. 1967. "Property Tax Reform," in *The Property Tax: Problems and Potentials*. Princeton: Tax Institute of America.

Hausman, J. 1981. "Labor Supply," in H. Aaron and J. Pechman (eds.), *How Taxes Affect Economic Behavior*. Washington, D.C.: The Brookings Institution.

Helms, L. 1983. "The Effect of State and Local Taxes on Economic Growth: A Time Series–Cross Section Approach," Department of Economics, University of California at Davis, Working Paper No. 211.

"Help the IRS Reform Tax Code." 1985. *Business Week* April 29:128.

"Heritage Offers Solution to the Social Security Dilemma." 1982. *Heritage Today* November/December:1, 4.

"Higher-Bracket Tax Revenue Rises." 1985. *The Miami Herald*. March 9:10A.

Holloway, R. 1983. "More Gambling, Less Tax?" *Lloyds Bank Review* October:31–43.

Holt, C. and J. Shelton 1962. "The Lock-In Effect of the Capital Gains Tax," *National Tax Journal* 15:337–52.

Howrey, P. and S. Hymans 1980. "The Measurement and Determination of Loanable-Funds Saving," in J. Pechman (ed.), *What Should Be Taxed: Income or Expenditure?* Washington, D.C.: The Brookings Institution.

"The Huge Stakes in 10–5–3 Depreciation." 1979. *Business Week* October 1:124.

Hurd, M. and M. Boskin 1981. "The Effect of Social Security on Retirement in the Early 1970s," NBER Working Paper No. 659.

Hyman, D. 1973. *The Economics of Governmental Activity*. New York: Holt, Rinehart, and Winston.

"Is There a VAT in America's Future?" 1979. *Business in Brief,* Chase Manhattan Bank March/April:2–3.

Jackson, S. and N. Jonas 1981. "Whittling Away at the Corporate Tax Burden," *Business Week* April 20:28.

Joint Economic Committee 1981. *State and Local Economic Development Strategy: A Supply Side Perspective*. Washington, D.C.: USGPO.

Kaldor, N. 1955. *An Expenditure Tax*. London: George, Allen, and Unwin, Ltd.

Keleher, R. 1979. *Supply-Side Effects of Fiscal Policy: Some Preliminary Hypotheses*. Research Paper No. 9. Atlanta: Federal Reserve Bank at Atlanta.

Kelley, P. 1970. "Is an Expenditure Tax Feasible?" *National Tax Journal* 23:237–53.

"The Key to Faster Write-Offs." 1979. *Business Week* September 3:85.

King, M. 1975. "Taxation, Corporate Financial Policy, and the Cost of Capital," *Journal of Public Economics* 4:271–79.

———. 1977. *Public Policy and the Corporation*. London: Chapman and Hall.

Klein, W. 1977. "Timing in Personal Taxation," *Journal of Legal Studies* June 1977:461–81.

Klott, G. 1984. "Filing the Return," *New York Times* March 4, Section 12:50.

Kochin L. 1974. "Are Future Taxes Anticipated by Consumers?" *Journal of Money, Credit, and Banking* 6:385–94.

Koretz, G. 1981a. "A Critic's Straight Talk about the Laffer Curve," *Business Week* January 17:12.

———. 1981b. "Economic Diary," *Business Week* May 4:16.

Kraus, M. 1979. "U.S. Sales Tax Is Preferable to VAT System," *The Wall Street Journal* October 24:22.

Krieger, R.A. 1982. "Supply-Side Economics: An Introduction," *The Chase Economic Observer* March/April:7–8.

Kristol, I. 1980. "Of Economics and Eco-Mania," *The Wall Street Journal* September 19:28.

Krzyzaniak, M. and R. Musgrave 1963. *The Shifting of the Corporation Income Tax*. Baltimore: The Johns Hopkins University Press.

Laffer, A. n.d. "Legislated Reductions in Tax Rates and the Economy." Mimeo:7–8.

———. 1981. "Government Expectations and Revenue Deficiencies," *Cato Journal* 1:Spring:18–20.

Laffer, A. and J. Seymour 1979. *The Economics of the Tax Revolt* New York: Harcourt Brace Jovanovich.

Lawson, G. 1978. "Company Profits: The Grand Illusion," *The Sunday Times* (London) July 30:61.

———. n.d. "Company Profitability and the U.K. Stockmarket," unpublished paper. University of Manchester Business School. Appendix 7B:1–13.

Lee, S. 1983. "Consider the Saving Grace of a Consumption Tax," *The Wall Street Journal* March 8:34.

Levy, Y. 1981. "American Emirates," Federal Reserve Bank of San Francisco *Weekly Letter* October 9:1–3.

Leimer, D. and S. Lesnoy 1980. "Social Security and Private Saving: A Reexamination of the Time Series Evidence Using Alternative Variables," U.S. Department of Health, Education, and Welfare Working Paper No. 19.

Lesnoy, S. and D. Leimer 1982. "Social Security and Private Savings: New Time Series Evidence," *Journal of Political Economy* 90:606–42.

Lindholm, R. 1970. "The Value Added Tax: A Short Review of the Literature," *Journal of Economic Literature* 8:1178–89.

———. 1976. *Value Added Tax and Other Tax Reforms*. Chicago: Nelson-Hall.

Long, R. 1978. "Remarks," unpublished paper. November 30:7.

Lucas, Jr., R. 1982. "The Death of Keynes," in T. Hailstones (ed.), *Viewpoints on Supply-Side Economics*. Richmond, Va.: Robert F. Dame.

McLure, C. 1967. "Tax Exporting in the United States," *National Tax Journal* 20:49–77.

304   **References**

1972. *Value Added Tax*. Washington, D.C.: American Enterprise Institute.

1973. "A Federal Tax on Value Added: U.S. View," *Proceedings of the Sixty-Sixth Annual Conference on Taxation*, National Tax Association.

1975. "General Equilibrium Analysis: The Harberger Model After Ten Years," *Journal of Public Economics* 4:125–61.

1978a. "Economic Constraints On State and Local Taxation of Energy Resources," *National Tax Journal* 31:257–62.

1978b. "A Status Report on Tax Integration in the United States," *National Tax Journal* 31:313–28.

1979. *Must Corporate Income Be Taxed Twice?* Washington, D.C.: The Brookings Institution.

1980a. "State and Federal Relations in the Taxation of Value Added," *The Journal of Corporation Law* 6:Fall:127–39.

1980b. "Tax Restructuring Act of 1979: Time for an American Value Added Tax?" *Public Policy* 28:Summer:301–22.

1981a. "Tax Exporting and the Commerce Clause: Reflections on Commonwealth Edison," NBER Working Paper No. 746.

1981b. "The Elusive Incidence of the Corporate Income Tax: The State Case," *Public Finance Quarterly* 9:395–413.

1981c. "The Elusive Case of the Corporate Income Tax: The State Case," NBER Working Paper 616.

"Making the Most of the New Tax Cuts." 1981. *Business Week* August 17:127.

Martin, E. 1981. "Coping With Chaos," *The Wall Street Journal* June 28:1, 18.

Mathews, R. 1975. *Report of the Committee of Inquiry into Inflation and Taxation*. Canberra: Australian Government Publishing Service.

1980. "The Structure of Taxation," in *The Politics of Taxation*. Sydney: Hodder and Stoughton.

1982. "Tax Effectiveness and Tax Equity in Federal Countries," Australian National University, Center for Research on Federal Financial Relations mimeo.

Maxwell, J. and J. Aronson 1977. *Financing State and Local Governments*. Washington, D.C.: The Brookings Institution.

Meade, J. 1978. *The Structure and Reform of Direct Taxation*. London: George, Allen, and Unwin, Ltd.

Meiselman, D. 1982. "Economic Policies and Interest Rates: Reconciling Supply-Side, Keynesian, and Monetarist Views," *Manhattan Report* July:9.

Merry, R. 1981a. "Congress Debating Extent, Effects of Regan's Depreciation Proposal," *The Wall Street Journal* April 28:33.

1981b. "Ways and Means Chief Criticizes Tax Cut of 30 Percent and Faster Write-Offs for Business," *The Wall Street Journal* April 10:3.

1981c. "The Delicate Art of Reforming a Tax Law," *The Wall Street Journal* April 15:28.

1981d. "Tax Break for 2 Earner Couples," *Wall Street Journal* June 24:3.

1983. "Conferees Clear Social Security Bill to Ensure Solvency Next 75 Years," *The Wall Street Journal* March 27:24C.

Metz, T. 1980. "New Issues Become the Rage Again, Riding on Stock Market's Strength," *The Wall Street Journal* November 17:31.

Mieszkowski, P. 1972. "The Property Tax: An Excise Tax or a Profit Tax?" *Journal of Public Economics* 1:73–96.

    1978. "The Choice of Tax Base: Consumption Versus Income Taxation," in M. Boskin (ed.), *Federal Tax Reform: Myths and Realities*. San Francisco: Institute for Contemporary Studies.

    1980. "Advisability and Feasibility of an Expenditure Tax System," in H. Aaron and M. Boskin (ed.), *The Economics of Taxation*. Washington, D.C.: The Brookings Institution.

Mikesell, J. 1971. "Local Sales Taxes," in J. Due, *State and Local Sales Taxation: Structure and Administration*. Chicago: Public Administration Service.

Minarik, J. 1981; "Capital Gains," in H. Aaron and J. Pechman (eds.), *How Taxes Affect Economic Behavior*. Washington, D.C.: The Brookings Institution.

Modahl, B. 1980. "Doubts about 10–5–3," *The Wall Street Journal* March 10:26.

Monthly Tax Features 1979. Tax Foundation May:3.

Morgan, Jr., D. 1964. *Retail Sales Tax: An Appraisal of New Issues*. Madison: The University of Wisconsin Press.

Morganthaler, E. 1982. "Business Is Good for Accountants . . . ," *Wall Street Journal* May 3:33.

Moszer, M. 1981. "A Comment on the Laffer Model," *Cato Journal* 1:Spring:23–44.

Mueller, J. 1981. "Lessons of the Tax-Cuts of Yesteryear," *The Wall Street Journal* March 5:24.

Munnell, A. 1976. "Private Pensions and Savings: New Evidence," *Journal of Political Economy* 84:1013–32.

    1977. *The Future of Social Security*. Washington, D.C.: The Brookings Institution.

    1980. "The Couple versus the Individual under the Federal Personal Income Tax," in H. Aaron and M. Boskin (eds.), *The Economics of Taxation*. Washington, D.C.: The Brookings Institution.

Musgrave, R. and P. Musgrave 1976. *Public Finance in Theory and Practice*. New York: McGraw-Hill.

    1980. *Public Finance in Theory and Practice*. New York: McGraw-Hill.

Mushkin, S. 1979. "The Case for User Fees." 2: *Taxing and Spending* April:16–19.

Myers, R. 1975. *Social Insurance and Allied Government Programs*. Homewood, Ill.: Richard D. Irwin.

Nash, N. 1984. "Investing with an Eye on the After-Tax Return," *The New York Times* March 4, Section 12:19–20, 28.

Nelson, C. 1972. "The Predictive Performance of the FRB–MIT–Penn Model of the U.S. Economy," *American Economic Review* 62:902–17.

    1973. *Applied Time Series Analysis for Managerial Forecasting*. New York: Holden Day.

Netzer, D. 1966. *Economics of the Property Tax*. Washington, D.C.: The Brookings Institution.

"The New NBER: Has Scholarship Been Hurt?" 1980. *Business Week* October 6:95–6.

Nobel, K. 1984. "Tax Shelters Boom as Sophisticates Seek Relief," *The New York Times* March 4, Section 12:25–6.

Nowotny, Ewald 1980. "Inflation and Taxation: Reviewing the Macroeconomic Issues," *Journal of Economic Literature* 18:1025–49.

O'Brien, E. 1979. "Reduction of Tax on Capital Gains Spears Investment," *The Wall Street Journal* October 31:24.

Olson, W. 1973. "A Birthday You May Want to Forget," *The Wall Street Journal* October 5:8.

Palash, C. 1980. "Recent Trends in the Federal Taxation of Individual Income," *Quarterly Review,* Federal Reserve Bank of New York: 5, 15–20.

"Paring Personal Taxes as the First Priority." 1980. *Business Week* December 29:68.

Paul, R. 1954. *Taxation in the United States.* Boston: Little, Brown and Company.

Peacock, A. 1978. "Do We Need to Reform Direct Taxes?" *Lloyd's Bank Review* July:28–40.

Pechman, J. 1977. *Federal Tax Policy.* Washington, D.C.: The Brookings Institution.

(ed.) 1980. *What Should Be Taxed; Income or Expenditure?* Washington, D.C.: The Brookings Institution.

1982. "Tax Policies for the 1980s," in J. Pechman and N. Simler (eds.), *Economics in the Public Service.* New York: W. W. Norton and Company.

(ed.) 1984. *Options for Tax Reform.* Washington, D.C.: The Brookings Institution.

(ed.) 1985. *A Citizen's Guide to the New Tax Reforms.* Totowa, N.J.: Rowman and Allanheld.

Pechman, J., H. Aaron, and M. Taussig 1968. *Social Security: Perspectives for Reform.* Washington, D.C.: The Brookings Institution.

Pechman, J. and B. Okner 1974. *Who Bears the Tax Burden?* Washington: The Brookings Institution.

Peterson, G. et al. 1973. *Property Taxes, Housing and the Cities.* Lexington, Mass.: Lexington Books.

Phares, D. 1980. *Who Pays State and Local Taxes.* Cambridge, Mass.: Oelgeschlager, Gunn, and Hain.

Pierson, J. 1980. "Controversy Flares Over Proposals to Ease Tax Burdens on Savings and Investments," *The Wall Street Journal* May 2:48.

"Taxing Problem." 1980 *The Wall Street Journal* May 2:48.

"Plan to Shift Taxes' Focus Is Proposed." 1979. *Washington Star* September 2:1, 6.

Pollock, O. 1980. "The 1978 Capital Gains Tax Reduction: An Emerging Breakthrough in U.S. Tax Policy," *Research Report.* New York: Ingalls and Snyder.

1981a. "Revenue Effects of the 1978 Capital Gains Tax Reduction: New and Important Data," *Research Report.* New York: Ingalls and Snyder.

1981b. "The 1978 Capital Gains Tax Reductions: A Breakthrough in U.S. Tax Policy," *Research Report.* New York: Ingalls and Snyder.

Price Waterhouse and Company 1980. *Disclosure of the Effects of Inflation: An Analysis, Financial Reporting and Changing Prices.* New York.

Quarterly Summary of Federal, State, and Local Tax Revenue. 1983. Washington, D.C.: Bureau of the Census.

Quarterly Summary of Federal, State, and Local Tax Revenue. 1985. Washington, D.C.: Bureau of the Census.

Rabushka, A. 1978. "The True Wealth of Nations," *The Wall Street Journal* December 6:6.

Ratliff, C. 1962. Interstate Apportionment of Business Income for State Income Tax Purposes. Chapel Hill: University of North Carolina Press.

"Reagan's Go-for-Broke Package." 1981. *Business Week* March 2:22–3.

"Reagan Signs Tax Bill." 1981. *Durham Morning Herald* August 14:2A.

"Review and Outlook." 1981. *The Wall Street Journal* April 8:28.

Ricardo-Campbell, R. 1981. "How to Keep Social Security Taxes from Rising," *The Wall Street Journal* March 5:24.

Roberts, P. 1978. "The Breakdown of the Keynesian Model," *The Public Interest* Summer:20–33.

    1981. "Reagan's Tax-Cut Program: The Evidence," *The Wall Street Journal* May 21:26.

    1983. "Marginal-Rate Madness as Social Security Reform," *The Wall Street Journal* March 11:26.

Rosen, H. 1980. "What Is Labor Supply and Do Taxes Affect It?" *American Economic Review* 70:171–76.

    1982. "Taxes, Labor Supply, and Human Capital," *NBER Reporter* Spring:6.

Rossana, R. 1981. "Structuring Corporate Taxes for a More Productive Economy," *Business Review,* Federal Reserve Bank of Philadelphia January-February:16.

Runyon, H. 1982. "Indexation and Bracket Creep," *Weekly Letter,* Federal Reserve Bank of San Francisco April 30:1.

"Saving Social Security." 1983. *The Miami Herald* January 10:16A.

Schulz, J. et al. 1974. *Providing Adequate Retirement Income: Pension Reform in the United States and Abroad* Hanover: University Press of New England.

Schuyler, M. 1984. *Consumption Taxes: Promises and Problems.* Washington: Institute for Research on the Economics of Taxation.

Seidman, L. 1980. "The Personal Consumption Tax and Social Welfare," *Challenge* 23:September-October:10–16.

    1981. "A Personal Consumption Tax: Can It Break the Capital Formation Deadlock?" *Federal Reserve Bank of Philadelphia Business Review* January/February:3–9.

Seltzer, L. 1951. *The Nature and Tax Treatment of Capital Gains and Losses.* New York: National Bureau of Economic Research.

Senate Finance Committee 1984. "Deficit Reduction Tax Bill of 1984," *Standard Federal Tax Reports.* Chicago: Commerce Clearing House.

Shannon, J. 1967. "Full Disclosure Policy – The State's Role in the Assessment Process," in *The Property Tax: Problems and Potentials.* Princeton, N.J.: Tax Institute of America.

Sheils, M., M. Frons, and M. Lord 1981. "A New Tax Reform?" *Newsweek* March 16:82.

Shoup, C. 1969. *Public Finance.* Chicago: Aldine.

Shoven, J. and J. Whalley 1972. "A General Equilibrium Calculation of Effects of Differential Taxation of Income from Capital in the U.S.," *Journal of Public Economics* 1:281–321.

Siegfried, J. 1974. "Effective Average U.S. Corporation Income Tax Rates," *National Tax Journal* 27:245–59.

Simon, J. 1980. "Revenue Increase Bolsters Romero Tax-Cut Policy," *The San Juan Star* May 25.

Simons, H.C. 1983. *Personal Income Taxation*. Chicago: University of Chicago Press.

Slemrod, J. 1982. "Stock Transactions Volume and the 1978 Capital Gains Tax Reduction," *Public Finance Quarterly* 10:3–16.

Smith, A. 1937. *The Wealth of Nations*. New York: Random House.

Social Security Administration 1982a. *History of the Provisions of Old-Age Survivors, and Disability, and Health Insurance 1935–1981*. Washington, D.C.: USGPO.

1982b. *Your Social Security*. Washington, D.C.: U.S. Department of Health and Human Services.

Social Security Bulletin 43:February 1980.

"Social Security Forced to Borrow." 1982. *The Miami Herald* December 25:8A.

"Social Security: Personal Security Accounts Called Key to Long-Term Reform, Solvency." 1983. *The Stanford Observer* January, Section 2:1–2.

"Special Purpose Units Multiply as Local Jurisdictions Splinter." 1982. Tax Foundation, *Monthly Tax Features* 26:October:3.

Steuerle, E., R. McHugh, and E. Sunley 1978. "Who Benefits From Income Averaging?" *National Tax Journal* 31:19–32.

Stiglitz, J. 1973. "Taxation, Corporate Financial Policy, and the Cost of Capital," *Journal of Public Economics* 2:1–34.

1976. "The Corporation Tax," *Journal of Public Economics* 5:303–11.

Stinson, T. 1977. *State Taxation of Mineral Deposits and Production*. Washington, D.C.: Office of Research and Development of U.S. Environmental Protection Agency.

Strout, R. 1978. "Value Added Tax Tempts Long," *The Christian Science Monitor* December 4:5.

Stuart, C. 1981. "Swedish Tax Rates, Labor Supply, and Tax Revenues," *Journal of Political Economy* 89:1020–38.

Studenski, P. and H. E. Krooss 1952. *Financial History of the United States*. New York: McGraw-Hill.

Sullivan, C. 1966. *The Tax on Value Added*. New York: Columbia University Press.

Summers, L. 1978. "Tax Policy in a Life Cycle Model," NBER Working Paper No. 302.

Sunley, E. 1978. "Tax Neutrality Between Capital Services Provided by Long-Lived and Short-Lived Assets," in M. Kaufman and G. Robbins (eds.), *Office of Tax Analysis Papers*. Washington, D.C.: U.S. Department of the Treasury.

Tait, A. 1981. "Is the Introduction of a Value Added Tax Inflationary?" *Finance and Development* 18:June:38–42.

Tate, D. 1979. "Value Added Tax To Be Pushed." *The Durham Morning Herald* November 16:5A.

Tatom, J. and J. Turley 1978. "Inflation and Taxes: Disincentives for Capital Formation," *Review*, 60:Federal Reserve Bank of St. Louis January:1–8.

"Tax Briefs." 1982. *Business Week*. April 26:61.

"Tax Forms Billion-Hour Citizen Task." 1982. *Durham Morning Herald* April 16:10A.

Tax Foundation 1982a. "Tax Index Sets New High," *Monthly Tax Features* 26:February:1–2.

1985. "Federal Income Taxes Paid by High- and Low-Income Taxpayers," *Monthly Tax Features* 29:May:1.

"Taxman." 1985. *The Durham Morning Herald.* April 30:9B.

Taxation Review (Aspery) Committee 1974. *Preliminary Report.* Canberra: Australian Government Publishing Service.

Thompson, L. 1983. "The Social Security Reform Debate," *Journal of Economic Literature* 21:1425–67.

Thuronyi, V. 1980. "The Expenditure Tax as a Saving Incentive," *Tax Notes* March 3:276.

Thurow, L. 1975. "The Economics of Public Finance," *National Tax Journal* 28:185–94.

1981. *The Zero-Sum Game.* New York: Penguin Books.

1982. "Redesigning Social Security," *Newsweek* May 24:26.

Tideman, T. and D. Tucker 1976. "The Tax Treatment of Business Profits under Inflationary Conditions," in H. Aaron (ed.), *Inflation and the Income Tax.* Washington, D.C.: The Brookings Institution.

Tobin, J. 1967. "Life Cycle Saving and Balanced Growth," in *Ten Economic Studies in the Tradition of Irving Fisher.* New York: John Wiley and Sons.

1980. "Stabilization Policy Ten Years After," *Brookings Papers on Economic Activity* No. 1:42.

"Truth in Taxation." 1979. *The Wall Street Journal* August 23:22.

Ture, N. 1985. *Tax Reform Savaging of the Puerto Rican Economy.* IRET Op Ed No. 4. Washington, D.C.: Institute for Research on the Economics of Taxation.

Ullman, A. 1980. "A Tax Policy for the 1980s," *Challenge* March/April:52–5.

"Ullman Introduces Value Added Tax Bill That Calls for Sweeping Change in Code." 1979. *The Wall Street Journal* October 17:3.

"Updating Depreciation." 1979. *Business Week* October 1:44.

"The U.S. Bias against Saving Leads to High Inflation, Weak Dollar, Slow Growth, Declining Productivity," *Business Week* December 11:90–6.

U.S. Bureau of the Census 1974. *Statistical Abstract of the United States.* Washington, D.C.: USGPO.

1983. *Governmental Finances in 1981–82.* Washington, D.C.: USGPO.

U.S. Department of the Treasury 1977. *Blueprints for Basic Tax Reform.* Washington, D.C.: USGPO.

1980 and 1984. *Your Federal Income Tax.* Washington, D.C.: USGPO.

1981. *Statistics of Income 1978, Individual Income Tax Returns.* Washington, D.C.: USGPO.

1982. *Highlights of 1982 Tax Changes.* Publication 553, Internal Revenue Service. November:9.

1984. *Tax Reform for Fairness, Simplicity, and Economic Growth.* Washington, D.C.: USGPO.

Vanderford, D. 1980. "Building a Supply Side Model: The Permanent Money Balances Hypothesis," *Taxing and Spending* 3:Winter:21–42.

Van de Water, P. 1979. "Issues in Social Security Financing," *Tax Review* April 1979:13–16.

Vedder, R. and L. Gallaway 1985. "Soaking the Rich Through Tax Cuts," *The Wall Street Journal* March 26:30.

Vickery, W. 1947. *Agenda for Progressive Taxation.* New York: Ronald Press.

Von Furstenburg, G. 1975. "Individual Income Taxation and Inflation," *National Tax Journal* 28:117–25.

"VAT of 1% Nets $11 Billion TF Study Shows." 1979. *Monthly Tax Features*, 23:Tax Foundation June/July:3.

Walker, C. and M. Bloomfield (eds.) 1984. *New Directions in Federal Tax Policy for the 1980s.* Cambridge, Mass.: Ballinger.

Wanniski, J. 1978. *The Way the World Words.* New York: Simon and Schuster.

Watson, R. 1973. "Lotteries: Can the Public and State Both Win?" Federal Reserve Bank of Philadelphia *Business Review* July:3–14.

Weaver, C. 1982. *The Crisis in Social Security: Economic and Political Origins.* Durham: Duke University Press.

Wetzler, J. 1977. "Capital Gains and Losses," in J. Pechman (ed.), *Comprehensive Income Taxation.* Washington: The Brookings Institution.

1981. "Comments," in H. Aaron and J. Pechman (eds.), *How Taxes Affect Economic Behavior.* Washington, D.C.: The Brookings Institution.

"What President Carter Can Learn from Germany and Japan: Eliminating Gains Taxes Brings Rapid Economic Growth." 1978. *The Christian Science Monitor* September 26:5.

"When to Put Your Money into Gems." 1981. *Business Week* March 16:158–61.

White, F. 1983. "Trade-Off in Growth and Stability in State Taxes," *National Tax Journal* 36:103–114.

"Why Washington Likes Consumption Taxes." 1983. *Business Week* June 13:80–2.

Wilke, J. and C. Harris 1985. "At the IRS," *Business Week* April 29:109,112.

Witte, A. and D. Woodbury 1985. "The Effect of Tax Laws and Tax Administration on Tax Compliance," *National Tax Journal* March 38:1–13.

Witte, J. 1985a. "The Income Tax Mess: Deviant Process or Institutional Failure?" Annual Meeting of the American Political Science Association August 29–September 1:1–20.

1985b. *The Politics and Development of the Federal Income Tax.* Madison: the University of Wisconsin Press.

Wright, C. 1967. "Some Evidence of the Interest Elasticity of Consumption," *American Economic Review* 57:850–55.

"Your Stake in the Fight over Social Security." 1981. *Consumer Reports* September:503–10.

Yinger, J. 1978. "Economic Advisor's Staff Paper Challenges Capital Gains Study," *Tax Notes* 10:October 9:428.

Zucker, S. 1978. "The Gains from Cutting Capital Gains," *Business Week* August 14:24.

1980. "A Spectacular Debunking of Social Security Critics," *Business Week* September 22:25.

Index